studies in jazz

Institute of Jazz Studies
Rutgers—The State University of New Jersey
General Editors: Dan Morgenstern and Edward Berger

1. BENNY CARTER: A Life in American Music, *by Morroe Berger, Edward Berger, and James Patrick, 2 vols., 1982*
2. ART TATUM: A Guide to His Recorded Music, *by Arnold Laubich and Ray Spencer, 1982*
3. ERROLL GARNER: The Most Happy Piano, *by James M. Doran, 1985*
4. JAMES P. JOHNSON: A Case of Mistaken Identity, *by Scott E. Brown;* Discography 1917–1950, *by Robert Hilbert, 1986*
5. PEE WEE ERWIN: This Horn for Hire, *as told to Warren W. Vaché Sr., 1987*
6. BENNY GOODMAN: Listen to His Legacy, *by D. Russell Connor, 1988*
7. ELLINGTONIA: The Recorded Music of Duke Ellington and His Sidemen, *by W. E. Timner, 1988; 4th ed., 1996*
8. THE GLENN MILLER ARMY AIR FORCE BAND: Sustineo Alas / I Sustain the Wings, *by Edward F. Polic;* Foreword *by George T. Simon, 1989*
9. SWING LEGACY, *by Chip Deffaa, 1989*
10. REMINISCING IN TEMPO: The Life and Times of a Jazz Hustler, *by Teddy Reig, with Edward Berger, 1990*
11. IN THE MAINSTREAM: 18 Portraits in Jazz, *by Chip Deffaa, 1992*
12. BUDDY DeFRANCO: A Biographical Portrait and Discography, *by John Kuehn and Arne Astrup, 1993*
13. PEE WEE SPEAKS: A Discography of Pee Wee Russell, *by Robert Hilbert, with David Niven, 1992*
14. SYLVESTER AHOLA: The Gloucester Gabriel, *by Dick Hill, 1993*
15. THE POLICE CARD DISCORD, *by Maxwell T. Cohen, 1993*
16. TRADITIONALISTS AND REVIVALISTS IN JAZZ, *by Chip Deffaa, 1993*
17. BASSICALLY SPEAKING: An Oral History of George Duvivier, *by Edward Berger;* Musical Analysis *by David Chevan, 1993*
18. TRAM: The Frank Trumbauer Story, *by Philip R. Evans and Larry F. Kiner, with William Trumbauer, 1994*
19. TOMMY DORSEY: On the Side, *by Robert L. Stockdale, 1995*
20. JOHN COLTRANE: A Discography and Musical Biography, *by Yasuhiro Fujioka, with Lewis Porter and Yoh-ichi Hamada, 1995*
21. RED HEAD: A Chronological Survey of "Red" Nichols and His Five Pennies, *by Stephen M. Stroff, 1996*
22. THE RED NICHOLS STORY: After Intermission 1942–1965, *by Philip R. Evans, Stanley Hester, Stephen Hester, and Linda Evans, 1997*
23. BENNY GOODMAN: Wrappin' It Up, *by D. Russell Connor, 1996*
24. CHARLIE PARKER AND THEMATIC IMPROVISATION, *by Henry Martin, 1996*
25. BACK BEATS AND RIM SHOTS: The Johnny Blowers Story, *by Warren W. Vaché Sr., 1997*
26. DUKE ELLINGTON: A Listener's Guide, *by Eddie Lambert, 1998*
27. SERGE CHALOFF: A Musical Biography and Discography, *by Vladimir Simosko, 1998*

Jazz Fiction

A History and Comprehensive Reader's Guide

David Rife

Studies in Jazz, No. 55

THE SCARECROW PRESS, INC.
Lanham, Maryland • Toronto • Plymouth, UK
2008

SCARECROW PRESS, INC.

Published in the United States of America
by Scarecrow Press, Inc.
A wholly owned subsidiary of
The Rowman & Littlefield Publishing Group, Inc.
4501 Forbes Boulevard, Suite 200, Lanham, Maryland 20706
www.scarecrowpress.com

Estover Road
Plymouth PL6 7PY
United Kingdom

British Library Cataloguing in Publication Information Available

Library of Congress Cataloging-in-Publication Data

Rife, David, 1937–
    Jazz fiction : a history and comprehensive reader's guide / David Rife.
        p. cm.—(Studies in jazz ; no. 55)
    Includes bibliographical references and index.
    ISBN-13: 978-0-8108-5907-4 (pbk. : alk. paper)
    ISBN-10: 0-8108-5907-6 (pbk. : alk. paper)
    1. Fiction—20th century—History and criticism. 2. Jazz in literature.
3. Jazz—Fiction—Bibliography. I. Title.
PN3352.J39R54 2008
809'.393578—dc22   2007028048

♾™ The paper used in this publication meets the minimum requirements of American
National Standard for Information Sciences—Permanence of Paper for Printed Library
Materials, ANSI/NISO Z39.48-1992.
Manufactured in the United States of America.

To the memory of my mother, Dorothy Langdon Fisher
(1913–2005)

"... if I'd a knowed what a trouble it was to make a book I wouldn't a tackled it and ain't agoing to no more."

—*The Adventures of Huckleberry Finn* by Mark Twain

Contents

Editor's Foreword

The bulk of David Rife's *Jazz Fiction* is a meticulously compiled and annotated bibliography, but it is much more. It combines sheer volume—some 687 works by 524 authors—with important introductory essays and lists that enrich it as both a work of criticism and a definitive reference book. It is the product of a professor of English who combines thirty-five years of teaching and writing about fiction with a love and knowledge of jazz and its artists. Indeed, he is a founding associate editor of a periodical specifically devoted to the linkage between this creative music and creative writing, *Brilliant Corners: A Journal of Jazz and Literature*. David Rife knows this literature, and the vast majority of his annotations derive from the most primary of sources—his own reading of the works.

Readers of this volume, a greatly expanded work based on two articles in the *Annual Review of Jazz Studies*, will do well to turn first to Dr. Rife's introductory essays, which first trace the history of jazz novels and short stories from 1912 through recent works (including a work in progress) and then turn to a number of prominent genres of jazz fiction, including works for the very young to futuristic science fiction and quasi-biographical fiction based on actual jazz artists. Not only does he survey the multitude of crime and mystery fiction—something of a Rife specialty and a form that so often employs jazz as a suitable literary soundtrack—but he even warns jazz lovers about fiction devoid of jazz but which uses "jazz," "swing," or related terms as a form of bait-and-switch advertising. For me, the breadth of his effort is symbolized by his global outreach; his survey includes authors from some twenty nations, plus a number by immigrants to America.

Finally, I should call attention to parts 2 and 3, which guide readers with specialized interests. Part 2 lists some selected and significant works from a number of genres. Part 3 offers two short-lists, one of stories and one of novels, which are Dr. Rife's choices for introductions to fiction that combine literary interest with significant incorporations of jazz as an art form, its artists, and/or the social and racial issues that jazz fiction often treats.

For both literary insight and bibliographical scope, this is a definitive volume.

David Cayer
Guest Editor

Acknowledgments

I would like to express my gratitude to several institutions and individuals who helped me with this sprawling project. Thanks to Lycoming College for research grants and released time; and to the staff (especially Janet Hurlbert and Marlene Neece) of the Snowden Library of Lycoming College for their cheerful efficiency in answering questions and procuring materials. Thanks, too, to Dan Morgenstern, Edward Berger, and the staff at the Institute of Jazz Studies, Rutgers University, for giving me access to its research materials and for encouraging my study.

I am also greatly indebted to David Powell and Sascha Feinstein for advice and criticism, and to Bill Ford for his careful reading of the manuscript and for offering several ideas concerning the way fiction writers appropriate jazz techniques in their writing. My editor, David Cayer, provided the kind of steady guidance that every writer craves, and I am grateful. Bill Moody supplied me with a couple of valuable insider tidbits that I was able to use, and Sheran Swank rescued me from disaster many times with her technological expertise.

Several people helped me enormously with foreign language materials. Michael Molasky introduced me to the world of Japanese jazz fiction; Cornelius Partsch provided leads and information on German jazz fiction of the post–World War I era. Three translators have been immensely helpful: David Haley, for his rendition of a German novel; Garrett Heysel, for several extended passages from the French; and Lisa Harris Fehling, for a collection of stories from the Dutch. If the sections on international jazz fiction are as original as I think they are, these folks deserve much of the credit.

Since, like Huck Finn, I have no intention of producing any more books, I'd like to take this first—and final—opportunity to thank some folks (and a critter) who supported me in ways they couldn't begin to understand: my daughters, Gabriela and Ariana Rife, and their mother, Sandy Rife; my long-time spousal equivalent, Janice "Squeezie" Yaw; and my hero grandpup, Scotch E. Werner. Love and thanks to all.

Part 1

FROM MUSIC TO STORY

Chapter One

Bibliographic Overview

If the concept of *jazz fiction* is not as improbable as, say, *dance architecture*, it nevertheless resists easy definition. For instance: does the term refer to those stories and novels that employ a jazz setting and use the music as subject matter to promote the theme? Or is the term elastic enough to embrace the novels of Jack Kerouac, to name just one writer who refers frequently to bebop artists within the mode of "jazzy" language? And what of works like Alice Adams's haunting novel, *Listening to Billie*, in which the legendary singer Billie Holiday makes a brief, dramatic appearance toward the beginning, disappears immediately, and yet profoundly affects the contingent life of the protagonist? Surely the term is accommodating enough to include all such works and others beside. For this study, which was designed to be as comprehensive as possible, the term *jazz fiction* will denote those stories and novels in which the music figures in the narrative; it will also include those works, like Ralph Ellison's masterpiece, *Invisible Man,* that are obviously imbued with the spirit of the music, even though their discernible jazz content might seem negligible or even nonexistent.

EARLY WORKS

Jazz fiction got off to a promising start in 1912 with the publication of James Weldon Johnson's *The Autobiography of an Ex-Colored Man,* the story of a light-skinned mulatto who achieves success by applying his mastery of classical piano to ragtime. But instead of following his dream of converting ragtime into respectable art, thus legitimating the African-American experience, he masquerades as white and succumbs to a life of ease, nevertheless regretting that he had betrayed his race by selling his "birthright for a mess of pottage." This early work adumbrates certain important elements that became increasingly persistent as both the music and its literature achieved greater popularity: the artist-patron (especially black artist-white patron) dynamic, the relationship between the races, the painful mystery of identity, and the potential of music to elevate not only the welfare of an individual but, indeed, a race.

After this provocative start, jazz fiction did little to distinguish itself over the next quarter-century, though scattered works of interest occasionally appeared. Two humorous pieces, the first by a black writer, the second by a white, are worth noting. In rhythmic style, Rudolph Fisher's "Common Meter" depicts a cutting contest between two bands in Harlem in the late 1920s. As usual a woman caused the competition between the bands, who have to "fight it out with jazz" because knives and brass knuckles are forbidden. Octavus Cohen's "Music Hath Charms" hinges on the comeuppance of a con man who claims to blow a mean horn but can neither read nor play a note. In another early short work, however, Hermann Deutsch's "Louis Armstrong," the title character can play as many notes as his horn can handle. This vernacular account of Armstrong's rise from ragamuffin to renowned musician provides an early example of a story that blurs the boundaries between fact and fiction.

It wouldn't seem right if F. Scott Fitzgerald and his followers didn't make an appearance on this list. After all, it was Fitzgerald who gave the Jazz Age its name. Julian Street's "The Jazz Baby" is typical of the stories that try to capture the frenetic spirit of that time. The story involves a generational dispute that arises when a New York matron discovers that her collegiate son has fallen in love with the saxophone. When she asks him if it is "a fire extinguisher, or a home-brew outfit," he replies, "No—home blew" and commences to sing a chorus of "Those Home-Brew Blues" before winding up his spirited performance with a saxophone solo. The dispute continues when the son and a buddy take their dates uptown to Harlem to see a show called *Jazzbo* instead of going to a more culturally respectable event in a socially acceptable part of town.

By now everyone is familiar with the brouhaha caused by the jazz played at Jay Gatsby's parties in Fitzgerald's *The Great Gatsby*, but few are familiar with his "Dice, Brassknuckles & Guitar," a comical ("silly" is more accurate) story dramatizing the implacability of the rich and the cultural divide between the American North and South. The protagonist gives guitar lessons (and "Bachelor of Jazz" degrees to those who complete the course) and claims that his students become so rhythmic after a few sessions that "you'd think some of 'em was colored."

More substantial than these minor effusions are the works of two ranking black writers, Claude McKay and Langston Hughes. In *Home to Harlem* McKay traces the parallel paths of two young urban black males who are trying to find their way in a racist society. Jazz and blues are always close to the action of this novel as the characters spend most of their nonworking hours in cabarets and speakeasies where they hope to find release from the pain of their wretched lives through music and dancing. More than in any other work, the term *jazz* and its variants are used in innovative ways. *Banjo* is also drenched in music and race. Lincoln Agrippa Daily is known to everyone as Banjo for the beloved instrument he plays. Banjo and other poor blacks from all over the world subsist by panhandling, whoring, drinking, and making music on the seedy waterfront of Marseilles during the 1920s. Banjo's sustaining dream is to build an orchestra, but the best he can manage to get together is a short-lived quartet consisting of a flute, tiny horn, guitar, and, of course, banjo. The racial and musical dimensions of the novel collide often, as when, for instance, Banjo's buddy chides him for his instrument, saying "Banjo is bondage. . . . the instrument of slavery. Banjo is Dixie. The Dixie of the land of cotton and massa and missus and black mammy. . . ." A clever commentator could doubtless argue that the novel's plotlessness, its improvisatory nature, is intended to mimic the jazz that Banjo loves so dearly.

The works of Langston Hughes are also laced with references to jazz and race. In his novel, *Not without Laughter,* Hughes focuses on the daily life of a poor African-American family in a small Midwestern community who, along with their fellow blacks, achieve a sense of community through music and dancing. One chapter, "Guitar," nicely captures this phenomenon in its representation of a loving man who brings folks closer together through his music. Several of Hughes's shorter works are also centrally concerned with jazz. For instance, in "The Blues I'm Playing," set during the Harlem Renaissance, Hughes explores the conflict between classical music and jazz. The disparate philosophies represented by these musical forms are presented through the conflict between Oceola Jones, a black pianist, and her wealthy white patron, Mrs. Ellsworth, reminding us of the cultural conundrum regarding the influence of white stewardship on African-American artists. In "Bop," Hughes's series character, Simple, a lover of bebop, explains to the dubious narrator that the music is more than just nonsense syllables, that in fact its name derives from the sound made when cops hit blacks on the head with their billy clubs, thus creating an authentic "colored boys" music. "Jazz, Jive, and Jam" presents a less caustic picture of racial matters as Simple argues to his woman, who has been dragging him to talks on integration, that jazz would be far more effective in promoting racial harmony than any number of seminars on the issue because, since everyone loves the music, blacks and whites would dance together, and racial discord would disappear. "Old Ghost Revives Atavistic Memories in a Lady of the DAR" also combines race, music, and dancing (after a fashion) when a D.A.R. member disturbs a very genteel meeting of her club by raising the race issue, the "Negro Question." This summons forth the ghost of Blind Boone, who arranges himself at the piano and proceeds to play bebop and boogie, causing the ultra-refined, deeply prejudiced Mrs. Palmer "to dance, to boogie and, as the music modulated, even to be-bop" and to cry out "ah, do it, daddy" before her "ancient carcass squatted in one final scoop and swished like a duck, 'Hucklebuck, baby! Hucklebuck!'"

The best-known work of jazz fiction's first quarter-century is Dorothy Baker's *Young Man with a Horn* (1938), whose lasting fame undoubtedly owes a considerable debt of gratitude to a Hollywood movie of the same name (1950). Inspired by the music but not the life (so the author claims) of Bix Beiderbecke, *Young Man* offers yet another portrait of the doomed artist as a young man, in this case, Rick Martin, an outsider who has neither family nor education to speak of. What Rick does have in abundance is a genuine feel for music, especially improvisation; in fact, a major conflict (a familiar one in jazz literature) revolves around Rick's powerful desire to express his own individuality through music while being chained to the big band charts. Rick is the prototype of the self-destructive jazz hero who achieves apotheosis a few years later in the lives and legends of Charlie Parker and Chet Baker, among others. Although *Young Man with a Horn* is far from distinguished as a novel, it does place the music on center stage and, in so doing, opens the floodgates to jazz fiction.

THE 1940s THROUGH THE 1960s

Jazz fiction proliferated in the decades following the publication of *Young Man with a Horn* and broadened its base of inquiry. Dale Curran contributed two novels and George Willis three during the 1940s. Curran's *Dupree Blues* tells the story of a refugee from the middle class who plays in a New Orleans-style jazz band near Memphis. When he falls in love with the band's marginally talented singer, he gets in over his head financially and his life spirals out of control—an exemplum of the blues life. Curran's other, more substantial jazz novel, *Piano in the Band,* concerns itself with the mechanics of a dance hall jazz band: the tedious on-the-road existence, the frustrations of rehearsals, and the stock conflict that inevitably crops up when some band members want to create "real" music rather than follow the rigid routines imposed on them by their leader. At the end, the protagonist breaks away from the group to join a predominantly black band where he will be free to create and, perhaps, help to loosen the rigid color barrier.

Willis's trilogy (as he called it) relentlessly underscores the problems faced by jazz musicians. The dispiriting first volume, *Tangleweed*, involves swing band musicians who are serious about their music but reduced by circumstances to play in dives where they are always under pressure to commercialize their product while booze and women further complicate their lives. The following volume, *The Wild Faun*, recounts the story of a good-looking young pianist who prostitutes his talent by hustling the middle-aged women who hang all over him at the cocktail lounge where he works. The final installment in the series, *Little Boy Blue*, follows the career of Midwestern trumpeter Low Carey who dreams of having a band of his own until one day he meets a woman willing to bankroll him.

If Curran's and Willis's novels of the jazz life are bleak, so are most of the others in this period. Clifton Cuthbert's *The Robbed Heart* and Jack Baird's *Hot, Sweet and Blue* are cases in point. In the first of these, well-born Denis Sloane is a music critic who takes jazz very seriously. His devotion to this music takes him frequently to Harlem where he meets and falls in love with the beautiful, intelligent, light-skinned Judy Foster, daughter of a prominent Harlem businessman. While the novel is primarily concerned with chronicling the complexities of this interracial relationship, it also comments on the debasing compromises musicians are forced to make in order to ply their trade professionally. One of Sloane's black friends is in fact forced to deal dope because he can't survive on what he makes playing trumpet. *Hot, Sweet and Blue* also involves an interracial relationship. Growing up under the meanest conditions imaginable, Johnny Burke perseveres to become the leader of the best jazz band in Pittsburgh. Then he falls in love with a beautiful black singer, and the two of them make beautiful music together, both literally and metaphorically, until the bigotry of the day brings them resoundingly to earth.

As in *The Robbed Heart*, the persistent theme of artistic compromise is also important in Annemarie Ewing's *Little Gate* and Robert Sylvester's *Rough Sketch*. Obsessed with jazz and accepted equally by black and white musicians, Ewing's Joe "Little Gate" Geddes leaves his small Midwestern town for the big city, where he establishes a reputation before being reduced to playing his sax in a band that headlines novelty numbers, causing him to retreat to Harlem after hours for the music he loves. Later, when "Little Gate" forms a band of his own and produces a hit record, he discovers that he and his music have become commodities over which he has no control. (Like *Young Man with a Horn*, this novel seems to borrow heavily from the life of Bix Beiderbecke.) The section of *Rough Sketch* that concerns jazz (part 2) also has interesting things to say about the economics of the music industry, as well as the rise of jazz in the 1920s and 1930s. The lead character, Tony Fenner, had once been a musicians' agent, a role that leads to discussions about the impact of the burgeoning music industry on the music itself.

Harold Sinclair's *Music Out of Dixie* is more concerned with the rise of jazz itself than the industry that formed around it. Growing up in the slums near New Orleans toward the beginning of the twentieth century, Dade Tarrent is moved by music early in his life. He masters first the piano and then the clarinet, achieves success, and then suffers defeat. But he doesn't give up. At the end he has become an artist-composer and is heading for New York. Jelly Roll Morton makes a brief but important appearance.

Several other novels of this period portray characters similar to Tarrent, but very few of them experience the qualified optimism of *Music Out of Dixie*. More typically, jazz fiction is riddled with tormented, self-destructive characters like Dorothy Baker's Rick Martin. One of the more striking of these is Virgil Jones from Stanford Whitmore's *Solo*. Jones is reminiscent of Herman Melville's enigmatic Bartleby ("Bartleby, the Scrivener") in his obduracy, his almost total disconnectedness, and his aura of mystery. Jones proclaims himself the last individual in the world; he plays his piano and lives his life exclusively for himself. And the music he produced "was always new, always daring yet never tangled with badly conceived innovations, always a special brand of jazz that no one could imitate." When a manager and a music critic team up to exploit Jones, he resists, though he places himself at great risk by doing so. He is always true to his own peculiar nature.

James Updyke's Royal, from *It's Always Four O'Clock*, is another eccentric, enigmatic pianist, but he is even more self-destructive than Virgil Jones. Readers may find this narrative interesting for its focus on a group of musicians in Los Angeles after World War II trying to forge a new kind of jazz. The group's efforts to produce serious *new* music within a nightclub setting are often met with antagonism. George Lea's *Somewhere There's Music* is another postwar novel with a self-destructive musician at its center. By the time 21-year-old Mike Logan returns to his hometown in Michigan after serving in the Korean War, he has given up swing and Dixieland in favor of the new "cool" jazz, and he's also exchanged his clarinet for a baritone sax. As in every other soldier-home-from-the-war narrative, Mike is disoriented on his return: he has no plans, prospects, or marketable skills — only an abiding love of music, which unfortunately leads him into the company of jazz musicians and the world of narcotics and alcohol.

Several novels of these decades, including a few already noted, dramatize the big band experience. One early (1943) example of this is R. Pingank Malone's *Sound Your "A": The Story of Trumpeter Tom Stewart in Full-Length*

Novel Form, a book that was serialized in *Metronome*. In a story that would
be suitable for teenagers, most of the characters are young musicians with
jazz aspirations who are relegated to playing in a pit band. When one of them,
Tom Stewart, gets a chance to fill in with a name band famous for its "tickety-tockety" style of music, the bandleader falls in love with Tom's corny
playing, unaware that Tom is mocking the music.

Two longer, more serious works concerned with big bands are Osborn
Duke's *Sideman* and Henry Steig's *Send Me Down*, both of which are lengthy
and comprehensive in their explorations of the mechanics and frustrations of
big band life. *Sideman* offers a panoramic survey of the professional and personal lives of several members of a large post–Korean War dance band. The
story centers on sideman Bernie Bell, who leaves college in Texas to play
trombone in a band in Southern California, where he hopes to moonlight by
composing "serious" music. In short, this novel presents another portrait of
the artist as a young man. *Send Me Down* is equally lengthy but valuable for
its realistic descriptions of life on the road, the economics of the music business, the conflict between art and entertainment, and the destructiveness of
marijuana to the world of swing music. The plot revolves around two working-class brothers and a buddy growing up in New York City between the
wars. At considerable sacrifice to their parents, the boys develop sufficient
musical skill to pursue jazz as a career, disappointing their parents who consider such music trash. The brothers soon go their own musical ways, one going on the road with a small group, the other building a big band that eventually plays at Carnegie Hall.

The decades following World War II saw a good deal of pulp (or "soft
porn") jazz fiction, most of which has completely disappeared from view. The
few that have survived must be considered rare. Take, for example, Jack Hanley's *Hot Lips*. The cover of this "Intimate Novel #18" pictures one sexy
woman playing torrid sax and another dancing—just as torridly—while a man,
tie akimbo, watches them, transfixed (or maybe just blitzed). The story is surprisingly simple. When the lead saxophonist of an all-girl band is hospitalized
with delirium tremens, a replacement materializes almost immediately. She is
the beautiful, talented 19-year-old Althea Allen, desperate to escape her evil
stepfather who, in concert with the book's musical motif, "wanted to fiddle"
(with Althea, of course). Band manager Pete Dwyer falls instantly in love with
Althea, but so does fellow band member Mona Storm, who is unencumbered
for the moment because her second husband absconded with her wardrobe in
order to enter a drag contest. The band prospers, Althea becomes a star, and
she and Pete have taken the first steps toward living happily-ever-after by the
end. Readers of this "racy" 1952 novel must have been disappointed to learn
that the title refers only to the playing of musical instruments.

Joe Wiess's *Passion Blues* contains a plot every bit as ingenious—and convincing—as *Hot Lips'*. Trumpeter and leader of a hot jazz combo, Hank Miller develops an interest in gorgeous young singer Sherry. An experienced jazz singer himself, Hank takes it upon himself to mentor Sherry, at one point urging her to listen repeatedly to the recordings of Sarah Vaughan, Billie Holiday, and Doris Day. Sherry of course starts to fall for Hank, a serious plot complication since Hank is already involved with two other women, one of whom, Linda, turns out, to Hank's vast surprise, to be a lesbian. So when Linda then entices Sherry into her own bed, Hank is freed to hook up with his one true love, Hope, who likes Hank and his lovemaking so much that she fixes him up with her mother, thereby gaining maternal sanction for the forthcoming marriage between Hank and Hope.

If indeed, as has been claimed, the artifacts of popular culture are more useful than highbrow objects in helping us to decode our environment, then it's too bad so many books like the two summarized above have been lost to history. As a matter of incidental interest, the musical content of some of these trashy works is as solid as that found in more serious efforts.

To move from the ridiculous to the sublime, it is fair to say that one of the benchmarks of jazz fiction, Ralph Ellison's *Invisible Man*, appeared near mid-century. The story of a young black man's struggle to forge an identity within a discriminatory society, *Invisible Man* might seem not to qualify as a jazz work. After all, apart from thematically significant reference to Louis Armstrong's early rendition of "Black and Blue," it makes little overt mention of music of any kind. But the book—its style and technique—are clearly imbued with the spirit of the music. Note, for example, the "jazziness" of this typical passage:

> I too had stridden and debated, a student leader directing my voice at the highest beams and farthest rafters, ringing them, the accents staccato upon the ridgepole and echoing back with a tinkling, like words hurled to the trees of a wilderness, or into a well of slate-gray water; more sound than sense, a play upon the resonances of buildings, an assault upon the temples of the ear. . . .

Another novel from the 1950s, Harold Flender's *Paris Blue,* is also centrally concerned with racial matters. Eddie Cook moved to Paris a dozen years ago to escape the racial prejudice he had encountered in his Midwestern hometown and has made a comfortable life for himself, playing sax with his combo and generally evading stress and responsibility. But then he falls in love with a vacationing African-American school teacher who convinces him that the racial climate back home has improved immensely during Eddie's absence. At the end Eddie is contemplating going back to find out for himself if this is true.

Two novels from the 1960s still worth reading are Herbert Simmons's *Man Walking on Eggshells* and William Melvin Kelley's *A Drop of Patience*. *Man Walking* tells the story of Raymond "Splib" Douglas, who represents the hope of the future for African-Americans before squandering his impressive potential through drugs. Set during Prohibition in St. Louis and Harlem, the book contains much discussion of race and jazz and prominently refers to St. Louis "home boy" Miles Davis. *A Drop of Patience*, on the other hand, presents an affecting portrait of blind-from-birth horn player, Ludlow Washington, who leaves the South for New York and Chicago where he is finally recognized for his contribution to the new music of jazz, undoubtedly bebop. After being exploited and betrayed by commercialism and racism, Washington (already alienated by his color, blindness, and genius) suffers a breakdown but then recovers and sets out to find a place where he can make the music he loves in peace.

Charlie Parker and the writers of the Beat Generation became dominant forces beginning in the mid-1940s and their influence has continued into the twenty-first century. Three representative works on Parker's legendary (and legendarily short) life should suffice to indicate the range of interest in this towering figure. In *The Sound*, Ross Russell (who knew Parker personally) recounts the story of piano player Bernie Rich. He is torn between joining a big band and touring on the college circuit, with its financial security, or becoming involved in the more vibrant but less stable music scene in Harlem, where Red Travers (the Parker figure) is playing a major role in transforming jazz from swing to bop. The musical dimension of this often sensationalistic novel is extensive, well articulated, and gives the impression of having been written by an insider.

John A. Williams's *Night Song* is less sensational than *The Sound* but generates as much musical interest. The story has much to say about the exploitation of musicians by the music industry and the perennial issue of race. The racial question culminates in a scene toward the end in which Richie Stokes (the Parker figure) is beaten by white cops while Stokes's white friend looks on and does nothing to help. When Stokes—"The Eagle"—disintegrates and dies, he immediately becomes a folk hero, with graffiti cropping up everywhere, proclaiming "Eagle Lives" and "The Eagle Still Soars," echoing the response to the real Charlie Parker's death. (*Bird Lives!*, not incidentally, is the title of Bill Moody's 1999 mystery novel featuring jazz pianist-turned-sleuth Evan Horne.)

In one of the bibles of the Beat Generation, *The Horn*, John Clellon Holmes dramatizes the comeback attempt of Edgar "The Horn" Pool (a composite of Parker and Lester Young). Pool had been a ranking saxophonist until dissipation eroded his skills and affected his mind. This jazz-drenched novel shows Pool's painful effort to regain his place among the top musicians, some with striking resemblances to actual musicians, including Billie Holiday and Thelonious Monk.

Another, more famous bible of the Beat Generation, Jack Kerouac's *On the Road,* like all of Kerouac's novels, is shot through with references to jazz and its players and contains a few scenes depicting music in performance. But these generally superficial qualities don't make the book a jazz fiction. Rather, the book's methodology—its style and structure—makes it a jazz novel of consequence, an essential work of jazz fiction. Like James Baldwin, Kerouac expressed the desire to write in the same way a jazz musician blows, and there are extended passages in *On the Road* where the writer "blows" prose as boppish as anything that had appeared in fiction up to that time. In his essay, "Essentials of Spontaneous Prose," Kerouac describes his manner of writing fiction in a way that would be immediately recognizable to a bop musician as a description of *his* art.

THE 1970s AND BEYOND

Beginning in the 1970s, Don Asher (himself a jazz musician) wrote two diverting jazz works. Dedicated to Hampton Hawes and Jaki Bayard, the first of these, the breezy *The Electric Cotillion*, depicts the scruffy existence of the suggestively named Miles Davey, a pianist who wants to continue playing jazz in a world that has turned to rock 'n' roll. In order to work at all, Davey is forced to debase himself by accepting gigs at such events as a gay costume ball. In this novel, the persistent theme concerning the relegation of jazz to a position of unimportance is at least treated humorously. Asher's story, "The Barrier," presents a serious account of a white pianist who catches the bebop bug in the 1950s and insinuates himself into the black worlds of Boston and New York, hoping to learn to swing. If he never acquired the chops he hoped for, he nevertheless developed self-respect in his quest.

Ishmael Reed and Albert Murray also published notable jazz works beginning in the 1970s. Reed's unclassifiable, hyperactive novel *Mumbo Jumbo* parodies the overlapping histories of voodoo and jazz within the framework of a metaphysical mystery. Albert Murray's tetralogy (so far) is more comprehensive— and comprehensible—as it details the challenges of growing up gifted and black in an often farcical world. The sequence begins with *Train Whistle Guitar* in which young Scooter (later Schoolboy) falls under the powerful influence of a couple of bluesmen in rural Alabama in the 1920s. Scooter's college matriculation and growing maturation are depicted in *The Spyglass Tree*. In *The Seven League Boots* Schoolboy first becomes a bassist and then leaves the band to write music for the movies before joining the expatriate community in France. In the final installment to date of this ongoing work, *The Magic Keys* (2005), Scooter has put his musical ambitions on hold for the time being to return to New York City, marry his college sweetheart, pursue a graduate degree in the humanities, and reconsider what he wants to do with his life. In all of these novels, Murray appropriates, in syntax and structure, certain properties associated with African-American music while referring frequently to the music itself, especially jazz and the blues.

Two other jazz novels published in the 1970s should be noted for the variety they add to those already discussed. The first of these is Pat Richoux's *The Stardust Kid* whose eponymous high school hero, Mike Riley, plays a hot trumpet in Connor City, Nebraska, during World War II. The familiar narrative contour concerns Mike's desire to become a professional musician against his mother's wishes. She's "been there" and wants her son to avoid the fate of her ne'er-do-well ex-husband, Mike's dad. This coming-of-age novel provides a nostalgic backward look at small-town America when the prospect of a one-night stand by Horace Heidt and His Musical Knights could raise goosebumps. E. L. Doctorow's *Ragtime* also takes place in the past, though the past here is early twentieth century New York when the United States was experiencing—as it so often does—a period of great ferment. In its dramatization of the intersecting lives of three radically different families, *Ragtime* fuels speculation about how America came to achieve its protean identity. Although the actual musical content is not great, the title, the epigraph from Scott Joplin, and the syncopated style make it difficult to read the book without hearing the music of Joplin in your head.

The two decades closing out the twentieth century also provide a pleasing array of jazz fictions. David Ritz published two novels in the same year (1989), both of which are wacky, raunchy, and drenched in jazz. After an acknowledgment to "the many immortal saxists—Pres being the most prominent—who've brought me closer to God," *Barbells and Saxophones* tells the story of 27-year-old Vince Viola who lives for body-building, birds, sex, and his saxophone, and these often overlapping passions, along with a truly bizarre family situation, create the kind of conflicts that lead Vince to the psychiatrist's couch. Ritz's other jazz novel, *Blue Notes under a Felt Hat,* also features an obsessive protagonist, 23-year-old Danny who is gaga over sex, hats, and jazz in post–World War II New York. In a jazz club on 52nd Street, where bebop is fast overtaking swing, Danny meets a gifted but unknown black pianist-singer, Cliff Summer, and the two of them go on a series of travel adventures designed to bring Summer the fame and fortune Danny thinks he deserves. At the end Danny is selling hats and jazz records (hence the title) from his business in Harlem.

Like *Blue Notes*, Percival Everett's *Suder* also contains picaresque elements, as its dropout from a disastrous career in professional baseball, Craig Suder, encounters cocaine smugglers, a young runaway, and an elephant named Renoir during *his* peregrinations. A high point in young Craig's life when he was still in the South was the appearance of Bud Powell, who moved in with the Suders, soon calling Craig "Bird" because of the boy's alleged resemblance to Charlie Parker. Craig of course took up the saxophone and later in life included the instrument on his list of sacred objects, the things without which life would not be worth living. Another object on that list was a recording of Parker's "Ornithology," which Craig carried with him everywhere, along with a phonograph to play it on.

In the 1980s and 1990s several writers tested the limits of jazz fiction by deliberately appropriating certain characteristic techniques and structures of the music for their narratives, picking up where Ralph Ellison and Jack Kerouac, among others, left off. In both *Be-Bop, Re-Bop* and *Muse-Echo Blues,* for instance, Xam Wilson Cartiér often tries (sometimes successfully) to create the prose equivalent of an improvised jazz solo by borrowing certain techniques usually identified with poetry: metrical complexity, assonance, internal rhyme, and alliteration, to name a few. In *Be-Bop, Re-Bop* the narrator is a black woman who recounts her life growing up in St. Louis and later as a single mother on the West Coast. The narrator of *Muse-Echo Blues* is a jazz pianist-composer who has fallen prey to creative inertia in San Francisco in the early 1990s. To escape this dilemma, she time-travels back half a century and finds inspiration in a soul sister whose life has been energized by the fervent jazz scene of the times, including Billy Eckstine's and Count Basie's bands.

Nathaniel Mackey's ongoing work, *From a Broken Bottle Traces of Perfume Still Emanate*, is strikingly different from Cartiér's novels, starting with style and technique: Cartiér's novels are told from the black urban vernacular, Mackey's from the written tradition; Cartiér's are first-person narratives, Mackey's are epistolary novels. The two novels in Mackey's work-in-progress, *Bedouin Hornbook* and *Djbot Baghostus's Run*, consist of a series of letters from "N." to his correspondent, "Angel of Dust." These letters contain constant references to jazz and its musicians, as well as lengthy theoretical and analytical discussions of jazz in performance and recording. Often it seems as if the letter writer were consciously attempting to transform the music under discussion into the words on the page — and hoping for a similar response from Angel of Dust. Otherwise, why does N. tell his correspondent that the letter will be accompanied by a tape of the music N. has been meditating over? N. may be trying to give his readers a clue to his aesthetic intentions when he quotes from the liner-notes to John Coltrane's *Coltrane Live at the Village Van-guard Again!* In the notes Coltrane is quoted "as having said that he was 'try-ing to work out a kind of writing that will allow for more plasticity, more via-bility, more room for improvisation in the statement of the melody itself.'" This is followed immediately by N.'s admitting that maybe that is what he is trying to do (in his writing?) as well.

Unlike Mackey's unfathomable narratives, Toni Morrison's *Jazz* does con-tain discernible plot strands, the central one of which involves a middle-aged man's murder of his young girlfriend and his wife's subsequent jealous at-tempt to mutilate the girlfriend's corpse at the funeral. But it is the telling of this tale, not the tale itself, that fans and scholars alike of jazz fiction will find most provocative. To be specific, not only is the language "jazzy," but so is the structure: the narrative proceeds through multiple points of view, after the fashion of a musical performance in which first one and then another musi-cian takes the floor and, after letting the audience know he's been hearing what the other soloists have had to say, shapes the music according to his own will and personality. The structure of the novel, in other words, seems as spontaneous and improvisational as a Charlie Parker riff. Toni Morrison has often declared that she would like her writing to emulate jazz. If the critical commentary on *Jazz* is any indication, she has succeeded, possibly to a greater extent than any previous jazz fiction writer with a similar objective.

Even as the music continued to suffer serious commercial decline, how-ever, jazz fiction fairly flourished in the second half of the 1990s and demon-strated a striking variety of subjects and themes. David Huddle's novella, *Tenorman*, is draped around an unusual premise: an African-American horn man-composer, whose life has seemingly bottomed out, is brought back to the United States from Sweden under the auspices of the National Endowment for the Arts and provided with all the necessities of life on the condition that he allow every aspect of his daily existence to be studied and recorded. Just being associated with a genuinely creative person transforms the lives of the sterile researchers in a positive way.

People are also transformed through jazz in Jon Hassler's *Rookery Blues*. The setting is northern Minnesota at an academic backwater during the 1960s. When five faculty members discover their common love of jazz, they form a combo, "The Icejam Quintet," and this association provides their lives with a meaningful sense of community. But the togetherness they had struggled so hard to achieve is disrupted when the first labor union in the college's history comes to campus, forcing the combo members to follow their scattered alle-giances.

Anthony Weller's *The Polish Lover*, on the other hand, follows a jazz clar-inetist's obsessive globetrotting pursuit of an enigmatic woman and his reflections, a decade later, on the meaning of their strange relationship. The solid jazz content of this novel includes a significant appearance by Adam Makowicz and analytical discussions of the harmonic ideas in John Coltrane's music. It can also be said that the improvisational nature of jazz influences the structure, style, and theme of the story. What can't be said is that the author provides convincing motivation for his characters' actions—but fans of jazz fiction may consider this a minor blemish.

With a title from a Kenny Dorham composition and a dust jacket photo by William Claxton, Bart Schneider's *Blue Bossa* flaunts its jazz credentials. The story takes place in San Francisco during the time of the Patty Hearst kidnapping and concerns Ronnie Reboulet, whose motivations, like those of Anthony Weller's characters, are occasionally obscure. Reboulet resembles Chet Baker: he's a jazz trumpeter who had once been famous for his boyish good looks as well as his music and, at the height of his fame, lost everything to drugs: his teeth, his lip, and his looks. Now he's trying, with the help of a strong, caring woman, to get himself and his career back together. The novel contains excellent descriptions of music-making, refers frequently to beboppers, and provides certain musicians (Charlie Parker among them) with cameo roles.

Several nonfictional musicians also play roles in Rafi Zabar's epic *The Bear Comes Home,* including Charlie Haden and Ornette Coleman. The protagonist is a sax-playing talking bear who experiences love and transcendent bliss through music. The book overflows with jazz. The descriptions of music-making are superb, and the portrayal of the musician's life seems authentic: the constant challenges of the improvisational process, the mind-numbing tediousness of life on the road, and the seeming economic futility of a musical career. *The Bear Comes Home* brings jazz fiction in the twentieth century to an impressive close.

And jazz fiction has also provided a healthy handful of impressive novels in the first lustrum of the twenty-first century. Two long, unusually expansive works ushered in the new century. Stanley Crouch's *Don't the Moon Look Lonesome* provides a kaleidoscopic look at the culture of the United States in the waning stage of the twentieth century through the consciousness of a white female jazz singer who is shakily married to a black saxophonist. Jack Fuller's *The Best of Jackson Payne* concerns a white middle-aged musicologist who is writing a biography of a black saxophonist, "the last towering colossus of jazz." The titular Payne seems to be a composite of every agonized artist in the history of modern jazz.

Also long and expansive, Frederick Turner's *1929* presents an exuberant fictional biography of the short-lived Bix Beiderbecke in the context of his tumultuous times. The publication of the book was timed to coincide with the centennial of the great musician's birth. Alan Goldsher's *Jam* traces the friendship of two young boys who discover a mutual love for jazz. One of the boys grows famous by creating a unique fusion of rock 'n' roll and bebop, while the other rejects commercialization and remains true to the purity of jazz. Adam Mansbach's *Shackling Water* details the musical apprenticeship of a young black saxophonist whose total commitment to jazz is jeopardized by complicated relationships with a white woman and a black dope dealer.

The five novels thumbnailed above are serious, accomplished works, and as such they predict a productive future for jazz fiction.

If the short story and international fiction seem to be slighted in this overview, there are reasons. First, two excellent collections of jazz stories are available (though currently out-of-print). Both Marcela Breton's *Hot and Cool* and Richard Albert's *From Blues to Bop* contain informative introductions and judicious selections. The works of a variety of international writers are to be found in *B Flat, Bebop, Scat,* edited by Chris Parker. Many additional selections are to be found in the annotations that follow. Finally, to give proper credit to the considerable contribution foreign writers have made to jazz fiction, I have appended separate chapters on **immigrant and international jazz fiction** as well as several other thematic clusters.

Chapter Two

"Jazz" Fiction sans Music

Scholars and fans of jazz fiction should be forewarned: many works that represent themselves—or seem to represent themselves—as jazz-related in fact contain little or no musical content. Take, for instance, Charles Newman's *White Jazz* and Melissa Scott's *The Jazz*. Although the titles imply a musical connection, there is none. Both novels are concerned with cybernetics; "the jazz" actually refers to the code word for international communication systems.

What jazz in the title of Victor Suarez's *Latin Jazz* refers to is anyone's guess since this novel of a Cuban-American family's problems with dislocation contains no references to the music, though it does contain a functional salsa scene. The title of Tracy Ryan's *Jazz Tango* is even more mystifying: in its exploration of a woman's consciousness, the novel contains neither music nor dancing. The literary journalist Edmund Wilson shouldn't be blamed for employing a misleading title; after all, *The Higher Jazz* was edited into existence after his death, and the title was chosen by the editor. It does involve music but not jazz. Craig Holden's *The Jazz Bird* is a different story. A researched novel set in the Jazz Age year of 1927, it does contain a character with the titular name and makes fleeting references to jazz clubs and circles of the time, but its musical content is finally negligible. A self-contained story cut from the original manuscript of this novel and published in editor Robert Randisi's jazz-mystery anthology, *Murder . . . and All That Jazz*, "The P & G Ivory Cut Whiskey Massacree," discloses not a single whiff of music of any kind. Readers are advised that the stories in Randisi's collection contain, with a few exceptions, disappointingly little musical content. Nor does Jill Shure's *Night Jazz* fulfill the promise of its title; it's a time-bending romance whose protagonist is transported back to the Jazz

Age. Neal Holland Duncan's *Baby Soniat: A Tale from the Jazz Jungle*, while set in New Orleans and including "jazz" in the subtitle, likewise contains only a jazz funeral for musical content.

On the other hand, Julie Smith's title, *The Axeman's Jazz*, seems deceitful. On the cover a skeleton is pictured playing on a muted trumpet. That, in addition to the New Orleans setting and the double jazz reference in the title, would lead the wariest of readers to anticipate a story with a strong jazz component. Incredibly, there is none. Perhaps literature should be made to conform to truth-in-advertising guidelines. Even if this were to happen, James Ellroy's *White Jazz* would probably slip through the cracks. The novel does, after all, make glancing reference to a few jazz artists, and broken jazz records provide a clue to the mystery, but this hardly qualifies it as a jazz novel. Jazz in the title is probably used to torque up the dense noir atmosphere. Bobby Jo Mason's "Jazz," in her story "With Jazz," was not likely intended to mislead, deceive, or "torque up." It is rather an attempt to give a zippy name to a decidedly unmusical character.

Both James Baldwin and William Melvin Kelley have written impressive works of jazz fiction, so jazz buffs might be excused for thinking that their novels, *If Beale Street Could Talk* and *A Different Drummer,* respectively, embody musical themes. It turns out, of course, that neither contains any references to jazz. No one would accuse Baldwin or Kelley or their publishers of setting out to mislead an unwitting reading public. Unfortunately, the same can not be said for Lucinda Roy's *Lady Moses*. The novel's protagonist is nicknamed Jazz, and Nikki Giovanni's dust jacket blurb further suggests that the reader should expect to find an abundance of bebop and blues between the covers. "I was not there," Giovanni writes, "when Charlie Parker started playing between the notes; I could not be there when Billie Holiday pondered the fruit of southern trees; I was unable to sit at a table when Miles Davis gave birth to the Cool but the musicians aren't the only ones who sing and I am here when Lucinda Roy makes her startling debut with *Lady Moses*." It is shocking, after all this, to find no jazz content of any sort in the novel.

No one would accuse the Library of Congress of setting out to deceive or mislead, but it could be charged with naively relying on the accuracy of the writers whose works it collects. In its Cataloguing-in-Publication Data the Library classifies Rett MacPherson's *Killing Cousins* as a novel about a jazz singer. In fact, this genealogical mystery is frequently referred to as a jazz novel even though its sole claim to the status is its reference to a dead jazz singer. There is no music. Nor is there any music in a two-part story that not only declares itself as jazz fiction but appears in a magazine devoted to jazz. "Eddie and the Two-Dollar Bet" appeared, anonymously, in *Jazz Today* and contains no musical references.

It would be futile to list all the works that seem or pretend to be jazz fictions and aren't. Some of the authors of these works no doubt intend their titles to contribute bluesiness or jazziness to the tone; others probably use "jazz" in an offhanded way, to indicate unspecified things, as in the phrase "all that jazz"; still others doubtless hope that the term will imbue the narrative with an element of edginess or sexiness. Whatever their intentions, however, it remains clear that many fictions containing the word in question are really only masquerading as jazz fictions. (For a novel that employs the slippery, protean term in unusual ways, see Claude McKay's *Home to Harlem*.) The annotated bibliography in this volume should go far to help aficionados of jazz literature identify the real thing—the authentic jazz fiction—and select the works that come closest to meeting their needs.

Chapter Three

Fiction for Juveniles and Young Adults

Jazz fiction provides copious examples of stories aimed at young audiences, from toddlers through young adults. It would of course be a stretch to designate most such works aimed at the very young as stories because invariably the texts are subordinate to the illustrations. Like other subjects, jazz provides a convenient platform from which to spread ideas, promote moral values, and raise the burning issue of feelings. In a more immediate and organic way, however, jazz clearly inspires vibrant colors, intriguing shapes, and ear-catching sound patterns in children's literature.

Sherry Shahan's *The Jazzy Alphabet* provides an example of a book designed to help tots master the alphabet. What infant wouldn't be beguiled to be introduced to *B* via "boogie woogie bebop a boogaloo. Bim-bam blues!" With minimal narration, Chris Raschka's *Charlie Parker Played Be Bop* and *John Coltrane's 'Giant Steps'* introduce young readers to the styles of the eponymous artists and teach them to *hear* the music in their minds. The concept behind the Coltrane work is quite unusual, as the narrator first introduces his very young audience to the artist's "sheets of sound" and then has a box, some raindrops, and a kitten illustrate this theoretical concept. It brings a smile to imagine listening to Coltrane with a friend and hearing his—or your—two-year-old blurt out "sheets of sound." Matthew Golub's *The Jazz Fly* is also interested in introducing the very young to principles of jazz, especially scat singing in this instance. He does this by creating a story in which a jazz-speaking fly asks different critters how to get to town; when they answer him, he hears music in their *oinks* and *rrribits*, inspiring him to perform an outstanding solo that night at a supper club. This book is packaged with a CD of the author, accompanied by a jazz quartet, narrating the story.

Several books aimed at roughly the same audience provide fictionalized portraits of jazz greats; generally speaking, all warts are removed from the artists' lives in order to protect the innocent. For instance, Louis Armstrong's early life, as presented in Alan Schroeder's *Satchmo's Blues,* seems sweetly picturesque as young Louis buys his first horn at a pawn shop, aims it at the heavens, and vows someday to blow the stars clean out of the sky. Andrea Davis Pinkney's *Ella Fitzgerald, the Tale of a Vocal Virtuoso* relates the story of Fitzgerald's life, emphasizing her invaluable contribution to scat singing; the story is told by female narrator Scat Cat Monroe in "the infectious rhythms of scat." In *Lookin' for Bird in the Big City,* Robert Burleigh dramatizes the story of Miles Davis's search for his idol, Charlie Parker, and how Parker immediately recognizes the young trumpeter's special gift, allowing the two of them to make beautiful bebop together. In contrast, Harold D. Sill, in *Misbehaving with Fats: A Toby Bradley Adventure,* has a political point to make. In this story, young New England white boy, Toby Bradley, is able, through the miracle of time travel, to hang out with his hero Fats Waller and learn what it was like to grow up talented and black in segregated America.

As the target audience for jazz fiction grows older, the strategies of presentation and the fictional objectives change accordingly. There are of course more (and larger) words and fewer illustrations, and these longer works comprise unmistakable stories, many of which contain more complex moral or didactic implications than the works aimed at a younger audience. It is not unusual for these stories to include an older relative as a conduit for the young protagonist's growing wisdom.

Both Jerome Cushman's *Tom B. and the Joyful Noise* and Arnold Dobrin's *Scat!* contain the stock figure of the churchly grandmother who tries to dissuade her grandson from becoming involved in jazz—that "sinful music." In the first story, Thomas Boynton Fraser ("Tommy B." to his friends) is a cocky little black kid who uses his shoeshine kit as a passport to wander about New Orleans; when he stumbles one night upon the French Quarter, he becomes immediately enthralled by the music and vows to learn to play the trumpet. As Tommy's devotion to jazz grows, his schoolwork suffers and his grandma's ire increases. In the tradition of such stories, however, everything is nicely resolved in the end. Everything turns out well for eight-year-old Scat, too. His father plays jazz trumpet, and Scat wants to do the same but his grandmother disapproves. In a nice, ironic twist, when grandma dies Scat remembers her sage advice always to follow his heart and so he conveniently allows this wisdom to prevail over her disdain for jazz—and teaches himself to play the harmonica.

Grandfathers and uncles occasionally serve to counterbalance the sternly disapproving grandmothers in jazz fiction, though seldom if ever in the same story. In Don Carter's *Heaven's All-Star Band*, for instance, the young grandson had heard his beloved Grandpa Jack so often refer to bebop as heavenly that when the old man died the boy imagined him to be in a heaven filled with the music of Dizzy, Monk, Bird, and Trane, among others. The grandfather figure is also central to Arna Bontemps's *Lonesome Boy*, a longer, richer, more ambiguous story than most aimed at a preteen audience. As trumpet-loving Little Bubber, who lives with his grandfather in the country, grows closer to his instrument, he grows further apart from his surrogate father and his wise counsel, until—inevitably—Bubber leaves his country home for the bright lights and seductive music of New Orleans. Predictably, he quickly becomes a success and just as quickly is corrupted by that success. When he returns home, his grandpa tells him to always seek out the company of others when he is lonesome and to play the trumpet only when other people are around. This unusually suggestive story may owe a debt of gratitude to Nathaniel Hawthorne's classic, "Young Goodman Brown."

Debbie A. Taylor's *Sweet Music in Harlem* contains neither such suggestiveness nor a grandfather. What it does have is ebullient joy and Uncle Click, a famous Harlem horn man who loses his signature hat just as a photographer from *Highnote* magazine is on his way to take his picture. So Uncle Click dispatches his doting nephew C. J. (horn man in waiting) to scour the neighborhood for his beloved chapeau. In going on this mission of love, C. J. unwittingly sets in motion a lovely occasion of musical camaraderie. The story was inspired by Art Kane's famous 1958 photograph *A Great Day in Harlem.*

As the jazz fiction audience grows into its teens and beyond (the amorphous "Young People" category), the literature directed at it becomes more thematic, didactic, and racially resonant. It's not surprising to find the coming-of-age theme predominant in these works, since this motif, especially in the United States, has long been preeminent in the literature aimed at a youthful audience. The same can be said of the racial question, which has arguably been the central conflict in American culture practically from the beginning.

Nat Hentoff's *Jazz Country* is as interested in civil rights issues as it is in jazz. It depicts the dilemma of a white boy who is influenced by black musicians and can't decide whether to go to college or pursue a career in jazz. Hentoff's *Does This School Have Capital Punishment?* provides a good story with a strong musical component wrapped around the dilemma of another young man. Sam Davidson is one of those kids stalked by trouble, so when he enrolls at one of New York City's most prestigious high schools, everyone wonders how long he will last. But Sam seems to adjust well to his new environment; he even becomes absorbed by an oral history assignment that brings him into close association with a legendary jazz trumpeter, Major Kelley, who dramatically saves Sam's skin when the boy is wrongfully accused of possessing marijuana—a nice example of a black man risking his own well-being to rescue a privileged white boy.

Haskel Frankel's *Big Band* is heartwarming in another way. Here high-schooler Bob Allen plays trumpet so well that he has been encouraged to drop out of school to attempt to make a career of music. Enter father, who makes a deal with his son: if you can successfully arrange a summer band tour, he tells his son, you can quit school and immerse yourself in music. Everyone— probably even young readers—knows how this challenge is going to work itself out.

Richard Hill's coming-of-age novel, *Riding Solo with the Golden Horde*, is interesting for its setting in time and place. It takes place in St. Petersburg, Florida, in the late 1950s and involves its white saxophone-playing protagonist, Vic Messenger, in the world of black jazz during segregation. Louis Armstrong makes a cameo appearance, and Gene Quill plays a significant role.

Through a shocking twist Howard Brett's *Memphis Blues* extends the boundaries of the maturation subgenre. The story takes place during Beale Street's heyday and involves mulatto Harold Green's rise from the gutter to relative prominence. When a good-hearted whore is killed, young Harold avenges her death by slitting the throat of her killer, thus becoming "a real, honest-to-God black man."

Seemingly a world away from *Memphis Blues* is Roderick Townley's sanguine *Sky: A Novel in Three Sets and an Encore*, which is set in 1959 Manhattan and features nerdy, tongue-twisted teenager, Sky (né Alec Schuyler), whose problems are more predictable and far less violent than those in the previous Beale Street novel: namely, what to do about a beautiful, brainy girlfriend, a problematic future, and a father who despises the jazz that Sky lives to play. The three sets of the subtitle are "Moanin'," "'Round Midnight," and "I Should Care"; the encore is "Circle in the Rain," and the dedicatees are pianist Lennie Tristano and drummer John Weisman. In short, this novel deserves to be nominated for "The Jazziest Jazz Fiction for Young Readers."

Erika Tamar's *Blues for Silk Garcia* isn't nearly as jazzy or ultimately cheerful as *Sky*, but it is nevertheless refreshing because it is written by and about a female, an unusual if not quite rare phenomenon. Fifteen-year-old Linda Ann Garcia sets out to find her father, whose only legacies to her are a striking physical resemblance, a guitar, and a recording of a song, "Blues for Linda Ann." Linda Ann is disappointed to find that her father is dead but grateful to discover that he reinvented jazz theory and was a genius of jazz guitar. She also finds out that he was a wretched human being, more than likely a psychopath. Through her quest, Linda Ann comes to understand that the only human feelings her father experienced were distilled into his music. This epiphany leads her to accept her father for who and what he was. Now, knowing she is no longer just "the daughter of Silk Garcia," she can go on to discover who *she* is.

Lisa Tucker's *Shout Down the Moon* is another novel by a female about a female and, arguably, primarily for females of high school age or slightly beyond. Twenty-one-year-old Patty Taylor simply wants to make a life for herself and her two-year-old son, but all occasions conspire against her: an alcoholic, psychologically destructive mother; a scary ex-husband who is determined to reenter her life; and a prejudiced music industry that would exploit a woman's appearance over her talent. When Patty lands a gig as lead singer of a serious all-male jazz quartet, she becomes the bad guy: just another pretty face and shapely body hired to make the band commercially viable while forcing it to compromise its artistic ideals. But against formidable odds plucky Patty vows to master jazz and transform herself from decorative pop singer to estimable musician. At the end she is well on the way to gaining the respect, if not the love, of the quartet. A dissertation is somewhere waiting to be written on the effect of the intrusion of the female singer on the male jazz group. It's nice to see this important motif from the woman's perspective—for a change.

Chapter Four

Women

No one should be surprised to learn that male writers of jazz fiction, like their sisters, have produced work that focuses on females. After all, throughout literary history the men have tried their hand at creating memorable female characters, sometimes with striking results. It is disappointing—but not surprising—to report that neither the men nor the women in this subgenre can yet claim an Emma Bovary, Hester Prynne, Anna Karenina, or Carrie Meeber. Fortunately, this does not mean that there aren't titles, by both sexes, in this category worth seeking out.

Alan V. Hewat's *Lady's Time* is a serious novel that raises provocative questions that nicely complement its portrait of a lady. The lady of the title, Winslow (not Day), is an attractive woman of mixed blood passing for white in New England after escaping from an abusive life in turn-of-the-century New Orleans. She supports herself by giving music lessons and playing ragtime piano at a local inn. Her mysterious early death leads the reader to suspect that she had entered into a pact with voodoo spirits back home in Louisiana—a variation, with a racial twist, on the age-old Faust theme.

Stanley Crouch provides a more expansive exploration of a woman's psyche in *Don't the Moon Look Lonesome* in his depiction of a white female jazz singer from North Dakota married to a black saxophonist from Houston. This particular configuration allows the writer to assess the state of the union as he filters, through the consciousness of a single sympathetic observer, some of the central issues of the time, the end of the twentieth century. These include, but are no means limited to, matters relating to marriage and family, race, dope, and jazz.

Hal Glatzer's *Too Dead to Swing* couldn't be less serious or ambitious. It is included here for its radical contrast with the previous two works. The first and most obvious difference concerns its subgenre; it's a light-hearted period mystery. The second is its milieu: it features an all-woman swing band, the Ultra Belles, whose violinist turns up dead, possibly from hatpin misadventure, leading their saxophonist Katy Green to become an amateur detective as well as den mother to the other girls.

The novels by women that center on female swing bands are considerably less cheerful than Glatzer's effort. Shannon Richards-Slaughter's dissertation novel, "The Blossoms of Jazz: A Novel of Black Female Jazz Musicians in the 1930s," concerns a nostalgic reunion concert of the Blossoms, a black trio that had faded from memory after making it big years earlier. As the daughter of one of the Blossoms decides to write a biography of the group, she discovers—among other things—the not-so-surprising fact that the black women had been reluctant to perform in the South. Jeanne Westin's *Swing Sisters* follows a similar plot line: the reunion of an all-woman (white, in this case) big band that had flourished toward the end of the Depression before being "forgotten in their own time." Serious musicians all, the women are soon disillusioned to learn that "pretty faces mean pretty profits." Even when they blow the roof off a house, the reviews emphasize their clothing at the expense of their musicianship. This long, generally depressing researched work is valuable for the insights it provides into the mechanics of a women's orchestra during the heyday for such groups. This is a neglected area of jazz fiction and scholarship.

One species of jazz fiction that has, unfortunately, not been neglected embodies the works written by women for women, especially those with an aversion to the real world. Because the plots of these works are so deliciously (albeit unintentionally) camp, they are great fun to read about; in fact, the novels themselves, in small doses, can provide diversion from the travails or banality of everyday life.

First case in point: Elizabeth Jordan's *Blues in the Night* has it all: geographical and historical sweep; world war and revolution (including a cameo appearance by "Che" Guevara); racial conflict; booze and drugs; witch doctors and foreign gangsters; and, through all of this, love, love, love. Dessie is a southern blonde with a proclivity for the blues, thanks largely to her old black nanny down home. A momentary indescretion results in Dessie's birthing an illegitimate child, causing her to flee in shame to New York, where she soon auditions for a gig as a jazz singer. After being shocked to be told that she would never make it in show biz in the big city unless she stripped, Dessie, against daunting odds, becomes a tremendous success as jazz chanteuse—before returning, almost immediately, to obscurity and destitution. She soon finds herself in Mexico where she learns Spanish in record time, allowing her—*literally*—to sing for her supper. At the end the plucky gal seems destined to reestablish herself as the finest jazz singer of her generation.

Carolee Burns, from Stella Cameron's *Tell Me Why,* had also been a world-class jazz musician before mysteriously disappearing from public view, surfacing only occasionally to perform at a small club outside Seattle far from the bright lights and madding crowd. Enter Max Wolfe, former professional football star, "the man no woman had managed to tame." Attracted to the sadness enveloping Carolee, Max determines to unravel the mystery of her melancholy and, of course, cure it. Well, very shortly nostrils flare, pulses quicken, accidents happen, secrets are revealed, and—surprise!—love conquers all. Through all of this, there always seems to be a piano in the shadows beckoning Carolee to return to the international stage whence she had so abruptly vanished.

Unlike the previous two "women's novels," Andrea Smith's *Friday Nights at Honeybee's* has an all-black dramatis personae and features two protagonists whose radically different lives converge in Harlem at Honeybee Mc-Color's place, the locus of the Harlem music scene, where every musician of note (and many of little note) stops by from time to time for the rolling jam session always in progress and the scrumptious soul food in abundant supply. This "sisterhood" novel contains more jazz than the other two combined. It refers to many actual jazz musicians and provides some of them with walk-on parts; it nicely renders the musical apprenticeship and development of one of the protagonists; and it describes the grinding life on the road of marginal musicians. It is a folksy novel told in the African-American vernacular and contains a hopeful denouement.

Lisa Tucker's *Shout Down the Moon* also contains a hopeful outcome and is clearly designed for an audience of young females. It traces the troubled existence of twenty-one-year-old Patty Taylor, who encounters formidable obstacles as she struggles to make a life for herself and her two-year-old son. Luck seems to be with her when she lands a gig as lead singer of a serious jazz quartet. But this good fortune soon sours when the guys in the band give her the cold shoulder; after all, they are serious musicians and her presence— the presence of a female singer—means that they will have to compromise their lofty standards in order to become commercially viable. But Patty doesn't crumble under this hostility. Rather she does what she believes to be the right thing: she learns jazz and transforms herself from pretty pop singer into serious musician, gaining the respect of the band. Another work with a young female protagonist is Mandy Sayer's *Mood Indigo*, a novel-in-stories that is clearly not intended exclusively for an audience of young females. It dramatizes ten or so years in the life of a young Australian girl, Rose, whose everyday existence and prospects for the future are bleak. Rose is sustained by her love for her dad and the music he makes as an itinerant jazz pianist. Unfortunately, her dad aspires to be a serious musician, and not many customers want to listen to serious music during Happy Hour. At one climactic—and dispiriting—moment, just as Rose's dad begins to play "Mood Indigo," management informs him that such music is inappropriate for an afterwork crowd who have come to a saloon to have their spirits lifted. Several *serious* jazz pianists are referred to.

A few other novels by women-about-women present protagonists who are more mature or become more mature than the previous two. These works generally promote a feminist perspective and, more specifically, if the three books that follow are typical—as surely they are—a black feminist agenda. At the center of Gayl Jones's *Corregidora* is a blues singer who tries to come to terms with her abysmal life by singing; when asked what the blues does for her, she reflects, "It helps me to explain what I can't explain." Although this novel portrays the kind of lives from which the blues spring and refers to notable jazz and blues figures, it is much more about black feminism and the legacy of slavery. Ntozake Shange's *Sassafrass, Cypress and Indigo* also advances the cause of African-American feminism as it recounts the intertwining stories of three African-American sisters and their mother who start out in Charleston before branching out in different directions. All of the women have artistic inclinations, and two of the sisters are involved with jazz men, one of whom seems doomed to live out his life on the fringes of the dope world while the other, a musician and composer, dedicates himself to his art. Devotees of jazz fiction will find interest in this dichotomy.

The jazz novel by a woman about a woman that presents the most comprehensive portrait of a female jazz artist is Candace Allen's *Valaida*, a researched roman á clef based on the life of Valada (later Valaida) Snow, the small-town girl from the South who grew up to travel the world as a trumpeter and showbiz personality. The author has taken the few murky recorded biographical facts of the subject's childhood and fleshed them out in an effort to imagine how her past might have influenced the mature artist who spent most of her creative life on the road. The novel explores questions of race, prejudice, and suffering from a variety of perspectives and imaginatively recreates how these might have affected one gifted African-American individual caught, as it were, in the middle. Ethel Waters, Earl Hines, Coleman Hawkins, and Billie Holiday play significant roles in this largely psychological inventory of a remarkable artist.

Another historical novel, Toni Morrison's *Jazz,* is also most assuredly a jazz novel by a woman, but it makes no attempt to create a larger-than-life protagonist. Rather, it employs multiple narrative perspectives (or, perhaps, a single narrator speaking in different voices, like Benny Carter or Yusef Lateef going from one instrument to another on a single tune) in recounting several unsavory episodes in the lives of rural southern characters who have relocated to Harlem in the 1920s. The central incident involves 50-year-old Joe Trace's murder of his young girlfriend Dorcas and Joe's wife's subsequent attempt, in a jealous rage, to mutilate the corpse at Dorcas's funeral. Although the jazz content is not significant at the level of plot, it is, as the title implies, everywhere apparent in the book's style and structure.

First, the style is—for lack of a less redundant word—jazzy. Note, for example, how the elliptical constructions and nonstandard punctuation (or lack of punctuation) of the following passage collaborate to reflect the busy-ness of the big-city experience:

> The city is smart at this: smelling and good and looking raunchy; sending secret messages designed as public signs: this way, open here, danger to let colored only single men on sale woman wanted private room stop dog on premises absolutely no money down fresh chicken free delivery fast.

Second, the multiple points of view of *Jazz* suggest a musical performance in which first one, then another, musician takes center stage and, after letting the audience know he's been listening to his predecessor(s), bends the music to his own will and personality. Everything about the novel's structure seems designed to feel spontaneous and improvised—like a prime Charlie Parker riff.

Nobel laureate Toni Morrison has often spoken about how she would like her art to emulate certain characteristics of jazz. In *Jazz* she has probably accomplished this with greater success than can be argued for any other American novel. The cottage industry of literary criticism that has sprung into existence over this novel lends force to this assertion.

So one must conclude that though neither the male nor female writers of jazz fiction have yet bodied forth a truly memorable female character, they have together generated a sufficient variety of worthy fictions featuring women to pique the interest of the ardent fan of such literature for some time to come.

Chapter Five

Works Based on the
Lives of Actual Musicians

The surprise isn't that there are fictions based on the lives—or events in the lives—of jazz artists but that there aren't more of them. But then, come to think on it, there are few autobiographies and far fewer biographies of jazz musicians that do justice to the lives that were often as not filled with enough dramatic events and creative contemplations to fill a massive multivolume work. Thanks to the wondrous elasticity of fiction, works in this category are occasionally able to make provocative forays into the artist's mind and imagination, encouraging readers to reconsider what they think they have learned through empirical data.

A striking example of this kind of work is Michael Ondaatje's *Coming through Slaughter*, a breathtaking psychological portrait of one of jazz's innovators, Buddy Bolden. Starting with the few known facts of Bolden's life, Ondaatje has imagined for us what it might have been like to inhabit Bolden's deranged mind as he forged dramatic relationships with both his music and women before—and while—his personality suffered something like total disintegration. The author brilliantly employs poetic techniques to supercharge his prose, resulting in a convincing depiction of how a psychopathic genius was *consumed* by the frenetic music he heard in his head and on the streets. Long before the end, the reader feels he knows how music sounded, felt, and, yes, looked to this tortured artist.

Another "inventor" of jazz, Jelly Roll Morton, is given rounded treatment in Samuel Charters's researched novel, *Jelly Roll Morton's Last Night at the Jungle Inn*, in which the egomaniacal title character anecdotally tells the story of his life, taking full credit whenever possible for his own invaluable contributions to the birth and evolution of the music.

Although Louis Armstrong is not even present in the first quarter of the novel, he steals the show once he comes on stage in Roddy Doyle's *Oh, Play That Thing,* and one could argue that the novel fizzles when he exits. Armstrong and the story's protagonist, Henry Smart, engage in a series of energetically entertaining adventures during Armstrong's Hot Fives period. Much of this part of the novel dramatizes the strategies Armstrong employs to gain credit for being the world's best musician, the difficulties he has in accomplishing this lofty objective in an industry controlled by whites, and the problems he has with women. For instance, when Smart reminds Armstrong that one of his women wants to take credit for his success, Armstrong replies: "That fair. . . . She put my name up in lights, first one to. And she showed me how to carry a hat. I ain't denying nothing. But listen here, Pops. On whose big mouth be the chops that blow the horn?"

Both Annemarie Ewing's *Little Gate* and Dorothy Baker's *Young Man with a Horn* should qualify as romans á clef for the eerie resemblances between their protagonists and Armstrong's contemporary, Bix Beiderbecke, though neither writer mentions him by name. (Baker does acknowledge in an introductory note that her novel was inspired by "the music, but not the life" of Beiderbecke.) As a young man Ewing's Joe "Little Gate" Geddes is accepted by blacks and whites alike in his small Iowa hometown. In short and predictable order, he moves to Chicago, where he lands a long-running gig in a speakeasy run by mobsters. He then moves on to New York, where he finally forms his own band, travels to the West Coast and back, makes a bestselling record, becomes famous, and discovers that he and his music have become commodities and that he's helpless to do anything about it.

Baker's young man with a horn is Rick Martin, an outsider who has a real feel for jazz, especially improvisation. Like Little Gate, he feels a powerful need to break free of the orchestral charts that bind him. Rick is the prototype of the tortured, self-destructive jazz hero who is predestined for a short, intense life — a twentieth-century reincarnation of the romantic hero.

Frederick Turner's *1929,* on the other hand, makes no bones about who its hero is based on. The story begins and ends in the present at Davenport, Iowa, at the annual Bix Fest. But in between we observe the history of Beiderbecke mastering his instruments in unorthodox ways (and without being able to read music), playing in a Chicago speakeasy frequented by mobsters, traveling to the West Coast and back with Paul "Pops" Whiteman's "Symphonic Jazz Orchestra," becoming absurdly famous, and always suffering from a superabundance of alcoholism and creativity. This dervish of a novel provides one of the fullest and most satisfying presentations of a jazz artist in the context of his times.

Billie Holiday is surely as interesting and deserving a subject as the other artists under discussion, but she hasn't yet found the right "biographer" to bring her back to life. In fact, Alexis DeVeaux's *Don't Explain: A Song of Billie Holiday* and Jeremy Reed's *Saint Billie* may not even qualify as fictional works in the strict sense of the term. For example, *Don't Explain* is a book-length prose poem that is organized chronologically around selected, generally familiar, key events in the singer's life. Although sadness suffuses the book, Holiday's inner strength and courage ultimately win out—as one can only wish they had in her corporeal existence.

Sadness also permeates Jeremy Reed's *Saint Billie*, a collection of poems and prose pieces intended to illuminate Holiday's inner life. At the center of the book is a section titled "Billie's Novel in Ten Chapters"; like the other seventeen prose pieces, these "chapters" are less than a page each—in short, a *very* abbreviated novel. The point of departure for each of the Holiday pieces is a quotation relating to the singer. For instance, one chapter dramatizes Holiday's ruminations over Carmen McRae's comment regarding the relationship between Holiday's life and her music: "Singing is the only place she can express herself the way she'd like to be all the time. Only way she's happy is through a song. I don't think she expresses herself as she would want to when you meet her in person. The only time she's at ease and at rest with herself is when she sings." In the title piece the author imagines a meeting between Holiday and another outsider "saint," the French writer, Jean Genet.

Another blues singer (though country rather than city) who is given a pseudo-biographical (and hence fictional) treatment is Huddy "Leadbelly" Ledbetter in Richard M. Garvin and Edmond G. Addeo's *The Midnight Special: The Legend of Leadbelly*. The book claims to be carefully researched but nevertheless exploits the sad and sordid contours of a life pretty much confined to sex, violence, and music. The theme of prejudice is prominent in the book as it traces Leadbelly's trajectory from the cotton fields of Louisiana to the "Promised Land" of New York where he encounters the same kind of racism he had hoped to escape. The story ends in melodramatic irony as Leadbelly's song, " Goodnight, Irene," sells two million copies six months after his death even as his widow stands in lines hoping to find menial employment.

Given his flamboyant life, early death, and inestimable contribution to jazz, it is not surprising to find Charlie Parker portrayed in several works of fiction. Ross Russell, a record producer who actually knew Parker, wrote *The Sound*, which contains several scenes depicting the vibrant post–World War II music scene in Harlem, where Red Travers (the Parker figure) is transforming jazz from big band to bebop. In its preponderance of sex and drugs, the novel is often sensationalistic, but it rings true frequently enough to make the reader feel he has gotten a sense of the man behind the myth.

John A. Williams's *Night Song* provides another solid portrait of the legendary Parker, even as it interests itself in questions concerning the exploitation of the artist by the recording industry and, inevitably, race. In fact, in the culminating scene in the novel Richie Stokes (the Parker figure) is beaten by white cops as his white friend simply looks on. When Stokes—"The Eagle"—disintegrates and dies, he immediately becomes a folk hero, with graffiti proclaiming "Eagle Lives" and "The Eagle Still Soars" popping up everywhere (and echoing the actual response to Parker's death).

Argentine writer Julio Cortázar dedicated his novella, "The Pursuer" ["El Perseguida"] to "C. P.," underscoring its debt to the great saxophonist. Although the story depicts certain key events toward the end of Parker's life, much of its dramatic interest derives from the relationship between Bruno, a jazz critic, and his subject, Johnny Carter (the Parker figure). As Johnny says after reading Bruno's critical biography of him, "What you forgot to put in is me."

Parker is also a felt presence in much Beat literature, especially John Clellon Holmes's *The Horn*, in which Edgar "The Horn" Pool (who is actually a composite portrait of Parker and Lester Young) tries to regain his status as ranking saxophonist only to discover that his musical skills and psychological condition have deteriorated too far for a successful comeback. The theme of Parker's cataclysmic decline and collapse are central to most of these works about him.

If none of the works based on the life of Parker come close to providing a rounded portrait of the artist, the same can be said of the only full-length novel based on Miles Davis's life, Walter Ellis's *Prince of Darkness: A Jazz Fiction Inspired by the Music of Miles Davis.* The subtitle sets up expectations that are never fulfilled: that the novel will provide insight into the origins and development of Davis's art. Unfortunately for the reader interested in such crucial matters, the novel is much more concerned with exploring the deterministic factors underlying the trumpeter's lifelong anguish: racism and an alcoholic mother. Despite an interesting structure, the novel falls short of making a case for Davis as "prince of darkness," let alone a principal jazz musician of his time.

In his relative obscurity, unobtrusive demeanor, and outwardly ordinary life, Warne Marsh was probably the antithesis of Parker and Davis—in every way but the important one of thinking about and producing music. In *Out of Nowhere: The Musical Life of Warne Marsh*, Marcus M. Cornelius has produced a fictional autobiography of the saxophonist who was involved with practically every jazz musician of note in the golden years beginning shortly after World War II. Not by any means a great novel, this book is nevertheless intrinsically interesting for its exploration of the growth and development of

an artistic sensibility; it is one of the very few jazz novels to take us inside the
head of the artist as he ruminates, often at length, about music. As the dedication to the novel says: "This book is inspired by and dedicated to the music of perhaps the most inventive improviser in the history of music in the
West. It is an account of his life as he might have told it: *his song set to
words*" [italics added].

Jazz fiction fans who read French should be aware of Robert Pico's *Jackson Jazz,* which appears to be a full-scale fictionalized biography of Milt
Jackson, who is here credited with being the creator of bebop. The author
seems to have culled all the known facts of Jackson's life and cobbled them
together as a novel. Every club date and concert; every recording and road
trip; every sideman and setback are duly noted. And of course Jackson's long
association with the Modern Jazz Quartet is meticulously chronicled.

The approach that Geoff Dyer takes in his *But Beautiful* could not be
more different from Pico's and most other authors of fact-based jazz fiction.
Dyer refers to his method as "imaginative criticism," by which he means
that he takes key episodes from the lives of selected musicians and creates
his own fictionalized versions of these events. The musicians are Lester
Young, Thelonious Monk, Bud Powell, Ben Webster, Charles Mingus, Chet
Baker, and Art Pepper. In one sense, this is about as good as jazz fiction
gets: the writing is very stylish, the events are well chosen, and the musicians are limned with loving care. In another sense, however, it can be argued that Dyer misinterpreted or misunderstood the characters of some of
his musicians and that he did the music itself a disservice by placing so
much emphasis on the pain, sadness, and neurosis of the jazz life.

Those three qualities are also abundantly present in Candace Allen's
Valaida, another full-dress fictionalized biography, like Pico's, that follows
its subject from cradle to grave. Allen has taken the scattered few facts from
Valada (later Valaida) Snow's early life and fleshed them out in an effort to
understand how Snow's early existence helped to shape the later career of the
woman who became a phenomenal trumpeter and showbiz personality. On
the basis of her original research, Allen also claims to set the record straight
regarding Snow's legendary incarceration in Denmark during World War II.
Many readers will applaud the author's portrayal of the inner life of a remarkable African-American woman; some, on the other hand, may find such
inner-directedness distracting.

Whereas the books under discussion have all focused on fictionalized biographical and autobiographical elements of the lives of actual musicians,
there is an altogether different species in this genre, and it can be more interesting than its fact-based cousin: the "biography" of a fictitious jazz musician
who is not based on a single real-life counterpart but who, in the case of Jack

Fuller's *The Best of Jackson Payne,* is a composite of almost every agonized jazz musician in the history of modern jazz. The story is told by musicologist Charles Quinlan who has undertaken to write a biography of Jackson Payne, "the last towering colossus of jazz." In trying to get at the truth of Payne's tortured existence and also to understand Payne's increasingly complex musical ideas, Quinlan is compelled to wrestle with the intricacies and ambiguities of his own life. The range and seriousness of this novel can be inferred from a partial list of its thematic concerns: race, sex, drug addiction, the process of creativity, the search for absolute originality and, through that, the realization of spiritual transcendence.

Several works in this chapter (those on Bolden and Holiday, for example) deliberately resort to lyricism in their presentations. Can it be that their authors felt—or, perhaps, realized—that "straight" prose was inadequate to the task of bringing their musical subjects to fictive life?

Chapter Six

Fantasy and Science Fiction

The subgenre of jazz fantasy and science fiction isn't extensive or generally outstanding, but it contains a moderately interesting variety of subject matter and themes—and one work that may approach greatness. More than in most such subgenres, this variety is best represented through short stories where, to take an overview, we find pieces that concern a machine that converts the sounds of jazz into the feelings that produced them, causing the black narrator to smash the machine with his trumpet while reflecting that, although whites may continue to exploit blacks in every way imaginable, they had better not "come scuffling for our souls" (Richard Matheson, "Jazz Machine"). And, speaking of souls, we also find several stories that riff on the Faust theme (partial thanks, no doubt, to the Robert Johnson-at-the-crossroads myth). In one such story a guitar-playing hobo at the turn of the twentieth century goes in search of a hoodoo doctor to put him in touch with the devil; it turns out in this variation-on-a-theme that the guitarist learns that in order to gain supremacy over his instrument, he must first get in touch with his origins, especially those relating to his slave progenitors (Julio Finn, "Blue Bayou"). Another Faustian story has the musician seeking surpassing talent and outfoxing the devil by embracing "cool" West Coast jazz instead of the "hot" jazz mandated by the devil (Robert Tilley, "The Devil and All That Jazz").

Less soulful but more pseudoscientific are the science fiction works, which characteristically concern spacemen, extraterrestrials, and space travel. In one slight piece spacemen land on Earth in search of Art Blakey recordings and information about what had happened to jazz on Earth after the Jazz Messengers (Amiri Baraka, "Answers in Progress"). In another, a scientist's spacecraft crashes on an unknown planet; fortunately, his recording gear is unscathed, and this allows him to listen, over and over, to his beloved recording of Duke Ellington's "Ko-Ko." One day he hears "Ko-Ko" coming back at him. When he investigates he discovers that the sound emanates from an elephantine extraterrestrial. The two of course become friends, bonded through their love of jazz (Robert Tilley, "Something Else"). Another variation on the space travel theme depicts the plight of several miners on Titania who overcome serious obstacles in order to compete in a jazz competition millions of miles away (Damon Knight, "Coming Back to Dixieland").

Time travel is as characteristic of science fiction as spaceflight, and two stories in the jazz subgenre of the former category have similar contours. In the first, a jazz buff in 2078 shuttles back to the 1930s to locate the jazz saxophonist who had made "Willie's Blues" famous before he died (Robert Tilley, "Willie's Blues"). In the other one, a nagging wife causes her wealthy old husband to transport himself back 200 years to Storyville where he can surround himself with his beloved jazz and where, too, he can receive a rousing jazz funeral with all of the great musicians of the past sending him off in flamboyant style (Chad Oliver, "Didn't He Ramble").

Finally, to round things out, three stories with supernatural elements. In the first of these the wraith of Archduke Ferdinand returns to the land of the living, New Orleans in this case, where he enlists an accomplice to help him assassinate the individual behind the rise of Mussolini, vowing to spare the lives of only those people who are listening to jazz when the vendetta commences (Poppy Z. Brite, "Mussolini and the Axeman's Jazz"). In the middle story, when a professor who is secretly writing a book on jazz learns that drummer JoJo Jones and his band are coming to town, he takes his girlfriend to hear the music. Later, the professor discovers that his girlfriend has been hanging out with the band behind his back and has apparently become hooked on jazz—and heroin as well. Jones and his men are described in vampirish terms (Robert Bloch, "Dig That Crazy Horse"). Ghosts, goblins, and things that go bump in the night, rather than vampirish musicians, characterize the final long story in the category under discussion, as a grad student at Columbia discovers to his great surprise and delight that legendary saxophonist "Hat" is not only still alive but has an extended gig in town. So the student goes to hear his idol night after night, finally ingratiating himself enough with the older man to get him to agree to an interview—on Halloween. The story Hat tells the narrator took place in the South many years ago and involves a dead white woman in the black section of town and appropriate mysterious events. The interpolated story, like the interview, happened on Halloween (Peter Straub, "Pork Pie Hat").

Jazz fantasy and science fiction are also represented by full-length novels. In Paul Beardmore's *Jazz Elephants*, for instance, two African elephants escape from a London zoo not because they were mistreated or humiliated but because they wanted to play their trumpets on the *outside;* in other words they wanted a situation in which to exercise their creativity without any restrictions. When they meet up with other musicians (human variety) escaping to freedom, they decide to form a band. This long fantasy for adults apparently intends to satirize the age-old theme concerning the desire for freedom within a repressive society.

The music that is submerged by thematic concerns in the previous book shines consistently through the narrative of Piers Anthony and Ron Leming's *The Gutbucket Quest*, a fantasy in which blues guitarist Slim Chance is struck by lightning and transported thereby to Armadillo, Tejas, a wondrous place where harmony prevails and music—especially the blues—possesses supernatural powers. The complication occurs when a corporate villain steals a magical guitar named Gutbucket and threatens to use it to eliminate both music and magic from the world. The plot unfurls as Slim and his elder, African-American sidekick, Progress Hornsby, set out to retrieve Gutbucket and make the world paradisiacal once again. That Progress has a gorgeous, fantastically talented blues-singer daughter adds spice to a piquant plot.

Another jazz fantasy with plenty of plot and an abundance of exoticism is David Wyn Roberts's *The Alchemist's Song*, a novel set in strange, mysterious places and shot through with references to alchemy, folklore, mythology, and Native American spiritualism. The story involves a matched pair of trumpets forged in the eighteenth century: "the first brass instruments to be adorned with triple side-mounted Viennese valves . . . [giving] them access to the full chromatic scale over nearly three octaves." When one of these marvelous instruments falls into the hands of late twentieth-century jazz musician Harry Holborn, he becomes obsessed with locating its mate. After he dies under problematic circumstances, his wife continues his quest, which by now has assumed metaphysical proportions.

Adam Lively's *Blue Fruit* also has an eighteenth-century, twentieth-century matrix, though much more in the traditional science fiction context of time travel. The story's protagonist, John Field, a young ship's surgeon on an eighteenth-century whaling vessel, finds himself transported to twentieth-century Harlem where he is taken in by a black family. He is soon befriended by a talented, avant-garde saxophonist who guides him through the jazz dives of Harlem where Field—and the reader—undergoes several vivid experiences involving improvisational jazz.

Other science fiction jazz novels fall into the post-apocalyptic category. Mitch Berman's *Time Capsule* begins as young Max Debrick ("Debris" to his buddies) and his combo are in the middle of a recording session on the outskirts of Manhattan when a nuclear bomb of unimaginable magnitude brings the world to a halt and, presumably, an end. Miraculously, Max and his beloved saxophone are spared and so he sets out in search of other survivors, sustaining himself on roaches and rodents along the way. In Pennsylvania, Max finally finds another survivor and the two of them embark on a quest to see whether the holocaust had spared others. Caveat: the first several chapters of this novel will grieve anyone, especially New Yorkers, I suspect, who were in any way connected to the tragic events of September 11, 2001.

If awards were given in the various subgenres of jazz fiction, Kathleen Ann Goonan would win, hands down, for science fiction. She has produced a futuristic tetralogy that is often dense with jazz reference, and she discusses the relationship of jazz to her novels on her home page (http://goonan.con/essay.html).

In the first novel in the series, *Queen City Jazz,* nanotech plagues have decimated mankind and the protagonist, Verity, her dog, Cairo, and the corpse of her best friend, Blaze, set off in search of the Enlivened City of Cincinnati, where Blaze might be returned to life. Blaze is—was—a jazz pianist who had been on the verge of making a musical breakthrough on the order of, say, Charlie Parker's. Fans of jazz science fiction (surely a select group) should be amused, if not delighted, by a scene late in the book involving a professional baseball game featuring jazz musicians: Billie Holiday is on the pitching mound, Dizzy Gillespie in the outfield, and Charlie Parker blasts a game-winning home run. Science fiction is no fan of probability theory.

The sequel to this novel, *Mississippi Blues*, continues the adventures of Verity and Blaze while incorporating several important new characters and employing multiple narrative perspectives. Here Verity assumes the responsibility of helping the emancipated but still vulnerable citizens of Cincinnati to reach the mysterious city of New Orleans, where (it is rumored) salvation awaits. To accomplish her lofty goal, Verity supervises the construction of a monstrous riverboat designed to take the survivors to their destination. This novel is saturated with the blues: when the characters aren't listening to the blues, they are playing, composing, or studying them. Most of the chapter titles are named after blues songs. And one of the characters (a professor of the blues) has gone so far as to create a virtual blues show in which, on one occasion, she duets with Robert Johnson.

The third novel in the series, *Crescent City Rhapsody,* returns the musical emphasis to jazz. Duke Ellington is a character, and in fact the title derives from a piece he was (in the context of the novel) commissioned to write. There is also a character named Sun Ra who is presumably the female reincarnation of the *Space Is the Place* orchestra leader. The story itself, like the others in the tetralogy, takes place in the near future and involves, among other plot strands, a worldwide communications blackout. When a brilliant astronomer discovers the source of the calamity, he places at risk everything in the world of importance to him. In an afterword, the author claims that Ellington's *Music Is My Mistress* provided the musical scaffolding for the novel.

In the final installment in this quartet of jazz science fiction novels, *Light Music,* outsiders attack Crescent City, forcing the community to flee for their lives. As two of the founders escape westward, they encounter talking animals, conscious machines, and toys that long to be real. There is only one overt reference to jazz, but apparently it is intended to carry considerable dramatic, and thematic, weight.

The work that defies classification (and approaches greatness) is Rafi Zabor's *The Bear Comes Home.* Although it contains one overwhelming element of fantasy, its taxonomy is finally as elusive as Franz Kafka's world masterpiece about a man who becomes an insect, "The Metamorphosis." One reason both works resist facile classification is that they begin with an impossibility (man turning into bug and bear who talks and plays sax) and then proceed after the fashion of realistic narratives.

But our Bear, unlike Kafka's bug, has always been a bear; he didn't become one overnight. His bearness underscores his outsider status: he's an artist—and a genius at that—in a materialistic society. The long, sprawling story dramatizes the awesome challenges confronting the creative artist who is called upon, night after night, to be spontaneous and innovative and the pure joy—the ecstasy even—that can result when these challenges are met. The descriptions of music in performance, of the improvisational process, of the tedium of life on the road with a jazz band, and of the grim reality of the professional jazz artist's life—all of these are richly, lovingly detailed, often technical, and always convincing. As a nice bonus, several nonfictitious musicians make appearances: Lester Bowie, Charlie Haden, and Ornette Coleman, to name just three.

What can be said, finally, about the presence of jazz in the literature of fantasy and science fiction? Certainly nothing definitive. It may be enough to state what seems to be the obvious: that things of the spirit—genuine artistic things in this case—possess certain perdurable qualities that allow them to transcend the terrestrial and temporal limitations that bind the rest of us. At least, one suspects, that's what some of the authors of such works want (and want their readers) to believe. As a famous Jazz Age character says, "Isn't it pretty to think so?"

Chapter Seven

Mystery and Crime

Vast and various, the broad category of mystery and mayhem jazz fiction comprises a large number of often overlapping subgenres: amateur detective, hard-boiled private investigator, and police procedural among the more familiar. The one constant across these various subdivisions is the commission of a crime, often murder. The ways in which the crimes are investigated and the tone of the proceedings vary, however, from a little to a lot. Often the mystery itself is subordinated to other elements.

Take, for instance, Dallas Murphy's Artie Deemer series, each of which is named after a jazz standard: *Lover Man, Lush Life,* and *Don't Explain.* Few would pick up one of these novels for the mystery. They seem designed to entertain on a subcerebral level, not to provide a ratiocinative challenge. Private investigator Artie has a cash-cow dog, Jellyroll (famous for a television commercial), who likes to curl up with his master and listen to jazz, especially Charlie Parker and Thelonious Monk, among other boppers. In *Lush Life,* Johnny Hartman provides the background music when Artie takes his new girlfriend to bed for the first time, with spectacular results that would no doubt have been vastly different if late Coltrane or Ornette Coleman had been on the stereo.

Reluctant amateur detectives Trevor Chaplin and his sweetheart Jill Swinburne occupy stage center of Alan Plater's lighthearted Beiderbecke trio: *The Beiderbecke Affair, The Beiderbecke Tapes,* and *The Beiderbecke Connection.* Readers will have to guess the name of the famous jazz musician around whom these novels revolve. In the last-named title, Trevor helps a mysterious refugee (who may well be a bad guy) because he likes Bix Beiderbecke and Duke Ellington, and people who like such geniuses "wouldn't do anything wrong."

Equally high-spirited is John Wainwright's *Do Nothin' Till You Hear from Me,* with Lucky, a wisecracking bandleader protagonist whose obsessive goal in life is to assemble the best band in all of creation. When he receives a parcel containing a human ear and a note suggesting that a kidnapping is underway, Lucky is enlisted by a clarinet-playing homicide detective to help solve the crime. This story is unusual because its mystery is pretty much swamped by Lucky's ruminations on jazz and the mechanics of building a high-quality orchestra.

Jerrilyn Farmer's *Perfect Sax,* as the title hints, is even frothier. Set among the haute monde of Los Angeles and featuring caterer and event-planner Madeline Bean, the story is triggered by a "perfect" saxophone that is auctioned off for a king's ransom before disappearing. When a corpse is found in Madeline's bedroom, mayhem follows. The novel tries hard to be jazzy: some chapters are named after jazz compositions—"Mood Indigo," "Nutty," "I Want to Talk about You," and "Jeeps Blues" [*sic*], to name a few—and the acknowledgments honor the music, but it's fair to say that the novel's musical content is as frothy as the story itself.

Jessica Fletcher and Donald Bain's *Murder in a Minor Key,* on the other hand, contains a surprising amount of musical substance. While in New Orleans to attend a conference, Jessica Fletcher—Maine's own version of Miss Marple—befriends a music critic who has become obsessed with locating some rumored early cylinder recordings of legendary trumpeter and voodooist, Little Red LeCoeur. When Jessica's friend dies "by misadventure," she springs into action, not only solving the murder case but unearthing the priceless recordings in the process. This book is a novelization of an episode from the *Murder, She Wrote* television series.

Several jazz mysteries are set within the swing band milieu and usually take place in the late 1930s or early 1940s. For the most part these works, like those just discussed, don't take themselves very seriously; they lack the gritty verisimilitude characteristic of hard-boiled mysteries and police procedurals. Following the example of Agatha Christie's *Ten Little Indians,* big band entertainments are often built around the mystifying serial deaths within a group in a controlled environment, in this case band members working in a nightclub or ballroom.

Ngaio Marsh's *Swing, Brother, Swing* (published as *A Wreath for Rivera* in the United States) provides a convenient early example. In roughly the first third of this novel, Breezy Bellair and his boogie-woogie band prepare to unveil a new novelty number involving the mock killing of various band members. The music in this daffy mystery stops when the killings begin.

Someone's also out to get the members of King Grayson's London swing band in Ray Sonin's *The Dance Band Mystery,* causing Sam Underhill of the

Dance Band News to team up with Scotland Yard to get to the bottom of things. In unmasking the culprit, Underhill finds himself playing piano with the orchestra in a case that broadens to include the distribution of potent reefers to musicians, clandestine children's dolls imported from the United States, and—surprise!—a scorned woman. Band members in Ida Shurman's *Death Beats the Band* are also being murdered. Since the orchestra and patrons are marooned in the club by a blizzard, the band's new bassist takes it upon himself to play detective and solve the killings.

The milieux of Robert Avery's *Murder on the Downbeat* are the swing clubs in midtown Manhattan and the after-hours joints in Harlem. Recording company scout and jazz columnist Malachy Bliss assumes the role of amateur detective when first one and then another jazz musician is murdered and his girlfriend is jailed as a suspect. Although this book moves breezily along after the fashion of Dashiell Hammett's Thin Man series, it nevertheless carries a modest but meaningful racial subtext in its portrayal of Harlem as a place where musicians, both black and white, can go after work "to play honest, uninhibited jazz with the best musicians in the world." Brandon Bird's *Downbeat for a Dirge* also portrays murder and mystery within the dance band context, but more than the other works under discussion it provides solid descriptions of the mechanics of a band at work, including the drudgery of life on the road. The band sticks to the charts, playing some Stan Kenton kinds of things but leaving "goatee jazz to other bands."

A fair number of period pieces crop up in jazz mystery fiction. Kathleen Anne Fleming's *The Jazz Age Murders* and Jill Shure's *Night Jazz* are typical. In the first of these a young woman is able to solve a murder mystery in the present by studying the history of the club where the killing occurred. The club had been around since the Jazz Age (as the title implies). In *Night Jazz* a successful ad executive is miraculously transported back to the Jazz Age as she tries to get to the bottom of her brother's mysterious disappearance. Once back in time, our protagonist immerses herself in the culture of the period, especially women's fashions. Neither of these novels contains significant jazz content.

Hal Glatzer's period piece, *Too Dead to Swing,* however, does contain matters of interest for the lover of jazz fiction. This is largely to do with its focus on an all-women swing band and its plucky protagonist, Katy Green, who plays violin and alto sax with equal adroitness. When one of the Ultra Belles turns up dead, Katy assumes the dual role of detective and den mother as the girls travel from one gig to another by train; they need guidance and chaperoning because their nonworking hours are filled with booze, drugs, and sex.

Peter Duchin and John Morgan Wilson's two Philip Damon novels are also period pieces with a swing orchestra setting—or perhaps neo-swing since they take place in the early sixties. In the first of these books, *Blue Moon,* society bandleader and pianist Philip Damon is forced into detective work when he becomes the prime suspect in two murders. The melancholy title song plays a significant role. In the second novel, *Good Morning, Heartache,* Damon is again thrust into the role of amateur detective when his substitute horn man, an ex-junkie, turns up dead after sitting in with Cannonball Adderley at Howard Rumsey's Lighthouse. Both novels contain scenes of the orchestra in action and make frequent references to jazz and swing musicians. Coauthor Duchin, like Philip Damon, is a prominent piano-playing bandleader like his father before him. Another writer with swing connections, Rupert Holmes, takes his retro swing mystery, *Swing: A Mystery,* a step further than Duchin and Wilson take theirs: Holmes includes a CD whose swing tunes (composed and arranged by the author and referenced in the text) contain clues designed to help the reader solve the mystery. The convoluted plot takes place at the 1940 Golden Gate International Exposition and involves, among other things, a coded message that could threaten the safety of the free world.

Harper Barnes's *Blue Monday,* Jon A. Jackson's *Man with an Axe,* and Hunton Downs's *Murder in the Mood* would probably not qualify as period pieces, but they all take place in or depend heavily on the past. In *Blue Monday,* a jazz-loving idealistic reporter in 1935 Kansas City suspects that Bennie Moten's death during a tonsillectomy was in fact murder. By employing his considerable investigative talents, he is able to resolve the questions surrounding Moten's death. Lester Young, Ben Webster, and Count Basie, among others, make brief appearances in the novel. *Man with an Axe* also features a jazz-loving detective (but a professional one) who immerses himself in a very mysterious event—in this case, the enigma of what actually happened to Jimmy Hoffa one long-ago weekend at an isolated African-American resort community on the Great Lakes. "Fang" Mulheisen of the Detroit police department reflects often on the bop and free jazz movements and many of the musicians who matriculated in the "old" Detroit. One important character had played sax for Phil Woods, while another, in a neat novelistic twist, turns out to be the daughter of Albert Ayler.

The past is also present in *Murder in the Mood*, a sweeping, researched thriller (*thoroughly* researched, it would seem) involving Nazis, neo-Nazis, drug cartels, the new billionaires, and—more to the point—speculation as to what happened to Glenn Miller during Hitler's reign of terror. The plot turns on the discovery in the present of a "Secret Broadcast" disc that Miller had recorded in 1944.

Another jazz novel concerned with Nazism is W. M. Ellis Oglesby's *Blow Happy, Blow Sad*, though in the nomenclature of mystery fiction it should properly be categorized as an espionage novel. A black American cornetist,

Chops Danielson, risks his life aiding the Resistance in Nazi-occupied Denmark. His performances in underground jazz venues send coded military messages to England, while he simultaneously seeks to rescue his Danish sweetheart, a classical violinist, from the occupiers. (The story is reminiscent of members of the French Resistance who used the numbers of Louis Armstrong records as code.)

Two other panoramic thrillers are moderately interesting for their jazz content, Martin Cruz Smith's *Stallion Gate* and Andrew Klavan's *Hunting Down Amanda*. Set in New Mexico in the mid-1940s, the former features J. Robert Oppenheimer and Klaus Fuchs, among others, as they go about their top secret business at the most secret installation of World War II, the test site for the first atomic weapon. The protagonist is an American Indian soldier from the Southwest who had played piano with Charlie Parker and dreams of opening a jazz club after the war. Although the jazz content of this novel remains in the background, the scene in which Klaus Fuchs dances a "Hapsburg ballroom number" to bebop may be worth the price of admission. Blake, the protagonist of *Hunting Down Amanda,* is also a jazz musician, but he's black, plays sax, and becomes involved in a plot involving supernatural elements, such as a young girl with miraculous healing powers. The novel contains a solid chapter or two of Blake at work and at least one passage worth noting: when Blake bests the bad guys, their leader says: "I should never have sent you guys up against a jazz musician. Those guys are dangerous."

Dangerous forces are also at play in Ernest Borneman's *Tremolo*, a novel more in the Hitchcockian suspense mode than thriller. The protagonist, Mike Sommerville, was one of the first northern whites to catch on to New Orleans-style jazz before he gave up performing to design and manufacture jazz instruments and live the good life with his picture-perfect family—until things start to go bump in the night. At first Mike and his wife believe that their house is haunted, but then they suspect each other of psychological instability. The story contains a good bit of music, including descriptions of jam sessions—and Mike has a dog named Buddy Bolden.

Jazz fiction generally turns grittier, darker, and more violent when it teams up with the more realistic precincts of mystery literature: the crime story, the hard-boiled detective caper, the police procedural, and the noir novel. There is of course significant overlap between the first three categories and the atmospheric noir.

Paul Pines's *The Tin Angel* and J. R. Creech's *Music and Crime* provide good examples of crime fiction. *The Tin Angel* is a vividly recounted tale set in Manhattan's Lower East Side in the 1970s, involving missing finances, a mysterious death, and drugs. Bowery bums, plainclothes cops, scam artists, and a colorful jazz club owner, Pablo Waitz, comprise the dramatis personae.

The author actually owned a club called "The Tin Angel" on the Bowery, and his familiarity with operating such an establishment shines through on every page. *Music and Crime* also rings depressingly true as it traces the descent of two competent jazz musicians, living on the nether edges of the music world in Los Angeles and New York, into a life of street crime. In the process of this downward transformation, they discover what they would rather not have known about the cutthroat music industry. Sadly, the music that should have liberated these musicians made their lives wretched.

Bart Spicer's *Blues for the Prince* provides a solid example of the hard-boiled subgenre. It is particularly interesting for its Ellingtonian echoes. The Prince of the title (Harold Morton Prince) is the best jazz pianist and composer of the last two decades. When he is murdered, his right-hand man is charged with the crime after claiming—or threatening to claim—that *he* had written the music that made The Prince famous. The book contains a chapter (17) that brings together a group of nonfictitious jazz all-stars for a jam session to memorialize The Prince.

A group comprising everyone who is anyone in the jazz world, including representatives from *Downbeat* and *Metronome*, also gathers to give trumpeter Dandy a rousing send-off in John Farr's *The Deadly Combo*, a hard-edged mystery that might better be labeled pulp noir. Mac Stewart is a plain-clothes detective and devotee of jazz who determines to track down the killer of onetime trumpet great Dandy, who may have brought on his own death by bragging to some unscrupulous stranger about the gold horn he had once been awarded (without mentioning that he had long ago pawned the instrument). Everything in the novel seems to start around 3 A.M., and everyone—especially Stewart—speaks in the clipped, staccato dialogue characteristic of the B-movies of the day.

Malcolm Braly's *Shake Him Till He Rattles* is another hard-edged jazz novel with noir overtones. Bass saxophonist Lee Cabiness is stalked by a narcotics detective whose obsession with nailing Cabiness, we discover later, derives from his own addiction. The San Francisco beatnik scene is well rendered, and the novel contains an excellent description of a cutting contest among three saxophonists. Douglass Wallop's *Night Light* is almost pure noir in its feverish, obsessive atmosphere, as a young New York widower loses his daughter to a random killing. His compulsion to understand and avenge his daughter's death plunges him into an amoral nocturnal world dominated by jazz clubs.

Excessive behavior is also prevalent in John Harvey's brooding series of police procedurals set in Nottingham, England. The detective is Charlie Resnick, who loves jazz and listens to bebop to wind down in his rare spare moments, sometimes reading *The Penguin Guide to Jazz* as accompaniment.

He has four cats, all named after bebop greats: Dizzy, Miles, Bird, and Pepper. One of these gritty, well written novels (*Still Waters*) begins with the "flow and swing" of Milt Jackson's music and ends against a background of Duke Ellington music as Resnick pursues a serial killer. A collection of twelve short stories featuring Resnick is called *Now's the Time*; all of the stories but one take their titles from the Charlie Parker songbook. Underscoring the jazz relationship to these stories are a "Coda," in which the author talks briefly about the jazz foundation of the stories, and "A Partial Soundtrack," which lists Resnick's favorite jazz recordings. In the final novel in the Resnick series, *Last Rites,* jazz as usual contributes significantly to the story's rich atmosphere, but its most interesting relationship to the music comes in the "Coda," where Harvey writes: ". . . I think that it was jazz that kept Charlie sane, that provided him with both release and inspiration. Me, too. In the writing of these books I have relied, again and again, on the music of Duke Ellington, Billie Holiday, Thelonious Monk, Spike Robinson, Ben Webster with Art Tatum, and Lester Young. Let it live on." Harvey's newsletter, not incidentally, is called *In a Mellotone.*

Two other mystery series should be mentioned in closing: Charlotte Carter's Nanette Hayes novels and Bill Moody's Evan Horne series; both protagonists are musicians who become amateur detectives. Nanette is profane, sassy, sexy, and plays sax on the streets of Manhattan. She facetiously claims to be Django Reinhardt's illegitimate gypsy granddaughter in one book, and says she has accepted Thelonious Monk as her personal savior in another. In the first of the three novels she has so far appeared in, *Rhode Island Red,* she enters into a passionate relationship with a mysterious man who has enlisted Nan to teach him the essence of Charlie Parker, one of whose saxophones plays a major role—including giving the book its title—in this breezy mystery. In the second, *Coq au Vin,* she goes to Paris to search for a missing relative. While there she teams up with André, a black American street-jazz violinist who is passionate about jazz history, especially as it relates to African-American expatriates in Paris. The third in the series, *Drumsticks,* names its chapter titles after jazz tunes, refers to Charlie Rouse in the first sentence, and is dedicated "To the Bennys: Carter, Golson, and Green. . . ." Nan goes on a case that takes her across Manhattan and into Brooklyn as she tries to find the killer of a Harlem folk artist.

Although quite different in many ways, Bill Moody's Evan Horne series packs at least as much jazz per page as Carter's. The protagonist is a jazz pianist who becomes an amateur sleuth after injuring his hand in an auto accident. In the first novel (*Solo Hand*) Horne tries to protect two musicians whose careers are jeopardized by a blackmail scam. The novel is also interesting for its portrayal of the mechanics of the CD industry. In *Death of a*

Tenor Man, the second in the series, Horne travels from his home base in Los Angeles to Las Vegas (a familiar pattern in the series) to help an English professor friend research the suspicious death of Wardell Gray, who died under questionable circumstances in Las Vegas in 1955. Horne also returns to the past in the third book in the series, *The Sound of the Trumpet*, which revolves around an audiotape that may contain the last recording of legendary trumpeter Clifford Brown, who died in a car accident at twenty-five. The story gains considerable interest from its interesting technique: Moody incorporates a series of "Interludes" in which he imaginatively recreates the final days of Brown's life. (In a neat life-imitating-art twist, the actual lost tape of Brown's last recording was unearthed after this novel was published and is rumored to be languishing in Blue Note's vaults until red tape can be cut through.)

In the next number in the series, *Bird Lives!*, somebody's killing off the Kenny G-like smooth jazz musicians and Horne is called in—by the FBI, no less—to help solve the serial murders. Finally, in the most recent book in the series to date (2005), *Looking for Chet Baker*, Horne is in London for a gig at Ronnie Scott's famous jazz emporium and hoping to get back in a serious musical groove and leave crime detection behind when his old chum Ace Buffington materializes with a problem: it seems that Ace has contracted to do a book on Chet Baker and has promised his publisher that Horne would collaborate on the manuscript. Horne refuses Ace's pleas but nevertheless follows his friend to Amsterdam. When Horne reaches Ace's hotel room (which had also been Chet Baker's room), he find's Ace's notes and briefcase but no Ace. Horne's consequent search for his missing buddy also involves him in unriddling the mysterious death of Chet Baker.

All of Moody's Evan Horne novels are packed with references to jazz. In fact, the committed reader can—possibly—enjoy a transformative experience if he stokes up his stereo with the music mentioned in the text and using that as background accompaniment for his reading.

This survey suggests why jazz finds a congenial host in mystery fiction, just as jazz so often provides "appropriate" background music for crime films and television shows. It provides simultaneously a context for a significant art form performed by noted artists and a music that was so often associated with late nights, disreputable venues, liquor and drugs, and, of course, sex—all of them characteristic of this form of fiction.

Chapter Eight

Immigrant and International

Jazz fiction is well represented by immigrant and foreign contributions. The works concerning **immigrants** are few but memorable, with three titles in particular distinguishing themselves for their breadth, seriousness, and organic use of the music: Diana Abu-Jabar's *Arabian Jazz*, Oscar Hijuelos's *The Mambo Kings Play Songs of Love*, and Edgardo Vega Yunque's *No Matter How Much You Promise to Cook or Pay the Rent You Blew It Cauze Bill Bailey Ain't Never Coming Home Again* (henceforth *Bill Bailey*).

Set in upstate New York from the 1960s to the 1990s, *Arabian Jazz* focuses on one of the persistent concerns of immigrants as dramatized in the literature of their plight, in this case an Arab-American family's struggle with assimilation: how is it possible, the familiar question runs, to reconcile the traditions of the "old country" with the lifestyles of the new? This question centers on Jemorah, whose very identity is jeopardized by her more or less equal attachment to both cultures. Although the novel's jazz content is sporadic, it is thematically essential. Jem's father, Mattussen Ramoud, plays the drums exuberantly at every opportunity and believes implicitly that the drumbeat is the pulse of human existence. It is through her father and his powerful musical beliefs that Jem comes to understand that the ostensibly incompatible combination of American jazz and Arabic trills can actually engender harmony. How this epiphany relates to the central question posed by the book needs no gloss.

The Mambo Kings Sing Songs of Love is less about assimilation than the equally persistent immigrant theme concerning the pursuit of the American Dream. Two mismatched but loving brothers, Cesar and Nestor Castillo, leave their Cuban homeland in 1949 to chase their dream of becoming mambo stars like their heroes Desi Arnaz and Xavier Cugat. In New York they work at menial jobs by day and play their beloved music at night, finally approaching the region of their aspirations as, first, they produce bestselling 78 records and then are asked to perform with Desi Arnaz on his popular television series, *I Love Lucy*. The value of this novel lies not only in its realistic description of the mechanics of band life but also in its dramatization of the music that cross-pollinated with American jazz to produce "Cu-bop," which is fully and lovingly described here; for instance, we are told in a long, energetic footnote that Cu-bop is

> the term used to describe the fusion of Afro-Cuban music and hot be-bop Harlem jazz. Its greatest practitioner was the bandleader Machito, who with Mario Bauzá and Chano Pozo hooked up with Dizzy Gillespie and Charlie Parker in the late 1940s. The American jazz players picked up the Cuban rhythms and the Cubans picked up jazzier rhythms and chord progressions. Machito's orchestra, with Chico O'Farrill as arranger, became famous for dazzling solos played over extended vamps called montunos. During these furious breaks, when drummers like Chano Pozo and players like Charlie Parker went nuts, dancers like Frankie Pérez took to the center of the ballroom floor, improvising turns, dips, splits, leaps around the basic mambo steps, in the same way that the musicians improvised during their solos.

These dancers were "feeling cu-bop crazy, man." Readers of this work will feel that they are getting a beautifully dramatized history of Cuban-American jazz, as well as an affecting story, during one of the music's golden moments.

Bill Bailey also overflows with dramatic events and centers on Latinos, but primarily Afro-Ricans rather than Cuban Americans. As in *Arabian Jazz*, the central figure is a young female setting out on the rocky road to maturity, hoping to discover who she is along the way. Half Puerto Rican and half Irish American, Vidamía Farrell journeys from the affluent suburbs of New York City down to Manhattan's Lower East Side, where her birth-father, Billy Farrell, lives with his second family under conditions vastly different from those Vidamía left behind. Billy had once been such a promising pianist that Miles Davis had asked him to join his band. But Billy went to Vietnam instead and there lost two fingers and his best buddy, causing him to develop post-traumatic stress disorder and damaging his musical aspirations. After being lovingly accepted into her new family, Vidamía and her newfound siblings purchase a piano to lure Billy back into a jazz groove. The plan works. Billy regains his artistry and lands a gig at the Village Gate. Meanwhile, Vidamía enters into a relationship with an up-and-coming African-American saxophonist. But then, just as everything is looking up for the Farrell family, devastating events obtrude. Nevertheless, Vidamía perseveres, comes ever closer to discovering her essential self, and, chin high, prepares to face the future. This abundant novel is very suggestive on questions of race and ethnicity—black, white, and Latino.

The **international** or **foreign** contribution to jazz fiction is fairly vast and often qualitatively impressive. Many are aware of the jazz crazes that swept over much of Europe following the two world wars, but few, I suspect, are familiar with the parallel phenomenon that took place in Asia. For instance, Shanghai had a small but significant African-American jazz community by the 1930s. This came about largely because of the increased opportunities offered by transpacific steamship travel (which provided many musicians with jobs as entertainers and waiters) and by the opportunities afforded by Shanghai's impressive array of nightclubs. Even before this, however, jazz was popular in **China**, and not just in Shanghai. Before the influx of African-Americans, Russian bands dominated the Chinese jazz scene; in fact, as early as 1927 at least ten Russian jazz orchestras were active in Beijing's flourishing nightclub and hotel venues.

Much of the jazz fiction that concerns itself with the infiltration of Asia by African-Americans carries a political agenda. It is typical for such works to portray the plight of the black outsider caught up in a consumerist culture. A good example of this theme can be found in Mu Shiying's "Five in a Nightclub," in which a black drummer is forced by economic circumstances to perform even as his wife lies in a coma after delivering a stillborn child earlier in the day. For information on the neglected cranny of Chinese jazz fiction, see Andrew F. Jones's illuminating essay, "Black Internationale: Notes on the Chinese Jazz Age," in *Jazz Planet*, pp. 225–43, edited by E. Taylor Atkins (Jackson: University of Mississippi Press, 2003).

It is considerably less surprising, given the post–World War II relationship between the United States and **Japan**, to learn that jazz had—as it continues to have—a shaping influence on Japanese culture, especially its literature. Michael Molasky's summary statement on this issue could not be more germane or instructive and deserves to be quoted in full:

Despite the dearth of scholarship on the topic of jazz in Japanese literature, the music has exerted a particularly powerful and tangible impact on Japan's literary world since the mid-1950s. Conversely, Japanese poets and novelists have helped glorify the image of jazz as the music of choice for aspiring artists or intellectuals with an anti-authoritarian bent. Poets such as Shiraishi Kazuko have attempted to infuse their poetic language with the rhythms and improvisational qualities of jazz, often reading poems to live musical accompaniment. And although fewer "jazz novels" have been written in Japanese than in English, many of Japan's leading novelists have paid deference to the music in their works of fiction and cultural criticism. Many acclaimed writers, including 1994 Nobel Prize winner, Oe Kenzaburo, have written about jazz being a major force in their intellectual and ideological development. Numerous bestselling writers have similarly remarked that jazz has played a salient role in mediating their relationship to American culture. They include Murakami Haruki (who ran a jazz bar before becoming a writer and whose collection of jazz recordings exceeds 6000 discs), Murakami Ryu (no relation; he grew up near a large U.S. naval base and has produced a jazz CD), Itsuki Hiroyuki, and Tsutsui Yasutaka. (Itsuki and Tsutsui have each written several books of fiction about jazz musicians, including Tsutsui's collection, *Jazz Stories*.) Even Ishihara Shintaro, Tokyo's controversial governor (mayor) and co-author of the notorious book, *The Japan That Can't Say No,* first made his reputation as a writer of stories and filmscripts during the mid-1950s, and quite a few of these works used jazz—as both a musical and countercultural icon—to portray a new breed of postwar Japanese youth as rebellious, sexually uninhibited, and thoroughly Americanized in both style and attitude. (Quoted by permission of the author from a work in progress, tentatively titled *Jazz in Japanese Culture: From Akira Kurosawa to Haruki Murakami.*)

Jazz fiction from the West is, predictably, both more numerous and more accessible than that of the East—and it is more often available in translation (though surely dozens if not hundreds of European and perhaps Russian jazz novels have disappeared from the record or lie untranslated in the dustbin of the past). One work that has half-escaped such a fate is Hans Janowitz's *Jazz: Roman* (1927), which has been republished in the original **German** and partially translated into English. *Jazz* is of interest not only because of its early appearance in the history of jazz fiction but also, and most significantly, because it is the earliest novel in any language to appropriate the techniques and structures of jazz within a novelistic frame. The story, such as it is, concerns a group of musicians—calling themselves at first the Jazz-Band-Boys and later the Jazz-Symphonists—whose "mission in life . . . [is to translate] the whole world into jazz." This lofty endeavor takes place primarily at a nightclub, allowing the author to cobble together a wide variety of characters and events. When he feels like ending his story, the self-reflexive speaker does so, more or less, simply by stopping in the middle of the narrative, rationalizing (or explaining) that "A jazz novel has the right to fade out quietly, and just come to an end in the midst of a thematic repetition."

Hermann Hesse's *Steppenwolf* was published in the same year (1927) and language as Janowitz's exuberant novel but is infinitely more famous, no doubt because its author was a Nobel laureate whose works have been translated into many languages. Although the novel's jazz content is not great, it is symbolically significant. The conflicted middle-aged protagonist, Harry Haller, suffers from the weight of existence. He feels so spiritually bereft that he contemplates suicide. But just as he prepares to give in to the darkness, he meets a handsome, amoral, bisexual saxophone player who introduces Harry to the idea of the pleasure principle. Thus one of the functions of jazz in the novel is to introduce the notion that mankind would be much more content, or at least less miserable, if it acted on instinct and pursued pleasure instead of continuing to lead the stultifying life of the mind. The novel is also interesting for its depiction of the influence of African-Americans and their music on European culture—a familiar motif in the Continental literature of the day.

Ruth Feiner's *Cat Across the Path* could not be more different from the previous two books. Its histrionic plot concerns the relationship of two mismatched young Berliners who are united by their love of music and their profound attraction to a luminous young woman. One, Fritz, moves to Paris, where he becomes the golden boy of the new jazz. When it becomes clear that he is destined for stardom, he adopts an Americanized name—Johnny Groves—and soon becomes known as the Jazz King of the Western World. The value of this book lies in its dramatization of the vibrant German jazz scene on the threshold of World War II.

Although **France** has long enjoyed the reputation for providing a warm, enthusiastic welcome to expatriate American, especially African-American, jazz musicians, it seems to have produced surprisingly little literature that reflects that phenomenon. One early exception may be Stephane Manier's *Sous le Signe du Jazz*, which was published in 1926. Like other international works published during the 1920s, this novel is much concerned, sometimes even fascinated, with black American musicians and their syncopated rhythms.

The world of jazz fiction would not be a lesser place had at least two French novels *not* been translated into English. They are worth mentioning only for their oddity. The first of these is Jacques de Loustal-Paringaux's *Barney and the Blue Note*, a novel in cartoons that exploits all of the worst myths and stereotypes of the jazz life. The story concerns the deterioration of one Barney whose fame as a jazz musician in the 1950s had caused him to retreat from the world and squander his musical gift through heroin, booze, and existential remoteness. The second curious French work is Daniel Odier's *Cannibal Kiss*. It is decidedly a free-form novel as it moves from one picaresque exploit to another of its 15-year-old protagonist, a girl named Bird with a cat called Lester Young. This novel may in fact be an effort to provide the novelistic equivalent of an inspired Charlie Parker solo. If that is the case, the translation obscures rather than illuminates the intention.

More conventional—and substantial—examples of the French jazz novel are to be found in Gerard Herzhaft's *Long Blues in A Minor*, Christian Gailly's *An Evening at the Club*, and Daniel Maximin's *Lone Sun*. *Long Blues* is triggered by the relationship between an African-American soldier, Sugar, and a teenage French boy, Champollion, during the French liberation. When Sugar returns to the States, he gives the boy his record collection, introducing him to "the America of the blues." Years later, Champollion, now a man, quits his lucrative job to follow his passion, the blues. After insinuating himself into

Chicago's black community, he finally meets up with his hero, Big Johnny
White, and the two of them bus to Clarksdale, Mississippi, where Champollion experiences segregation for the first time, leading him to the conclusion
that the blues were not so much "music as a state of mind."

It is difficult to say if any life-lessons are learned in *An Evening at the Club*,
a short, existential novel concerning an influential jazz pianist, Simon Nordis,
who inexplicably one day gives up music and the life that goes with it. Much
later, after years as a nine-to-fiver, Simon is asked by a coworker to stop by a
jazz club for drinks after work. When the band goes on break, Simon is drawn,
as if by a magnet, to the piano. Shortly after he begins to play, he is joined by
an attractive jazz singer, who is also drawn as if by a magnet to Simon. Then,
practically at the moment they enter into the inevitable sexual relationship, Simon's wife dies in an auto accident. That, enigmatically, is it.

Lone Sun, on the other hand, is not so much enigmatic in the unmotivated
behavior of its characters and the arbitrariness of its events as in the seemingly
willful strangeness of its postmodern technique: a mélange of dreams, snippets
of stories, folktales, Creole aphorisms, diary entries, and legends, all in the in-
voluted service of a novel-within-a-novel whose objective is to explore the unrecorded Caribbean past. The style and substance of the narrative are strongly
influenced by African-American and Afro-Cuban jazz, and the story itself
mentions jazz musicians, dramatizes music in performance, and contains two
powerful extended passages concerning one of Coleman Hawkins's renditions
of "Body and Soul." Born in Guadaloupe but longtime resident of France, author Maximin *may* be a major jazz fictionist but unfortunately most of us will
not be able to make that judgment until his other works are translated into English. Curiously, no translator is credited for *Lone Sun.*

Speaking of novels set in the **West Indies**, L. Edward Brathwaite (later Edward Kamau Brathwaite) has much of interest to say on the subject in a series of essays published in *BIM* [11, no. 44 (1967): 275–84; 12, no. 45 (1967):
39–51; 12, no. 46 (1968): 115–26]. Although the novels he discusses do not
usually include jazz as subject matter, he argues that they do appropriate
structures and techniques of the music to a significant extent. As he says of
Robert Mais's *Brother Man*, for example, this novel

> reveals certain rhythmic, thematic and structural features which justify . . . com-
> paring it to music. Its specific relationship to New Orleans jazz comes with its
> peculiar sense of union and unity, its contrasting "duets," its "improvisation"
> and correspondences and above all its *pervasive sense of community* (its *collec-
> tive* improvisation. . . . [author's emphasis]

Given its long-standing enthusiasm for jazz, it comes as no surprise to learn that
the **United Kingdom** has made substantial contributions to the world of jazz

fiction. John Wain's *Strike the Father Dead* is a case in point. This serious **English** novel underscores the barriers—philosophical, racial, and emotional—that separate people. When the young protagonist, Jeremy, commits himself to jazz, for instance, he separates himself from his father, a classics professor. Through his friendship with a black American horn player, Jeremy is later able to come to terms with his music and his life. This novel nicely captures the moment when the new post–World War II developments in jazz were filtering across the ocean and often comfortably combining with the French existential philosophy that was in the air.

Alan Plater's *Misterioso* also involves the search for a father, though in this case it is the daughter doing the searching. After her mother dies in an accident, Rachel discovers that the man she had thought was her father was not her father at all, so she sets out to find her biological parent armed with only a few clues to guide her: he loved jazz, adopted the names of jazz musicians as pseudonyms, and used *misterioso* as his all-purpose signature word. When Rachel finally finds her dad (at the Café Misterioso, of course), she learns things that very much complicate her life, including her conception of who she actually is. This often funny novel is drenched in jazz-related materials, and Thelonious Monk's famous tune "Misterioso" is the glue that binds them together. Author Plater has also produced a series of lighthearted detective novels revolving around the works of Bix Beiderbecke.

John Harvey's *In a True Light* also involves the search for a relative, this time of a father for a daughter. John Sloane, fresh out of prison for art forgery, learns that he had fathered a child with a well-known abstract-expressionist painter nearly forty years ago. So Sloane, at the behest of his dying former sweetheart, sets out to find the daughter he didn't know he had and do what he can to rectify an unpleasant family situation. His quest takes him to New York, and his return triggers flashbacks to his involvement in the vibrant art and music scenes that flowered there in the 1950s. Sloane's daughter turns out to be a singer—a jazz artist like her parents before her. The novel contains a memorable scene involving Thelonious Monk and John Coltrane gigging at the Five Spot. Author Harvey has also produced a series of detective novels and stories that contain significant jazz content.

Patrick Neate's *Twelve Bar Blues* could not be more different from the other British novels discussed above: it sprawls across three continents, two centuries, and multiple points of view. One locus of the story involves Fortis "Lick" Holden, a descendant of African slaves and a pioneer, in New Orleans, in the new music there, playing with Louis Armstrong, among others, and becoming "the greatest horn player that was ever lost to history." The novel's second field of interest centers on Lick's granddaughter Sylvia, a London-reared former prostitute and currently unemployed jazz singer who travels to the United States in an effort to solve the mystery of her multiracial heritage and, thereby, find out who she actually is. This energetic and ambitious but often chaotic novel won the prestigious Whitbread Award.

One of the most compelling jazz fictions to come out of England, Geoff Dyer's *But Beautiful: A Book about Jazz*, could hardly be classified as a novel, chaotic or otherwise. Rather it more nearly resembles the so-called New Journalism as the author, in keeping with the subject matter, improvises on events in the lives of jazz musicians: Lester Young, Thelonious Monk, Bud Powell, Ben Webster, Charles Mingus, Chet Baker, and Art Pepper. Dyer's strategy was to take a legendary episode from the life of each artist and create his own imaginative version of it. The result is a wondrously evocative combination of re-creation and reflection, with one possible flaw in the overall design: the author occasionally distorts the characters of the musicians he borrowed for this literary experiment, causing jazz purists to cry "foul."

No one would mistake John Murray's *Jazz, Etc.* for anything other than what it is: a wacky, wildly inventive novel involving several varieties of jazz by a writer clearly besotted, after the fashion of Anthony Burgess, by language. The story wobbles back and forth between Cumbria, England, and Portugal with an important stopover in Manhattan. The "hero," Enzo Mori, is a brilliant Italian Cumbrian thoroughly in thrall to his Oxford University contemporary, Fanny Golightly, who becomes internationally famous on the jazz guitar. Unfortunately for Enzo, Fanny is as fixated on someone else as Enzo is on her—a legendary Portuguese musician by the name of Toto Cebola. Another important plot strand of this zany novel involves Enzo's father, Vince, who harebrainedly pursues his often overlapping passions of women, the clarinet, and his "trad band," The Chompin Stompers, all the while hilariously mutilating the English language. Sooner or later, everyone in the story is spellbound by jazz. Even the supporting characters are often depicted in musical terms, as if they were intentionally adapting their verbal behavior to the structures of jazz.

England isn't the only member of the United Kingdom to have contributed to the body of jazz fiction. **Wales**, **Scotland**, and **Ireland** (which is, of course, only partially in the U.K.) have generated entries in this category. Roger Granelli's *Out of Nowhere* contains a violent, overheated plot centering on Welshman Frank Magnani, who leaves Britain at the encouragement of friends and other musicians to see if he can make his mark on jazz guitar in New York. After an early lucky break, Frank soon becomes disillusioned and then loses his job. Frank further complicates his tenuous existence by sleeping with his older benefactor's sweetheart and becoming embroiled with a dope dealer. Although the book suffers from debilitating novelistic weaknesses, its musical content is solid. The author is a professional musician.

More artistic and, in vastly different ways, compelling are two **Scottish** novels, both by black writers. The first of these is Jackie Kay's *Trumpet*, a story told from multiple viewpoints concerning the life and death of Joss Moody, who is revealed to have been a woman despite a long-term marriage to Millie. This work resonates with questions regarding the indefinability of gender and identity and the ways in which these can be complicated and enriched through jazz. Luke Sutherland's *Jelly Roll* is a violent, scatological, drug-ridden novel that has much more to do with race and general nastiness than gender or identity. When their psychotic saxophone player drops out of the ironically named Sunny Sunday Sextet, the five remaining band members resolve to find a replacement, go on tour, and gain a new musical lease on life. They soon acquire a brilliant sax man whose Irish background and black pigmentation cause instant turmoil among the other musicians, all of whom are white, Scottish, and (with one exception) furiously bigoted. Much of this long book focuses on the unspeakable racism and other prejudices that are generated by the appearance of this gifted outsider. Although there are some descriptions of jazz in performance, the primary center of musical interest lies in the rounded depiction of the volatile chemistry of the band as it goes on its tour of the Highlands. Many readers will have to strain to overcome the long opening section of this novel: it is in Scots dialect and overflowing with obscenity and assaultive language. Author Sutherland is a professional songwriter and musician.

Irishman Roddy Doyle's *Oh, Play That Thing* may indeed embody an equal measure of sex, violence, obscenity, and racism as *Jelly Roll*. It begins with IRA assassin Henry Smart fleeing Ireland, where he is a marked man, and landing in New York, hoping to remake himself and maybe even pursue the American Dream. After experiencing the truly grim realities of the disenfranchised, Henry escapes to Chicago, at which point the book becomes a jazz fiction. Henry soon encounters Louis Armstrong, who makes Henry his "white man"—that is, his means of traversing black and white societies in his quest for fame and fortune. Henry and Armstrong—the Irish immigrant fugitive and his southern African-American companion—constitute a truly odd couple as they go about their picaresque business in this, the longest, most absorbing part of the novel. Toward the end, Henry becomes expendable as Armstrong, now in Harlem, is being promoted as the world's greatest musician. The novel describes, often beautifully, jazz in performance, it incorporates several other actual musicians from the period, and it depicts a famous recording session of Armstrong and the Hot Five. If you listen closely, you just might hear an Irish tenor chiming in.

Other countries have contributed to the substantial body of international jazz fiction. The great **Argentine** writer, Julio Cortázar, for instance, is well represented by several stories, a novella, and a novel. In fact the first nineteen chapters of the novel, *Hopscotch,* read like the ne plus ultra of jazz fiction with their constant references to jazz and its practitioners and frequent provocative discussions of the music. And the novella, "The Pursuer," constitutes a major addition to the literature under discussion. Not only is it dedicated to "Ch. P.," but it is based on several key events in the great saxophonist's life. Similarly, the **Sri Lankan** (now Canadian) writer, Michael Ondaatje, took the few known facts of one of jazz's innovators, Buddy Bolden, and wove them into a stunning novel, *Coming through Slaughter,* which uses modernistic techniques to dramatize Bolden's psychological disorder and its relationship to his creativity.

Edward O'Connor's *Astral Projection* couldn't be more different. A native **Canadian**, O'Connor has produced a classic coming-of-age narrative focusing on a teenager whose home life in 1967 Miami is in shambles until he finds purpose and comfort in the jazz guitar. In part one—*The Album*—the chapters are called "Tracks" and each is named after a famous jazz composition: "Them That's Not," "All or Nothing at All," "Dancing on the Ceiling," "I Didn't Know What Time It Was," and so forth. Review copies of the book were accompanied by a CD containing many of the jazz pieces figuring in the text, underscoring the novel's strong jazz content.

If **Spain**'s Antonio Muñoz Molina's award-winning *Winter in Lisbon* were similarly promoted, the music would resemble the soundtrack of a noir movie. In fact this ranking jazz novel would be very comfortably classified as jazz noir with its smoky jazz venues, bibulous musicians, mysterious women, and exotic intrigue. The main characters are jazz musicians who play and hang out in jazz clubs with names like Lady Bird and Satchmo while meditating on the nature and meaning of their music. Although this work has been translated into sixteen languages, including English, it has yet to be distributed in the United States.

Perhaps the best known international jazz fiction writer is the **Czech** (now Canadian) Joseph Ŝkvorecký who characteristically uses jazz for political purposes in several stories and novels, three of which—"The Bass Saxophone," *The Cowards,* and *The Swell Season: A Text on the Most Important Things*—form a trilogy set in Nazi- and later Russian-occupied Czechoslovakia toward the end of World War II. The protagonist of these works is Danny Smiricky, a saxophonist who seeks solace from the pain of his repressive world through jazz, which has been outlawed by the totalitarian regime. Throughout these and Ŝkvorecký's other jazz-related works, the music often accents questions relating to freedom and slavery, reminding us of Thelonious Monk's comment that jazz means freedom.

As I have implied, the numerous examples of international jazz fiction that I cite above and in the annotations probably constitute only a fraction of the actual total. Who knows how many works in this broad category have gone undetected because they have not been translated or have slipped through the net of research? Until such time as data bases are refined and polylingual jazz fiction scholars developed, these works, like the aftermath of a live jazz performance, will remain disappeared in the air. The good news, of course, is that the literature, unlike the music, can be restored. The bad news, if anecdotal evidence can be trusted, is that publishers, even scholarly ones, grow ever more reluctant to traffic in translations.

Chapter Nine

For Further Reading

An Annotated Bibliography of Jazz Fiction and Jazz Fiction Criticism. Compiled by Richard N. Albert. Westport, CT: Greenwood, 1996.

Baker, Houston. *Blues, Ideology, and Afro-American Literature: A Vernacular Theory.* Chicago: University of Chicago Press, 1984.

Bell, Bernard W. *The Afro-American Novel and Its Tradition.* Amherst: University of Massachusetts Press, 1987.

B Flat, Bebop, Scat: Jazz Short Stories and Poems. Edited by Chris Parker. London: Quartet, 1986.

Breton, Marcella. "An Annotated Bibliography of Selected Jazz Short Stories." *African Review* 26 (1992): 299–306.

Cataliotti, Robert H. *The Music in African American Fiction.* New York and London: Garland, 1995.

Cowley, Julian. "The Art of the Improvisers: Jazz and Fiction in Post-Bebop America." *New Comparison* 6 (1988): 194–204.

From Blues to Bop: A Collection of Jazz Fiction. Edited by Richard N. Albert. Baton Rouge: Louisiana State University Press, 1990.

Grandt, Jürgen E. *Kinds of Blue: The Jazz Aesthetic in African American Narrative.* Columbus: The Ohio State University Press, 2004.

Gysin, Fritz. "From 'Liberating Voices' to 'Metathetic Ventriloquism': Boundaries in African-American Jazz Fiction." *Callaloo* 25, no. 1 (2002): 274–87.

Hot and Cool: Jazz Short Stories. Edited by Marcella Breton. New York: Plume, 1990.

Jarrett, Michael. "Four Choruses on the Tropes of Jazz Writing." *American Literary History* 6, no. 2 (1994): 336–53.

The Jazz Cadence of American Culture. Edited by Robert G. O'Meally. New York: University Press, 1998.

Jazz Parody (Anthology of Jazz Fiction). Edited by Charles Harvey. London: Spearman, 1948.

Jazz Planet. Edited by E. Taylor Atkins. Jackson: University Press of Mississippi, 2003.

Jones, Gayl. *Liberating Voices: Oral Tradition in African American Literature.* Cambridge, MA and London: Harvard University Press, 1991.

Moment's Notice: Jazz in Poetry and Prose. Edited by Art Lange and Nathaniel Mackey. Minneapolis: Coffee House Press, 1993.

Rice, Alan J. "Finger-Snapping to Train-Dancing and Back Again: The Development of a Jazz Style in African American Prose." *Yearbook of English Studies* (London) 24 (1994): 105–6.

Rife, David. "Jazz Fiction: A Bibliographic Overview." *Annual Review of Jazz Studies* 10 (1999): 17–34.

Rife, David, with Ellen Caswell. "Jazz Fiction: An Annotated Bibliography." *Annual Review of Jazz Studies* 11 (2000–2001): 125–215.

Sudhalter, Richard M. "Composing the Words That Might Capture Jazz." *New York Times,* Sec. 2, 29 August 1999: 1, 24.

Part 2

JAZZ FICTION BY
SELECT CATEGORIES

Many readers may wish to use the annotated bibliography that comprises most of this volume to search for works in particular genres or subject matters (e.g., mystery novels or works about women in jazz), some of which were summarized in the preceding chapters. What follows is a listing of works that most strongly fit these—and a few other—particular categories. Please note that fictional works written for *preteenage* children are adequately listed in the preceding chapter on "Juvenile and Young Adult Fiction."

TEEN AND YOUNG ADULT

Blakemore, Charles. *The Subjective Truth*
Bontemps, Arna. *Lonesome Boy*
Burnap, Campbell. "A Bit of a Scrape"
Catling, Patrick Skene. *Jazz Jazz Jazz*
Collier, James Lincoln. *The Jazz Kid*
Frankel, Haskel. *Big Band*
Glaser, Elton. "Blue Cat Club"
Hannah, Barry. "Testimony of Pilot"
Hentoff, Nat. *Does This School Have Capital Punishment?*
———. *Jazz Country*
Hill, Richard. *Riding Solo with the Golden Horde*
Howard, Brett. *Memphis Blues*
Hsuki, Hiroyuki. *Young Man in Search of a Barren Plain (Seinem Wa Kovya o Mezasu)*
Lamb, David. *The Trumpet Is Blown*
Malone, R. Pingank. "Sound Your 'A': The Story of Trumpeter Tom Stewart in Full-Length Novel Form"
Martin, Kenneth K. "The End of Jamie"
Newton, Suzanne. *I Will Call It Georgie's Blues*
Richoux, Pat. *The Stardust Kid*
Simon, George T. *Don Watson Starts His Band*
Tamar, Erika. *Blues for Silk Garcia*
Townley, Roderick. *Sky: A Novel in Three Sets and an Encore*
Tucker, Lisa. *Shout Down the Moon*
Young, Al. *Snakes*

FANTASY, HORROR, AND SCIENCE FICTION

Anthony, Piers, and Ron Leming. *The Gutbucket Quest*
Austin, Alex. "Dancers"
Beardmore, Paul. *The Jazz Elephants*
Berman, Mitch. *Time Capsule*

Bloch, Robert. "Dig That Crazy Horse!"
Boyczuk, Robert. "Jazz Fantasia"
Branham, R. V. "Chango Chingamadre, Dutchman, & Me"
Brite, Poppy Z. "Mussolini and the Axeman's Jazz"
Cohen, Elaine. "Blevins' Blues"
Dawson, Fielding. *Will She Understand?*
Finn, Julio. "The Blue Bayou"
Frost, Gregory. "Attack of the Jazz Giants"
Gardner, Martin. "The Devil and the Trombone"
Goonan, Kathleen Ann. *Crescent City Rhapsody*
——. *Light Music*
——. *Mississippi Blues*
——. *Queen City Jazz*
Klavan, Andrew. *Hunting Down Amanda*
Knight, Damon. "Coming Back to Dixieland"
Leiber, Fritz. "The Beat Cluster"
Lively, Adam. *Blue Fruit*
Marshall-Courtois, Rebecca. "The Place Where Colored Notes Play"
Marvin, Bryan. "Hath Charms to Soothe"
Matheson, Richard. "The Jazz Machine"
McMartin, Sean. "Music for One Hand Only"
Oliver, Chad. "Didn't He Ramble"
Perlongo, Robert A. "Jollity on a Treadmill"
Reed, Ishmael. *Mumbo Jumbo*
Roberts, David Wyn. *The Alchemist's Song*
Shure, Jill. *Night Jazz*
Stewart, John. "The Americanization of Rhythm"
Straub, Peter. "Pork Pie Hat"
Tilley, Robert J. "The Devil and All That Jazz"
——. "Something Else"
——. "Willie's Blues"
Zabor, Rafi. *The Bear Comes Home*

BLUES

Anthony, Piers, and Ron Leming. *The Gutbucket Quest*
Atkins, Ace. *Crossroad Blues*
——. *Dark End of the Street*
——. *Dirty South*
——. *Leavin' Trunk Blues*
Bambara, Toni Cade. "Mississippi Ham Rider"
Beaumont, Charles. "Black Country"
Bell, Madison Smartt. *Anything Goes*

Biggie, Patrick. "St. Louis Blues"
Brickman, Marshall. "What, Another Legend?"
Chappell, Fred. "Blue Drive"
Cohn, David L. "Black Troubador"
Curran, Dale. *Dupree Blues*
Dubus, Andre III. *Bluesman*
Flowers, Arthur. *Another Good Loving Blues*
Guralnick, Peter. *Nighthawk Blues*
Hellenga, Robert. *Blues Lessons*
Herzhaft, Gerard. *Long Blues in A Minor*
Hood, Mary. "Lonesome Road Blues"
Howard, Brett. *Memphis Blues*
Hughes, Langston. *Not without Laughter*
Johnson, Clifford Vincent. "Old Blues Singers Never Die"
Jones, Gayle. *Corregidora*
Kelley, William Melvin. "Cry for Me"
Lee, George Washington. *Beale Street Sundown*
Leonard, Elmore. *Tishomingo Blues*
Major, Clarence. *Dirty Bird Blues*
McCarthy, Albert J. "My Home Is a Southern Town"
Mitchell, Adrian. *If You See Me Comin'*
Mosley, Walter. *RL's Dream*
Moss, Grant. "I Remember Bessie Smith"
Ohio, Denise. *Blue*
Phillips, Freeman. "Little Nooley's Blues"
Phillips, Jane. *Mojo Hand*
Piazza, Tom. *Blues and Trouble*
Woods, G. Arthur. *The Jazz and the Blues*

BIG BAND AND SWING

Baker, Dorothy. *Young Man with a Horn*
Curran, Dale. *Piano in the Band*
Downs, Hunton. *Murder in the Mood*
Duchin, Peter, and John Morgan Wilson. *Blue Moon*
———. *Good Morning, Heartache*
Duke, Osborn. *Sideman*
English, Richard. *"Strictly Ding-Dong" and Other Swing Stories*
Ewing, Annemarie. *Little Gate*
Fairweather, Digby. "The Killers of '59"
Fisher, Rudolf. "Common Meter"
Frankel, Haskel. *Big Band*
Garceau, Phil. "The Price of Swing"

Glatzer, Hal. *Too Dead to Swing*
Green, Benny. *Fifty-eight Minutes to London*
Holmes, Rupert. *Swing: A Mystery*
Malone, R. Pingank. "Sound Your 'A': The Story of Trumpeter Tom Stewart in Full-
  Length Novel Form"
Murray, Albert. *The Seven League Boots*
Reed, Harlan. *The Swing Music Murder*
Robinson, Peter. "Memory Lane"
Rundell, Wyatt. *Jazz Band*
Shurman, Ida. *Death Beats the Band*
Sonin, Ray. *The Dance Band Mystery*
Steig, Henry. *Send Me Down*
——. "Swing Business"
Stephens, Edward. *Roman Joy*
Tate, Sylvia. *Never by Chance*
Tormé, Mel. *Wynner*
Wainwright, John. *Do Nothin' Till You Hear from Me*
Willis, George. *Tangleweed*

BEBOP

Asher, Don. "The Barrier"
Baldwin, James. "Sonny's Blues"
Braly, Malcolm. *Shake Him Till He Rattles*
Brossard, Chandler. *Who Walk in Darkness*
Cartiér, Xam Wilson. *Be-Bop, Re-Bop*
Conroy, Frank. *Body and Soul*
DeVries, Peter. "Jam Today"
Flender, Harold. *Paris Blues*
Forman, Bruce. *Trust Me*
Fuller, Jack. *The Best of Jackson Payne*
Gilbert, Edwin. *The Hot and the Cool*
Goldsher, Alan. *Jam*
Holmes, John Clellon. *The Horn*
Huddle, David. *Tenorman*
Hughes, Langston. "Bop"
——. "Jazz, Jive, and Jam"
James, Stuart. *Too Late Blues*
Johns, Veronica Parker. "Mr. Hyde-de-Ho"
Joseph, Oscar. "Suite for a Queen"
Kelley, William Melvin. *A Drop of Patience*
Kerouac, Jack. *On the Road*
Lombreglia, Ralph. "Jazzers"

Loustal-Paringaux, Jacques de. *Barney and the Blue Note*
Mansbach, Adam. *Shackling Water*
McCluskey, John. *Look What They Done to My Song*
Miller, Warren. *The Cool World*
Rainer, Dachine. "The Party"
Russell, Ross. *The Sound*
Sadoff, Ira. "Black Man's Burden"
Schneider, Bart. *Blue Bossa*
Simmons, Herbert. *Man Walking on Eggshells*
Smith, J. P. *Body and Soul*
Updyke, James. *It's Always Four O'Clock*
Weller, Anthony. *The Polish Lover*
Zabor, Rafi. *The Bear Comes Home*

WORKS BASED ON THE LIVES OF ACTUAL MUSICIANS

Allen, Candace. *Valaida* [Valaida Snow]
Baker, Dorothy. *Young Man with a Horn* [Bix Beiderbecke]
Baraka, Amiri. "A Monk Story" [Thelonious Monk]
Brown, Beth. "Jazzman's Last Day" [Lee Morgan]
Charters, Samuel. *Jelly Roll Morton's Last Night at the Jungle Inn*
Cliff, Michelle. "A Woman Who Plays Trumpet Is Deported" [Valaida Snow]
Cornelius, Marcus M. *Out of Nowhere: The Musical Life of Warne Marsh*
Cortázar, Julio. "The Pursuer" [Charlie Parker]
Deutsch, Hermann. "Louis Armstrong"
DeVeaux, Alexis. *Don't Explain: A Song of Billie Holiday*
Doyle, Roddy. *Oh, Play That Thing* [Louis Armstrong]
Ellis, Walter. *Prince of Darkness: A Jazz Fiction Inspired by the Music of Miles Davis*
Ewing, Annemarie. *Little Gate* [Bix Beiderbecke?]
Federman, Raymond. "Remembering Charlie Parker or How to Get It Out of Your System"
Garvin, Richard M., and Edmond G. Addeo. *The Midnight Special: The Legend of Leadbelly* [Huddy Ledbetter]
Grennard, Elliott. "Sparrow's Last Jump" [Charlie Parker]
Holmes, John Clellon. *The Horn* [Charlie Parker and Lester Young]
Jones, James. "The King" [Bunk Johnson?]
Ondaatje, Michael. *Coming through Slaughter* [Buddy Bolden]
Phillips, Jane. *Mojo Hand* [Lightnin' Hopkins]
Pico, Robert. *Jackson Jazz* [Milt Jackson]
Reed, Jeremy. *Saint Billie* [Billie Holiday]
Russell, Ross. *The Sound* [Charlie Parker]
Salinger, J. D. "Blue Melody" [Bessie Smith]
Schneider, Bart. *Blue Bossa* [Chet Baker]

Scott, Tony. "Destination K. C." [Charlie Parker]
Shaw, Artie. "Snow White in Harlem, 1930." [Artie Shaw and Willie "The Lion" Smith]
Turner, Frederick. *1929* [Bix Beiderbecke]
Welty, Eudora. "Powerhouse" [Fats Waller]
Williams, John A. *Night Song* [Charlie Parker]

CRIME, MYSTERY, AND NOIR

Anderson, Beth. *Night Sounds*
Avery, Robert. *Murder on the Downbeat*
Barnes, Harper. *Blue Monday*
Bird, Brandon. *Downbeat for a Dirge*
Blaine, Laurence. *Sweet Street Blues*
Borneman, Ernest. *Tremolo*
Braly, Malcolm. *Shake Him Till He Rattles*
Brown, Carter. *The Ever-Loving Blues*
Carter, Charlotte. "Birdbath"
———. *Coq au Vin*
———. *Drumsticks*
———. *Rhode Island Red*
Coggins, Mark. *The Immortal Game*
Collins, Max Allan, and Matthew V. Clemens. "East Side, West Side"
Connelly, Michael. "Christmas Even"
———. *Lost Light*
Creech, J. R. *Music and Crime*
Edwards, Grace F. *Do or Die*
Estleman, Loren D. *Lady Yesterday*
Farmer, Jerrilyn. *Perfect Sax*
Farr, John. *The Deadly Combo*
Fox, F. G. *Funky Butt Blues*
Fulmer, David. *Chasing the Devil's Tail*
———. *Jass*
Glatzer, Hal. *Too Dead to Swing*
Gorman, Ed. "Muse"
Harvey, John. *Cold Light*
———. *Cutting Edge*
———. *Easy Meat*
———. "Favor"
———. *Last Rites*
———. *Living Proof*
———. *Lonely Hearts*
———. *Now's the Time*
———. *Still Water*

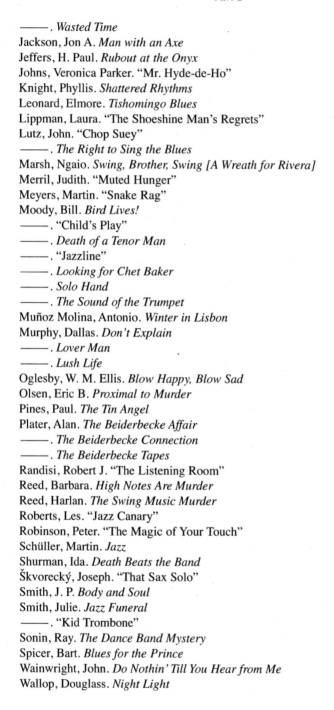

—— . *Wasted Time*
Jackson, Jon A. *Man with an Axe*
Jeffers, H. Paul. *Rubout at the Onyx*
Johns, Veronica Parker. "Mr. Hyde-de-Ho"
Knight, Phyllis. *Shattered Rhythms*
Leonard, Elmore. *Tishomingo Blues*
Lippman, Laura. "The Shoeshine Man's Regrets"
Lutz, John. "Chop Suey"
—— . *The Right to Sing the Blues*
Marsh, Ngaio. *Swing, Brother, Swing [A Wreath for Rivera]*
Merril, Judith. "Muted Hunger"
Meyers, Martin. "Snake Rag"
Moody, Bill. *Bird Lives!*
—— . "Child's Play"
—— . *Death of a Tenor Man*
—— . "Jazzline"
—— . *Looking for Chet Baker*
—— . *Solo Hand*
—— . *The Sound of the Trumpet*
Muñoz Molina, Antonio. *Winter in Lisbon*
Murphy, Dallas. *Don't Explain*
—— . *Lover Man*
—— . *Lush Life*
Oglesby, W. M. Ellis. *Blow Happy, Blow Sad*
Olsen, Eric B. *Proximal to Murder*
Pines, Paul. *The Tin Angel*
Plater, Alan. *The Beiderbecke Affair*
—— . *The Beiderbecke Connection*
—— . *The Beiderbecke Tapes*
Randisi, Robert J. "The Listening Room"
Reed, Barbara. *High Notes Are Murder*
Reed, Harlan. *The Swing Music Murder*
Roberts, Les. "Jazz Canary"
Robinson, Peter. "The Magic of Your Touch"
Schüller, Martin. *Jazz*
Shurman, Ida. *Death Beats the Band*
Škvorecký, Joseph. "That Sax Solo"
Smith, J. P. *Body and Soul*
Smith, Julie. *Jazz Funeral*
—— . "Kid Trombone"
Sonin, Ray. *The Dance Band Mystery*
Spicer, Bart. *Blues for the Prince*
Wainwright, John. *Do Nothin' Till You Hear from Me*
Wallop, Douglass. *Night Light*

WOMEN

Adams, Alice. *Listening to Billie*
Allen, Candace. *Valaida*
Angelou, Maya. "The Reunion"
Baker, Dorothy. "Keely Street Blues"
Bambera, Toni Cade. "Medley"
Cameron, Stella. *Tell Me Why*
Carter, Charlotte. "Birdbath"
——. *Coq au Vin*
——. *Drumsticks*
——. "A Flower Is a Lovesome Thing"
——. *Rhode Island Red*
Cartiér, Xam Wilson. *Be-Bop, Re-Bop*
——. *Muse-Echo Blues*
Cliff, Michelle. "A Woman Who Plays Trumpet Is Deported"
Coleman, Wanda. "Angel Baby Blues"
——. "The Blues in the Night"
——. "The Man Who Loved Billie Holiday"
——. "Jazz at Twelve"
Coxhead, Nona. *Big-Time Baby*
Cresswell, Jasmine. *Contract: Paternity*
Crouch, Stanley. *Don't the Moon Look Lonesome*
Davis, Genie. *Dreamtown*
Daugherty, Tracy. *Axeman's Jazz*
Deaver, Jeffery Wilds. *Mistress of Justice*
DeVeaux, Alexis. *Don't Explain: A Song of Billie Holiday*
Edwards, Grace F. *Do or Die*
Gibney, Shannon. "How I Remade Coltrane"
Glatzer, Hal. *Too Dead to Swing*
Gould, Philip. *Kitty Collins*
Grime, Kitty. "Seeing Her Off"
Hewat, Alan V. *Lady's Time*
Hughes, Langston. "The Blues I'm Playing"
Hunter, Kristen. *God Bless the Child*
Johns, Veronica Parker. "Mr. Hyde-de-Ho"
Jones, Gayle. *Corregidora*
Jordan, Elizabeth. *Blues in the Night*
Kennett, Frances. *Lady Jazz*
Kitt, Sandra. *Serenade*
Knight, Phyllis. *Shattered Rhythms*
Lewis, Ellen Jordis. "Miss Brown to You"
Ohio, Denise. *Blue*
Petry, Ann. *The Street*

Phillips, Jane. *Mojo Hand*
Reed, Jeremy. *Saint Billie*
Rhys, Jean. "Let Them Call It Jazz"
Richards, Susan Starr. "Calling Up Billie"
Richards-Slaughter, Shannon. "The Blossoms of Jazz"
Sayer, Mandy. *Mood Indigo*
Shange, Ntozake. *Sassafrass, Cypress and Indigo*
Shure, Jill. *Night Jazz*
Smith, Andrea. *Friday Nights at Honeybee's*
Tamar, Erika. *Blues for Silk Garcia*
Tucker, Lisa. *Shout Down the Moon*
Westin, Jeane. *Swing Sisters*
Wheeler, Susan. *Record Palace*

IMMIGRANT AND INTERNATIONAL

Abu-Jabar, Diana. *Arabian Jazz* [Immigrant]
Accame, Jorge. *Concierto de Jazz* [Argentina]
Clapham, Walter. *Come Blow Your Horn* [England]
Cortazár, Julio. "Bix Beiderbecke" [Argentina]
———. *Hopscotch (Rayuela)*
———. "Lucas, His Pianists"
———. "A Place Named Kindberg"
———. "The Pursuer" ("El Perseguidor")
Deelder, J. A. *Verhalen en Gedichten* [Netherlands]
Denver, Paul. *Send Me No Lilies* [England]
Diniz, Tailor. *O Assassino Usava Batom* [Brazil]
Downs, Hunton. *Murder in the Mood* [England]
Doyle, Roddy. *Oh, Play That Thing* [Ireland]
Dyer, Geoff. *But Beautiful* [England]
Feiner, Ruth. *Cat Across the Path* [Germany]
Frank, Bruno. *The Persians Are Coming (Politische Novelle)* [Germany]
Fuller, John. *Tell It Me Again* [England]
Gailly, Christian. *An Evening at the Club (Soir au Club)* [France]
Granelli, Roger. *Out of Nowhere* [Wales]
Grant, James. *Don't Shoot the Pianist* [England].
Green, Benny. *Blame It on My Youth* [England]
———. *Fifty-eight Minutes to London*
Grime, Kitty. "Seeing Her Off" [England]
Harvey, John. *Cold Light* [England]
———. *Cutting Edge*
———. *Easy Meat*
———. *In a True Light*
———. *Last Rites*

————. *Living Proof*
————. *Lonely Hearts*
————. *Now's the Time*
————. *Still Water*
————. *Wasted Years*
Henk, Michael. *Die Trompete* [Germany]
Herzhaft, Gerard. *Long Blues in A Minor* [France]
Hesse, Hermann. *Steppenwolf* [Switzerland]
Hijuelos, Oscar. *The Mambo Kings Sing Songs of Love* [Immigrant]
Hsuki, Hiroyuki. *Young Man in Search of a Barren Plain* (*Seinen Wa Korya o Mezasu*) [Japan]
Islas, Arturo. *La Mollie and the King of Tears* [Immigrant]
Janowitz, Hans. *Jazz: Roman* [Germany]
Kawana, Phil. "Dead Jazz Guys" [New Zealand]
Kay, Jackie. *Trumpet* [Scotland]
Kelly, Rod. *Just for the Bread* [England]
Kennett, Frances. *Lady Jazz* [England]
Leistra, Ben. *Het Jazz—Requiem* [Netherlands]
Lively, Adam. *Blue Fruit* [England]
Loustal-Paringaux, Jacques de. *Barney and the Blue Note* [France]
Manier, Stéphane. *Sous le Signe du Jazz* [France]
Marsh, Ngaio. *Swing, Brother, Swing* (also published as *A Wreath for Rivera*) [New Zealand, England]
Maximin, Daniel. *L'Ile et Une Nuit* (*The Island and a Night*) [Guadaloupe, France]
————. *Lone Sun* (*L'Isolé Soleil*)
————. *Soufriéres* (*Sulfur Mines*)
Mendez Carrasco, Armando. *Dos Cuentos de Jazz* [Chile]
Mitchell, Adrian. *If You See Me Comin'* [England]
Mu, Shiying. "Five in a Nightclub" [China]
Murray, John. *Jazz, Etc.* [England]
Neate, Patrick. *Twelve Bar Blues* [England]
O'Connor, Patrick. *Astral Projection* [Canada]
Odier, Daniel. *Cannibal Kiss* [France]
Ondaatje, Michael. *Coming through Slaughter* [Sri Lanka, Canada]
Pico, Robert. *Jackson Jazz* [France]
Plater, Alan. *The Beiderbecke Affair* [England]
————. *The Beiderbecke Connection*
————. *The Beiderbecke Tapes*
————. *Misterioso*
Reed, Jeremy. *Saint Billie* [England]
Rhys, Jean. "Let Them Call It Jazz" [England]
Rigter, Bob. *Jazz in Oostzee* [Netherlands]
Rimanelli, Giose. *Una Posizione Sociale* [Italy]
Robinson, Peter. "Memory Lane" [England]
Roelants, Maurice. "The Jazz Player" [Netherlands]

Roos, Olle. "Naer Negerjazzen kom till Björkåsen" [Sweden]
Ross, Sinclair. *Whir of Gold* [Canada]
Salaverría, José. "The Negro of the Jazz Band" [Spain]
Sayer, Mandy. *Mood Indigo* [Australia]
Schickele, René. *Symphonie für Jazz* [Germany]
Schüller, Martin. *Jazz* [Germany]
Škvorecký, Joseph. "The Bass Saxophone" [Czech Republic, Canada]
———. "The Bebop of Richard Kambala"
———. *The Cowards*
———. "Eine Kleine Jazzmusik"
———. "That Sax Solo"
———. *The Swell Season*
———. *The Tenor Saxophonist's Story*
Sonin, Ray. *The Dance Band Mystery* [England]
Suarez, Virgil. *Latin Jazz* [Immigrant]
Sutherland, Luke. *Jelly Roll* [Scotland]
Tsutsui, Yasutaka. *Jazz Stories* (*Jazu Shosetsu*) [Japan]
Vega Yunqué, Edgardo. *No Matter How Much You Promise to Cook or Pay the Rent You Blew It Cauze Bill Bailey Ain't Never Coming Home Again* [Immigrant]
Vian, Boris. "Cancer" [France]
———. "A Chorus for the Last Judgement"
———. "Letter to Santa Klaus"
———. "Round about Close to Midnight"
Wain, John. *Strike the Father Dead* [England]
Wainwright, John. *Do Nothin' Till You Hear from Me* [England]
Williams, Mike. *Old Jazz* [England, Australia]
XuXi. "Jazz Wife" [Immigrant]
———. "Manky's Tale"
Zinik, Zinovy. "A Ticket to Spare" [Russia]

INTERNET

Burns, Mary. "The Sound of Dreaming"
De Niro, Alan. "Tetrarchs"
Ewing, Debora. "Coloring Outside the Lines"
Green, David Paul. "Blues Man"
———. "Bohemian Jazz Boys Hit the Town"
Honea, Whit. "Jazz"
Jeyapalan, Renuka. "The Jazz Singer"
Marshall-Courtois, Rebecca. "The Place Where Colored Notes Play"
Mass, Rochelle. "Rozogov and Jazz"
Moore, John. "The Art of Improvisation"
RogueStar. "Jazz"

Sexton, Kay. "Traveling Magic"
Spechler, Diana. "Inheritance"
XuXi. "Jazz Wife"
———. "Manky's Tale"

NOVELIZATIONS

Boyd, Frank. [Henry Kane.] *Johnny Staccato*
Dail, Hubert. *The Singing Fool*
Fletcher, Jessica, and Donald Bain. *Murder in a Minor Key*
Gade, Sven. *Jazz Mad*
Gilmour, H. B. *All That Jazz*
James, Stuart. *Too Late Blues*
Johnson, Grady. *The Five Pennies*
Kane, Henry. *Peter Gunn*
Kanin, Garson. *The Rat Race*
Pine, Les, and Tina Rome. *A Man Called Adam*
Woodley, Richard. *The Jazz Singer*

PULP AND SMUT

Austin, William A. *Commit the Sins*
Baird, Jack. *Hot, Sweet, and Blue*
Bunyan, Pat. *I Peddle Jazz*
Casey, Scott. *One More Time*
Gwinn, William. *Jazz Bum*
———. *A Way with Women*
Hanley, Jack. *Hot Lips*
Nemec, John. *Canary's Combo*
Novak, Mike. *B-Girl*
Sand, Carter. *Two for the Money*
St. James, Blakeley. *A Festival for Christina*
Vining, Keith. *Keep Running*
Weiss, Joe. *Passion Blues*

Part 3

JAZZ FICTION SHORT-LISTS

For those who would like to learn more about jazz fiction but don't know where to begin, I offer the following two short-lists, which modestly presume to furnish exemplary specimens of their respective genres, not "Best of Jazz Fiction" compilations. A few of the stories do indeed aspire to literary greatness—for instance, Baldwin's "Sonny's Blues," Welty's "Powerhouse," McCluskey's "Lush Life," and Wideman's "The Silence of Thelonious Monk." If the novels don't contain any masterpieces, they nevertheless offer an impressive variety of themes and techniques, and all but a couple duly incorporate a significant degree of music in their narratives. It would be difficult to imagine, for example, any four works of similar quality, in any genre or art form, more different from each other than Muñoz Molina's *Winter in Lisbon*, Murray's *Jazz, Etc.*, Ondaatje's *Coming through Slaughter*, and Zabor's *The Bear Comes Home*. Thus, these and the other compelling works on both lists provide a convenient point of departure for jazz fiction aficionados and the potential to supply them with a deeply rewarding literary-musical experience.

Two final notes: Many of the stories can be found in two anthologies published in 1990: Richard N. Albert's *From Blues to Bop* and Marcela Breton's *Hot and Cool: Jazz Short Stories*. And, in the interest of full disclosure, three of the stories first appeared in *Brilliant Corners*, a journal I have helped edit since its inception.

SHORT FICTION

Angelou, Maya. "The Reunion"
Asher, Don. "The Barrier"
Baldwin, James. "Sonny's Blues"
Bambara, Toni Cade. "Medley"
Baraka, Amiri [LeRoi Jones]. "The Screamers"
Beaumont, Charles. "Black Country"
Brown, Frank London. "Singing Dinah's Song"
Cohen, Octavus. "Music Hath Charms"
Coleman, Wanda. "Jazz at Twelve"
Cortázar, Julio. "The Pursuer"
Delancey, Kiki. "Swingtime"
Foote, Shelby. "Ride Out"
Greenlee, Sam. "Blues for Little Prez"
Hughes, Langston. "The Blues I'm Playing"
Kawana, Phil. "Dead Jazz Guys"
Lutz, John. "The Right to Sing the Blues"
McCluskey, John. "Lush Life"
Moody, Bill. "The Resurrection of Bobo Jones"
Petry, Ann. "Solo on the Drums"

Reed, James. "The Shrimp Peel Gig"
Škvorecký, Josef. "The Bebop of Richard Kambala"
Southern, Terry. "You're Too Hip, Baby"
Welty, Eudora. "Powerhouse"
Wideman, John Edgar. "The Silence of Thelonious Monk"
Yates, Richard. "A Really Good Jazz Piano"

NOVELS

Allen, Candace. *Valaida*
Baker, Dorothy. *Young Man with a Horn*
Cornelius, Marcus M. *Out of Nowhere*
Crouch, Stanley. *Don't the Moon Look Lonesome*
Doyle, Roddy. *Oh, Play That Thing*
Dyer, Geoff. *But Beautiful*
Fuller, Jack. *The Best of Jackson Payne*
Hijuelos, Oscar. *The Mambo Kings Sing Songs of Love*
Hoey, Allen. *Chasing the Dragon: A Novel about Jazz*
Holmes, John Clellon. *The Horn*
Huddle, David. *Tenorman*
Kay, Jackie. *Trumpet*
Kelley, William Melvin. *A Drop of Patience*
McKay, Claude. *Banjo: A Story without a Plot*
Moody, Bill. *The Sound of the Trumpet*
Morrison, Toni. *Jazz*
Muñoz Molina, Antonio. *Winter in Lisbon*
Murray, Albert. *The Seven League Boots*
Murray, John. *Jazz, Etc.*
Ondaatje, Michael. *Coming through Slaughter*
Russell, Ross. *The Sound*
Schneider, Bart. *Blue Bossa*
Simmons, Herbert. *Man Walking on Eggshells*
Turner, Frederick. *1929*
Weller, Anthony. *The Polish Lover*
Williams, John A. *Night Song*
Zabor, Rafi. *The Bear Comes Home*

Part 4

ANNOTATED BIBLIOGRAPHY
OF JAZZ FICTION

Abu-Jaber, Diana. *Arabian Jazz*. New York: Harcourt Brace, 1993.

Set in a poor white community in upstate New York from the 1960s to the 1990s, this novel recounts an Arab-American family's struggle with assimilation: how is it possible to balance the traditions of the "Old Country" with the lifestyles of the new? This conflict soon centers on Jemorah, whose very sense of identity is jeopardized by her attachment to both cultures. The jazz content, such as it is, flows from Jem's father, Mattussem Ramoud, who plays drums exuberantly in a jazz band in his spare time, believing that the drumbeat is the pulse of existence. Through her father and his musical theory, Jem comes to realize that the strange combination of American jazz and Arabic trills actually reconciles — brings into harmony — two seemingly incompatible worlds. The book begins and ends with significant references to jazz and contains sparsely scattered references to the music and its players throughout.

Accame, Jorge. *Concierto de Jazz*. Buenos Aires: Grupo Editorial Norma, 2000.

Apparently a lyrical, postmodernist novel about the relationship between jazz and erotic love. Seen but not translated.

Adams, Alice. *Listening to Billie*. New York: Knopf, 1978.

The protagonist, a young unmarried pregnant woman at first, is in a New York nightclub to hear Billie Holiday. The physical presence — and the music — of the great singer makes an indelible impression on the young woman and sets the tone (of sadness, loss, contingency) that characterizes the novel. The theme concerning the growth of a self is nicely realized here, and that alone goes far to negate and perhaps even triumph over the heavy losses the protagonist suffers in the course of a vividly experienced life that is still in midcareer at the end of the book. As in some of Holiday's greatest songs, strength can flow from suffering and loss.

Adrian, James. "Last Jam: Documentary." *Nugget* 9 (April 1965): 26–28, 66.

For twenty of his thirty-four years, Cy has dedicated himself to becoming the best jazz drummer he can be; he "considers himself as good a rhythm man as Morello, as good a technician as Rich, as hard a cooker as Blakey." But now, just as he had accomplished all he had "set out for in life," rock and roll came along, making Cy and his like "walking corpses" — those serious jazz musicians who could not or would not capitulate to the new order. Badly in need of a payday, Cy accepts a one-shot recording gig with a rock group comprising a white teenage star singer surrounded by black sidemen. Cy, of course, cannot play "dirty" (i.e., sloppy) enough for the group and so is fired. At the end he gets back in touch with his ex-wife, who is overjoyed to learn that Cy is ready to "pick out a gray flannel suit." One wishes that writers of stories on this theme had followed up with "five-years-later" epilogues. Calling "Last Jam" a "documentary," the author clearly intended this story to represent what was happening on a large scale among serious jazz musicians in the mid-1960s.

Albert, Richard N., ed. *From Blues to Bop*. Baton Rouge: Louisiana State University Press, 1990.
A sterling collection of short jazz fiction with an informative introduction. A reader with deep interest in the subject could not do better than this and Breton's anthologies (q.v.). See entries for Allen, Steve; Anderson, Alston; Baker, Dorothy (*Young Man with a Horn*); Baldwin, James ("Sonny's Blues"); Barthelme, Donald; Brickman, Marshall; Brown, Beth; Culver, Monty; Feather, Leonard ("I Invented Jazz Concerts!"); Foote, Shelby; Grennard, Elliot; Holmes, John Clellon ("The Horn"); Hughes, Langston ("Dance"); Hunter, Evan (*Streets of Gold*); Kerouac, Jack ("Jazz of the Beat Generation"); Manus, Willard ("Hello Central, Give Me Dr. Jazz"); Painter, Pamela; Powers, J. F.; Škvorecký, Josef ("Eine Kleine Jazzmusik"); and Welty, Eudora. Titles are given in parentheses when the author is represented by more than a single entry in this bibliography.

Allen, Candace. *Valaida*. London: Virago, 2004.
A long, earnest, fact-based fictional biography of Valada (later Valaida) Snow, a small-town gal from Chattanooga who later traveled the world as a phenomenal jazz trumpeter and show-biz personality. The novel endeavors to flesh out the skimpy, obscure details of the real-life Snow's early years in an effort to illuminate how her past might have impacted on the mature artist who spent most of her adult life on the road. Using original research, the author also claims to set straight the story behind Snow's legendary incarceration in Denmark during World War II. The novel explores questions of race, prejudice, and suffering from several angles and dramatizes the effect these had on a single individual caught in the middle, as it were. Snow's bête noire, Ethel Waters; her onetime lover, Earl Hines; and her expatriate pal Coleman Hawkins are given vivid scenes—and Billie Holiday (like Snow, a victimized outsider) is a felt presence throughout the narrative. Although the novel does contain striking musical passages, some might argue that their force is weakened by a torrent of largely psychological analysis. In short, the inner life of a remarkable African-American woman overshadows the music that made her so.

Allen, Steve. *Bop Fables*. New York: Simon and Schuster, 1955.
Four fairy tales "as they might be told by a 'progressive' musician." Allen wrote these, apparently, to edify adults so that they might understand what their jive-talking children were saying, and also because he found himself "amused by jazz language for its own sake." The retold fables are "Goldilocks and the Three Cool Bears," "Three Mixed-up Little Pigs," "Crazy Red Riding

Hood," and "Jack and the Real Flip Beanstalk." To use the language of the fables, this book is "like the end, ya know?"

Allyn, Doug. "The Sultans of Soul." 1993. In *Murder of Music: Musical Mysteries from Ellery Queen's Mystery Magazine* and *Alfred Hitchcock's Mystery Magazine*. Eds. Cynthia Manson and Kathleen Halligan, 29–54. New York: Carroll and Graf, 1997.

A stooped, prematurely aged black man hires private eye Axton to recoup the delinquent royalties for a song he had written for the Sultans of Soul thirty years earlier. The song, "Motor City Mama," became a hit on the race charts but none of the artists received any money. Now the lead singer is in a nursing home and in dire need of financial support. In trying to get to the bottom of this issue, Ax becomes embroiled in questions involving mistaken identity and problematic paternity.

Anderson, Alston. "Dance of the Infidels." *Lover Man*, 150–67. Garden City, NY: Doubleday, 1959; London: Cassell, 1959.

When the young black speaker encounters a man with his ear up to the juke box in a southern café, he knows he's found a soul brother—someone who loves the music as much as he. But when they get together to listen to their beloved jazz, the speaker discovers that Ronald is not only a piano player but also a dope addict. When they reunite later in New York City the speaker discovers the depth of, and infers some of the reasons for, Ronald's addiction. The story is named after a Clifford Brown composition. Other stories in this collection make passing reference to classic jazz artists like Duke Ellington and Earl Hines.

Anderson, Beth. *Night Sounds*. San Diego: Clocktower Books, 2000.

For young Chicago jazz pianist Joe Barbarello, life could hardly get any better: on the same night he lands a recording contract to die for and beds the woman of every arrested adolescent American male's damp dreams, Zoey Baver, who is not only beautiful and sexy but rich to boot. After three days of sexual satiation, he is shocked to discover that his new sweetheart is suspected of having brutally knifed to death a former lover just days earlier. Joe becomes a suspect, too, and the first crime branches into several others. Although the author, in her "Dedication," lavishes thanks on several members of the jazz community, including the Director of the Chicago Metropolitan Jazz Orchestra, the music itself (except for the opening scene and another toward the middle of the novel) is pretty much swallowed up by the plot mechanics of the mystery.

Angelou, Maya. "The Reunion." In *Confirmation: An Anthology of African American Women*, edited by Amiri Baraka and Amina Baraka, 54–58. New York: Morrow, 1983.

An often funny story in which black jazz pianist Philomena Jenkins encounters a white girl from her past, Beth Ann Baker, in a South Side Chicago club— in the company of a handsome black man no less! Beth Ann's family, it turns out, had employed Philomena's family down home in Georgia. Now Beth Ann wants to know how to handle her dilemma of wanting to marry a black man; when she says to Philomena, "He's mine. He belongs to me," Philomena tells her to go to hell and returns to the deep satisfaction of her status-free music.

Anthony, Piers, and Ron Leming. *The Gutbucket Quest.* New York: Tor, 2000.
A fantasy in which blues guitarist Slim Chance is struck by lightning straight from the ground, transporting him, when he returns to consciousness, to Armadillo, Tejas, a wondrous place where harmony prevails and music— especially the blues—possesses supernatural properties. But the key force behind the blues, a magical guitar named Gutbucket, has been stolen by a corporate villain, who threatens to eliminate both music and magic from the world. So Slim sets out, in the company of his elder, African-American mentor, Progress Hornsby, to retrieve the Gutbucket and to turn his own music into a supernatural weapon against the threatening forces. Along the way, Slim proves himself worthy of the love of Progress's gorgeous, fantastically talented blues-singer daughter, Nadine. The authors' deep love for the blues shines through in this narrative. One of the collaborators, Ron Leming, is a Texas (not *Tejas*) blues musician.

Arrhenius, Peter. *The Penguin Quartet.* Minneapolis: Carolrhoda Books, 1998. [First published as *Pingvinkvartten.* Stockholm, Sweden: Bok Forlaget Natur och Kultur, 1996.]
An illustrated book for young children. Bored with watching over their soon-to-be-hatched eggs in the South Pole, four father penguins, all named after jazz greats (Herbie, Charlie, Miles, and Max), decide to form a jazz quartet and play the cool jazz clubs in New York City. They do just that, become a rapid-fire success, but then rush home, happy to have undertaken their adventure but even happier to be back with their families.

Asher, Don. "The Barrier." *Angel on My Shoulder: Stories*, 46–67. Santa Barbara, CA: Capra, 1985.
A white piano player catches the bebop bug in the 1950s and takes himself into the black worlds of New York and Boston in order to learn to swing—in short, to see if he can adopt the black qualities that will make him a first-rate jazz musician. After several years and setbacks, he is accepted by the hip blacks he plays with. He never makes it all the way to jazz distinction, but he gets close enough for self-respect. A well- and hiply told story with powerful musical content and provocative racial overtones. Asher is a professional jazz musician.

————. *The Electric Cotillion*. Garden City, NY: Doubleday, 1970.

Dedicated to Hampton Hawes and Jacki Byard, with an epigraph quoting Dizzy Gillespie to Benny Carter, this novel limns the scruffy existence of Miles Davey[!], a lapsed Jew who wants to continue playing jazz in a world that has turned to rock and roll. Reduced to playing in a band-for-hire, Davey humiliates himself by performing for events like a gay costume ball. He soon falls into a relationship with a teenager from Utah (he's 40) whose rock-and-roll sensibility clashes with his serious jazz perspective. A breezy-flaky novel set in San Francisco in the late 1960s. Art Tatum makes a cameo appearance. Much booze and drugs.

Atkins, Ace. *Crossroad Blues: A Nick Travers Mystery*. New York: St. Martin's, 1998.

Former New Orleans Saint and current blues historian at Tulane University, Nick Travers becomes involved in a case related to the mysterious death of the legendary blues musician Robert Johnson and to the whereabouts of a rumored stash of Johnson's hitherto unheard recordings. The narrative shuttles among Memphis, Clarksdale (Mississippi), and New Orleans—always with an emphasis on the blues and its history—as the past is called upon to solve the mystery in the present.

————. *Dark End of the Street*. New York: William Morrow, 2002.

Nick Travers's third adventure in freelance sleuthing starts out as a favor for one of his dearest friends, Loretta Jackson, who has long played the role of Nick's surrogate mother. She wants him to locate her brother, Clyde James, a ranking soul singer during the 1960s, who disappeared after his wife and good friend were murdered. Despite persistent rumors that Clyde had died years ago, Nick sets out from New Orleans to Memphis (where Clyde had last lived) and the casinos of Tunica, Mississippi. Along the way, he becomes embroiled in gubernatorial politics, a neo-Confederacy conspiracy, the Dixie Mafia, and a truly bizarre hit man who believes that Elvis communicates with him on the lower (i.e., stranger) frequencies. As always in the Nick Travers series, there is much reference to the blues, but in this novel the music is often overshadowed by violence. It is interesting to note that Nick refers to himself in this novel as a "blues teacher"—one who records oral histories or hunts information on dead or forgotten musicians, which means that he crisscrosses "the Delta or Chicago or parts of Texas searching for hundred-year-old birth certificates or trying to find folks who'd rather stay hidden."

————. *Dirty Bomb*. New York: William Morrow, 2004.

Blues historian Nick Travers becomes embroiled in the rapacious, violent world of contemporary music when a former New Orleans Saints teammate asks him to help find a large sum of money that has been hustled from a fifteen-year-old rap star. The negligible musical content in this, the fourth mystery in the Travers series, has been reduced to blues artists and the Mississippi Delta.

————. *Leavin' Trunk Blues: A Nick Travers Mystery*. New York: Thomas Dunne Books, 2000.
The second in the series of mysteries featuring Nick Travers, the New Orleans blues historian. In this case, Nick travels north to Chicago during the frigid Christmas season to solve the mystery surrounding the murder of blues producer Billy Lyons that sent his lover and accused killer (one of the greatest blues singers in the history of a great blues town) to prison forty years earlier. A very gritty, atmospheric novel steeped in the blues and saturated with violence. If this series is any indication, you have not only to be persistent but tough as nails to be a blues historian.

Austin, Alex. "Dancers." In *Jazz Parody (Anthology of Jazz Fiction)*, edited by Charles Harvey, 21–26. London: Spearman Publishers, 1948.
An end-of-the-world fantasy in which a "she" ends up dancing with a "he." Although the musical references are to jazz and blues, they could as easily have been to the polka and minuet.

Austin, William A. *Commit the Sins*. Chicago: Newsstand Library, 1961.
In this "Adult Reading" paperback original, tall, "slim hipped and flat chested" taxi driver Patricia Warren is frustratingly conflicted over her own sexuality. Although she is seriously attracted to one of her female passengers, she soon becomes equally attracted to Champ, a jazz trumpeter who "looks like people want jazz men to look . . . and acts like they want them to act . . ." The tension (if a pulp novel like this can be said to contain tension) is generated by Pat's sexual quandary, which does have an unusual resolution. Despite the fact that much of the action takes place in Detroit jazz clubs in the late 1950s with jazz musicians as characters, the musical dimension of this story does not exude authenticity.

Avent, Emily. "Jazz Bar." http://www.state.sc.us/arts/fictionproject/2005/avent.htm (11/15/2005).
Lost on her way to a party in a "not-so-big city," the speaker stops at a jazz bar, becomes entranced by the music, and ends up, after hours, dancing very sensually with the female bartender.

Avery, Robert. *Murder on the Downbeat*. New York: Mystery House, 1943.
A mystery that tries, sometimes successfully, to be breezy, after the fashion of Dashiell Hammett's Thin Man series. Recording company scout and jazz

columnist, Malachy Bliss, presses himself into service as an amateur detective when first one and then another ranking jazz musician is murdered, and his girlfriend is jailed as a suspect. The milieu is the swing clubs in midtown Manhattan and the after-hour joints in Harlem where musicians, both black and white, can go after work "to play honest, uninhibited jazz with the best musicians in the world." Good musical description toward the beginning.

Baird, Jack. *Hot, Sweet, and Blue.* New York: Gold Medal, 1956.
    Growing up in Pittsburgh on the wrong side of the tracks with a drunken musician father, Johnny Burke yearns to play jazz; after acquiring a cornet at a pawn shop, Johnny takes lessons and eventually becomes the leader of the best jazz band in town. He falls in love with a black singer, Lily, and the two of them make beautiful music together, literally and metaphorically, but their love is not strong enough to overcome racial barriers. All the stereotypical trappings of the jazz life are here: booze, sex, violence.

Baker, Dorothy. "The Jazz Sonata." *Coronet*, April 1, 1937, 27–32.
    Hilda Means had been famous in Montana as an interpreter of Liszt and as a music teacher, but the stakes are higher here in New York as she prepares to give a Beethoven recital and the pressure is getting to her. Enter Archie Grove, jazz pianist, who comforts her in unexpected ways, while demonstrating that music is music, whether by Jelly Roll Morton or Mozart.

————. "Keeley Street Blues." In *O. Henry Memorial Award: Prize Stories of 1939*, 65–76. New York: Doubleday, Doran, 1939.
    Geraldine Evans has a plan to get out of the home for delinquents where she was sent by mistake. She will win the twenty-five dollar prize at the Bijou Theater's amateur night for singing "I've Got a Right to Sing the Blues." Then she will surely get an audition with her idol, Duke Ellington, who will hire her on the spot. The trouble is, the audience proclaims an off-key blonde the winner, leaving Geraldine doubting that her dream will ever come true.

————. "They Called It Swing." In *My Favorite Stories*, edited by Maureen Daly, 119–35. New York: Dodd, Mead, 1948.
    In this section from *Young Man with a Horn* (q.v.) Rick Martin has begun to make a name for himself and is about to have the opportunity to make the big time.

————. *Young Man with a Horn.* New York: Houghton Mifflin, 1938.
    The author claims that this novel was inspired by the music—but not the life—of Bix Beiderbecke. It is yet another *Bildungsroman*, this time a portrait

of the Artist as a Young Man Who Didn't Live Very Long at All. Rick Martin is an outsider; he has no family to speak of and no education but a real feel for music and improvisation. In fact, a central conflict involves his powerful desire to improvise while being restricted to the big band charts. Rick is the prototype of the self-destructive jazz hero of the kind who achieves apotheosis a few years later in the life and legend of Charlie Parker. Although this was the first "important" jazz novel and remains the most famous in the genre, its fame derives as much from a movie adaptation as its literary distinction.

Baldwin, James. *Another Country*. New York: Dial, 1962; London: Corgi, 1962.
A long, prosy novel that attempts to explore the issues of sex, gender, race, and identity. Apart from the fact that a central character, Rufus (who commits suicide early on), was once a promising jazz musician and his sister, Ida, is a fledgling singer, the book contains surprisingly little jazz content.

——. *If Beale Street Could Talk*. New York: Dial, 1974; London: Michael Joseph, 1974.
If Beale Street *could* talk, it would—astonishingly—have nothing to say about jazz!

——. "Sonny's Blues." *Partisan Review* 24 (1957): 327–58.
The most widely anthologized jazz story and still one of the best. Two brothers, separated by age and outlook, are poignantly brought together through the medium of the blues. Through music, the older, school-teacher brother comes to understand Sonny's suffering and, through that, the suffering of the black race. The description of the music in the transcendent moment when this occurs could not be better.

Ballenger, Walter. "Strand." *Chicago Review* 11, no. 2 (Summer 1957): 19–35.
Pork Chops plays his trombone wherever he can. He has no other life, no other name, no past, and certainly no future. When a young drummer acquaintance is beaten to death by a white man, Pork Chops goes to the viewing hoping to get some much-needed grub. While there, Pork Chops is accused by the victim's mother of not having come to her son's aid—even though Pork Chops had not been present when her son was attacked. At story's end, Pork Chops is still hungry.

——. "When the Saints Go Marching In." *Chicago Review* 10, no. 4 (Winter 1957): 25–39.
Because his parents were social climbers and he was enthralled by Dixieland jazz, Park Cudahy ran away from home when he was eleven and never looked

back. Now about fifty and living hand-to-mouth, he is astonished to discover that his parents had died, leaving him a mansion and $50,000. So Park leaves his Chicago gig and, in the company of musician friends, returns to his parental home in Ohio, where he and his fellow revelers threaten to throw the staid community into chaos with their loud music and socially unacceptable behavior. In the end, Park and company lead the town in a riotous march (to the strains of "The Saints") to the train station, where they prepare to return to Chicago, Park having covertly donated what was left of his fortune to the local college.

Bambara, Toni Cade. "Medley." *The Sea Birds Are Still Alive: Collected Stories*, 103–24. New York: Random House, 1977.
A very funny, tartly told tale concerning the breakup between the speaker, Sweet Pea, and her live-in lover, Larry, a mediocre jazz musician but a fun lover. Their cavorting in the shower together evokes the making of music—specifically a jazz medley. Many jazz references, especially to bassists and singers.

———. "Mississippi Ham Rider." *The Massachusetts Review* (Summer 1964): 621–30.
Two representatives (one black, one white) for a New York recording company go south to try to coax old-time bluesman Ham Rider to come north with them to make some recordings. Badly in need of money, he agrees—but only on his own terms. A case of the exploiters getting a taste of their own medicine.

Bankier, William. "The Dog Who Hated Jazz." In *Ellery Queen's Prime Crimes*, edited by Eleanor Sullivan, 38–47. New York: Dial, 1983.
When blind pianist Joe Benson lands a gig at a piano bar, his jazz-hating dog has to be sequestered in the manager's office, whence he is instrumental in solving a mystery. When Joe is asked if he was conflicted by playing "Flying Home" on a Saturday night and "Harvest Home" on Sunday morning, he replies: "If God had meant us to create music only in church . . . he wouldn't have given us Art Tatum and Oscar Peterson."

Baraka, Amiri [LeRoi Jones]. "Answers in Progress." 1967. In *The Fiction of LeRoi Jones/Amiri Baraka*, 219–22. Chicago: Lawrence Hill, 2000.
Spacemen land in Newark in search of Art Blakey records and information concerning what happened to music after the Jazz Messengers on planet Earth.

———. "Dig This! Out?" *Tales of the Out & the Gone*. New York: Akashic Books, 2007. 152–57.
"The Blood," or "a replacement for himself but from a different planet," delivers himself of two parabolic poems, both of which make significant

(though fuddling) references to jazz, the first involving Charlie Parker who represents "The Soul/ of/ Blackness."

————. "A Monk Story." *Brilliant Corners* 2 (Summer 1997): 57–60.
Months after attending Thelonious Monk's funeral, the speaker runs into the dead pianist on the streets of Newark.

————. "Norman's Date." *Playboy*, July 1983. *Tales of the Out & the Gone.* New York: Akashic Books, 2007. 49–64.
Norman's really an on-the-scene kind of guy and a good storyteller to boot, so when he embarks on what seems like a shaggy dog story at the local saloon, his buddies give him their attention. It was not hard for them to do so since the story involves a beautiful blonde and sensational sex. Norman's story begins at the Five Spot, where Thelonious Monk and John Coltrane are cutting loose and symbolically providing musical accompaniment to Norman's verbal solo.

————. "Now and Then." 1967. In *The Fiction of LeRoi Jones/Amiri Baraka*, 213–18. Chicago: Lawrence Hill, 2000.
Based on the Ayler brothers and the free jazz movement, this story concerns racial issues and Albert Ayler. None of the characters are actually named, and the nature of the racial issues is obscure, but the style is definitely influenced by jazz: "The musician and his brother always talked about spirits. They were good musicians, talking about spirits, and they had them, the spirits, and soared with them, when they played. The music would climb, and bombard everything, destroying whole civilizations, it seemed . . ."

————. "Rhythm Travel." *Dark Matter*, 2000. *Tales of the Out & the Gone.* New York: Akashic Books, 2007. 162–64.
A very slight work of fantasy/science fiction involving technology that allows the listener to disappear and reappear whenever certain pieces of music are played. Duke Ellington, Sun Ra, and Thelonious Monk are the primary jazz referents.

————. "The Screamers." *Genesis West* 2, no. 5 (1963): 81–86.
When a group of jazz musicians follow their honking saxophonist leader outside the club where they are playing, the patrons follow them into the street creating, for a brief moment, the spirit of revolution. Many references to honking tenor saxophonists like Illinois Jacquet, all of whom are portrayed in mythic terms.

————. "Yow." In "6 Persons." In *The Fiction of LeRoi Jones/Amiri Baraka*, 251–72. Chicago: Lawrence Hill, 2000.

This is chapter 2 of Baraka's hitherto unpublished autobiographical fiction, *6 Persons* (1974). It is an interior monologue wherein the protagonist revisits his formative years and reflects on the experiences and influences that shaped him. Among these, jazz plays a central role, with frequent reference to such icons as Miles Davis, Charles Parker, Louis Armstrong, Amos Milburn, Stan Getz, Paul Desmond, and Dave Brubeck.

Barnes, Harper. *Blue Monday*. St. Louis: Patrice, 1991.
A young idealistic reporter with a love of jazz suspects that Bennie Moten's death during a tonsillectomy was really murder. He plays detective and solves the questions surrounding Moten's death. Set in Kansas City in 1935, the novel contains much about the interrelationships among the jazz scene, the Pendergast political machine, and racial issues. In addition to Moten, Lester Young, Ben Webster, and Count Basie (among others) make brief appearances. And, yes, there's a nice love affair too.

Barthelme, Donald. "The King of Jazz." *New Yorker*, February 7, 1977, 31–32.
An absurdist parody of a cutting contest between Hideo Yamaguchi, "The top trombone man in all of Japan," and the American king of jazz, Hokie Mokie, whose music generates "the real epiphanic glow." When Hideo wins, it seems like Hokie will lay down his horn for good, but then he enters into another contest with Hideo and wins back his crown—no King Emeritus for him, thank you!

Beardmore, Paul. *The Jazz Elephants*. 1991. London: Abacus, 1993.
A fantasy for adults concerning the escape of two African elephants from a London zoo. It's not that Rumpus Pumpus and Finta Fanta were mistreated by their caretakers or the crowds who flocked to see them; rather, they wanted to play their trumpets on the outside. In other words, they yearned for the kind of freedom that would allow them to fully express themselves. While escaping, they encounter Henri, a human trombonist who is also escaping toward freedom. Together they decide to seek out other jazz musicians in order to form a group. Meanwhile, the authorities are expending every effort to apprehend the beasts. The jazz content (never great to begin with) pretty much gets swallowed up at this point. This long novel apparently intends to satirize the perdurable conflict between freedom and bureaucratic repression but does so in a decidedly edentulous (etuskulent?) way.

Beaumont, Charles. "Black Country." *Playboy* 1954. *The Hunger and Other Stories*, 213–34. New York: Putnam, 1957.
Energetic story about legendary black trumpeter Spoof Collins and young white saxophonist Sonny Holmes, who takes over the band when Spoof dies

and seems to *become* Spook, in his playing at least. Drummer Hushup Paige relates the story in appropriately rhythmic—i.e., jazzy—language. At the climax, as Sonny's horn speaks for Spoof, "The melody got lost, first off. Everything got lost, then, while the horn flew. It wasn't only jazz; it was the heart of jazz, and the insides, pulled out with the roots and held up for everybody to see; it was the blues that told the story of all the lonely cats and all the ugly whores who ever lived, blues that spoke-up for the loser lamping sunshine out of iron-gray bars and every hophead hooked and gone, for the bindlestiffs and the city slickers; for the country boys in Georgia shacks and the High Yellow hipsters in Chicago slums and the bootblacks on the corners and the fruits in New Orleans, a blues that spoke for all the lonely, sad and anxious downers who could never speak for themselves . . ."

——. "Night Ride." *Playboy* 1957. In *The Howling Man*, edited by Roger Anker, 417–38. New York: Tom Doherty Associates (TOR), 1988.
A young pianist joins a band and plays with a depth of feeling seldom seen, making the octet (the Band of Angels) an outstanding group. Davey Green's remarkable ability is connected to the death of his young wife; he translates his grief into music. He meets another young woman, falls in love, gets engaged—and then the leader of the band ruins the relationship by claiming to have slept with Davey's fiancee, causing Davey to commit suicide, which creates a sense of loss among the other band members.

Beliveau, Kay. *Strike for the Heart.* Garden City, NY: Doubleday, 1947.
This novel contains scattered references to jazz musicians (Bunk Johnson, Woody Herman, Artie Shaw, et al.) and the protagonist falls in love with a jazz clarinetist-labor leader; in fact, the jazz man's attraction to the music is outlined in chapter 10. But generally speaking the music is overshadowed by political issues and the love affair at the novel's center.

Bell, Madison Smartt. *Anything Goes.* New York: Pantheon, 2002.
A year in the life of twenty-year-old blues musician Jesse, whose life to this point seems the very stuff of the music he plays: his mother disappeared not long after he was born and his father resented him before turning bitter and becoming alcoholic. But thanks to a gift for music, Jesse finds a livelihood and a family of sorts in a bar band called Anything Goes, after their signature composition. The novel details life on the road for this white blues group: long car rides between gigs, musty motels, meaningless sex, epic hangovers. When a female lead singer joins the band, it becomes better than anyone had thought possible, and Jesse gains in skill and confidence. At the end he is in the process of a positive transformation and looking toward a purposeful future.

Belton, Sandra. *From Miss Ida's Porch*. Illustrated by Floyd Cooper. New
    York: Four Winds Press, 1993.
    A children's narrative in which the neighborhood kids and their relatives
gravitate to Miss Ida's porch at sunset to hear memory stories about the famous
blacks who used to come to their small town. These notables—Duke Ellington
and Marian Anderson among others—would always stay in the homes of local
black families because the hotels in town wouldn't accept them.

Berger, Jerry, and Tommy Wolf. "No Coast Jazz." *Jazz New York*. New York:
    Jacques Willaumez Associates, 1956. Unpaginated.
    A spoof of the raging controversy in the mid-1950s over the differences be-
tween East and West Coast jazz. No Coast jazz is easier to deal with because
it has only one practitioner, "Armando (Big Jazz) Rooneyville, a plumber's
assistant during the day and a driving, vital, inspired original jazz voice at
night." But No Coast jazz contains within it the seeds of self-destruction, for,
since its "ultimate goal is to create 32 bars of utter musical silence, which, if
this should ever be superimposed upon another 32 bars of equally profound
silence in 19/16 time, would mean that musical expression had finally
reached a point beyond which it could not go."

Berman, Mitch. *Time Capsule*. 1987. New York: Ballantine, 1988.
    Young Max Debrick ("Debris" to his buddies) and his combo are in the mid-
dle of a recording session on the outskirts of Manhattan when a nuclear bomb
of unimaginable magnitude brings the world to a halt and, presumably, an end.
But Max and his beloved saxophone miraculously survive. Living on cock-
roaches and rats, Max sets out in search of other survivors. He finally encounters one in central Pennsylvania, a middle-aged black man by the name of
Charles E. Dewey, Jr. (nickname: "Wolf"), and the two set out together to determine whether the holocaust spared others. Indeed, they stumble onto a community of survivors and learn that there are at least two more such communities. This futuristic novel dramatizes the value of friendship and hope in a
vulnerable universe. Reviews and blurbs of the story make much of its jazz
connection, many of the titled chapters display the saxophone glyph, and the
cover copy of the paperback proclaims, "A jazz musician's epic journey
through an America devastated by nuclear war—an unspeakable gig he thinks
he's playing solo. . . ." But the jazz content is actually quite modest. Max's saxophone is mentioned on every page (or so it seems), there are at least two jam
session scenes (both related in flashbacks), and several ranking musicians are
referred to, but that's about it for this novel of more than 300 pages. (Readers
should be warned that the first several chapters will grieve anyone, especially
New Yorkers, connected in any way to the events of September 11, 2001.)

Bernhardt, Klaus. *Eins zu null für Jazz.* [*One to Nothing for Jazz*]. Illustrationen und Buchumschlag von Franz Reins. Erich Schmidt Verlag: Bielefeld, 1956.
A tale, in German, for young people concerning the New Orleans origins of jazz.

Biggie, Patrick. "St. Louis Blues." In *B Flat, Bebop, Scat*, edited by Chris Parker, 176–84. London: Quartet, 1986.
Through a chance encounter on a golf course in Cuba, a Foreign Service agent discovers that he and his wife occupy the former home of Thomas Lincoln McAndrews, a businessman and jazz connoisseur who had been forced to leave Cuba with little but the shirt on his back. While sorting through the possessions left behind, the new occupants hear, mysteriously, the sad strains of Sidney Bechet's "St. Louis Blues" emanating from the house, leading the narrator to bend his diplomatic status to send McAndrews in Florida a couple of items, including his treasured recording of "St. Louis Blues."

Bird, Brandon [George Evans and Kay Evans]. *Downbeat for a Dirge.* New York: Dodd, Mead, 1952.
Murder and mystery within the dance band milieu. Good descriptions of the mechanics of a band at work and of the travails of life on the road. The band sticks to the charts, playing some Stan Kenton kinds of things but leaving "goatee jazz to other bands."

Blaine, Laurence. *Sweet Street Blues.* Los Angeles: Holloway House, 1978.
After seven years in prison, Milton "Jazz" McGhee returns to the violent, drug-infested world of Detroit hoping to discover who had set him up and then to seek revenge. He is also hoping to come to terms with the phantoms from his past: his lost daughter, his lost sweetheart, his lost (and unknown) mother, and his lost dreams of becoming a ranking jazz musician. "Jazz" had been a hot musician who played sax and flute and also composed. There are inevitably some references to jazz and its "spiritual spontaneity," but the novel is marred by excessive violence, an unfocused narrative, and melodramatic coincidence. At the end, we learn that "Jazz" has been telling his story from a psychiatric hospital, where he has undergone seven years of counseling and rehabilitation. Not unlike a Donald Goines crime novel.

Blakemore, Charles. *The Subjective Truth.* Nashville: Winston-Derek, 1993.
A young and exceptionally gifted black pianist and a young and talented white drummer become best friends through their mutual love of jazz. They form a band, move from Chicago to New York, and achieve considerable success; meanwhile, their lives start to spiral downward because of booze and drugs. The

black, Jimmy, moves to Europe while his white buddy, Joe, returns to the Midwest where he embraces a middle-class existence. At Jimmy's funeral, Joe has an epiphany concerning the roots of Jimmy's music—its subjective truth. Many jazz references to and cameo appearances by such musicians as Eric Dolphy, Thelonious Monk, Charles Mingus, Duke Ellington, and Illinois Jacquet.

Blankfort, Michael. *Take the A Train*. New York: Dutton, 1978.
Almost all of the music in this book is contained in the title. The story involves the bonding relationship between a young Jewish man and an older black underworld figure from Harlem, where much of the narrative takes place after World War II. There is some jazz in the background, but you have to use an ear trumpet to hear it.

Bloch, Robert. "Dig That Crazy Horse!" In *Ellery Queen's Awards: 12th Series*, edited by Ellery Queen, 81–98. New York: Simon and Schuster, 1957.
When he discovers that the drummer JoJo Jones and his band are coming to town, Professor Talmadge (who is secretly writing a book on jazz) excitedly calls his girlfriend, Dorothy. They go to the club together. Later, Talmadge discovers that Dorothy has been hanging out at the club, has become friendly with Jones, and is talking like a jazz musician. Dorothy seems to have become addicted to Jones, and likely to heroin as well, for she mysteriously dies. Talmadge confronts Jones, with fatal results. Jones and his men are described in vampire-like terms in this tale of horror. Significant jazz content.

Bonnie, Fred. "Take a Seat, Not a Solo." *Wide Load*, 65–86. Ontario, Canada: Oberon Press, 1987.
A milquetoast harmonica player, Howard Metts, believes he can do great things with his harp, but is hampered by agoraphobia. But one night, in the company of friends and with the help of much beer, he sits in at the Blues Basin with Big Fredda and is a hit. During the second set, he is asked to do an encore; he attempts to do so, despite being drunk and in desperate need of the men's room. Confusion—chaos—follows; he ends up in jail overnight, and plays his harp for the cops next morning.

Bontemps, Arna. *Lonesome Boy*. Illustrated by Feliks Topoloski. Boston: Houghton Mifflin, 1955.
As little Bubber moves from childhood to adolescence, he grows closer to his trumpet and further from the wise counsel of his grandfather. Finally, Bubber leaves his country home to play in New Orleans, where he is corrupted by success. After unwittingly playing one mysterious night at "the devil's ball," Bubber returns to his grandpa's rural Louisiana home and his

generous wisdom: "You should have minded what I told you at the first. Blow your horn when you're a mind to, but put it down when you're through. When you go traipsing through the woods, leave it on the shelf. When you feel lonesome, don't touch it. A horn can't do nothing for lonesomeness but make it hurt worse. When you're lonesome, that's the time to go out and find somebody to talk to. Come back to your trumpet when the house is full of company or when people's passing on the street." A very suggestive story for young people—in a sense, an African-American version of Hawthorne's "Young Goodman Brown," with aesthetics taking the place of religion.

Booth, Christopher B. *Killing Jazz: A Detective Story.* New York and London: Chelsea House, 1928.
 As wealthy, puritanical Caleb Ballinger quietly communed with the spiritual world, "The Sabbath stillness of the quiet house was shattered by the sound of a riotous desecration, the crashing and the wailing of that heathenish, wicked music which is known as 'jazz'." Someone had diabolically defiled the sacredness of the day by playing a jazz record, knowing that the shock would likely kill Ballinger. Detective Jim Smith is called into service to get to the bottom of the fiendish crime in this early example of a mystery that incorporates jazz in its narrative. The musical component is interesting for the cultural bias it reveals: that jazz is the work of the Devil and fully capable of killing decent Christians like poor old Caleb Ballinger.

Borneman, Ernest. *Tremolo.* New York and London: Harper, 1948.
 The epigraph quotes Jelly Roll Morton on the relationship between tremolo and suspense. One of the first northern whites to catch on to New Orleans-style jazz, Mike Sommerville gave up the jazz life to design and manufacture jazz instruments and settle down in an idyllic house with his picture-perfect family. But mysterious things begin to disrupt the household order, leading Mike and his wife, Marge, at first to suspect that their house was haunted and then that one or both of them were psychologically disturbed. Just as things reach breaking point, Mike solves the mystery, removes its source—his own mother!—and succeeds in restoring his world to its Edenic state. Solid jazz content with descriptions of musical sessions, many references to Dixieland notables, and a dog named Buddy Bolden.

Bourjaily, Vance. *The Great Fake Book.* New York: Weidenfeld and Nicolson, 1986.
 A hodgepodge of literary techniques comprising letters, memos, calendar notations, journals, diaries, and a novel-within-a-novel, this book details Charles Mizzourin's quest to discover who his father really was. The father

died thirty years earlier when the son was an infant, so Charles has to rely on surviving artifacts from the past. One of these is the "Great Fake Book," his father's lost diary that contains a contraband collection of musical phrases from which a jazz musician performs. It is in these sections of the novel that we find the fairly considerable jazz content.

Boyce, David. "Special Arrangement." In *Jazz Parody (Anthology of Jazz Fiction)*, edited by Charles Harvey, 50–56. London: Spearman Publishers, 1948.
    A story with a musical structure ("First Chorus," "Modulation," etc.) focusing on a boy who becomes a drummer before becoming involved in the rackets. It begins: "Jake's life story started soft, like strings and muted brass, worked up to an exciting crescendo of daring chords and died away again mellow and peaceful like the tone of a blues-singer."

Boyczuk, Robert. "Jazz Fantasia." *On Spec* 5, no.4 (1993): 32–46.
    Former sax man Hamilton had had a gift: when he listened to the better jazz musicians, he could not only tell them what they were feeling but, after a while, exactly what they were thinking as well. But Hamilton lost his gift along with his musical expertise when he succumbed to booze. Now he occasionally thinks he hears the note of his dreams, but he can never locate the player. Quite likely Hamilton is hallucinating as he despairs over what he might have become had he not turned to alcohol. Jazz is omnipresent in this story.

Boyd, Frank. [Henry Kane.] *Johnny Staccato*. Greenwich, CT: Gold Medal, 1960.
    Hard-boiled private eye Johnny Staccato gave up trying to make a living in jazz some time ago, but as this story opens he's back at the keyboard jamming with some old friends. All too soon, however, he becomes involved in trying to solve the murders of a famous but universally despised disk jockey and the singer whose career he ruined. Although several scenes take place in Greenwich Village clubs and contain some jazz content, the book's primary emphases are on the rottenness of the pop music industry and the unriddling of the crimes. A novelization of the 1959–60 television series starring John Cassavetes.

Bragaglia, Anton G. *Jazz Band*. Milano: Edizioni "Corbaccio," 1929.
    Not seen.

Braly, Malcolm. *Shake Him Till He Rattles*. New York: Belmont, 1963.
    A noir novel set in San Francisco. Bass sax player Lee Cabiness is stalked by a member of the narcotics squad whose obsession with Cabiness, we discover late in the novel, derives from his own addiction. The beatnik scene is

well rendered, and there is a wonderful description of a cutting contest in which three saxophonists try to outdo each other. Frequent references to such jazz musicians as Cannonball Adderley, Charlie Parker, and Erroll Garner. Jazz musicians are referred to as "the original carriers of the Beat infection." The novel also touches on the persistent theme in jazz fiction of the artist-musician in pursuit of some indefinable aesthetic, possibly spiritual, goal.

Brand, Pat. "Headlines! Headlines!" In *Jazz Parody (Anthology of Jazz Fiction)*, edited by Charles Harvey, 5–20. London: Spearman Publishers, 1948.
   A legendary early jazz pianist, Lonnie da Silva, disappeared from the music scene twenty-five years ago, right after World War I, but has now been reported to be alive and well in South Wales, where he's been playing in a pub. A concert in London is arranged, but when Lonnie shows up to perform before 3,000 screaming jazz buffs, his appearance generates unexpected consequences.

Brandi Vera, Pascual. *Jazz: Novela*. Santiago, Chile: Editorial Nascimento [*sic*], 1935.
   Not seen.

Branham, R.V. "Chango Chingamadre, Dutchman, & Me." In *Full Spectrum 3*, edited by Lou Aronica, Amy Stout, and Betsy Mitchell, 380–92. New York: Foundation/ Doubleday, 1991.
   Bassist Mervyn Eichmann (M. E.—the "Me" of the title) relates this drug-drenched story about his attempt to save his buddy Chango, a bop drummer who was determined to sit in with the house band that night and play "secret music"—music in which no sound emanates from the instruments. The soundless music, beatnik ambiance, and fantasy mode of this story invite comparison to Thomas Pynchon's "Entropy" (q.v.). Several references to jazz musicians: Louis Armstrong, Charlie Parker, Miles Davis, and Dave Brubeck, to name a few.

Bratton, Elliot F. "The Wider World." *Jazz Son: Selected Poetry, Lyrics, and Fiction*, 147–73. Xlibris, 2003.
   Young music editor of a New York entertainment magazine, Lee Sanford, is thrilled to learn that the Hale Dodge Quartet is in town for the weekend. Lee's mind flashes back ten years to when he met Dodge, his favorite jazz musician, in Prospect Park, Brooklyn. The avant-garde musician was generous with his time and wisdom as he conversed with Lee about jazz. Now, ten years later, Lee undergoes, for the second time, a spiritual transformation while listening to Dodge's music. When the mysterious Dodge disappears after his gig, foul play is suspected. But years later, on assignment to interview a jazz trumpeter who has come out of retirement, Lee returns to Prospect Park

where he once again encounters his hero, who seems not at all surprised to see Lee. The younger man has apparently been liberated into "the wider world" through his responsiveness to Dodge's metaphysical free jazz.

Breton, Marcela, ed. *Hot and Cool: Jazz Short Stories*. New York: Plume, 1990.

An excellent, varied collection of many of the best jazz short stories with an informed introduction. See following entries: Angelou, Maya; Baldwin, James ("Sonny's Blues"); Bambara, Toni Cade ("Medley"); Barthelme, Donald; Cortazár, Julio ("The Pursuer"); De Vries, Peter; Fisher, Rudolph; Gardner, Martin ("The Devil and the Trombone"); Hughes, Langston ("The Blues I'm Playing"); Baraka, Amiri [LeRoi Jones], ("The Screamers"); Marsh, William; Petry, Ann ("Solo on the Drums"); Powers, J. F.; Škvorecký, Joseph ("Eine Kleine Jazzmusik"); Smith, C. W.; Southern, Terry ("You're Too Hip, Baby"); Welty, Eudora; Yates, Richard; Young, Al ("Chicken Hawk's Dream"). Titles are given in parentheses when the author is represented by more than a single entry in this volume.

Brickman, Marshall. "What, Another Legend?" *New Yorker*, May 19, 1973, 32–33.

Purporting to be liner notes for an album in a Giants of Jazz series, this story spoofs the efforts of jazz historians who tirelessly exhume long forgotten "great" musicians. The "greatness" of this story's subject, 112-year-old Pootie Le Fleur, can be inferred from the deadpan statement that after Le Fleur played for James P. Johnson, Johnson "urged him to go to New York or any other city a thousand miles away."

Brite, Poppy Z. "Mussolini and the Axeman's Jazz." In *Dark Destiny: Proprietors of Fate*, edited by Edward E. Kramer, 200–223. White Wolf Publishing, 1995.

A supernatural horror story that provides netherworld explanations for the events leading to the two world wars. After losing his life in Sarajevo, Archduke Ferdinand returns as a wraith to the land of the living—New Orleans in this case—to enlist the aid of an accomplice to kill the person behind the rise of Mussolini. When the time for action arrives, the characters of Ferdinand and his henchman merge into "The Axeman," who claims that his vendetta will spare only those people who are listening to jazz when the Axeman comes to wreak his gory vengeance.

Brossard, Chandler. *Who Walk in Darkness*. New York: New Directions, 1952; London: Lehman, 1952.

Set in New York's Greenwich Village not long after World War II, this novel focuses on several rootless and often jobless young acquaintances who seek to fill the void of their lives by hanging out in Harlem dance halls, participating in dope parties, and attending prize fights. The book employs considerable bop terminology and makes some references to jazz and jazz musicians, but in general music is used as background accompaniment to the actions of the self-absorbed characters.

Brown, Beth. "Jazzman's Last Day." *The North American Review* 268, no. 1 (1983): 16–17.
An inventory of the banal facts of Jimmy "The Truth" Jackson's last day. Inspired by Lee Morgan, whose mistress shot him while he was performing on stage.

Brown, Carlton. *Brainstorm*. New York and Toronto: Farrar and Rinehart, 1944.
An almost clinical account of one man's mental deterioration with sporadic references to jazz.

Brown, Carter. *The Ever-Loving Blues*. New York: Signet, 1961. [First published, in 1956, as *Death of a Doll*.]
Hard-boiled, wise-cracking private eye Danny Boyd is in Hollywood to find a missing woman, who was last seen in the company of jazz folks. The jazz trumpet player is a boozer and is also on the needle and talks hepcat talk; in short, he's a stereotype. Jazz in this mystery is pretty much window dressing; its function is to provide exotic appeal.

Brown, Frank London. "McDougal." *Phoenix Magazine*, Fall 1961, 32–33.
Trumpeter McDougal is the only white in a jazz combo. But because he's been beaten down by life and has a pregnant black wife and three brown children, he can play as soulfully as the rest.

———. "Singing Dinah's Song." In *Soon One Morning: New Writing by American Negroes, 1940–1962*, edited by Herbert Hill, 349–54. New York: Knopf, 1963.
A punch press operator, Daddy-O, deals with the assaultive noise and, more generally, his wretched life by singing amid the noise of the workplace. When the narrator asks Daddy-O what he is doing, Daddy-O says, "Baby, I'm singing Dinah's songs. Ain't that broad mellow?" After Daddy-O cracks up and is taken away, the speaker sings Dinah songs in rhythm with his machine.

———. "A Way of Life." In *Music '59: Downbeat Fourth Annual Yearbook*, 66–67. Chicago: Maher, 1959.

The speaker and his dying friend, Charlie, are waiting for an ambulance while the guy in the next room plays Sonny Stitt's recording of "Old Folks" over and over. Although Charlie hated music, he didn't want to go to the hospital because Stitt "played so goddamned pretty."

Bunyan, Pat. *I Peddle Jazz*. Fresno: Saber, 1960. [First published as *The Big Blues*. Newsstand Library, 1958.]

Paul Parto, the trumpet-playing bandleader and narrator of this rare novel, has a problem: how to manage a life that includes a wife and daughter; a common-law wife who has two children, a mother, and later a husband too; a day job as a journalist; a nocturnal career as a leader of a jazz combo; and a serious case of satyriasis that requires him (at 5'7" and 145 pounds, clearly the sexiest man on earth) to bed down every dame he encounters (usually several times per evening)—all of this while smoking and drinking incessantly. For most men this side of James Bond and Indiana Jones, such a life would be a stretch—but not for Priapic Paul, for whom—obviously—time expands to meet the need. What would probably have been called soft porn in its day would simply be called schlock today, as witness this typical passage: "I put my arms around her and we kissed. I felt her soft, sweaty flesh start to quiver as I became an octopus. Her breath got heavy. I pushed her up, turned out the light and pulled her over to the bed. I turned her towards me and crushed her in a passionate embrace, kissing, kissing, both of us making like savages. I pulled away and started to unzip her dress, my fingers impatient as hell, half-ripping, half-tearing it off. She unhooked her bra, and threw herself at me." And so on. Say what you will, they just don't write 'em like that anymore. Although the novel has a jazz focus and Paul claims to play from his soul, the music is overwhelmed by a surfeit of sex, violence, and decadence; in short, the book promotes many of the ugly stereotypes associated with jazz.

Burke, Jim. "He Would Never Let Anyone Down . . ." *Music Maker* [Australia] 37, no. 11 (April 1969): 8–9.

When advance ticket sales for the blockbuster jazz concert lag, promoter Maxie tries to generate publicity for the event by hiring a stranger wearing a fantastic disguise to play the drums, nonstop, for twenty-four hours. When the stranger leaves, Maxie receives a telegram informing him that the headliner ensemble, the International Jazzmen, had been involved in an airplane accident and were forced to cancel their tour. Fortunately, all of the musicians survived except the drummer, whose remains couldn't be found. The drummer (guess who?) had the reputation of never letting anyone down.

Burleigh, Robert. *Lookin' for Bird in the Big City*. San Diego: Silver Whistle, 2001.

Loosely based on fact, this illustrated book for children depicts Miles Davis's search in the big city for his idol, saxophonist Charlie "Bird" Parker. When Miles finally locates him, Parker recognizes that the young trumpeter has a special gift, and the two of them make beautiful bebop together.

Burnap, Campbell. "A Bit of a Scrape." In *B Flat, Bebop, Scat*, edited by Chris Parker, 72–92. London: Quartet, 1986.

Charlie Dunnicliff and three of his schoolmates become enamored of jazz and form an unofficial jazz society, listening attentively to classical jazz 78s and discussing them and matters related to the music. They form a band of their own, are asked to play for the school dance, and fear they will be ridiculed. But they give a dazzling performance, with Charlie outdoing himself on the washboard and winning the affection of his dream girl.

Burns, Mary. "The Sound of Dreaming." http:/mainHTML.cfm?page=mary burns.html_(12 October 2005).

Sexual fireworks seem inevitable when an unhappily married piano teacher arrives to give a horny housewife her piano lesson. But instead of making a pass, he relates to her a dream in which Louis Armstrong joins him in making music. Both characters are changed by their nonsexual encounter, and he is sure that the jazz composition he has been working on will fall into place that night.

Cabbell, Edward J. "The Soul's Sting." *Phylon* 30, no. 4 (Winter 1969): 413–19.

A saxophonist in a dance band in Harlem tells of a chance encounter with a young man who has recently come from the South, like the narrator himself four years earlier. The cycle will continue.

Cameron, Stella. *Tell Me Why*. New York: Kensington, 2001.

Carolee Burns had been a famous jazz pianist, playing to enthusiastic audiences all over the world. But then, a year and a half ago, she mysteriously dropped out of sight, surfacing occasionally to perform at a small club outside Seattle. Enter Max Wolfe, "the man no woman had managed to tame." Magnetized by the sadness enveloping Carolee, ex-Denver Bronco Max determines to get to the bottom of her melancholy. Have I mentioned that this is a woman's novel? Anyway, nostrils flare, pulses quicken, accidents happen, secrets are revealed, and—as most assuredly in real life—love conquers all. To be sure, a piano is always nearby, beckoning Carolee to return to the international stage, but the actual jazz content is ludicrously lacking.

Carter, Charlotte. "Birdbath." In *The Mysterious Press Anniversary Anthology*, edited by the Editors of Mysterious Press, 312–33. New York: Warner, 2001.
After witnessing a street crime at the annual Charlie Parker Fest in Tomkins Square Park (whence the title), street saxophonist and amateur sleuth Nanette Hayes takes it upon herself to get to the bottom of things. She discovers that the alleged pickpocket, now violently dead, had been a jazz musician and that the "crime" she saw was part of a scam involving female African-American models and blackmail. The story is told through a series of journal entries that Nanette is hoping someday to show her old boyfriend Andre, who is still in Paris (see *Coq au Vin*).

———. *Coq au Vin*. New York: Mysterious Press, 1999.
Nanette Hayes, the sassy heroine of this novel, plays sax on the streets of New York. In this second installment of a series, Nan returns to her beloved Paris to search for a missing relative. She soon teams up with expatriate Andre, who plays jazz violin and is passionate about jazz history, especially as it relates to black American expatriates in Paris. Nan facetiously claims to be Django Reinhardt's illegitimate gypsy granddaughter. Many references to black musicians who sought refuge from racism in Paris.

———. *Drumsticks*. New York: Mysterious Press, 2000.
Sassy, sexy, saxophone-playing Nanette Hayes is back home in New York after a disastrous sojourn in Paris (see *Coq au Vin*). Her life is seriously on the skids until she buys a mojo doll from Harlem folk artist, Ida Williams, which seems to turn her life around. When Nan lands a gig, she comps Ida to opening night. Halfway through the first set, Ida is shot and killed, sending Nan on a case that is improbably (but enjoyably) complicated as it stretches across Manhattan (with a brief segue into Brooklyn) and involves a strikingly disparate cast of characters. As always in this series, jazz is prominent: the novel titles its chapters after jazz tunes, refers to Charlie Rouse in the first sentence, and is dedicated "To the Bennys: Carter, Golson, and Green. . . ."

———. "A Flower Is a Lovesome Thing." In *Blue Lightning*, edited by John Harvey, 7–20. London: Slow Dancer Press, 1998; Chester Springs, PA: Dufour Editions, 1999.
Four years ago Big Martha Little had made it big rather late in her professional life as second lead in an all-black Broadway revue; now she is scraping along as a nightclub singer specializing in Bessie Smith covers and Duke Ellington compositions. On the night of the story, we are in Martha's mind most of the time as she reflects on her broken-down life.

———. *Rhode Island Red*. London and New York: Serpent's Tail, 1997.

Amateur sleuth Nanette is doing OK playing her saxophone on the streets of New York, but her life changes radically when an undercover cop dies in her apartment. She enters into a passionate relationship with a mysterious man who wants Nan to teach him the essence of Charlie Parker, one of whose saxophones plays a major role in this breezy series mystery. Many references to jazz musicians; chapters are titled after tunes associated with Thelonious Monk: "I Mean You," "Nutty," "Rhythm-a-ning," and so forth. In fact, early on Nan says: "When it comes to the piano . . . it's Monk whom I have accepted as my personal savior. All that quirky, absent-minded professor, mad as a hatter, turn-everything-on-its head brand of genius. Oh, do I love that man."

Carter, Don. *Heaven's All-Star Band*. New York: Knopf, 2002.

Grandpa Jack called the bebop he loved "heavenly," so now that he's in heaven his grandson imagines it to be a place filled with the music of Dizzy, Monk, Bird, Trane, et al.

Carter, Vincent O. *Such Sweet Thunder*. Steerforth: South Royalton, VT, 2003.

Set in Kansas City, Missouri, during the Depression, this long novel dramatizes black life through the eyes of young Amerigo Jones in a climate of racism, anti-Semitism, and widespread injustice. Jacket copy proclaims it "a jazz song of a book, a river of sound, clearly influenced by the big band jazz style that was pioneered in the Kansas City of [author] Carter's youth. . . ." *The Library Journal* also claims that the novel is "infused with the sounds and spirit of Kansas City jazz." Indeed, the novel is dedicated to Duke Ellington, takes its title from a famous Ellington composition, and contains references to such artists as Fats Waller, Jimmie Rushing, Bessie Smith, and Chick Webb and the members of his band. But it is probably the style more than anything else that evokes the spirit of the music, as in this passage: Amerigo "was swept into the thickening crowd of black folks where the song throbbed beneath the brutal clash of a cymbal, against the sobbing of an alto saxophone, quickening to the pulse of a bass fiddle, or the pertinent click of hickory sticks upon taut snares . . ." The novel was completed in the early 1960s but not published until 2003, twenty years after the author's death.

Cartiér, Xam Wilson. *Be-Bop, Re-Bop*. New York: Ballantine, 1987.

The narrator is a black woman who recounts her life as a child growing up in St. Louis and later as a single mother on the West Coast. Her father had schooled her in jazz. The novel contains many references to jazz and blues notables and to the cultural significance of the music for blacks. Like *Muse-Echo*

Blues (q.v.), it employs rhythmic, alliterative language, as if in an effort to emulate certain musical properties.

————. *Muse-Echo Blues*. New York: Harmony, 1991.
	Narrator Kat is a young African-American jazz pianist-composer in San Francisco in the 1990s. She has been afflicted with a frustrating case of creative inertia for reasons that are not hard to find: she is surrounded by black professionals (buppies) who drive BMWs, listen to black Muzak, and in general behave like their white counterparts. The souls of black folks (and thus their music) seems to have been etiolated by overexposure to the dominant culture. So Kat mind-travels back a half-century, where she finds inspiration in a soul sister, Kitty, whose life was energized by the fervent jazz scene of the time, including Billy Eckstine's and Count Basie's bands. In the tradition of such stories, Kat is reborn through her alter-ego Kitty and poised to regain her chops at the end. Sonny Stitt and Lester Young have small but vivid roles; a solo by Hamiet Bluiett is lovingly described, and references to jazz and its performers abound.

Casey, Scott. *One More Time!* New York: Tower, 1965.
	Dedicated to "George Probert, whose music inspired this book," this novel gets off to a rousing start as Cal Lewis (22-year-old white soprano saxophonist in an otherwise all-black combo led by his surrogate father Sully) first meets a femme fatale and then, after hours, gigs with Louis Armstrong. Cal's painfully complicated existence is made more so as he relinquishes his beloved Dixieland jazz to earn big bucks playing in a Lawrence Welk-like big band. One important character in this jazz-drenched novel, Page Jackson, seems to be based on Charlie Parker.

Catling, Patrick Skene. *Jazz Jazz Jazz*. London: Blond and Briggs, 1980; New York: St. Martin's, 1981.
	Thirteen-year-old Alan Poindexter, son of a prominent cotton broker in the New Orleans of 1913, is introduced to jazz by his friend Moses, the descendant of slaves, and becomes entranced by this powerful new music. The novel dramatizes the relationship between these two young men and their travels at the same time that it chronicles the evolution of jazz history from its beginnings through bop.

Chappell, Fred. "Blue Drive." *Moments of Light*, 1982. In *Stories of the Modern South*, edited by Ben Forkner and Patrick Samway, S.J., 77–100. New York: Penguin, 1986.
	When old-time bluesman Stovebolt Johnson reaches the place where he thinks he has a gig, he finds that its new owner has no time for an aged black

guitarist. Nevertheless, he hangs out at the saloon, whose guests greatly enjoy "the best music in the world" (according to Stovebolt). Scattered references to blues musicians like B. B. King and John Lee Hooker.

Charters, Samuel. *Jelly Roll Morton's Last Night at the Jungle Inn: An Imaginary Memoir by Samuel Charters*. New York: Marion Boyars, 1984.
A researched narrative, accompanied by photographs, in which the egomaniacal Jelly Roll Morton tells the anecdotal history of his life, never tiring of promoting his own invaluable contributions to the birth and development of jazz.

Christensen, Madonna Dries. *Swinging Sisters*. New York: iUniverse, Inc., 2004.
A wholesome, fact-based family chronicle focusing on a Depression-era all-girl swing band that bounced around the country in a hearse, playing their music wherever they could find an audience. The Texas Rangerettes were celebrated for their particular rendition of western swing—an amalgam of cowboy, hillbilly, folk, polka, jazz, and blues. Like all such bands, they struggled to be taken seriously and were constantly reminded that their largely male audiences were more interested in their garb and grooming than their musicianship. After a decade or so on the road, four of the gals from the band and their mother—the Jones women—experienced something like a collective epiphany, causing them to reject their rather superficial lives as itinerant musicians to become nuns in the Catholic Church.

Clapham, Walter. *Come Blow Your Horn*. London: Jonathan Cape, 1958.
During an unbearably hot summer, two teenagers—Danny and Elizabeth—coincidentally meet at an English seaside town where they behave as if they were performing in a romantic comedy. Rumors of wicked behavior circulate; one concerns mixed nude swimming by moonlight! Danny plays jazz trumpet and is never far from his beloved horn, though he is forced to pawn it at one point. He wonders how such great horn players as Chet Baker, Miles Davis, and Dizzy Gillespie ever found the time and place to hone their skills. Whenever he can, Danny goes to the beach and plays "to the sea and sky" or gets together at the Grotto with like-minded jazz enthusiasts. Music is always close by in this frothy novel but seldom at center stage.

Claverie, Jean. *Little Lou*. Mankato, MN: Creative Education, 1990.
Little Lou was exposed to the blues while still in the womb; then, growing up he hung out at a neighborhood bar where he was enthralled by the blues and jazz. After a thrilling encounter with gangsters, Little Lou (who must be about six) wins an opportunity to play piano with Earl Golson and his grown-up jazz

band. Set in the South in the 1920s, this children's book contains an introduction by bluesman Memphis Slim.

Cliff, Michelle. "A Woman Who Plays Trumpet Is Deported." *Bodies of Water,* 53–60. New York: Dutton, 1990.
Inspired by and dedicated to Valaida Snow, who escaped from a concentration camp, this story dramatizes the plight of an American black woman trumpeter in the 1930s who is forced (because of her color and instrument) to flee to Paris to practice her craft. When the club where she plays closes in 1940, she moves to Copenhagen, where she is imprisoned by the Nazi occupiers. The second paragraph effectively encapsulates the situation of the story: "A woman. A black woman. A black woman musician. A black woman musician who plays trumpet. A bitch who blows. A lady trumpet-player. A woman with chops." Candace Allen, in *Valaida* (q.v.), provides a much expanded version of this incident.

Coggins, Mark. *Candy from Strangers.* Madison, WI: Bleak House Books, 2006.
This is the third installment of an ongoing, hard-boiled series set in the San Francisco Bay area and featuring politically incorrect August Riordan, private investigator, jazz enthusiast, and bassist (when he can land a gig). The very busy, action-laden plot involves young women whose racy websites cause them to go missing—and sometimes turn up dead. In keeping with the hard-boiled tradition, the picture that emerges of the urban landscape, and indeed of human nature as Riordan scuttles about in his antiquated jalopy trying to put things to right, is not pretty. The first book in this series, *The Immortal Game* (q.v.), contained considerable jazz interest; the second, *Vulture Capital,* had none. This one provides modest jazz content in its occasional descriptions of music in performance, references to jazz and its musicians, and a subplot concerning a valuable stolen Begliomini bass.

———. *The Immortal Game.* Berkeley: Poltroon Press, 1999.
After being hired to investigate a case involving theft of chess software, private eye August Riordan takes the reader on a wisecracking, action-packed ramble through San Francisco's kinky sex milieux, including S/M and bondage emporia. Riordan is very much the jazz buff; he prides himself on his collection of straightahead recordings from the 1930s through the 1950s and even more on his hi-fi system made of components manufactured and sold before 1980, "before the introduction of digital recordings on CD ROM, and before stereo manufacturers started caring more about glitzy consoles with small footprints than they did about the quality of the sound." A purist, in other words. Riordan is also a semipro jazz bassist, who lugs his cherished

instrument wherever he can fill in on a gig. Chapter 10 ("in the key of g") contains solid descriptions of a combo in action, in one of the very few clubs in the area that still cares about the music.

Cohen, Elaine. "Blevins' Blues." In *B Flat, Bebop, Scat*, edited by Chris Parker, 150–74. London: Quartet, 1986.
Dipsomaniacal trumpeter J. A. Blevins had apparently entered into a compact with the devil years ago: his soul in exchange for musical expertise. Now in his final hours, Blevins has a phantasmagorical experience, beginning with an encounter with a mouse in his seedy New York hotel room, moving to a bar where he encounters a senator from his past and a whore from his present, and ending with a conflagration and his mouse in flight. Not much music.

Cohen, Octavus. "Music Hath Charms." *Dark Days and Black Knights*, 1–44. New York: Dodd, Mead, 1923.
A humorous story hinging on the comeuppance of a con man who claims to blow a mean horn when in fact he can neither read nor play a note.

Cohn, David L. "Black Troubador." In *A Caravan of Music Stories*, edited by Noah D. Fabricant and Heinz Werner, 247–53. New York: Frederick Fell, 1947.
Joe Moss is a three-harp black man who, "when he bears down hard on his two-bit harmonica . . . can make trouble leave your weary mind, set your tired feet to stomping, bring sweet Jesus to your back-sliding soul." And, according to him, his playing also causes men to shut their doors and send their women to the kitchen till he passes by.

Coleman, Wanda. "Angel Baby Blues." *Heavy Daughter Blues: Poems and Stories, 1968–1986*, 84–86. Santa Rosa, CA: Black Sparrow, 1987.
A black gal in the 1980s looks back on selected formative experiences in the Los Angeles of the 1950s, deciding to hang around a bit longer, hoping someday "to collect what's due me" for "having paid my dues *forevah*." The titular "blues" are in the melancholy tone, not in any particular musical reference.

——. "The Blues in the Night." *Heavy Daughter Blues: Poems and Stories, 1968–1986*, 120–23. Santa Rosa, CA: Black Sparrow, 1987..
Lying alone in bed, sad over her separation from her husband and in need of sex, the protagonist gets up, dances frenziedly to her husband's records, gussies up, and goes out "near midnight into the ultramarine cool of ghetto night," confident that the man of her damp dreams is waiting for her. Reference to soul music and blues and allusions to the title tune.

———. "Chocolate Chip." *African Sleeping Sickness: Stories and Poems*, 168. Santa Rosa, CA: Black Sparrow, 1990.
A very short (one paragraph) first-person anecdotal account of a woman who becomes sexually aroused in a store when she hears a Roy Ayers jazz fusion recording on the sound system. Even though she urgently wants sex, she rejects the clerk's insulting overture.

———. "Jazz at Twelve." *Brilliant Corners* 5: 33–41 (Summer 2001).
Moonlighting songwriter Babe and her husband, Kevin, are out on the town to see the hot James Ditzi Quintet. The story comprises Babe's reflections on her personal life, on jazz, and on the music industry in general. The technique of the story is both unusual and effective as it recapitulates future events while recording action in the present. Much reference to narcotics.

———. "Letter to Big Joe." *Heavy Daughter Blues: Poems and Stories, 1968–1986*, 210–13. Santa Rosa, CA: Black Sparrow, 1987.
A series of brief reminiscences in the form of a letter written by a woman who had once worked in a jazz joint owned by a man (Joe) who used to go around singing "Satin Doll" in a "scratchy yawn" and book "hot heavy" weekends of jazz to which, alas, no one came.

———. "The Man Who Loved Billie Holiday." *Heavy Daughter Blues: Poems and Stories, 1968–1986*, 47–52. Santa Rosa, CA: Black Sparrow, 1987.
Down on her luck and desperately looking for work, Francine stops at a diner for a cup of coffee, but a handsome older man sitting at the counter can tell she's hungry and so treats her to a meal. When she gobbles her food, her benefactor remarks that Billie Holiday used to eat like that, and then he lapses into an affecting reminiscence of his relationship with the great singer. In the end we understand that while the sweet-talking man has been putting the moves on Francine, she's been hustling him, too.

———. "Take It Up at the Bridge." *A War of Eyes and Other Stories*, 125–26. Santa Rosa, CA: Black Sparrow, 1988.
A very short, jazzy story about a night of the Professor of Play's music at the Club Reverb. The dancers are turned on by the music. Tomorrow the Professor will play another one-night stand in another city.

Collier, James Lincoln. *The Jazz Kid*. New York: Henry Holt, 1994.
Intended for a juvenile audience, this novel dramatizes the story of teenager Paulie Horvath who breaks from his blue-collar parents in order to become a jazz musician in the Chicago of the 1920s. Many references to gangsters and jazz musicians of the time.

Collins, Max Allan, and Matthew V. Clemens. "East Side, West Side." In *Murder . . . and All That Jazz,* edited by Robert J. Randisi, 47–67. New York: Signet, 2004.

In this period piece, a glamorous couple from Chicago are in New York to get married. When their maid of honor (Mae West, no less!) goes missing, they become a detective duo. A former jazz pianist, the male and his bride-to-be are delayed only slightly in their efforts to solve the case when he makes an unexpected guest appearance with the orchestra he used to play for.

Connelly, Michael. "Christmas Even." In *Murder . . . and All That Jazz*, edited by Robert J. Randisi, 109–34. New York: Signet, 2004.

In investigating a killing, series detective Harry Bosch discovers a saxophone in the decedent's closet and traces it to a musician he had once seen perform. Bosch's special affinity for the saxophone, as well as the Christmas season, compels him to seek out its owner and return it.

———. *Echo Park*. Boston-New York-London: Little Brown, 2006.

Jazz-loving LAPD detective Harry Bosch is working on a cold case concerning the disappearance of a young woman that has been on his mind ever since he first investigated it in 1995. Although there is little music in the narrative, one substantial jazz reference qualifies it for inclusion in this bibliography. When Harry's girlfriend-colleague asks him what he's playing on the stereo, he tells her it's the long-lost Carnegie Hall concert of Thelonious Monk and John Coltrane. He goes on to say that "it's a miracle to think that it was there all that time. It took the right person to find it. To recognize it." Thus a jazz recording provides an analogue to the baffling crime under investigation—and Harry, of course, will be "the right person" to recognize the clues that have been there all along.

———. *Lost Light*. Boston: Little, Brown, 2003.

In this hard-boiled detective novel, private investigator Harry Bosch reaches back into the past to seek justice for a young woman who was killed on his watch while he was still with the LAPD. Bosch is learning to play the saxophone and loves classic jazz, especially Art Pepper, in this series novel. The jazz content of this book is modest but interesting.

Conroy, Frank. *Body and Soul*. New York: Houghton Mifflin, 1993.

Yet another *Bildungsroman* dramatizing the rise from obscurity to fame of Claude Rawlings, child prodigy of the piano growing up in Manhattan in the 1940s. Although the musical content generally focuses on the developments occurring in the new classical music of the times, it also contains a few resonant passages relating to jazz, especially to the music of Art Tatum and

Charlie Parker. For instance, in one scene, as Claude and his mentor listen to a Parker recording, "The sharp sound of Parker's alto saxophone cut the air with a twisting, syncopated blues line, repeated after twelve bars. At the twenty-fifth bar two things happened: . . . the pianist . . . began to play the cycle of fifths based on Parker's bebop changes . . . and second, Claude began to play the twelve-tone composition he'd been working on all night." Claude's teacher soon realizes that "the two fit together harmonically, as if the bebop were accompaniment for the twelve-tone, or vice versa." And then, in chapter 20 of this long novel, there is a scene in which Claude plays a jazz duet with another pianist in London, and the two experience an epiphanic moment as they spontaneously create an entirely new harmonic base while escaping tonality. Devotees of jazz fiction might welcome the recommendation to read this chapter and skip the rest.

Cook, Bruce. "Just a Gig." *Michigan's Voices,* Winter 1962: 13–23.
    Family man Kelly receives a call from old friend Benny, who desperately needs Kelly to play trumpet that night. Kelly has been out of music for several years; first he was in detox, then he got married and had a child. Nevertheless, jazz is in his blood, so he joins Benny's group, performs well, has a terrifying experience, and returns to the bosom of his family, telling his wife that "It was just a gig."

Cornelius, Marcus M. *Out of Nowhere*: *The Musical Life of Warne Marsh.*
    Canberra, Australia: Aurora Nova, 2002.
    A curious, occasionally affecting, fictionalized autobiography of saxophonist Warne Marsh that contains as much musical content, page by page, as any other jazz fiction. It traces Marsh's genealogy, musical apprenticeship, and career. Along the way, the reader is exposed to reflections on the art and implications of improvisation and of music in general. Music, we are told in an epigraph, "comes out of nowhere, like the wind, and is gone." In his own words, Marsh was a stunningly unremarkable man—in every way except thinking about and producing music. He was involved with practically every jazz musician of note in the golden years beginning right after World War II, but especially with Lenny Tristano and Lee Konitz. And he has much to say about Charlie Parker and Lester Young, among others. The author researched this book for several years, and the result is that we are able vicariously to inhabit the consciousness of its subject. Here, for example, is Marsh reflecting on his young musical self: "I could already hear the melodies and harmonies in even the simplest song—the most moving often has a very simple melody—and spent a great deal of my time experimenting on how to build a melody to harmonize with another melody and realized then that I would be a soloist, or a scientist. To be a section man and just play parts would not be

possible; my ear could hear too many possibilities to ignore them. I have known men go to pieces when confronted with the challenge of creating a solo, and the intensity of the demand of being a soloist has put an end to more than a few musical careers, the way some pilots lose nerve after a crash. It is all to do with confidence built upon knowledge: true inspiration is always informed. . . ." As the dedication to the novel says: "This book is inspired by and dedicated to the music of perhaps the most inventive improviser in the history of music in the West. It is an account of his life as he might have told it: his song set to words." Though *Out of Nowhere* is not by any means a distinguished novel, it is nevertheless good to have a fictional account of a figure who has often been marginalized when not completely forgotten in discussions of post–World War II jazz history.

Cortázar, Julio. "Bix Beiderbecke." *Cuentos: Obras Completas I*, 1107–14. Barcelona: Galaxia Gutenberg, 2003.

As my friend the translator [David Powell] wrote me: "'Bix' is a wild celebratory reflection on the unity of jazz, sex, art, literature, classical music, and everything worth remembering, or experiencing, in life lived to its fullest." It is, I gather, a story as free-flowing as a jazz line, and it ends where one might expect it to begin. The postmodernist narrative concerns a Panamanian woman reminiscing about the time, over two decades earlier, when she lived (or didn't live) with the legendary Bix—a classic example of the unreliable narrator. The author did not live to complete his story (if he ever *intended to* close it), but it seems to me that it is nevertheless, even in its unfinished state, precisely the kind of story (like others I have read, albeit in translation, by the same author) that should redouble one's resolve to master Spanish.

———. *Hopscotch.* Translated by Gregory Rabassa. New York: Pantheon, 1966. [First published as *Rayuela*. Editorial Sudamericana Sociedad Anónima, 1963.]

A postmodernist novel recounting the astonishing adventures of Horacio Oliveira (an Argentinian writer living in Paris), his mistress, and their circle of bohemian friends. For the first nineteen chapters, this reads like the jazz novel to end all jazz novels, with constant reference to and provocative discussions of jazz and its musicians; after that, however, as the plot mechanics kick in, the musical content becomes sporadic.

———. "Lucas, His Pianists." *A Certain Lucas.* 1979. Translated by Gregory Rabassa, 157–58. New York: Knopf, 1984.

With piano music in the background, Lucas briefly reminisces about pianists, classical and jazz, he has enjoyed; one brief memory involves the time that Thelonious Sphere Monk threatened to pour beer on Lucas's date's hair.

Lucas resolves to ask to hear two things when he is at the point of death: "Mozart's last quintet and a certain piano solo on the theme of 'I Ain't Got Nobody.' If he [Lucas] feels that there won't be enough time, he'll only ask for the piano record. Long is the list, but he's already chosen. Out of the depths of time, Earl Hines will accompany him."

———. "A Place Named Kindberg." *We Love Glenda So Much* and *A Change of Light*. Translated by Gregory Rabassa. 185–98. New York: Vintage, 1984.

An interior monologue concerning a stop at a place called Kindberg by the speaker and a girl friend. References to Archie Shepp form a leitmotif; in fact, the story's style may be (though it's hard to say for sure, since this is a translation) an attempt to imitate the rhythms and structures of free jazz, as in this excerpt: "Predictable, poor little bear so content with her lettuce and her plan to swallow Spinoza in six months mixed with Allen Ginsberg and Shepp again; how many clichés would she parade out until the coffee came (don't forget to give her the aspirin, if she starts sneezing on me it'll be a problem, little snot-nose with wet hair face all sticky bangs the rain lashing her by the side of the road) but parallel between Shepp and the end of the goulash everything was kind of spinning in a short while, hanging, they were the same phrases and Spinoza or Copenhagen and at the same time different, Lina there across from him breaking the bread drinking the wine looking at him content, far away and near at the same time, changing with the spinning of the night, although far away and near wasn't an explanation, something else, something like a show, Lina showing him something that wasn't herself but what then, please tell me. . . ."

———. "The Pursuer." *End of the Game and Other Stories*, 182–247. Translated by Paul Blackburn. New York: Pantheon, 1967. [First published as "El Perseguidor," in *Las Armas Secretas*, 99–183. Buenos Aires: Sudamericana, 1959.]

Dedicated to "Ch. P.," this novella dramatizes certain key events in Charlie Parker's last days. Many references to sex, dope, and booze. Much of the story's dramatic tension derives from discussions between Johnny Carter (the Parker figure) and Bruno, the narrator, a jazz critic who has recently published a biography of Carter; particularly at issue is the unbreachable disparity between what the artist tries to accomplish through his music and how this is (mis)interpreted by the critic. Johnny is the pursuer of the title, a quester after the ineffable, but so is the narrator a parasitic pursuer of Johnny and reflected glory. In short the pursuer is also the pursued—and vice versa.

Cotterell, Roger. "Blues for Night People." *Jazz & Blues* 2, no. 7 (October 1972): 14–15.

Thanks to a popular album, pianist Lou is moving up in the music world. Now, he thinks, he will be able to play some "real" jazz—some music from the soul. But he soon discovers that if he wants to continue to land gigs, he will have to provide his audiences with the popular music he had become famous for, leaving his truly creative stuff for . . . another time.

Coxhead, Nona. *Big-Time Baby*. London: Magnum, 1981.

Targeted to women, this novel set in the Jazz Age stars flapper Ivy (Shaw) Darling, who runs away from her fiancé and the conventional life he represents to plunge herself into the heady world of New York City. There she eventually rises to stardom as a singer and dancer in jazzy musicals. Ivy, of course, is the "Big-Time Baby" (later the "little jazz baby") of the title, and the song of that title written in her honor becomes a showstopper. The story overflows with period references—celebrities, gangsters, bootleg booze, Harlem music—and is (very) mildly feminist, but its jazz content is shallow and predictable. For instance, although the music hovers over many scenes, specific references to musicians (Armstrong, Walker, Beiderbecke, et al.) and the exciting new music emanating from Harlem are sporadic and slight. In short, a rare but inessential work for jazz fiction lovers (except, perhaps, for collectors of Jazz Age arcana).

Creech, J. R. *Music and Crime*. New York: Putnam, 1989.

Living on the nether fringes of the music world in Los Angeles and New York, Ray the Face is an accomplished saxophonist and composer who simply can't make a career in music, so with his bassist partner Lonnie he takes to street crime. Along the way, he discovers what he'd rather not have known about the grim reality of the cutthroat music industry. Much of this novel's sadness derives from our witnessing artists whose lives are made wretched by the music that might have liberated them, had circumstances been different.

Cresswell, Jasmine. *Contract: Paternity*. Toronto and New York: Harlequin, 1997.

Although this romance is set in New Orleans and its heroine is a jazz singer and nightclub owner, it contains precious little jazz content, apart from glancing references to such musicians as Ernestine Anderson, Duke Ellington, and Billie Holiday. Rather, it concerns Antoinette "Toni" Delacroix's desire to have a baby—a plan she puts on hold in order to help disentangle her lawyer brother from a blackmail scheme.

Crouch, Stanley. *Don't the Moon Look Lonesome: A Novel in Blues and Swing*. New York: Pantheon, 2000.

A very long foray into American culture at the end of the twentieth century as filtered through the consciousness of a callipygous white female jazz singer from South Dakota (in other words, a white woman in a black woman's body or at least a woman embodying qualities and characteristics of both races) whose long-term relationship with a more successful black saxophonist is at risk. Set in Manhattan and Houston and almost totally lacking in dramatic action or conventional plot, this book resembles works of urban anthropology in its explorations of such matters as race, jazz, family, homosexuality, drugs, and city life in general. Crouch dedicates the novel to his "mentors," Albert Murray, Ralph Ellison, and Saul Bellow, and in fact it often reads as if the latter two giants had collaborated to produce an early draft of a novel provisionally titled *Invisible Man Meets Mr. Sammler's Planet*. Although the book contains powerful passages and ideas worth dramatizing, the reader who finds the protagonist, Carla Hamsun, less than thoroughly engrossing will tire of the novel long before the midway point.

Crow, Bill. "Andy's Ashes." *Brilliant Corners* 5 (Summer 2001): 42–45.

A macabrely humorous story concerning the disposition of trumpeter Andy's final remains. The setting is a midtown Manhattan tavern to which all the jazz musicians eventually gravitate. Author Crow is a professional jazz bassist and widely published jazz writer.

Culver, Monty. "Black Water Blues." *Atlantic Monthly*, May 1950: 34–38.

As the only white musician in an otherwise all-black band, pianist "Lion" Rohrs lives with the tension of an outsider. When trouble breaks out, he knows that the bandleader, Bump Roxy, will be quick to use him as a scapegoat.

Cundiff, Lucy. "Trumpet Man." *Saturday Evening Post* June 19, 1954, 31+.

Trumpet man Dan Daly lost his lip years ago, and his nightclub gig is in serious jeopardy until one night when a leading orchestra leader joins the audience, inspiring Dan to recover his musical mastery (for the moment). As a result, the song Dan wrote for his wife becomes a longtime hit, allowing Dan and Molly to open the little club of their dreams.

Curran, Dale. *Dupree Blues*. New York: Knopf, 1948.

A refugee from a middle-class existence in Duluth, the title figure, Dupree, plays in a New Orleans style jazz band not far from Memphis. A gambler and boozer with a sharp pain in his gut, Dupree falls in love with the beautiful but

marginally talented singer in the band. When he gets in over his head financially, his life crumbles and then comes apart. The novel intends Dupree to
represent the kind of little-guy folk hero that inspires the blues. Frequent and
considerable descriptions of gambling and music-making.

————. *Piano in the Band*. New York: Reynal & Hitchcock, 1940.
   Toward the end of the Depression, George Baker plays piano in a dance-
hall jazz band. Much attention is given to the on-the-road existence of such a
group: the frustrations and resulting tensions of rehearsals and constant
travel. These tensions peak when the bandleader hires a beautiful blonde
singer, affecting the group dynamics of the all-male band. Another conflict—
and a common one in jazz fiction—arises because some of the musicians
want to create "real" music rather than follow the strict routines of the bandleader, who plays it safe to ensure financial success. Finally, circumstances
make it possible for George to consider joining a largely black band where
he'll be free to create—and, presumably, where he will be able to help loosen
the rigid color line. Some booze and dope and much musical description.

Curtis, Christopher Paul. *Bud, Not Buddy*. New York: Delacorte, 1999.
   This novel for juveniles is set in Flint, Michigan, during the Great Depression. After his mother dies, ten-year-old Bud goes in search of his father. Because she never told him who his father was, Bud follows the only clue he can
find: flyers of "HERMAN E. CALLOWAY and his famous band, the Dusky
Devastators of the Depression!!!!!!" Bud eventually finds his dad and is
"adopted" by the band. At the end, it looks like Bud is on his way to becoming a jazz musician. In an afterword, the author identifies his grandfather and
his band, Herman E. Curtis and the Dusky Devastators of the Depression!!!!!!, as the model for his fictional band.

Cushman, Jerome. *Tom B. and the Joyful Noise*. Illustrated by Cal Massey.
   Philadelphia: Westminster, 1970.
   Thomas Boynton Fraser ("Tommy B." to his friends) is a cocky little black
kid who moves about New Orleans with his shoeshine kit as passport. When
he stumbles upon the French Quarter one night, he is immediately hooked by
the excitement, especially the music. Later, at Preservation Hall, he meets a
horn man who promises to teach Tommy B. to play the trumpet. Complications ensue, first when Tommy's schoolwork suffers because of his encom-
passing interest in jazz and then when he learns of his grandmother's opposi-
tion to the "sinful music." In the tradition of books for young people,
everything turns out well in the end. Jacket copy implies that the book is a roman à clef.

Cuthbert, Clifton. *The Robbed Heart*. New York: L. B. Fischer, 1945.

The only son of a well-to-do New York family, Denis Sloane is a music critic who takes jazz and jazz bands very seriously. His devotion to this music takes him frequently to Harlem, where he meets the beautiful, intelligent, light-skinned Judy Foster, daughter of a prominent Harlem businessman. The novel dramatizes the complexities of an interracial love affair. There are references to musicians of the time and to the dispiriting compromises musicians must make to ply their trade for money; one of Sloane's black friends, Bert, feels forced to give up his trumpet and deal dope in order to survive.

Dabinett, Ward. "Not Commercial." In *Jazz Parody* (*Anthology of Jazz Fiction*), edited by Charles Harvey, 62–68. London: Spearman Publishers, 1948.

When a songwriter enlists the aid of a poet to write lyrics to his melodies, the collaboration leads to an ironic twist.

Dail, Hubert. *The Singing Fool*. New York: Grosset and Dunlap, 1929.

A novelization, with stills, of the Al Jolson semi-talky movie by the same name, a follow-up to *The Jazz Singer*. Al is a waiter and a "singing fool" who aspires to become a songwriter. He is "discovered" by a Broadway producer one night when he is singing a song to impress a girl. He goes to Broadway, becomes a success, marries the girl, and they become headliners, with Al writing the songs that Molly sings. They have a child—Sonny Boy—Molly tires of Al, and the marriage dissolves. After hitting the skids, Al attempts a comeback.

Daugherty, Tracy. *Axeman's Jazz*. Dallas: Southern Methodist University Press, 2003.

When light-skinned mulatto Telisha Washington sets out to discover who she *really* is, she finds herself in the neighborhood in Houston where she was raised, a blighted, largely African-American section infested by drugs and gangs. Although the title, dust jacket (picturing jazz or blues musicians performing in a dive), and last word ("jazz") suggest heavy musical content, there is virtually none. The title refers to the myth of the murderous axeman (who favored Lucifer's music, jazz), and, while several scenes are set in a ramshackle jazz-blues club, the music stays decidedly in the background.

Davis, Clive. "I Could Write a Book." In *B Flat, Bebop, Scat*, edited by Chris Parker, 122–33. London: Quartet, 1986.

Insurance salesman and weekend jazz man, Scott dreams that his hero Miles Davis asks him to fill in for him while he drives to the airport to pick up a girl. Years later, Scott prepares to go to a Miles Davis concert in London to see Miles in his fusion mode and again fantasizes that Davis asks him to participate in the music-making.

Davis, David. *Jazz Cats.* Gretna, LA: Pelican, 2001.
A juvenile book—a story in rhyme—involving (according to the Library of Congress summary) "Cool cats entertaining crowds with their music in the French Quarter of New Orleans." Not seen.

Davis, Genie. *Dreamtown.* Corvallis and Lake Tahoe: The Fiction Works, 2001.
Jake Romero, a serious boozer and jazz guitarist, takes to the road after being discovered in bed with a jealous mobster's girlfriend. He runs out of gas—and gin—and stops in the only jazz bar in the area, Dreamtown. The band is auditioning for a guitarist. Jake is less interested in the group than the bar's gorgeous waitress, Ann Ryan, who coincidently composes jazz. For the first time in his life, Jake falls hopelessly in love and dedicates his life, first, to winning her affection, and second, to saving her from a life-threatening brain tumor. Although Jake seems only marginally literate, he masters the medical literature on Ann's condition at the Johns Hopkins library. Only a $50,000 operation offers a remote prospect of recovery. In desperation, he risks his own life to find his old girlfriend, the mobster's moll, and persuades her to hock a ring and lend him the money. *Does* love conquer all? You'll have to read this breathtakingly ludicrous novel to find out. The musical content is modest.

Dawson, Fielding. "The Blue in the Sky." *Will She Understand?*, 27–32. Santa Rosa, CA: Black Sparrow, 1988.
The narrator remembers the time when he and two of his young chums went to East St. Louis to hear Charlie Barnett and his orchestra. June Christy and Jo Jones triggered powerful emotions in the speaker who, after making eye contact with Jones, wonders what effect the experience might have had on the drummer. This and the following entries by Dawson should probably be classified as fantasies.

———. "Full Circle." *Will She Understand?*, 53–54. Santa Rosa, CA: Black Sparrow, 1988.
"The Poet" returns to the bar featured in "The Reason" (q.v.) and reports that the Miles Davis Quintet was "getting better and better and better." Always standing—never sitting while absorbing music—the young poet "knew how to listen to music, and he was listening to this music in that way of hearing new work that the opening outward of the inner ear does something to balance. In suspense hearing nothing but music, there was nothing but music, anywhere,

he was up in a world and the world was music." In short, a description of the Miles Davis group in action.

———. "Miles." *Will She Understand?*, 55–59. Santa Rosa, CA: Black Sparrow, 1988.
The poet remembers encountering Miles Davis and giving him a booklet of his poems and telling him of Robert Creeley's remark that Creeley's "poetic line follows your [Davis's] melodic line, on 'But Not for Me.'" When the poet and Davis meet again years later, Davis not only recognizes the poet but tells him he still has the book.

———. "The Planets." *Will She Understand?*, 49–51. Santa Rosa, CA: Black Sparrow, 1988.
Three young buddies in 1953 go to Le Downbeat to hear some music. When they get there they find Stan Getz, Bob Brookmeyer, Roy Haynes, Tommy Potter, and Al Haig jamming to an empty house. Miles Davis drops by and sits in with the group, playing a transcendent "The Way You Look Tonight."

———. "The Reason." *Will She Understand?*, 13–14. Santa Rosa, CA: Black Sparrow, 1988.
In 1957, a "fair-skinned lad with a powdered wig and big ears" listens to the Miles Davis Quintet at Café Bohemia and then, to Davis's astonishment, transcribes, note for note, the music the quintet had just played.

———. "September in the Rain." *Will She Understand?*, 47–48. Santa Rosa, CA: Black Sparrow, 1988.
The speaker ("the poet") has an epiphany while listening to Red Garland play "They Didn't Believe Me" in a nightclub.

Deaver, Jeffery Wilds. *Mistress of Justice*. New York: Doubleday, 1992.
Paralegal at a preëminent Wall Street law firm by day, jazz pianist by night (whenever she can land a gig), Taylor Lockwood becomes involved in crime in high places. Despite a mini-subplot concerning Lockwood's dream of landing a recording contract and thereby becoming rich and famous, this blockbuster novel contains disappointingly little jazz content apart from infrequent references to such musicians as Billy Taylor, Cal Tjader, Paul Desmond, Dave Brubeck, and Miles Davis.

Deelder, J. A. "Blind Date." *Jazz: Verhalen en Gedichten* [*Stories and Poems*], 52–65. Amsterdam: De Bezige Bij, 1992.
A fantasy, in Dutch, involving three jazz musicians who go to a mysterious gig arranged by an eccentric jazz pianist. When they get there, the narrator be-

up his rendition of "Nearer My God to Thee," a fierce thunderstorm strikes, and he wonders if God is punishing him for sacrilege. Slight jazz content.

Farmer, Jerrilyn. *Perfect Sax: A Madeline Bean Novel.* New York: William Morrow, 2004.

A frothy mystery set among the haute monde of Los Angeles and featuring series caterer and event-planner Madeline Bean. She seems to be on the verge of her greatest triumph, a charity jazz soiree. Then the perfect sax that was auctioned off (a one-of-a-kind sterling silver Mark VI tenor) disappears, and Madeline finds a corpse in her bedroom. Mayhem, of course, ensues. The acknowledgments, like the title, convey a jazz motif, and many chapter titles are jazz compositions (including "Mood Indigo," "Nutty," "I Want to Talk about You," and "Jeeps Blues" [*sic*]). But the jazz content, like the story itself, lacks substance.

Farr, John. *The Deadly Combo: The Sour Note of Blackmail.* New York: Ace Double Novel Books, 1958.

A hard-edged mystery, very much of its period—a good example of pulp noir. Plainclothes detective and jazz devotee Mac Stewart determines to track down the killer of onetime great trumpet player Dandy, who has long since resided in the gutter. Mac believes that Dandy may have brought on his own death by bragging to a stranger about the solid gold trumpet he had once received as a tribute to his playing—failing to mention that he had pawned it years earlier. The novel takes place in Los Angeles' Jazz Row; comprises considerable clipped, staccato dialogue, much of which seems borrowed from B-movies ("What do you want, you big gorilla?"); and is riddled with jazz references. When Dandy is buried, all of the jazz notables (including representatives from *Down Beat* and *Metronome*) show up to give him a proper send-off.

Feather, Leonard. "Bass Is Basic Basis of Basie." *Metronome*, April 1944, 26.

Under the pseudonym of Snotty McSiegel (sometimes Professor S. Rosentwig McSiegel), the jazz man-of-all-works Leonard Feather published irregularly a series of facetious jazz casuals in such magazines as the long-forgotten *Swing Magazine* (1940), *Metronome* during the 1940s, and *Down Beat* starting in the early 1950s. Feather portrays McSiegel as a pompous ass, eager to explicate, in overbearingly obvious terms, anything related to the history or performance of jazz in its several manifestations and to take full credit for any of the music's successes. (One suspects that these items originated as column fillers.) The "stories" themselves are generally self-annotating; that is, their titles tell the reader what to expect. When that isn't the case ("You Gotta Get Lucky," "How I Caught Music Red-Handed"), I provide light glosses.

————. "Nacht in Tunisië" ["Night in Tunisia"]. *Jazz: Verhalen en Gedichten [Stories and Poems]*, 73–78. Amsterdam: De Bezige Bij, 1992.

A solitary, melancholic 40-year-old newspaper reporter vacations in Tunisia, where, to his surprise, he bonds with the locals. When not with his new friends, he listens to desultory jazz at the hotel café. He requests his favorite song, "Night in Tunisia," and discovers that the band is made up of accomplished musicians, one of whom played sax with Chet Baker. On the last night of his vacation, a European vacationer invites the reporter and his Tunisian friends to his wife's birthday party. After a flirtation, the reporter and the wife walk together on the beach, and a wink leads the Tunisian friends to follow. The reporter proves impotent, but the five friends have sex with the woman while the reporter passes out drunk. The next day the friends rush him to the airport. On board, he is forced to sit next to the woman, and wonders what she told her husband; they are too embarrassed to speak to each other. Back home, he makes his humdrum existence tolerable by planning his next trip to Tunisia and reuniting with his friends. He arrives bearing gifts, dressed in an oversized white suit, and seeks his friends at a favorite café. When he approaches, they don't recognize him. It is surely redundant to observe that this is an unusual story. In Dutch.

————. "Swingkoning" ["Swing King"]. *Jazz: Verhalen en Gedichten [Stories and Poems]* 141–49. Amsterdam: De Bezige Bij, 1992.

After the seven Belgians comprising the jazz band Charles Remue and His New Stompers travel to London from the Continent to make some recordings, the fruit of their efforts—seven two-sided 10-inch 78 rpm records—quickly become collectors' items. Fast-forward to 1986 where we follow the speaker as he discovers the original, hand-numbered test prints of the Remue recordings in a bar in Brussels that once belonged to the wildly popular "Swing King" of Brussels, Stan Brenders. The story provides a glimpse of the 1940s Swing era in Nazi-dominated Europe and it also dramatizes the thrill the jazz aficionado experiences when he makes a rare discovery. In Dutch.

Delancey, Kiki. "Swingtime." *Brilliant Corners* 6 (Winter 2001): 47–57. In *Coal Miner's Holiday*, 89–106. Louisville: Sarabande Books, 2002.

A young boy describes his father's life in jazz—first a kind of rolling jam session at home, then success in the clubs and on record in New York City. The language of the story, like the father's life, is always in motion, crackling with the excitement of the music, as in this excerpt: "There was something about Jack Herman, something in him, that knew what my father was going to do. He'd put the end of the clarinet in his mouth, the black, oblique mouthpiece in his mouth. The song would start. Jack'd be tootling along, nothing special, kind of keeping up with everybody while my dad would come in with the vocals, give them the silky whispering thing, maybe a little of the be-bop singing he'd been picking up there in the city, the fast singing he'd been hearing down 52nd Street; they'd work their way to the break, the trumpet solo would strike up, a big virile shout like it always did, and then, bam, that clarinet would be right there, would wrap itself so tightly around the trumpet, climb up on its back, rip right up full-speed with it, almost past it, almost but never exactly past it: always right along with it, the same syncopation, the same instant drops and curls, and the rebounds, and the rises, impossibly tight but absolutely free, absolutely wild, and never the same way twice. Never the same way twice."

De Mexico, N. R. *Marijuana Girl.* Beacon 328, 1960.

Nice girl goes bad in this cult pulp fiction in which, according to promotional copy of a reprint, "The pot-smoking jazz scene is well described . . ." Not seen.

De Niro, Alan. "Tetrarchs." Strangehorizons.com/2004/20040503/tetrarchs .shtml (4 June 2005)

Two of the stories in this four-part collection of speculative literature are titled "A Love Supreme" and "But Not for Me." In the first of these, the horn-playing narrator negotiates with a street vendor for an orange, the buying of which, one by one, was one of his "favorite things." He then encounters a beautiful floating woman with whom he exchanges parables. When she begins to dematerialize, he hears her "croon a story . . . about a love supreme." In the second story the saxophonist narrator meets a woman in Manhattan's Alphabet City. When they go to her apartment, she tells him he sounds like John Coltrane. When he discovers he has misplaced his saxophone, she plays Coltrane's "My Favorite Things" and he has a mystical experience, culminating in his realization that when the woman finds him in a different time and place and attempts to reveal to him the TRUTH, it will not reach him. Truth may be good, "But not for me."

Denver, Paul. *Send Me No Lilies.* London: Consul Books, 1965.

At first Benny Carlton is just another young trumpet player in the sticks of England happy to be playing weekend gigs and longing to get married, settle down, and lead an ordinary life. Marry he soon does, but at the same time his combo turns pro and quickly establishes a reputation that makes it in demand in London and the Continent. Because Benny's very ordinary wife can neither understand jazz nor tolerate her status as jazz widow, their marriage soon dissolves. In the last scene, as Benny solos, a friend remarks to Benny's ex-wife: "I don't reckon to know much about the kind of thing Benny plays, but it's his life, isn't it? . . . It sounds like everything that means life to him is in his playing."

Deutsch, Hermann. "Louis Armstrong." *Esquire*, October 1935, 70+.
An early example in fiction (of any kind) of a work that blurs the distinction between fact and fiction; the author—or editor—in fact calls it "semifiction." The story is a vernacular account of Armstrong's rise from street kid to renowned musician. The writer's knowledge of black dialect would seem to derive from minstrel shows.

De Veaux, Alexis. *Don't Explain: A Song of Billie Holiday*. New York: Harper and Row, 1980.
A biographical novel—or novelistic biography—in the form of a prose poem, this ultimately uncategorizable book is organized chronologically around certain events of Billie Holiday's life. Although sadness suffuses the book (as clearly it did the life), the legendary singer's strength and courage win out—as one can only wish they had in life.

DeVries, Peter. "Jam Today." *New Yorker*, February 4, 1950, 34–35.
When the speaker takes a swing record to a platter party, he is embarrassed to discover that the host and the other partygoers are devotees of the new bebop and so he futilely tries to conceal his squareness. A humorous satire of jazz pretentiousness.

Diniz, Tailor. *O Assassino Usava Batom. [The Killer Wore Lipstick.]* Porto Alegre, Brazil: Mercado Aberto, 1997.
Based on the jacket copy and a skim-through, this is a crime novel set in Brazil (and in Portuguese) involving a murder investigated by detective Walter Jacquet. There are many references to jazz, especially to singers and Bill Coleman's recording of "Satin Doll"; in fact, the resolution of the crime relates to the music on the CDs the victim had been listening to when he died.

Dobrin, Arnold. *Scat!* New Work: Four Winds, 1971.
Eight-year-old Scat's dad plays jazz trumpet, and Scat wants to play an instrument too, despite the disapproval of his churchly grandmother. When she dies, however, he follows her advice to follow his heart and teaches himself the harmonica. For young readers.

Doctorow, E. L. *Ragtime*. New York: Random House, 1975.
An energetic historical novel dramatizing the ultimately intersecting lives of three radically different families toward the beginning of the twentieth cen-

tury in New York. Several historical figures such as J. P. Morgan, Harry Houdini, and Emma Goldman play cameo roles. It's hard to read this novel (which contains an epigraph from Scott Joplin) without hearing the titular music in your head, but in fact the musical content resides primarily in the syncopation of language and events and in one performance of Joplin's "Maple Leaf Rag" by a key character, Coalhouse Walker, a black professional pianist.

Douglass, Archie. "'Mrs. Hopkins Pays a Call.'" In *Jazz Parody (Anthology of Jazz Fiction)*, edited by Charles Harvey, 86–91. London: Spearman Publishers, 1948.
A breezy first-person narrative in which the speaker, a jazz trumpeter, sticks his nose where it doesn't belong and gets involved in a scheme relying on a female impersonator to play Cupid.

Downs, Hunton. *Murder in the Mood*. London: Wright, 1998.
A sweeping, researched thriller involving Nazis, neo-Nazis, drug cartels, the Mafia, the new billionaires, and—more important—speculation concerning what really happened to Glenn Miller during Hitler's reign of terror. The plot turns on the discovery in the present of a "Secret Broadcast" disc Miller recorded in 1944. The background material on Miller is solid.

Doyle, Roddy. *Oh, Play That Thing*. New York: Penguin, 2004.
Although this is a rambunctious, ambitious novel embodying a distracting variety of themes and literary modes, it is nevertheless often scintillating in its musical dimension. It begins in 1924 with IRA assassin Henry Smart fleeing Ireland, where he is wanted for his political involvement, and landing, like so many before and after him in life as in literature, in New York, intent upon re-making himself and maybe getting a slice of the American pie in the process. Living very much by his wits and his willingness to do anything to get by, he experiences the grim realities of the disenfranchised. When New York proves too dangerous, he moves on to Chicago, at which point the novel enters into the realm of jazz fiction, for it is here in his new home that Smart runs into Louis Armstrong, who makes Smart his "white man"—Armstrong's means of traversing black and white societies in his quest for fame and fortune. This, the longest and most absorbing part of the novel, is largely picaresque in its depiction of the Irish immigrant fugitive and his southern African-American companion experiencing a series of wild shenanigans culminating in Armstrong's, now in Harlem, being proclaimed (and packaged) as the world's greatest musician. Readers on either side of the Atlantic will argue whether the author captured the American voices authentically. Let them argue: the sections focusing

on Armstrong are unquestionably entertaining. For instance, when Smart reminds Armstrong that one of his wives claims to have made him, Louis replies: "That fair. . . . She put my name up in lights, first one to. And she showed me how to carry a hat. I ain't denying nothing. But listen here, Pops. On whose big mouth be the chops that blow the horn?" The novel describes, often beautifully, jazz in performance, it incorporates several other musicians in cameo, and it depicts a famous recording session of Armstrong and the Hot Five. A solid addition to the library of jazz fiction.

Dubus, Andre III. *Bluesman*. Boston and London: Faber, 1993.

A familiar coming-of-age tale concerning Leo Suther, a 17-year-old who lives in a small Massachusetts town. The time is 1967, and the Vietnam War and urban riots loom in the background as Leo tries to make sense of his life. As he confronts the obligatory obstacles on the way to maturity (love, politics, the past), the one constant in Leo's life is the blues harmonica, for which he has considerable talent; in fact, the musical dimension of this novel is significant as it simultaneously dramatizes Leo's apprenticeship on his instrument and urges the reader to regard this in metaphoric terms.

Duchin, Peter, and John Morgan Wilson. *Blue Moon: A Philip Damon Mystery*. New York: Berkley Prime Crime, 2002.

A romantic period piece mystery with a fox-trotty feel and an opening sentence that will hook many fans of jazz fiction: "I woke on the morning of October 20, 1963, with Duke Ellington's 'Sophisticated Lady' playing in my head." The story is set in Manhattan's and San Francisco's café societies in 1963; stars Philip Damon, pianist and bandleader (and son of big band leader Archie Damon); and features numerous celebrity characters, like Truman Capote, George Plimpton, and Joe Dimaggio. Damon is forced into amateur detectivehood when he discovers that he is the only link—and thus a suspect—in two murders. The musical content of this light story is fairly considerable: it contains scenes focusing on Damon's swing band in action, frequent references to jazz and swing musicians, and a nice set piece in which Damon sits in with Dizzy Gillespie at an after-hours jazz club. The title refers to the oft-recorded melancholy song, which plays a significant role in the book. Coauthor Duchin is a prominent bandleader, as was his father before him.

——. *Good Morning, Heartache*. New York: Berkley Prime Crime, 2003.

When bandleader and pianist Philip Damon takes his society swing band to Los Angeles in 1965 for a six-week gig at the legendary Coconut Grove, he once again is thrust into action as amateur detective, as in the previous novel in this series, *Blue Moon* (q.v.). Short a trumpet player, Damon hires, with considerable trepidation, a hornman-singer who had been one of the most promising jazz musicians of his time until he was busted for narcotics possession. Everything seems to be going well until Bixby turns up dead after sitting in with the Cannonball Adderley Quartet at Howard Rumsey's Lighthouse. Damon is joined by saxophone-playing ex-detective from San Francisco homicide, Hercules Platt, whom Damon had worked with in *Blue Moon* and who is now the only black in Damon's orchestra. As before, there are dozens of celebrity walk-ons with Rock Hudson and Claudette Colbert playing extensive roles as Damon and Platt, against the backdrop of the Watts riots, go about the business of solving crime.

Duke, Osborn. "Oh Jazz, Oh Jazz." In *Eddie Condon's Treasury of Jazz*, edited by Eddie Condon and Richard Gehman, 461–88. New York: Dial, 1956.
   The travails of a group of musicians shortly after World War II who want to make serious music and earn a living doing it. But there is no escaping a host of problems: living on a bus for days at a time, wildly erratic hours making normal life impossible, fiscal difficulties of every sort, and the omnipresent pressure of giving the audience what they want: popjazz.

——. *Sideman*. New York: Criterion, 1956.
   A very long, windy novel—a kind of panoramic survey of the lives, professional and personal, of several members of a large, post–Korean War dance band. The protagonist is sideman Bernie Bell, who leaves college in Texas to join the band in Southern California. Although Bernie plays his trombone for money, he moonlights by composing "serious" music; in short, another portrait of the artist as a young man. Much music talk and good descriptions of the improvisational process. Several references to such jazz men as Stan Kenton, Bill Harris, and Dizzy Gillespie—and some focus on race and marijuana. One character has a dog named Bijou after the Bill Harris recording.

Dumas, Henry. "Will the Circle Be Unbroken?" *Negro Digest*, November 1966, 76–80.
   Three young whites are reluctantly admitted to the all-black Sound Barrier Club in Harlem. They have come to hear Probe, who has recently returned from exile. But when Probe plays his "new-sound" jazz on his mystical instrument (one of only three afro-horns in existence), the vibrations and volume overwhelm and kill the interlopers.

Duncan, Alice Faye. *Willie Jerome*. New York: Macmillan Books for Young Readers, 1995.
   When summer comes, Willie Jerome plays jazz from the rooftop all day. His little sister Judy "feels" the music—the "sizzlin' red hot bebop" Willie plays on his trumpet. But everyone else regards Willie's music as noise until,

one day, Judy persuades her mother to "Just close your eyes. Rest your mind, and let the music speak to your spirit." Mom does as instructed and apologizes for having criticized Willie's playing. For young readers.

Duncan, Neal Holland. *Baby Soniat: A Tale from the Jazz Jungle*. Memphis: St. Luke's, 1989.
Although this novel is set in New Orleans and carries a subtitle implying significant jazz content, its only reference to the music is a jazz funeral; in short, a misleading title.

Dyer, Geoff. *But Beautiful: A Book about Jazz*. London: Jonathan Cape, 1991; New York: North Point, 1996.
The author defines this work as "imaginative criticism," explaining that he took many scenes from legendary episodes in the lives of jazz musicians and created his own versions of them—improvising, as it were, in keeping with the subject matter. Dyer devotes a chapter to each artist: Lester Young, Thelonious Monk, Bud Powell, Ben Webster, Charles Mingus, Chet Baker, and Art Pepper. This book is a wondrously evocative combination of re-creation and reflection. But some readers will be offended by the emphasis on the pain, sadness, and neurosis of the jazz life; others will put down the book in anger, knowing for instance that Dyer's Ben Webster barely resembles the original. If only Dyer had given fictitious names to his musicians . . .

"Eddie and the Two Dollar Bet." *Jazz Today* 2, no. 3 (April 1957): 29.
A first-person narrative about one wacky Eddie. Although identified as a jazz short story, it contains no musical content. (See also "The Two-Dollar Bet.")

Edwards, Grace F. *Do or Die: A Mali Anderson Mystery*. New York: Doubleday, 2000.
Another Harlem mystery featuring Mali Anderson, who has just returned from a jazz cruise on the QE2 to discover that the singer in her dad's jazz band has been brutally murdered, leaving the victim's father (also a member of the band) devastated. So Mali, naturally, takes to the streets, bars, barber shops, and beauty parlors of Harlem to find the killer before he strikes again. This novel contains more jazz content than the others in the series (listed below). In addition to referring to many well-known musicians, Mali occasionally points out areas where famous artists once lived: "I knew that in the back of memory, at least a few of these men also remember when Erroll Garner, Buck Clayton, Don Byas, Dizzy Gillespie and his wife, and Billy Eckstine

and his wife had, at one time or another, lived in the same apartment building at 2040 Seventh Avenue, just a few blocks away."

―――. *If I Should Die*. New York: Doubleday, 1997.
Although Mali Anderson, the series heroine, lives in Harlem, patronizes jazz clubs, makes references to jazz musicians, and has a jazz musician father, this and the following two mysteries contain negligible jazz content.

―――. *No Time to Die*. New York: Doubleday, 1999.

―――. *A Toast before Dying*. New York: Doubleday, 1998.

Ellis, Walter. *Prince of Darkness: A Jazz Fiction Inspired by the Music of Miles Davis*. London: 20/20, 1998.
A more accurate subtitle would substitute "life" for "music" because this book is, unfortunately, much more concerned with Davis's life than his art. Employing facile psychology, this novel attributes Davis's lifelong anguish to racism and a drunken mother, while failing to make a convincing case for his being "the prince of darkness." Although the book has an interesting structure, it falls far short of its colossal subject.

Ellison, Ralph. *Invisible Man*. New York: Random House, 1952.
In this landmark novel, an unnamed (hence "invisible") young southern black man moves north with "great expectations." A panoramic novel of American culture toward the midpoint of the twentieth century, *Invisible Man* is not, strictly speaking, a jazz novel, though jazz and blues do play a significant role in the way they give body to key thematic moments (as in references to Louis Armstrong's singing "What did I do to be so black and blue?") and also to the way they inform the technique and style, as in this passage in which the narrator, after hearing a moving speech, recalls his own addresses to fellow students: ". . . I too had stridden and debated, a student leader directing my voice at the highest beams and farthest rafters, ringing them, the accents staccato upon the ridgepole and echoing back with a tinkling, like words hurled to the trees of a wilderness, or into a well of slate-gray water; more sound than sense, a play upon the resonances of buildings, an assault upon the temples of the ear. . . ." Those who are interested in pursuing the relationship between Ellison's ideas about jazz and fiction will find much to ponder in the introduction to his essays, *Shadow and Act* (New York: Random House, 1964), and in the collection of letters he exchanged with his friend Albert Murray, *Trading Twelves: The Selected Letters of Ralph Ellison and*

Albert Murray. Edited by Albert Murray and John F. Callahan. New York: Random House, 2000.

Ellroy, James. *White Jazz*. New York: Knopf, 1992; London: Century, 1992.
    An ultraviolent crime novel set in the Los Angeles of the 1950s. Apart from some broken jazz records that provide a significant clue in a vicious crime and a few references to such jazz figures as Stan Kenton and Art Pepper, there is very little jazz content. The "jazz" in the title is apparently intended to torque up the already dense noir atmosphere.

English, Richard. *"Strictly Ding-Dong" and Other Swing Stories*. Garden City, NY: Doubleday, Doran, 1941.
    A dozen stories linked by their connection to swing and the occasional reappearance of Ding-Dong Williams, "the king of swing" and the hottest clarinetist in the land. In the title story, Ding-Dong has been contracted by Hollywood to provide the swing finale for a movie in production. The complication occurs when Ding-Dong reveals that he can neither read nor write music; but not to fret: where slapstick comedy is concerned, this turns out to be no problem at all. The humor of these stories is of the kind best encountered in Saturday morning movies on TV, as when Ding-Dong, announcing he is a "rug cutter," elicits this response from one of the studio people: "That's all right. . . . One of our best producers used to be a tailor." Ding-Dong's definition of swing goes far to characterize the language and tenor of these stories: "You can't explain swing. . . . You gotta be gut-bucket at heart to understand it. I've always been a gate, and gates swing wide. If you're a sender, you get to rug cutting when you're grooving a wax, what with the suitcase man being hot on the skin, and because you're not a paper man, you gotta lick it high and wild to be happy. Swingaroos are born with a lotta jive, and they just hafta play go-instruments, not icky or straight ones, and a union card riding a go-toy gets that old Dixie Land fever, and he's stomping it out before he knows it. The cats get to crying then, and when they twitch you know you've got 'em. That's swing."

Eskew, Robert. "Time of the Blue Guitar." *Coastlines*, Spring–Summer 1958. *Music '59: Downbeat Fourth Annual Yearbook*, 77–80. Chicago: Maher, 1959.
    Told in jazz idiom, this story concerns the difficulties a combo has with its leader, Zabe, a fast-talking hustler who finally talks himself out of the combo by alienating his players.

Estaver, Paul. *Smoke: A Jazz Novel in Verse*. Lewiston, NY: Edwin Mellen, 2003.

A compilation of poetic vignettes concerning the jazz life as lived by the musicians in the northeastern United States in the decade or so following World War II. How this book qualifies as a novel is anyone's guess, since it contains neither narrative thrust nor (with one or two *possible* exceptions) developing characters. Estaver was a jazz musician in northern New England for 25 years.

Estleman, Loren D. *Lady Yesterday*. Boston: Houghton Mifflin, 1987.
A hard-boiled mystery in which detective Amos Walker goes in search of a jazz musician who dropped out of sight twenty years earlier. Although Walker's investigation leads him into Detroit's rich jazz heritage, including the few remaining clubs where the music is still performed, the novel has only superficial jazz content.

Evans, Robert. "The Jazz Age." In *Jazz Parody (Anthology of Jazz Fiction)*, edited by Charles Harvey, 27–31. London: Spearman Publishers, 1948.
Hardly a story at all, but rather a species of free writing designed (apparently) to suggest the conventional idea that jazz originates in *real* experience, in pain and suffering and deprivation. A few interesting verbal riffs describing jazz in the making.

———. "There's a Great Day Coming . . ." In *Jazz Parody (Anthology of Jazz Fiction)*, edited by Charles Harvey, 77–85. London: Spearman Publishers, 1948.
In this continuation of or companion-piece to the author's "The Jazz Age" (q.v.), the writer tries to penetrate to the heart of jazz—its origins, meanings, and implications. Very much about jazz but very little "story" or parody.

Everett, Percival L. *Suder*. New York: Viking, 1983.
A picaresque novel featuring the madcap adventures of Craig Suder, a struggling black third baseman for the Seattle Mariners, who "drops out" when he suffers a humiliating slump in his career as well as in his home life. In his quest for fulfillment, Suder encounters cocaine smugglers, a young runaway, an elephant named Renoir, and his own past. It is in the scenes in the rural South past that the jazz content is most prominent. For instance, Bud Powell comes to live with the Suder family and starts calling young Craig "Bird" because of his resemblance to the legendary saxophonist. After Powell then convinces Craig that he has the lips for saxophone, he takes up the instrument, adding it, much later in his life, to the list of things he cannot do without. At one point Craig asks Powell what jazz is, to which Powell responds (while hitting and holding a chord), "Jazz is one step beyond, one giant step." He adds, after hitting another chord, "Charlie Parker is dead now,

but not really." Powell also engenders the novel's controlling metaphor when he adopts a stray dog (Django) and then sets him free. Along the way Craig becomes obsessed with Parker's "Ornithology" and carries a recording of it and a phonograph to play it on wherever he goes. At the book's climax, Craig goes to see Dizzy Gillespie at a club and requests that Dizzy play "Ornithology." When the group starts to play, Craig joins them on sax, causing pandemonium.

Ewing, Annemarie. *Little Gate*. New York and Toronto: Rinehart, 1947.
   Joe "Little Gate" Geddes is obsessed with jazz and is accepted as a young man both by blacks and other musicians. He leaves his small Iowa town for Chicago, where he lands a long-running gig in a speakeasy frequented by mobsters. He moves to New York after Prohibition and plays his sax in a band that does mostly novelty music, causing Joe to flee to Harlem after hours for the music he loves. Joe eventually forms his own band, goes on the road (all the way to Los Angeles and back), makes a hit record, becomes a celebrity, and discovers that he and his music have become commodities over which he has no control. Meanwhile, Joe's love life becomes seriously complicated. In his character and career, Joe Geddes is remarkably similar to Bix Beiderbecke.

Ewing, Debora. "Coloring Outside the Lines." *Jerry Jazz Musician*. http://www.jerryjazzmusician.com/mainHTML.cfm?page=ewing.html (10/29/2003).
   The speaker likes "jazz because it plays in different colors" and this parallels for her "the way people come in different colors." She's in bed with a man and enjoying the music that has been accompanying their sex until he lets her know that he doesn't like her kind of music. She suspects that he won't call her again.

Fairweather, Digby. "The Killers of '59." In *B Flat, Bebop, Scat*, edited by Chris Parker, 96–107. London: Quartet, 1986.
   After auditioning for and winning a place in a British dance band around 1960, "the trumpeter" encounters several stark realities of big band life, including the competitiveness of musicians, the technical challenges of producing live music night after night, and the treachery of booze.

Fales, Dean. "Solo on the Cornet." *Story*, 1941. In *A Caravan of Music Stories*, edited by Noah D. Fabricant and Heinz Werner, 30–48. New York: Frederick Fell, 1947.
   After hearing Joel Pulmacher play the cornet, the religious young narrator resolves to master the instrument at whatever cost. Years later, when he jazzes

up his rendition of "Nearer My God to Thee," a fierce thunderstorm strikes, and he wonders if God is punishing him for sacrilege. Slight jazz content.

Farmer, Jerrilyn. *Perfect Sax: A Madeline Bean Novel.* New York: William Morrow, 2004.

A frothy mystery set among the haute monde of Los Angeles and featuring series caterer and event-planner Madeline Bean. She seems to be on the verge of her greatest triumph, a charity jazz soiree. Then the perfect sax that was auctioned off (a one-of-a-kind sterling silver Mark VI tenor) disappears, and Madeline finds a corpse in her bedroom. Mayhem, of course, ensues. The acknowledgments, like the title, convey a jazz motif, and many chapter titles are jazz compositions (including "Mood Indigo," "Nutty," "I Want to Talk about You," and "Jeeps Blues" [*sic*]). But the jazz content, like the story itself, lacks substance.

Farr, John. *The Deadly Combo: The Sour Note of Blackmail.* New York: Ace Double Novel Books, 1958.

A hard-edged mystery, very much of its period—a good example of pulp noir. Plainclothes detective and jazz devotee Mac Stewart determines to track down the killer of onetime great trumpet player Dandy, who has long since resided in the gutter. Mac believes that Dandy may have brought on his own death by bragging to a stranger about the solid gold trumpet he had once received as a tribute to his playing—failing to mention that he had pawned it years earlier. The novel takes place in Los Angeles' Jazz Row; comprises considerable clipped, staccato dialogue, much of which seems borrowed from B-movies ("What do you want, you big gorilla?"); and is riddled with jazz references. When Dandy is buried, all of the jazz notables (including representatives from *Down Beat* and *Metronome*) show up to give him a proper send-off.

Feather, Leonard. "Bass Is Basic Basis of Basie." *Metronome*, April 1944, 26.

Under the pseudonym of Snotty McSiegel (sometimes Professor S. Rosentwig McSiegel), the jazz man-of-all-works Leonard Feather published irregularly a series of facetious jazz casuals in such magazines as the long-forgotten *Swing Magazine* (1940), *Metronome* during the 1940s, and *Down Beat* starting in the early 1950s. Feather portrays McSiegel as a pompous ass, eager to explicate, in overbearingly obvious terms, anything related to the history or performance of jazz in its several manifestations and to take full credit for any of the music's successes. (One suspects that these items originated as column fillers.) The "stories" themselves are generally self-annotating; that is, their titles tell the reader what to expect. When that isn't the case ("You Gotta Get Lucky," "How I Caught Music Red-Handed"), I provide light glosses.

———. "Be-bop? I Was Pre-bop!" *Metronome*, December 1948, 24.

———. "The Duke Ellington Story: As Hollywood Might Do It." *Down Beat*
1950s; in *Laughter from the Hip*, edited by Leonard Feather and Jack
Tracy, 45–53. New York: Da Capo, 1979.
The title tells it all: the embarrassingly ludicrous result if Hollywood decided
to do a biopic of Duke Ellington, as it had done with Gene Krupa and Benny
Goodman, among others. Told as a screenplay, the story does produce a chuckle
or two, as when we learn that Duke's sister Ruth is played by Patty Duke.

———. "Hi-Fi Fable I: The Class Treatment." *Down Beat*, 1950s; in *Laughter from the Hip*, edited by Leonard Feather and Jack Tracy, 87–92. New
York: Da Capo, 1979.
A bandleader's scheme to allow his black soloist to perform in the segregated South backfires. Not a McSiegel piece.

———. "How I Caught Music Red-Handed." *Down Beat*, 1950s; in *Laughter from the Hip*, edited by Leonard Feather and Jack Tracy, 132–34. New
York: Da Capo, 1979.
A spoof of the McCarthy hearings, which tried to make Americans believe
that there was a Red (i.e., Communist) under every bed.

———. "I Invented Bossa Nova!" *Down Beat*, 1950s; in *Laughter from the
Hip*, edited by Leonard Feather and Jack Tracy, 162–67. New York: Da
Capo, 1979.

———. "I Invented Jazz Concerts." *Down Beat*, 1950s; in *Laughter from
the Hip*, edited by Leonard Feather and Jack Tracy, 102–7. New York: Da
Capo, 1979.

———. "Le Jazz Hep." *Metronome*, June 1943, 15; July 1943, 17; August
1943, 15; September 1943, 18; November 1943, 19; December 1943, 19;
January 1944, 30; February 1944, 20; March 1944, 24; April 1944, 26.
Professor McSiegel's frivolous history of jazz and taxonomy of its instruments.

———. "McSiegel Blind at Christmas: *Metronome*'s Hindmost Authority
Returns to Take Special St. Nicksiegel-land-Type Test." *Metronome*, January 1951, 20–21.

———. "McSiegel's Method." *Metronome*, June 1945, 11.

_____. "Professor McSiegel Tells about Sax!" *Metronome*, October 1943, 44–45.

_____. "Slide, Snotty, Slide." *Metronome,* December 1943, 19.

_____. "You Gotta Get Lucky." In *Music '59: Downbeat Fourth Annual Yearbook*, 73–75. Chicago: Maher, 1959.
A light piece (like all of Feather's contributions to jazz fiction) in which Joe, the trumpet-playing narrator, tries to pull a fast one on Frankie Wood, the bandleader, by running away with the band's vocalist. But Frankie is too fast for Joe: when last heard from, Frankie was on the road with Helene and headed for a honeymoon, leaving Joe to reflect that some guys have all the luck.

——, and Jack Tracy. "High-Fi Fable II: Double Jeopardy." In *Laughter from the Hip*, edited by Leonard Feather and Jack Tracy, 115–19. New York: Da Capo, 1979.
The speaker thinks he has beaten the system by using technology (a tape recorder in this case) to land a job with a big band, but his scheme backfires.

Feather, Leonard, and Jack Tracy, editors. *Laughter from the Hip: The Lighter Side of Jazz.* New York: Horizon, 1963; reprinted, with an introduction by Leonard Feather, New York: Da Capo, 1979.
A collection of "anecdotes, facetiae, satire, etc.," designed to counterbalance the heavy seriousness and pretentiousness that had come to characterize jazz and, especially, its criticism by the 1960s. Of particular interest to readers of jazz fiction are these contributions by Feather: "Hi-Fi Fable I," "Hi-Fi Fable II," "How I Caught Music Red-Handed," "I Invented Bossa Nova," and "I Invented Jazz Concerts!" (qq.v.)

Federman, Raymond. "Remembering Charlie Parker or How to Get It Out of Your System." *Take It or Leave It: An Exaggerated Second-hand Tale to be Read Aloud Either Standing or Sitting*. New York: Fiction Collective, 1976. Unpaginated.
This story eulogizes Parker and promotes the notion that blackness is essential to the making of jazz, all of this around a concert performance by Parker of "Lover Man."

Feiner, Ruth. *Cat Across the Path*. Translated from the German by Norman Alexander. Philadelphia and London: J. B. Lippincott, 1935.
After meeting on the street, two young Berliners become fast friends, even though they couldn't be more different from each other. Fritz is handsome,

charming, and patrician; Alex is nondescript, sullen, and a burgher. Through
Fritz, Alex becomes deeply interested in music, becoming in time an accomplished pianist and composer. Meanwhile, Fritz moves to Paris to continue his
studies in music and quickly establishes a reputation as the golden boy of the
new jazz. When it becomes clear that Fritz is destined for stardom, he changes
his name to Johnny Groves and quickly becomes the Jazz King of the Western World. The central tension of the novel flows from the obsessions both
men develop for a transcendently beautiful young woman. The plot mechanics governing this triangular relationship are so contrived as to resemble a
soap opera. Nevertheless, the book is valuable as one of the few depictions of
the jazz scene in Germany shortly before World War II. Fritz's defense of the
new music to Alex is historically interesting: ". . . take it from me it [jazz] will
go on developing until one day it will conquer the whole world. Our operas
will be written in jazz, believe me! I admit that to-day it is somewhat exaggerated in form and in its early stages, but I think we are merely at the beginning of something which will one day take the world by storm. Jazz will
bring us melodies and harmonies of an unheard-of beauty!"

Finn, Julio. "The Blue Bayou." In *B Flat, Bebop, Scat*, edited by Chris Parker,
    137–45. London: Quartet, 1986.
Early in the twentieth century a hobo with a guitar enters the bayou country of Louisiana in search of the hoodoo doctor who can put him in touch with
the devil. Although the guitarist hopes to gain supremacy over music, he
learns that in order to accomplish this, he must first get in touch with his own
origins, especially those relating to the slavery of his progenitors.

Fisher, Rudolf. "Common Meter." Parts 1, 2. *Baltimore Afro-American*, Feb-
    ruary 8, 15, 1930, 11, 11.
A humorous piece involving a battle-of-the-bands in late-1920s Harlem
told in a lively, "jazzy" style with much tart dialogue and realistic descriptions of musical performance. As usual, a woman is the cause of the battle between the bands, and because "They can't use knives and they can't use
knucks . . . they got to fight it out with jazz."

Fitzgerald, F. Scott. "Dice, Brassknuckles & Guitar." *Hearst's International
    Magazine*, May 1923. In *The Price Was High: The Last Uncollected Sto-
    ries of F. Scott Fitzgerald*. Edited by Matthew J. Bruccoli, 46–68. New
    York: Harcourt Brace Jovanovich/Bruccoli Clark, 1979.
A comical ("silly" might be more accurate) story dramatizing the implaca-
bility of the rich and the cultural divide between the American North and South.
A leading character gives guitar lessons—and "Bachelor of Jazz" degrees to

those who complete the course—to young ladies who become so rhythmic after a couple of sessions that "you'd think some of 'em was colored."

Fleming, Kathleen Anne. *The Jazz Age Murders.* Berkeley: Creative Arts Book Company, 1999.
Cleary's Jazz Club on Chicago's North Side has been in operation for the better part of a century, since the original Jazz Age. When a young woman is found dead there, one of her friends takes an interest in the club and determines to investigate her friend's death. She discovers unnerving things about the history of Cleary's, and these help her solve the crime in the present, a solution that hinges on saxophone reeds soaked in amphetamines. Modest jazz content.

Flender, Harold. *Paris Blues.* New York: Ballantine, 1957.
Saxophonist Eddie Cook has been an expatriate African-American jazzman in Paris for twelve years and would probably have been content to live out his days there leading a bachelor existence had he not fallen in love with a vacationing African-American school teacher. The primary tension in their relationship derives from his negative memories of racial prejudice in his hometown of Kansas City and her much more positive view of the racial situation in America. Connie's argument combines with Eddie's love to lead him to consider returning home to see for himself whether the racial climate has indeed improved. This novel comprises much discussion of jazz and contains several scenes set in the jazz club where Eddie and his combo have an ongoing gig.

Fletcher, Jessica, and Donald Bain. *Murder in a Minor Key.* New York: Signet, 2001.
Based on the genteel *Murder, She Wrote* television series, the novelization takes Maine's own Miss Marple, Jessica Fletcher, to New Orleans to attend a writers' conference and plump for her new novel, *Murder in a Minor Key.* She meets music critic Wayne Copely, who is obsessed with tracking down rumored early cylinder recordings of legendary trumpeter Little Red LeCoeur, a voodooist. When Copley's body is found in a cemetery next to the grave of an old voodoo queen, Jessica swings into action and soon solves the mystery of her friend's death and locates the invaluable recordings. The book contains frequent references to jazz musicians (mostly from New Orleans), considerable jazz chat, and even snippets of jazz in performance. Interest in the book is, of course, compounded by the fact that it was coauthored by a fictitious character.

Flowers, Arthur. *Another Good Loving Blues.* New York: Viking, 1993; London: Secker and Warburg, 1993.

A love story involving bluesman Lucas Bodeen and conjure woman Melvira Dupree and the forces that threaten their relationship. The story takes place largely in Memphis on famed Beale Street, in the second decade of the twentieth century. Much reference to Delta blues and scattered references to the new music, jazz, which was still in its infancy.

Foote, Shelby. "Ride Out." *Jordan County: A Landscape in Narrative*, 1–52. New York: Dial, 1954. [First published in slightly different form as "Tell Them Goodbye." *Saturday Evening Post*, February 15, 1947.]
After Duff Conway is executed for killing a man, the county physician at the execution cobbles together, from accounts of Duff's friends and acquaintances, a biography of the man, who had been a remarkable cornetist. Born in the Deep South, Duff formed an ineradicable attachment to music at a young age; learned to master his horn, sometimes while behind bars; went north to Harlem, where he expanded his musical horizon; and then returned south to recuperate from tuberculosis. There he killed a man who had stolen his woman.

Forman, Bruce. *Trust Me*. Fort Bragg, CA: Lost Coast Press, 2003.
Sam Mann is a Jewish jazz guitarist in San Francisco who has a mystical affinity with animals. Sam's prospects seem to be too good to be true when he meets a mysterious stranger, Jimm Dibbook, who plays on Sam's vanity and cupidity to convince him that he can make Sam rich and famous. Dibbook soon becomes Sam's manager and sets his new career in motion, after first getting Sam's power of attorney and then convincing him to drop out of sight for several weeks. One doesn't need to be one of the world's deep readers to predict what's in store for Sam. The jazz content of this Faustian fable is solid: The two or three scenes depicting Sam performing with his group carry the ring of authenticity; many jazz artists, mostly beboppers, are referred to; and Sam frequently hums or whistles passages from the classical jazz repertory. A lovely bonus concerns the way Sam unintentionally turns an octogenarian on to jazz. Author Forman is a professional jazz musician.

Forrest, Leon. *The Bloodworth Orphans*. New York: Random House, 1977.
A phantasmagorical account of the complex relationships among the bastards and orphans sired by a slave-owning family, the Bloodworths. The story is told from the perspective of African-Americans who had migrated from the South to the urban ghettoes of the North, in this case the South Side of Chicago. The style and structure reflect the lyricism and improvisational nature of jazz as well as the oratorical style of black Baptist preachers. One major character, Ironwood "Landlord" Rumble, is a jazz musician, and he is at the center of some extended jams, especially in Part 2, Chapter 11, from which this typical paragraph is taken:

"Now from a tower burial lookout site, on the outskirts to the city, Ironwood became the high priest of the tribe, extemporizing upon his royal golden flute, with a faint jangle of the whispering tambourine, a psalm of memory to Lady Day. Celebrating in tongues her time-freezing, prison-love, muted-hypodermic-jellied, sight-blinding, knocking-bones, lean-honed, aching vision, in the frigid, dehydrated valley of bleached dry bones of love, Ironwood's rage-muted violin-sounding flute; and behind *that*, talking, dancing, spirit, meat shaking off their bones, as Big Maybelle, like the huge-hearted felt-flesh life, like Bessie inside the body and blood of Lady's delicate violin song of sorrows . . . Singing them all back to the foundling child in the path-road, tiny enough to fit into a mailbox . . . *Sometimes I feel like I'm almost gone.*"

Fox, Charles. "'Got the World in a Jug, Lawd!'" In *Jazz Parody (Anthology of Jazz Fiction)*, edited by Charles Harvey, 99–110. London: Spearman Publishers, 1948.

After young, enthusiastic cornetist Joe Dumaine is hired to play on a Mississippi riverboat, he believes he has "the world in a jug." Refreshingly, this story dramatizes the positive qualities of the jazz life.

Fox, F. G. *Funky Butt Blues*. New Orleans: St. Expedite, 1994.

A freelance librarian in New Orleans is interviewed by an eccentric old-line citizen to catalog the books of his estate. Early jazz records are found among the books; one of these is suspected of being the only recording of the first jazzman, Buddy Bolden. Much on early jazz and Bolden, more on New Orleans, and most on the mechanics of librarianship.

Frank, Bruno. *The Persians Are Coming*. Translated by H. T. Porter-Lowe. London: Knopf, 1929. [Originally published as *Politische Novelle*. 1928.]

Two sophisticated, liberal diplomats (one French, the other German) analyze the "disease" of Europe and propose possible cures. The disease of course is America with its glamour, wealth, and blacks who have mesmerized Europe with their "diabolical rhythms." One long section focuses on Becky Floyd (unmistakably based on Josephine Baker) and her stunning performance backed by a jazz band: "With a high, nerve-shattering whine the music broke out again, a sudden violent ensemble of all the percussion, tympani, and wind instruments, and all these Negro throats swelled upward in a burst of homage. Becky Floyd came down the steps and began to dance."

Frankel, Haskel. *Big Band*. Garden City, NY: Doubleday, 1965.

Highschooler Bob Allen plays a mean trumpet and is encouraged by early success to drop out of school and pursue a career as a musician. He makes a deal with his dad: if Bob can successfully arrange a summer band tour, then he can quit school to devote himself full-time to music. Bob of course jumps at the opportunity, assembles a band with some of his buddies, and takes to the road—with predictable results: flat tires, miscommunications, and shady managers. Bob and Dad achieve a lovely—if predictable—rapprochement.

Frost, Gregory. "Attack of the Jazz Giants." *Attack of the Jazz Giants and Other Stories,* 133–45. Urbana, IL: Golden Gryphon, 2005.
   Strange things begin to happen on a southern racist's plantation: massive musical instruments mysteriously materialize, as if dropped from heaven, and "jass" seems to crop up everywhere, until the racist, Doc, is killed by the instruments and the magnified sounds of jazz on the radio.

Fuller, Jack. *The Best of Jackson Payne.* New York: Knopf, 2000.
   White, middle-aged musicologist Charles Quinlan has devoted much of his life to the study of jazz and is now embarked on writing a biography of the titular Jackson Payne, a black tenor saxophonist and "the last towering colossus of jazz. Listening to his late works is like being in touch with an element as pure and reactive as free oxygen." In attempting to fathom the truth of Payne's rise and fall, of his tortured existence, of his increasingly—and dauntingly—complex musical ideas, and of his quest for TRUTH through music, Quinlan is compelled to wrestle with the often ambiguous complexities of his own life. This rich novel is notable for the number and variety of voices it employs as Quinlan interviews the folks who had known Payne and for the multifaceted portrait it paints of its protagonist, who is a composite of every agonized artist in the history of modern jazz. It is also notable for the clarity of its dramatization of questions relating to race, sex, drug addiction, the process of creativity, and the search for total originality and, through that, transcendence and spiritual deliverance. The epigraph from James Baldwin is particularly apt: "What one's imagination makes of other people is dictated, of course, by the laws of one's own personality, and it is one of the ironies of black-white relations that, by means of what the white man imagines the black man to be, the black man is enabled to know who the white man is."

Fuller, John. *Tell It Me Again.* London: Chatto & Windus, 1988.
   Hugh, a middle-aged British professor-composer, is in the United States to finish a concerto and to deliver a series of university lectures. In Manhattan he meets a black jazz vocalist, Virginia, and soon falls deeply in lust with her.

She travels with him to Dallas, where he has a visiting professorship. There they enjoy an idyllic relationship until Virginia disappears without warning, turning an erotic tale into a missing-person mystery. Music—classical and jazz—is at the heart of this novel. Not only do we see Hugh struggle with the creative process, but we experience his analyses of the music he listens to: "Hugh had barely time to notice the new effects produced at this tempo, the mockery behind the naïve breaking up of the syllables in 'fam-il-i-ar,' the infinitesimal delay at 'shy' that lent an incalculable sexual challenge to the confession, the rough near-lisp of 'lights'. . . ." Passages like this provide considerable interest and authority to the novel's musical dimension.

Fulmer, David. *Chasing the Devil's Tail*. Scottsdale, AZ: Poisoned Pen Press, 2001.

A researched novel set in New Orleans in 1907 and involving the serial killings of five Storyville prostitutes. "King" Buddy Bolden is a major character, and his loud brass and incipient madness dominate the colorful scene from time to time; at one point he becomes a suspect in the murders. Ferdinand La Menthe (aka Jelly Roll Morton) also makes an appearance and is seen in performance. Although "jass" is much in the air, we're assured, the musical content is rather modest.

———. *Jass: A Valentin St. Cyr Mystery*. Orlando: Harcourt, 2005.

It's 1909 and jass is the rage in the red-light district of New Orleans where, one by one, four players of this new music are murdered. In trying to get to the bottom of these killings, Creole detective Valentin St. Cyr discovers that all four victims had been members of the same band and that the group's only surviving member is in hiding. When Valentin tries to locate a mystery woman he thinks is the linchpin of the case, he becomes aware that certain powerful forces in the community want him to be reassigned, convincing him that larger issues than the deaths of a few black musicians are at play. Jelly Roll Morton is a key character in this atmospheric, researched mystery, which is a sequel to *Chasing the Devil's Tail* (q.v.). Although the spirit of jazz pervades the novel, it seldom occupies center stage.

Gade, Sven. *Jazz Mad: A Stirring Romance of Genius and Love, Based on the Motion Picture Story*. New York: Jacobsen-Hodginson, 1927.

When a luckless immigrant composer fails to get his classical symphony produced, he survives by conducting a gag jazz band—the Goulash Orchestra—that is so bad the management provides vegetables for the patrons to throw at it. Based on the silent movie of the same name starring Jean Hersholt. Not seen.

Gailly, Christian. *An Evening at the Club.* Translated by Susan Fairfield. New
York: Other Press, 2003. [Originally published as *Soir au Club.* Paris: Editions de Minuit, 2001.]

A brief, strange book about a ranking, influential jazz pianist, Simon
Nardis, who inexplicably renounces his calling and the life that goes with it
(e.g., nightclubs and booze). Years later, a coworker invites him to stop at a
jazz club for music and drinks. During intermission, Simon is ineluctably
drawn to the piano, begins to play, and is soon joined by an attractive jazz
chanteuse. Practically at the moment they enter into a relationship, Simon's
wife is killed in an accident. That's it. The novel refers to such musicians as
John Coltrane, Sonny Rollins, and Ornette Coleman, and contains passages
describing music in performance.

Garceau, Phil. "The Price of Swing." In *Jazz Parody (Anthology of Jazz Fiction)*, edited by Charles Harvey, 69–76. London: Spearman Publishers, 1948.

When great black swing bandleader Denny Fletcher falls in love, he compromises his music by becoming commercial in order to win over the beautiful dancer who has joined his band: "If you bought him a drink, he might tell
you how he strived to interpret the sincere music of his race. How a woman
persuaded him to play for the public. How she walked out on him . . . How
he thought he could revert to his beloved swing and still remain in the top
spot. How he flopped."

Gardner, Martin. "The Devil and the Trombone." *The Record Changer* 7
(May 1948): 10.

An allegorical fantasy in which the speaker walks into a chapel where an
angel is playing sonorous chords on the organ; soon the angel is joined by the
devil playing jazzy trombone. Through this collaboration, the speaker (a college professor) achieves an epiphany regarding the seemingly contradictory
nature of jazz. (The popularity of this piece led *The Record Changer* to open
its pages to fiction.)

———. "The Fall of Flatbush Smith." *Esquire*, September 1947, 44.

When the speaker, editor of *Hot Beat* (a magazine "dedicated to be-bop and
other heresies"), stops by a bar in the Flatbush section of Brooklyn, he encounters a jazz trio that is bad beyond compare. The trumpet player, Flatbush
Smith, has an uncanny ability to hit the wrong note. So the speaker hatches a
plan: he'll write an article decrying the egregiousness of Flatbush Smith's
music. Sure enough, the Dixieland magazine, *Blue Beat*, immediately lionizes
the horn man as "the modern master of the off-key note," making him the
man of the moment in jazz circles. But then Flatbush's playing begins to im-

prove to the point that he actually becomes a solid musician. The New Orleans crowd of course condemns Smith for going commercial and abandons him. He is soon hired as a sideman by Guy Lombardo. A spoof of jazz trendiness.

————. "The Trouble with Trombones." *The Record Changer* 7 (October 1948): 10.
A humorous story in which the narrator begins by reflecting on the clownishness of trombone players; then, one night while trying to impress a pretty girl in the audience by manipulating the slide with his toes, he injures himself. So she sits in, taking his place, and impresses everyone with her superior skills—and then disappears. The narrator tracks her down, finds her playing oboe in a symphony orchestra, sits in for her, and then replaces her as she in turn takes to the trombone. Both succeed in their new milieux, marry, and are destined to live happily ever after.

Garvin, Richard M., and Edmond G. Addeo. *The Midnight Special: The Legend of Leadbelly*. New York: Bernard Geis, 1971.
No stereotype is left unturned in this researched, fictionalized biography of Huddy Ledbetter, better known as Leadbelly, whose life in this account is circumscribed by sex, violence, and music, pretty much in equal measures. After early years in the cotton country of Louisiana, Leadbelly periodically finds himself in prison, where he experiences the most degrading, dehumanizing conditions imaginable. Yet, somehow, he is sustained and even, improbably, saved by his music; in fact it twice wins him gubernatorial pardons. Then the folklorists, John Lomax and his son Alan, seek out Leadbelly and attempt to help him capitalize on his talent. When he finally makes it to New York, however, Leadbelly finds not the Promised Land he had hoped for but the same racist conditions he had experienced in the South. Because he is managed by the Lomaxes and performs primarily for white audiences, Leadbelly is accused of Uncle Tomming. In one climactic scene, Josh White publically humiliates him on just such a charge. As inevitably happens in such tales, Leadbelly dies just as his fortunes seem to be turning in the direction of success. Six months later, his song, "Goodnight, Irene," sells two million copies, even as his widow looks for a menial job.

Gibney, Shannon. "How I Remade Coltrane." *Brilliant Corners* 5: 30–52 (Winter 2000).
A coming-of-age story about a Coltrane-obsessed young mulatto who discovers—and accepts—her lesbianism as she prepares to go away to college and a new life.

Gilbert, Edwin. *The Hot and the Cool*. Garden City, NY: Doubleday, 1953.

Music is very much at the center of this novel as it dramatizes the hectic career of a sextet that is coming to terms with the "new" jazz that appeared after World War II. When the band members are not performing, they are discussing the music or going to the city—Manhattan—just across the way from their gig in New Jersey to listen to it. As happens so often in jazz stories, just as the group achieves balance, a female singer materializes, changing the group dynamics and creating a negative impact on the music. Kip, the beloved pianist, falls in love with the vocalist beyond logic and his own considerable resistance (cf. Jake Barnes in Ernest Hemingway's *The Sun Also Rises*). The novel is chock full of references to jazz musicians, clubs, and— of course—the music itself. And, furthermore, it demonstrates the time-honored idea that art has the capacity to heal all.

Gilmour, H. B. *All That Jazz*. New York: Jove, 1979.

Novelization of choreographer-director Bob Fosse's autobiographical musical biopic of the last days of Joe Gideon's sordid, sex-driven life. The jazz is in the dancing.

Gilson, Jamie. *Dial Leroi Rupert, DJ*. New York: Lothrop, Lee & Shepard, 1979.

Three twelve-year-old boys have to come up with $30 in a hurry to pay off a debt, so in desperation they form a jazz trio—clarinet, violin, and comb. They make a few bucks playing "When the Saints Go Marching In" on the Chicago subway but lose it all moving from one car to another. When they then petition Leroi Rupert, popular disc jockey, for help, Rupert hatches a plan to save the day.

Glaser, Elton. "Blue Cat Club." *Louisiana Literature* 3 (1986): 22–27.

A new white boy in town, nine-year-old Luther Thibodeaux, is attracted, as if by a magnet, to the all-black Blue Cat Club and the sound of the jazz saxophone that emanates from it. Luther becomes the subject of a police raid occasioned by the violation of the segregation law but is not found. Instead, he becomes privy to a lovers' quarrel and witnesses a shooting that wounds a musician.

Glatzer, Hal. *The Last Full Measure: A Katy Green Mystery*. Palo Alto & McKinleyville, CA: Perseverance Press/John Daniel & Co., 2006.

The protagonist of this period mystery (the third in a series) is Katy Green, a swing musician equally adroit on sax and violin. She's out of work, and a cold winter looms when she lands the gig of her dreams: she's hired to join an all-girl band—"The Swingin' Sarongs"—on a cruise ship bound for Hawaii. Katy's dream gig is soon compromised, however, as she becomes embroiled in a murder case, international intrigue, and the encroachment of World War II.

———. *Too Dead to Swing: A Katy Green Mystery.* Santa Barbara, CA: Perseverance Press, 2002.
The first in a series of swing era mysteries featuring Katy Green, a saxophonist and violinist and amateur detective. Unemployed in California and eager to return to New York, she is offered a job touring with an all-woman swing band, the Ultra Belles, when their violinist turns up dead, possibly from a hatpin misadventure. Because the Belles' extraprofessional lives are bounded by liquor, drugs, and sex, Katy assumes the role of den mother as the band tours by train. And, because she once had a pleasant affair with the Belles' Lothario bandleader, she sets out to uncover the killer when other crimes follow. This lighthearted mystery refers to several jazz notables of the period and includes in the text original songs composed by the author. The most prominent is "Walking on Eggshells," which (coincidentally?) echoes the title of Herbert Simmons's serious jazz novel, *Man Walking on Eggshells* (q.v.).

Goldsher, Alan. *Jam.* Sag Harbor, NY: The Permanent Press, 2002.
Two pre-teen neighbors become fast friends when they discover their mutual love for jazz, especially bebop. And they are both prodigiously talented musicians, "jazz geek" Frank on percussion and wonderboy James (later "Jam") on any instrument that falls his way but especially sax. After high school they form a combo that "plays cool, obscure hard-bop tunes" and develops a solid local following. But because James wants more, they begin to blend their pure jazz with rock, creating a unique bop rock that thrills their fellow Chicagoans and captures the attention of a record company maven, who signs them to a contract, renames them "Jam," and records an album that rapidly climbs the charts. Much attention is paid to the mechanics of the cutthroat music business, the travails of touring, the high price of fame, and the deteriorating relationship between the egotistical James and the jazz purist Frank, who is going to make it through life by playing "jazzified pop ditties" as if they were Mingus compositions and by marrying his high school dream girl. Many mainstream jazz artists are mentioned, and jazz is very much at the center of this novel. Author Goldsher is a professional bassist.

Gollub, Matthew. *The Jazz Fly.* Illustrated by Karen Hanke. Santa Rosa, CA: Tortuga, 2000.

When a fly who speaks jazz asks different critters directions to town he hears music in their oinks and rrribits, inspiring him to perform an outstanding solo at a supper club that night. There is an "Author's Note" at the end explaining the book's relationship to jazz, especially scatting, and a CD of the author narrating the story accompanied by a jazz quartet. For young children.

Goonan, Kathleen Ann. *Crescent City Rhapsody.* New York: Avon Eos, 2000.
    One of author Goonan's so-called jazz novels, this one—like the others—takes place in the near future, at the moment when the world suffers a communications blackout: everything related to electronics and computer science fails. When a brilliant astronomer, using instruments of his own invention and manufacture, discovers the source of the calamity, he places himself, his family, and everything he loves at risk. Another plot strand involves a woman mob boss whose enormous wealth had allowed her to purchase resurrection insurance. The author, in her "Acknowledgments and Thanks," lists half a dozen books on jazz that provided her with "critical insights," and claims that Duke Ellington's *Music Is My Mistress* "provided the backbone of the musical framework of the book." Indeed, Duke Ellington is a character in the novel as, to a lesser extent, is Ellington's singer Ivie Anderson, and the title derives from a piece Ellington (in the context of the story) was commissioned to write. There is also a character named Sun Ra, who is presumably the female reincarnation of, appropriately for a science fiction novel, the *Space Is the Place* orchestra leader, and the chapters have jazz-related titles ("Diminuendo in D.C.," "Second Solo: Japanoiserie," and so on). Finally, the author thanks her father for "imprinting" her "with jazz from infancy."

——. *Light Music.* New York: Eos, 2002.
    In this, the author's final epic vision of a nanotechnological future, the haven called Crescent City has become vulnerable to attack by outsiders who covet the wealth and security it offers. When a pirate attack threatens, one of the original founders of the community, Jason Peabody, and his friend Dania flee westward to escape the onslaught. On their journey they encounter manifestations of surpassing strangeness, including talking animals, conscious machines, and toys that long to be real. As the Earth awaits another amazing transformation, it has been quieted by "the Silence" from space, and the survivors are drawn to the "light music" that is drawing them to the stars. The *only* reference to jazz—and it does seem to be an important one—occurs when one character observes another making music, causing him to reflect: "She is creating something entirely new. It's all jazz, of course. Jazz does not connect to the past. It connects to the present. It flows from the present. It's not reconstructed. It is improvisational. Wholly conscious. A field of poten-

tial called into physical being, instant by instant. Her mind resonates with other aspects of the improvisation that are not audible to most of us." The author discusses the relationship of jazz to her novels on her home page (http://goonan.con/essay.html).

―――. *Mississippi Blues*. New York: Tom Doherty, 1997.

This equally long sequel to *Queen City Jazz* (q.v.) continues the adventures of Verity and Blaze while adding several other important characters and employing multiple narrative perspectives. Here, Verity assumes the responsibility of helping the now-free but vulnerable citizens of Cincinnati to reach the mysterious city of New Orleans, where (rumor has it) salvation awaits. To accomplish this lofty goal, Verity causes a monstrous nanotech riverboat to be built. The novel is the account of this boat's journey to its destination. The blues are everywhere: when the characters aren't listening to the blues, they are playing, singing, composing, or studying them. One of the characters (a professor of the blues) has gone so far as to create a virtual blues show in which, for example, she duets with Robert Johnson. If that's not enough, the author has given all but a very few chapters blues titles: "Free-fall Blues," "Soul Change Blues," "Dead Men Blues," "Doppelgänger Blues," ad infinitum.

―――. *Queen City Jazz*. New York: Tom Doherty, 1994.

A very long, futuristic novel in which nanotech plagues have decimated the world population. The protagonist, Verity, her dog, Cairo, and the corpse of her best friend Blaze set off in search of the Enlivened City of Cincinnati, where Blaze might be brought back to life. They do indeed find the city, and Blaze is returned to life, but instead of the utopia they had imagined, they find a surrealistic nightmare of a place. Blaze, we learn two-thirds of the way through the novel, plays jazz piano and seems on the verge of making a musical breakthrough on the order of the one Charlie Parker made. As Verity's new acquaintance, saxophonist Sphere, says of Blaze: "He can do anything— Joplin, Jelly Roll Morton; he can sound like Oscar Peterson or Bill Evans but he's beyond that . . . he's burned through the whole history of jazz and he's just *himself*." In a baseball game between the Cincinnati Reds and the Atlanta Bees toward the end of the book, Billie Holiday pitches, Dizzy Gillespie plays outfield, and Charlie Parker hits a game-winning home run.

Gorman, Ed. "Muse." In *Murder . . . and All That Jazz*, edited by Robert J. Randisi, 185–222. New York: Signet, 2004.

Three small-town journalists—two guys and a woman—are connected by their love for jazz and the men's lust for the gorgeous gal, Dulcy. One of the guys, Dave, becomes famous almost overnight when his songs start to appear on the charts. When he returns from southern California (with a new face and persona) for a visit and to resume his pursuit of Dulcy, he is killed. A couple of years later, in a neat, amoral twist, Dulcy is becoming a famous jazz singer: she's up for four Grammys and has the third lead in the new Julia Roberts movie.

Gould, Philip. *Kitty Collins*. Chapel Hill, NC: Algonquin, 1986.

A long novel centering on the life of Kitty Collins, who becomes a jazz pianist. The book attempts to evoke the excitement of the New York jazz scene in the 1940s but succeeds primarily in cataloguing the names of clubs and musicians.

Granelli, Roger. *Out of Nowhere*. Bridgend, Wales: Seren, 1995.

Encouraged by friends and musicians, 27-year-old Welshman Frank Magnani, a guitarist, migrates to New York in 1957 to try his luck in the world of jazz. He wins a place in an otherwise all-black combo under a leader more interested in making money than making *real* music. Frank, anxious to be on the cutting edge of bebop, is dissatisfied and soon fired, after being taken under the wing of the group's older, wiser drummer, Pearson. But Frank soon has to leave town: not only has he slept with Pearson's young sweetheart but he thinks he may have killed a drug dealer in a fight. After a stint playing music in a home for mongoloids in Florida, he gets into another fight, flees to Greece, returns much wiser to New York, achieves musical and financial success, and is cut down by the drug dealer he had fought before. Perhaps his compositions will outlive him. Although the novel is weak, the author, a professional musician himself, provides generally solid musical descriptions, as in this typical excerpt: "Magnani played the introduction to 'Lover Man,' the old Billie Holliday [*sic*] ballad. The vibes man beat out a soft support on his keys and the bass player voiced complicated lines that felt their way to the heart of the song. Between them they gave Magnani the platform he needed. . . . He began with Holliday's [*sic*] phrasing but now arpeggiated his chords in the most innovative way he could, trying to achieve something smooth and round, but also fresh and his own. He sucked in confidence from the approbation of Pearson, from whom came the faintest whisper of 'play man, you've got 'em.'"

Grant, James. *Don't Shoot the Pianist*. London: Judy Piatkus, 1980.

Lew Jackson's life has gone downhill. He had made a name for himself as a jazz musician, but then his wife left him, his playing suffered, and jazz (since this is the 1960s) lost its cachet. Now he manages, with a partner, the South Bank Jazz Club, the antithesis of Ronnie Scott's clean, comfortable venue on the other side of London. Things start to look up when Lew finagles the support of a young entrepreneur to put on a spectacular jazz festival. Meanwhile, Lew's female interest, a Jamaican hooker, turns up missing, and the concert falls into the hands of an underworld boss. But, after the fashion of lighthearted crime stories, everything turns out well in the end: not only is the festival a success, but Lew is offered a plummy gig by Ronnie Scott himself. Some of the musicians who appear at the festival and play bit parts in the novel are Dave McKenna, Kenny Davern, Scott Hamilton, Clark Terry, Joe Williams, Dizzy Gillespie, Ray Curtis, and Big Mama Richards. Among musicians, the last two play the biggest roles. One suspects they are ringers. The festival itself is well described.

Gray, Denis. *Benny's Last Blast*. Pittsburgh: Dorrance, 2002.
Overworked jazz angel Sebastian B. Coles III ("Benny") is sent to Planet Earth by God and His Jazz Council to attempt to reinvigorate a once popular jazz club, Pete's Place, that has fallen on hard times. Benny is to do this by gigging on his heavenly trumpet in company with Bill Monday's Blue Monday Combo, which is comprised of four formerly great musicians who are now past their prime. The question is whether Benny will be able to perform this "miracle" or cause God and His Council to think They chose the wrong angel for the mission.

Green, Benny. *Blame It on My Youth*. London: MacGibbon and Kee, 1967.
An autobiographical novel in three parts concerning a young man (called "Benny Green") during World War II in England. He "resolved to become a jazz musician or die in the attempt" by the time he was sixteen. Part One, "Davensburg," contains most of the book's musical content as it focuses on Benny and his mostly "secular Jewish" friends, all of whom are enthralled by jazz. Davensburg is reputed to be a jazz genius, and much of Part One is devoted to Benny's pursuit of him and, perhaps, of reflected glory. Many classic artists and their music are mentioned, including Benny's two-night gig with Stan Kenton as a professional saxophonist.

———. *Fifty-eight Minutes to London*. London: MacGibbon and Kee, 1969.
An insider's view of struggling young musicians in the Brighton dance-hall scene of the 1950s. The narrator Tom and his buddy Landau are the struggling saxophonists in question; unfortunately they are jazzmen and the only work they can find is in dance bands with names like The Noveltones and Van Rhodes and the Modernaires. The boys amuse themselves from time to time by insinuating jazz into their routines, to the dismay of their boss and the delight of the dancers. Their threadbare lives are further complicated by tawdry romances and idiosyncratic politics.

Green, David Paul. "Blues Man." *Crosscurrents Magazine*, 1987. http://www
.davidpaulgreen.com/fiction/bluesman.html (3 June 2005).
The down-and-out harp-playing blues man of the title explains his commitment to the blues: "I only play one blues song—mine—and it ain't got no
name and it don't ever end and it don't ever sound like the same song. It's
kind of like time, set to music." He's in sunny Southern California, and the
world has become dauntingly complicated and vast, but he'll keep on playing
his blues anyway.

———. "Bohemian Jazz Boys Hit the Town." *Kola* [Montreal], 1993. http://
www.davidpaulgreen.com/fiction/jazzboys.html (4 June 2005).
The year is 1950 and Dexter Travis and his Bohemian Jazz Boys are the
hottest band in the land, especially since Dizzy and Bird are in Europe. When
Travis needs a horn player, he auditions a skinny, pathetic white guy who
looks too young to lift, let alone play, a trumpet. But when he puts horn to
lips, Peterson blows Travis away, and is hired on the spot. Although Peterson
is an hour late for his first gig, he amazes everyone with his energy and expertise. Nevertheless, he *was* late, and the club owner refuses to pay him. So
he quits, saying that the band was too tame for his taste anyway. The force of
the substantial jazz content of this story is seriously compromised when, after an extended description of a raucous performance of " 'Round Midnight,"
the speaker says they finished the piece "the way Diz wrote it, nice and easy."
Internal evidence suggests that the writer confused two composers *and* two
quite different pieces of music.

Green, Howie. *Jazz Fish Zen: Adventures in Mamboland*. Boston-Rutland, VT
and Tokyo: Charles E. Tuttle, 1992.
In this brightly illustrated philosophical fable, saxophone-playing wan-
derer, Jazz Fish, finds himself in Mamboland, where he undergoes an experience that leads him in the direction of enlightenment; this Zen experience requires Jazz Fish to reconceptualize his notions of reality.

Greenlee, Sam. "Blues for Little Prez." *Black World*, August 1973. In
NOMMO: A Literary Legacy of Black Chicago (1967–1987), edited by Carole A. Parks, 141–47. Chicago: OBAhouse, 1987.
Nicknamed after Lester Young, "Little Prez" "couldn' do nothin' else 'cep
rap an' he could rap like the real Prez blew, an' when Little Prez got big
everybody knew he was gonna blow tenor too." Trouble is, "Little Prez" can't
blow a lick so he squanders his life by shooting up, listening to jazz records,
and dying young. Told in urban black vernacular, this story raises provocative
questions about race, drugs, and jazz. Frequent references to jazz notables, especially Count Basie's men.

Grennard, Elliott. "Sparrow's Last Jump." *Harper's*, May 1947, 419–26.

Based on Charlie Parker's notorious "Lover Man" recording session, which the author (himself a professional musician) had attended, this story underscores the Parker figure's (Sparrow's) disintegration from drugs and mental incapacity.

Grime, Kitty. "Seeing Her Off." In *B Flat, Bebop, Scat*, edited by Chris Parker, 22–30. London: Quartet, 1986.

Obnoxious vocalist Gennie succeeds in the unfeeling, male-dominated world of jazz—but her success doesn't last long. The story is structured around telephone conversations and answering-machine messages.

Guralnick, Peter. *Nighthawk Blues*. New York: Seaview, 1980.

A young white music promoter in the Northeast tracks down a legendary old bluesman, Screamin' Nighthawk (real name: Theodore Roosevelt Jefferson), in Mississippi and tries to turn him into a national star, even though he is old and feeble. Readers interested in the recrudescence of the Delta blues in the 1960s will find much of interest here.

Gwinn, William. *Jazz Bum*. New York: Lion, 1954.

A very pulpy story featuring Vic Ravenna, son of immigrants living in New York's Lower East Side. As a teenager, Vic becomes seriously interested in mastering jazz clarinet; at the same time he develops an interest in reefer, booze, and Zora, who becomes an obsession with him. Vic spends a year in a reformatory, where he hones his musical skills. When he gets out, he starts playing professionally, eventually abandoning swing for progressive jazz, at which he becomes the "crown prince." Meanwhile, Zora has become a chanteuse (and a slut to boot). For over 15 years Vic has not been able to get Zora out of his head—but when he encounters her, he sees through her for the first time, allowing him to transcend his obsession and declare his love to his nice-Nelly sweetheart. The last lines of the book are spectacular in their badness: "'What? Wh-what d-did you say?' There was a loveable little catch in that pretty voice when she was breathless. 'I want to say it real andante, so you'll hear it.' 'Say it! Please say it, Vicky, before I faint!' 'I love you, apple,' Vic said."

――――――. *A Way with Women*. New York: Lion, 1954.

This, too, like the author's *Jazz Bum* (q.v.), which was published in the same year, concerns a jazz bum with a woman problem. John Brian Connaught plays guitar in a nightclub. He is involved with three babes and in debt to the bad guys for over $11,000. When his troubles threaten to overwhelm him, he plays his violin on the streetcorner. There are a few references to music in performance and to buying guitar strings and the like, but the musical content is pretty light (and lame). There must be hundreds of these paperback originals from the 1950s that are lying undiscovered in the dustbin of schlock fiction. R.I.P.

"Hamlet's Clown." *Jazz Today* 2, no. 2 (March 1957): 29.

A maudlin story about Roger, who hadn't been a very good musician. When he was drafted (World War II), he was sent South. One night he sought out some jazz, went into the black part of town, and was beaten to death.

Hanley, Jack. *Hot Lips*. New York: Designs Publishing, 1952.

An extremely rare pulp novel that proclaims itself to be much, much more lurid than it actually is. The cover depicts one woman playing torrid sax and another dancing sexily, while a man, tie akimbo, sits transfixed. The cast of characters includes bandleader Solly Royall, "Midwife to the music of a collection of drunks, tarts, hoydens, tea-hounds, and 'nice girls.'" Many readers of this "Intimate Novel #18" must have been disappointed to discover that the title refers only to the playing of musical instruments. The story is unsurprisingly simple: when the lead saxophonist of the all-girl band is hospitalized with delirium tremens, a replacement materializes almost immediately, the beautiful and talented 19-year-old Althea Allen. She is desperate to escape her evil stepfather who, in concert with the musical motif, "wanted to fiddle" (with Althea, of course). Band manager Pete Dwyer falls instantly in love with Althea, but so does fellow band member Mona Storm, whose second husband has stolen her clothes to enter a drag contest. The vagabond (i.e., traveling) band prospers, Althea becomes a star, and she and Pete are destined to live happily-ever-after. Descriptions of the band's rehearsing and performing are approximately as convincing as the plot.

Hannah, Barry. "Testimony of Pilot." *Airships*, 17–44. New York: Knopf, 1978.

A coming-of-age account of two boys who play together in the high school band and later, in college, put together a group called "Bop Friends." The piano-playing narrator, William, becomes deaf but makes it through college anyway, while his saxophone-playing chum becomes a pilot and goes to Vietnam. Slight jazz content apart from scattered references to jazz artists of the day (including Stan Kenton, Paul Desmond, and Joe Morello).

Hardwick, Elizabeth. *Sleepless Nights*. New York: Random House, 1979.

Part Three of this memory quilt of a novel contains reflections on the doomed Billie Holiday, including the artist's strange relationship with her mismatched mother. Minimal jazz content otherwise.

Harvey, Charles, ed. *Jazz Parody (Anthology of Jazz Fiction)*. London: Spearman, 1948.
A collection of parodic fictions. See entries in this volume for Austin, Alex; Boyce, David; Brand, Pat; Dabinett, Ward; Douglas, Archie; Evans, Robert; Fox, Charles; Garceau, Phil; McCarthy, Albert J.; Ramsey, Frederick, Jr.; Shirley, Peter.

Harvey, John. *Cold Light*. New York: Henry Holt, 1994; London: Heinemann, 1994.
A pretty conventional plot revolving around a psychopathic killer. Jazz lover Charlie Resnick presides over this gritty procedural. In his leisure time, this British detective tends his four cats, all named after bebop musicians (Dizzy, Miles, Bud, and Pepper), listens to jazz, and reads *The Penguin Guide to Jazz*.

———. "Cool Blues." In *Blue Lightning*, edited by John Harvey, 127–44. London: Slow Dancer Press, 1998; Chester Springs, PA: Dufour Editions, 1999.
Jazz-loving detective Charlie Resnick is called in on a case involving a handsome con man who has been fleecing the women he so expertly picks up. Resnick recognizes the con man's aliases as little known brass men from Duke Ellington's orchestras and is thus able to solve the case.

———. *Cutting Edge*. New York: Henry Holt, 1991.
In the few leisure moments when Charlie Resnick is away from a case involving increasingly violent attacks against staff members of a large teaching hospital, he listens to Art Pepper and Clifford Brown. Charlie's friend, jazz musician Ed Silver, makes a prominent appearance.

———. "Drummer Unknown." In *Murder . . . and All That Jazz*, edited by Robert J. Randisi, 69–84. New York: Signet, 2004.
It's the London jazz scene in the 1950s, and the junkie drummer of the title is coerced by a bad plainclothes bobby to supply information on drug use among musicians, but the drummer does the right thing when the cop oversteps the terms of their agreement.

———. *Easy Meat*. New York: Henry Holt, 1996; London: Heinemann, 1996.
British cop Charlie Resnick is a jazz aficionado whose primary form of unwinding is reading about and listening to jazz, primarily straightahead bebop, like Lester Young, Howard McGhee, and Thelonious Monk. The music goes far to characterize Resnick as a deeply caring person whose ability to sympa-

thize with others derives from his own suffering. The characters in this violent police procedural do truly dreadful things to each other.

——. "Favor." In *Like a Charm: A Novel in Voices*, edited by Karin Slaughter, 177–96. New York: HarperCollins, 2004.
Private investigator Jack Kiley gets a much needed assignment to keep watch over jazz singer Dianne Adams, who has a gig at Ronnie Scott's jazz club. Kiley then manages to get an old friend hired to play sax in Adams's backup group. Just as Kiley starts to wonder why he's been hired, he finds himself embroiled in a dangerous bit of business emanating from a brief affair Adams had had with another woman the last time she was in London.

——. *In a True Light*. London: William Heinemann, 2001; New York: Carroll and Graf, 2002.
After serving two years in prison for art forgery, Sloane returns to his studio in North London to find a delinquent letter from the successful abstract-expressionist painter—Jane Graham—he'd had a passionate affair with four decades earlier in New York. Sloane goes to Pisa, where Jane lies dying, to discover that he had fathered a child with Jane. She now wants him to locate their daughter and attempt to effect a posthumous reconciliation with her. In his attempt to locate and then protect his daughter, Sloane returns to New York, and his return there triggers flashbacks to the vibrant art and music scenes of the 1950s. Sloane's daughter turns out to be a jazz singer, following in the tradition of Sloane's parents. The novel contains many references to the artists, writers, and musicians of the 1950s, including Frank O'Hara, Jackson Pollock, and Thelonious Monk, all of whom are seen in one kind of action or another. One scene in particular, depicting Monk and John Coltrane at the Five Spot, is truly memorable. One wonders if the digressive technique of the novel is intended to reflect the improvisational nature of jazz. Whoever referred to this book as "bop noir" came up with a catchy phrase, but perhaps the novel is ultimately too sanguine to feel comfortable in the noir category.

——. *Last Rites*. London: William Heinemann, 1998; New York: Henry Holt, 1999.
In this, the tenth and final novel in the Charlie Resnick series, the detective goes in search of a prisoner who had been released on compassionate furlough before disappearing into the lower depths of Nottingham, where a crime wave threatens to engulf the city. As usual, jazz contributes significantly to the novel's rich atmosphere, but the book's most interesting relation to the music comes in the "Coda," where Harvey writes, "I think that it was jazz that kept Charlie sane, that provided him with both release and inspira-

tion. Me, too. In the writing of these books I have relied, again and again, on the music of Duke Ellington, Billie Holiday, Thelonious Monk, Spike Robinson, Ben Webster with Art Tatum, and Lester Young. Let it live on." Harvey's newsletter, not incidentally, is called *In a Mellotone.*

————. *Living Proof.* New York: Henry Holt, 1995.
Apart from a saxophonist-in-action on the cover and a nice reference to Art Tatum and Ben Webster, this book contains little jazz content, as Detective Charlie Resnick tries to get to the bottom of a series of attacks in Nottingham's red-light district.

————. *Lonely Hearts.* New York: Henry Holt, 1989.
In this, the first in the Charlie Resnick police procedurals, Charlie goes in search of the killer or killers who prey on lonely women who make the mistake of seeking companionship through the lonely hearts column of the newspaper. Charlie's love of jazz surfaces whenever he is home with his four cats, all named after American jazz greats. At one point Charlie overhears someone whistling the Glenn Miller songbook and resolves to get him (or her) some Ellington for Christmas; at another, he reflects on the sad life of Billie Holiday as he analyzes one of her recordings. Billie Holiday with Lester Young seems a perfect combination for a novel of lonely hearts.

————. *Now's the Time: The Complete Resnick Short Stories.* London: Heinemann, 2002. [This is an updated and slightly expanded edition of the book published under the same title: London: Slow Dancer, 1999.]
The first eleven stories in this collection take their titles from the Charlie Parker songbook, the last from Billie Holiday's: "Now's the Time," "Dexterity," "She Rote," "Confirmation," "Bird of Paradise," "Cheryl," "Work," "Stupendous," "My Little Suede Shoes," "Cool Blues," "Slow Burn," and "Billie's Blues" (the only story that doesn't appear in the earlier edition). Although all of the stories connect somehow to their musical titles, the first one and the final two contain the most significant jazz content. The opening story, "Now's the Time," is in fact much more interesting for its musical content than for its feeble mystery, which involves Charlie having his pocket picked by a pathetic young whore. Unrelated to the "case," Charlie's friend, saxophonist Ed Silver, dies shortly after lamenting the deaths of all the old beboppers. The story ends at the renowned jazz club, Ronnie Scott's, where Charlie sits, alone, listening to one of his favorite tenor players, Spike Robinson, who dedicates the final song of the set ("Now's the Time") to the memory of Ed Silver. The penultimate story in the collection, "Slow Burn," begins with Resnick nursing his insomnia by listening to Thelonious Monk in the

wee, small hours, when he is called out on a case involving a jazz club that went up in flames leaving a scorched body inside. Charlie's investigation brings him together with the club's owner, a longtime acquaintance, and jazz dominates their conversation. A symbol-monger would doubtless make much of the incinerated jazz club at the story's center. In the final story, "Billie's Blues," Charlie is reacquainted with a prostitute he had known from an earlier case, as he tries to track down the killer of a fifteen-year-old hooker. Billie Holiday's blues provides melancholy accompaniment to the broken-down lives of the characters in the story, including those of Charlie and Eileen. Underscoring the jazz relationship to these stories are a "Coda," in which the author talks briefly about the jazz underpinnings of the stories, and "A Partial Soundtrack," in which are listed Charlie Resnick's favorite jazz recordings.

––––––. *Still Water*. New York: Henry Holt, 1997.
This ninth Charlie Resnick procedural begins with the "flow and swing" of Milt Jackson's music as Charlie goes in search of a serial killer and ends with Charlie closing in on his prey against a background of Duke Ellington music.

––––––. *Wasted Years*. New York: Henry Holt, 1993.
In this case, Charlie Resnick struggles with his own past as he tries to get to the bottom of a nasty series of robberies that are becoming ever more violent. Quite a few references to jazz musicians (including Paul Gonsalves, Charlie Mariano, and Ella Fitzgerald) and magazines (*Jazz FM*, *Jazz Monthly*), a scene in a jazz club, an interesting exchange over the album, *The Unique Thelonious Monk*, and an explanation of how Charlie came to name his cats after Dizzy Gillespie, Miles Davis, Art Pepper, and Bud Powell.

Harvey, John, ed. *Blue Lightning*. London: Slow Dancer Press, 1998; Chester Springs, PA: Dufour Editions, 1999.
An apparently commissioned collection of "eighteen brand new stories," each of which revolves around music of some kind. For jazz- and blues-related stories, see entries for Carter, Charlotte ("A Flower Is a Lovesome Thing"); Harvey, John ("Cool Blues"); Moody, Bill ("Grace Notes"); Mosley, Walter ("Blue Lightning"); Robinson, Peter ("Memory Lane"); Sallis, James; Thompson, Brian. Titles are given in parentheses when the author is represented by more than a single entry in this bibliography.

Hassler, Jon. *Rookery Blues*. New York: Ballantine, 1995.
A long campus novel that takes place in the turbulent 1960s. Rookery State College in Rookery, Minnesota, is an academic backwater in a place that's about as far north as you can get and still be in the United States. Five faculty members, all yearning for some sort of community, almost miraculously discover the

kind of companionship that brings deep satisfaction to their lives; they accomplish this through the jazz combo they form one frigid winter afternoon, The Ice-jam Quintet. But when the first labor union in the school's history comes disruptively into town, the musicians must struggle with their various allegiances.

Hautman, Chad. *Billie's Ghost.* 2002. New York: Plume, 2004.

Casey was a pretty ordinary (and not very interesting) guy whose existence was made meaningful by his relationship with his wife, Virginia, so when she dies in an auto accident, he gives up on life and wallows in self-pity, drinking to forget and listening to the wonderful jazz that had helped bring them so close. One night a mysterious black woman may or may not materialize in his home; if she does, she may—or may not—be a reincarnation of Billie Holiday. Indeed, she resembles the great singer and sounds like her, too. Few readers will not be able to predict what happens next. Yes, her influence leads Casey to reembrace life to the extent that he is reaching out to help others at the end. This short, generally hokey novel contains many references to jazz, especially to the person and music of Billie Holiday. In fact, whenever Casey's black benefactress is present, she sings snippets from Lady Day's signature songs as a way of bringing dramatic emphasis to the scene-at-hand.

Hellenga, Robert. *Blues Lessons.* New York: Scribner, 2002.

Martin Dijksterhuis is quite contented growing up in an agricultural community in Michigan during the 1950s. He finds comfort in his extended family and in the reassuring patterns and rhythms of the natural world. But his life changes irrevocably during his junior year in high school when, through the influence of the migrant workers who come north every year to pick fruit, he discovers his true calling—the blues—and falls in love with Corinna Williams, the daughter of the black foreman of the fruitpickers. These related complications conspire to take Martin far from home, both literally and metaphorically, before returning him years later in a way he could never have envisioned. Very much a blues story: Martin's apprenticeship on the guitar is detailed; many blues musicians are referenced, not always just in passing; and several scenes contain music being performed. The song "Corinna, Corinna" is prominent and so is the issue of race.

Henk, Michael. *Die Trompete.* Stuttgart: Franckh' sche Verlagshandlung, W. Keller, 1963.

A novel, in German, each chapter of which contains an epigraph from a famous jazz musician—Dave Brubeck, Turk Murphy, Lester Young, Duke Ellington, et al. One passage that I was able to translate suggests that it is a story of love and jazz: "I actually found everything in this city: you and jazz."

Hentoff, Nat. *Does This School Have Capital Punishment?* New York: Delacorte, 1981.

In school, trouble seems to follow Sam Davidson around, so when he enrolls in New York's prestigious Burr Academy everyone wonders how long he will last. At first, Sam seems to be making a comfortable adjustment; he even becomes absorbed by an oral history assignment that brings him into close contact with a legendary jazz trumpeter, Major Kelley. When Sam is wrongfully accused by a teacher of possessing marijuana, his school career is jeopardized. But Major Kelley comes to the rescue—a black man saving a privileged white kid. This young adult novel contains significant jazz content, from references to jazz musicians to the history of the genre.

———. *Jazz Country*. New York: Harper, 1965.

Intended for a juvenile audience, this is the story of a white boy who is influenced by black musicians to become a jazz trumpeter. As in many "Young Adult" works, the protagonist is faced with the dilemma of whether to go on to college after graduation or try to make it as a musician. The novel is at least as much interested in civil rights as it is in jazz.

Hermanos, Steve. *Strange Jazz.* San Jose: Writers Club, 2001.

A narrative that shuttles effectively between an exhausted Midwestern area and the chaotically vibrant East Village scene of Manhattan during the 1970s and 1980s. The narrator is Jack Pierce, one of three brothers to leave their Kansas homestead for the bright lights of the big city. One of Jack's brothers, Benji, is a sickeningly successful Wall Street yuppie, while the other, Archie, is an idealistic journalist. When Archie creates a shelter for the homeless after the Tompkins Square riots, infuriating Benji, music-critic Jack tries to restore familial peace. Although the author claims to have written under the influence of jazz, the book contains only modest musical content. There are references to jazz musicians, including a very nice set piece on Billy Higgins at Bradley's; a scene in which Jack blunders in trying to interview a female, up-and-coming baritone saxophonist; and a recurring character, Cal Klontz, who had played with Ellington, Parker, and Davis but is now—like jazz—on the skids.

Herzhaft, Gerard. *Long Blues in A Minor*. Translated by John Duval. Fayetteville, AR and London: University of Arkansas Press, 1988. [Originally published as *Un long blues en la mineur*. Editions Ramsay, 1986.]

During the French liberation in World War II, a teenage French boy is befriended by a black American soldier, Sugar, who gives the boy his stacks of comics and records when he returns to the States. Much later, the boy (now a man) plays the records for the first time and discovers "the America of the blues." Then Champollion starts playing the guitar to the accompaniment of Sugar's records. After that he takes to playing in the streets until he is roughed up several times by the gendarmes. So he gets a good job, makes a success of it, and then, to the amazement of all, quits to pursue his interest in the blues. After seeing an American blues singer in Paris, he determines to go to Chicago to follow his passion. There, he insinuates himself into the black community, where he attempts to locate the legendary Big Johnny White. When he finds his quarry, the two of them bus to Clarksdale, Mississippi, where the protagonist experiences segregated America for the first time. After his encounter with black America, "The blues stuck to my skin, not a music but a state of mind." In short, a novel with a sociological perspective and a message that you don't have to be black to experience the blues.

Hesse, Hermann. *Steppenwolf*. Translated by Basil Creighton. New York: Henry Holt, 1929. [Originally published as *Der Steppenwolf*. Berlin: Fischer, 1927.]

Nearing 50, Harry Haller is a victim of his time: because of the alienation and fragmentation of the modern world, he feels spiritually empty and even suicidal. Yet although he is the quintessence of civilized man, he feels the tug of another, repressed dimension of his personality—the part that urges him to act on instinct and embrace freedom. Just as Harry approaches the nadir of his existence, he encounters several reality teachers. One of these is saxophonist Pablo, a handsome, amoral, bisexual sensualist who, when Harry defends the music of the masters over the purveyors of transitory music like jazz, replies that qualitative differences between different kinds of music are irrelevant because the only objective of the musician is to perform as well as he can and provide pleasure to his audience. In short, modern man should abandon intellection in favor of hedonism and instinct. Jazz functions in the novel to express this idea and at the same time to represent, for Haller, the degradation of European culture as represented by the influence of American music and the influx of African-Americans.

Hewat, Alan V. *Lady's Time*. New York: Harper and Row, 1985.

The Lady of the title is Winslow, not Day, and she is an attractive woman of mixed blood passing for white in New England after fleeing an abusive life in turn-of-the-century New Orleans. She supports herself and her son by giving music lessons and playing ragtime piano at a local inn. When she dies mysteriously in 1919, some suspect murder, others mischance. The reader, knowing more than the characters, believes that Lady Winslow's death is her debt for making a pact with voodoo spirits to save her son from premature death. The

late William Matthews's jacket blurb is too lovely—and accurate—not to
quote in part: "At the heart of *Lady's Time* is Alan Hewat's understanding of
how ragtime and jazz both subverted and transcended the racially pained culture that nourished them. And of how that music, for the brave, came to be
about freedom and the acceptance of death. . . ."

Hijuelos, Oscar. *The Mambo Kings Play Songs of Love.* New York: Farrar
    Straus Giroux, 1989.
A lush, exuberant, nostalgic novel that traces the lives of brothers Cesar and
Nestor Castillo as they move from their native Cuba to New York in 1949, hoping to become mambo stars like their heroes Desi Arnaz and Xavier Cugat. They
succeed to the extent that they and their band, the Mambo Kings, make popular
recordings and are asked, in 1955, to perform with Arnaz in his beloved television series *I Love Lucy.* This novel holds special interest for the reader of jazz
fiction for its dramatization of the music that cross-pollinated with American
jazz to create "Cu-bop," a phenomenon that is here fully and lovingly described.

Hill, Richard. *Riding Solo with the Golden Horde.* Athens, GA: University of
    Georgia Press, 1994.
Aimed at a teenage audience, this coming-of-age novel involves a high
school student, Vic Messenger, whose burning ambition is to become a jazz
saxophone artist rather than just a talented performer. Set in St. Petersburg,
Florida, in the late 1950s, it involves Messenger in the world of black jazz in
a segregated time and place. Much reference to jazz and jazz musicians and
the burgeoning civil rights movement. The spirits of Billie Holiday and Charlie Parker hover over the novel, Louis Armstrong has a walk-on role, and
Gene Quill plays a significant part. Drugs, booze, and sex are central factors
in Messenger's growing maturation.

Hoey, Allen. *Chasing the Dragon: A Novel about Jazz.* Philadelphia: Xlibris,
    2006.
A thoroughgoing, researched jazz novel that dramatizes several overlapping narrative strands: the narrator's quest to get to the bottom of his friend
Wardell Gray's death two years earlier (and, of course, to discover who *he* is
in the process); the author's attempt to characterize the lives of jazz musicians—to portray what it's like to participate in "the Life," as it were; and the
Irish Catholic East Coast narrator's developing relationship with an African-
American West Coast woman. The author's love and knowledge of jazz shine
through on every page. His descriptions of musical technique and jazz in performance are frequent and exemplary.

Nick Flynn is a jazz journalist, a white man involved in an essentially black world. Nick is thus, like the musicians he writes about, an outsider—and he becomes even more so when he falls in love with a black woman. In his obsession to find out how Wardell Gray died in Las Vegas in 1955, Nick's investigation takes him on a crisscrossing journey across the United States and back and puts him in touch with a fascinating array of characters, all of whom were connected to Gray and most of whom are historical persons. Nick's discursive journey is interspersed by a substantial number of mostly interior monologues rendered in the voices of mid-century jazz icons—Art Pepper, Billie Holiday, Charles Mingus, John Coltrane, and Coleman Hawkins, among them. Together, these "interludes" provide a richly textured mosaic of "the Life"—what's it's like, in other words, to be constantly on the road in a philistine culture, separated from loved ones, and giving yourself up completely to a poorly compensated, underappreciated art form.

It is no accident that Nick's life (except for the compensation) parallels that of the black artists he writes about and that his love for Sarah parallels their complicated devotion to their music. Intimately—and tragically—associated with "the Life," of course, are drug addiction and racism, and this novel's exploration of these overarching themes is both convincing and provocative. Readers come to understand the vulnerability of the artist who knows the dragon (narcotics) is waiting around the corner but is helpless to change direction. Add this title to your list of essential jazz fictions.

Holden, Craig. *The Jazz Bird*. New York: Simon and Schuster, 2002.
A researched novel set in Cincinnati during the Jazz Age year of 1927 involving a struggle for power, love and betrayal, and a spectacular trial. Despite the title, the setting, and a major character referred to as "the Jazz Bird," this book contains precious little musical content apart from fleeting references to jazz clubs and circles of the time. The following is fairly typical of the novel's jazz substance: "Cincinnati was full of jazz clubs now. The Salvation Army had recently obtained an injunction against a new one because it was next door to a home for wayward girls. The babies born there, it claimed, would develop 'jazz emotions' from hearing it."

——. "The P & G Ivory Cut-Whiskey Massacree." In *Murder . . . and All That Jazz*, edited by Robert J. Randisi, 1–10. New York: Signet, 2004.
This period piece set in Cincinnati in the 1920s contains gangsters, speakeasies, bootleg booze, and ultraviolence but not a whiff of music. How this story (cut from the manuscript of the author's novel, *The Jazz Bird* [q. v.]) was chosen to lead off an anthology of jazz mystery fiction is itself a mystery.

Holmes, John Clellon. *Go!* New York: Scribner's, 1952.

A roman à clef based on the self-destructive exploits of such renowned members of the Beat Generation (before it became known as such) as Jack Kerouac, Allen Ginsberg, Neal Cassady, and Herbert Hunke. The wonder is that there is so little jazz.

————. *The Horn.* New York: Random House, 1958.

As Edgar "the Horn" Pool tries to regain his stature as ranking saxophonist, his skills, as well as his psychological condition, rapidly deteriorate. Pool is likely a composite of Charlie Parker and Lester Young, and other characters also derive from actual jazz figures: the model for Junius Priest, as the name implies, is Thelonious Monk and another character closely resembles Billie Holiday. A bible of the Beat generation, this jazz-soaked novel frequently relates jazz artists to nineteenth-century American romantic writers.

Holmes, Rupert. *Swing: A Mystery.* New York: Random House, 2005.

A period piece set around the 1940 Golden Gate International Exposition, the West Coast's answer to the New York World Fair. Tenor saxophonist Ray Sherwood is touring with Jack Donovan and his Orchestra at the baronial Claremont Hotel in Oakland, California, when he accepts a commission to orchestrate an award-winning composition for piano, *Swing.* Although Ray is reluctant to take on extra work, the co-ed composer is very ingratiating (not to mention fetching). But when the body of a woman Ray had met earlier drops from the air and lands at his feet, he finds himself involved in a convoluted mystery that involves not only several more dead bodies but two of the Axis powers. A breathlessly hokey but nevertheless enjoyable multimedia novel that contains illustrations and is accompanied by a CD whose swing tunes (composed and arranged by the author and referenced in the text) contain clues designed to help the reader solve the mystery. Swing music is at the heart of this story; in fact, the titular composition turns out to contain a coded message that could threaten the safety of the Free World. The father of Tony Award-winning author Holmes played sax for the Red Norvo orchestra.

Hond, Paul. *Mothers & Sons.* New York: Random House, 2005.

Moss Messinger is an irritating, neurotic, 27-year-old New Yorker who acts and behaves as if he were half or even a third his age. Incredibly, he has a girlfriend who is his opposite in several important ways: she's beautiful, grounded, and productive. On the single occasion when they have unprotected sex, she becomes pregnant. Meanwhile, Moss's 44-year-old mother, Nina, returns to Manhattan from California to look after her son's emotional needs; she had pretty much abandoned him ten years earlier to go on an extended jazz tour of Europe. As mother and son try, ineffectually, to achieve rapprochement, she sleeps with Moss's best friend and, wouldn't you know, becomes, like Moss's girlfriend, pregnant after a single bout of unprotected sex. One fetus is aborted, the other is born, and the book ends (unconscionably late) with the characters facing indeterminate futures. The modest musical content of the novel revolves around Nina, a jazz pianist inspired by Elmo Hope and influenced by Bill Evans. A couple of scenes depict her in nightclub performance, and occasionally we are made privy to her thoughts regarding the "meaning" of music to her life.

Honea, Whit. "Jazz." *The Blue Moon Review*. http://www.thebluemoon.com/fiction/whonea.shtml (19 August 2003).
A free-association ramble by an American in Paris who claims that "Jazz is my Junk" but seems nevertheless to be at the mercy of drugs or some other hallucinatory agent as he recounts several predominantly sexual episodes from his past.

Hoobler, Dorothy, Thomas Hoobler, and Carey-Greenberg Associates. *Florence Robinson: The Story of a Jazz Age Girl*. Parsippany, NJ: Silver Burdett, 1997.
When Flo's father returns to Mississippi after serving in France in World War I, he can no longer tolerate the racism he had left behind, so he goes to Chicago in search of a better life for his family. Flo, who must be around 10, discovers what it means to live where she is not excluded because of her race; and, thanks to her father who has a gift for jazz piano, she is also introduced to jazz, whose "secret," she comes to realize, is "what it meant to be free." For juveniles.

Hood, Mary. "Lonesome Road Blues." *The Ohio Review* 33 (1984): 34–51.
The blues in the title refers both to a bluegrass tune and the experience of a woman who goes to a county fair to hear her hero, Edmun Lovingood, takes him home for a shower and a good country meal, and then returns him for the evening performance where she learns he already has a sweetheart. In short, country blues: no less forlorn than black Delta blues but different.

Horowitz, Mikhail. "Blindfold Test: Orpheus." *Brilliant Corners* 9 (Summer 2005): 42–43.
A droll spoof of the *Down Beat* Blindfold Test using characters from Greek mythology as the musicians under review by Orpheus.

Horveno, Grégoire. *Mamie Blues*. Ville La Salle, Québec, Canada: Hurtubise HMH, 1993.

A short novel for children (in French) with illustrations. Mamie is a jazz devotee with the dream of going to New Orleans. But she has neither the resources nor the family support to pursue her project until her young daughter comes to her aid. The book contains an appendix of educational exercises comprising crossword puzzles and multiple-choice quizzes.

Houston, James D. *Gig*. New York: Dial, 1969.
One night in the life of piano bar pianist Roy Ambrose, who would much rather be able to support himself by composing and playing jazz. Unfortunately, the 1960s zeitgeist is not conducive to that kind of music. Ambrose gears the songs he plays to what he perceives to be the audience's needs: "Tea for Two" for dancers, "Embraceable You" for lovers, "Roll a Silver Dollar" for singalongers, and so on.

———. "Homage to the Count." *The Men in My Life and Other More or Less True Recollections of Kinship*, 125–29. Berkeley: Creative Arts, 1987.
A fictionalized memoir of the writer's disappointment in seeing his hero, Count Basie, at 79 unable to employ "the famous Basie right hand."

Houston, Margaret Belle. "The Jazz Heart." *Collier's*, February 15, 1930, 14+.
Terry, a Yankee conventioneer in New Orleans, wrangles an introduction to the enchanting (and enchantingly named) Cydalise, who is engaged to marry her cousin Leon—a marriage of convenience. As Terry tells Cydalise about life back home in Indiana, he mentions his hometown jazz band, leading her to exclaim, "Me . . . I have a jazz heart." Terry says he does too, they arrange to spend a jazz evening together, and . . . love prevails, leaving cousin Leon fuming.

Howard, Brett. *Memphis Blues*. Los Angeles: Holloway House, 1984.
A fact-based fiction involving Harold Green, a fair-skinned mulatto orphan who works his way up from the gutter to relative prominence during Beale Street's heyday. When a good-hearted whore is killed, Harold avenges her death by slitting the throat of her killer, becoming "a real, honest-to-God black man." Much emphasis is given to Beale Street as the vital center of black life and the blues that flows from that experience. Many of the epigraphs to individual chapters contain blues references, and jazz and blues musicians are frequently mentioned.

Howard, Clark. "Horn Man." *Ellery Queen's Mystery Magazine*, June 2, 1980: 54–65.

When trumpeter Dix returns to New Orleans after serving sixteen years in prison for a murder he didn't commit, he has only one thing in mind: to find the woman he took the rap for. Even though he is offered an old silver trumpet that had been the property of a legendary Vieux Carré horn man, Dix claims to have no interest in returning to music. But when he discovers that the woman he is seeking will be unavailable for quite a long while, he picks up the trumpet and seems destined to once again make jazz the center of his existence.

Hower, Edward. *Night Train Blues*. Sag Harbor, NY: The Permanent Press, 1996.
The sensitive, rebellious "hero" of this book is deeply moved as a young man when he hears Pinetop Smith's recording of the title piece, and then, in a much later scene, he sits down at the piano and plays a series of blues songs from memory, but that is pretty much the extent of the musical content.

Hsuki, Hiroyuki. *Seinen Wa Kovya o Mezasu* [*Young Man in Search of a Barren Plain*]. 1967.
A youth novel (in Japanese) about an aspiring young Japanese trumpeter who sets out, through the USSR, for Europe, hoping to gain the necessary experience to give his music the emotional depth he feels it is lacking.

Huddle, David. *Tenorman: A Novella*. San Francisco: Chronicle, 1995.
For tenorman-composer Eddie Carnes, jazz was his life. Seemingly at the end of the road, he is brought back to the United States from Sweden by a branch of the National Endowment for the Arts and supplied with all the necessities of life on the condition that he allow every aspect of his daily existence to be studied and recorded. Through the process of this experiment, the lives of the researchers are changed in positive ways: Eddie's commitment to his art has brought to their lives newfound depth and intensity, making them more fully human. Much jazz reference to such figures as Joe Henderson, Stan Getz, Johnny Griffin, Sonny Stitt, and David Murray—and a surprise cameo appearance by Branford and Wynton Marsalis.

Hughes, Langston. "The Blues I'm Playing." *Scribner's*, May 1934, 345–51.
Oceola Jones and Mrs. Dora Ellsworth come from different worlds: Jones is a young black pianist with southern roots and Ellsworth is an elderly white blue-blood patron of the arts in New York City. Mrs. Ellsworth wants Oceola to sacrifice everything—including her medical school boyfriend and her racial identity—to become an artist in the classical tradition, but Oceola cannot relinquish

her love for the jazz-blues-gospel music of her heritage or her desire to live a balanced life. A story rich in implication, including the questions of the struggling black artist and the wealthy white patron. One cannot resist wondering whether Bessie Smith might have ended up sounding like Kate Smith if she had had the "proper" patronage.

————. "Bop." *The Best of Simple*, 117–19. New York: Hill and Wang, 1961.
Hughes's series character, Simple, a lover of bebop, explains to the dubious narrator that the music is more than just nonsense syllables, that in fact its name derives from the sound made when cops hit blacks on the head with their billy clubs, thus creating an authentic "colored boys" music.

————. "Home." *The Ways of White Folks,* 32–48. New York: Knopf, [1934] 1969.
After playing the violin in a jazz orchestra in Europe for eight years, Roy Williams returns to racist Missouri to see his family and rest his ailing body. Although Roy has played jazz at night, he did so in order to learn the classics by day. Back in the United States, he is regarded as uppity and loses his life because of his color.

————. "Jazz, Jive, and Jam." *Simple Stakes a Claim*, 186–91. New York: Holt, Rinehart and Winston, 1957.
This story presents a conciliatory picture of the racial issue as Simple argues to his woman, who has been dragging him to talks on integration, that jazz would be far more effective in promoting racial harmony than any number of seminars on the topic because, since everyone loves jazz, blacks and whites would dance together to the music, and racial differences would dissipate.

————. *Not without Laughter*. New York: Knopf, 1930.
A picturesque novel focusing on the daily life of a poor African-American family in a small town in Kansas. Although it is not a jazz novel per se, it contains many references to jazz, blues, and dancing, and at least three chapters in which music is a dominant presence. Chapter V, "Guitar," tells the story of guitarist and singer Jimboy, who brings people together. Chapter VIII, "Dance," exuberantly dramatizes the importance of music and dance to African-American culture:

> "Whaw! Whaw! Whaw!" mocked the cornet—but the steady tomtom of the drums was no longer laughter now, no longer even pleasant: the drum beats had become sharp with surly sound, like heavy waves that beat angrily on a granite rock. And under the dissolute spell of its own rhythm the music had gotten quite beyond itself. The four black men in Benbow's wandering band were exploring

depths to which mere sound had no business to go. Cruel, desolate, unadorned was their music now, like the body of a ravished woman on the sun-baked earth; violent and hard, like a giant standing over his bleeding mate in the blazing sun. The odors of bodies, the stings of flesh, and the utter emptiness of soul when all is done—these things the piano and the drums, the cornet and the twanging banjo insisted on hoarsely to a beat that made dancers move, in that little hall, like pawns on a frenetic checkerboard.

The final chapter, XXX, "Princess of the Blues," tells of an encounter between the young protagonist and some family members with a jazz-blues singer from their past, now performing in a variety show in Chicago before a "typical Black Belt" audience.

———. "Old Ghost Revives Atavistic Memories in a Lady of the DAR." *Chicago Defender,* 2 July 1949 (no pagination).

A delightful, very genteel meeting of the Daughters of the American Revolution is disturbed when one of the members raises the "Negro question." Soon after, the ghost of Blind Boone enters the room, sits at the piano, and begins to play bebop and boogie, causing the ultra-refined, deeply prejudiced Mrs. Palmer "to dance, to boogie and, as the music modulated, even to bebop" and to cry out "ah, do it, daddy" before her "ancient carcass squatted in one final scoop and swished like a duck, 'Hucklebuck, baby! Hucklebuck!'"

———. "Rejuvenation through Joy." *The Ways of White Folks,* 66–95. New York: Knopf, [1934] 1969.

A satirical story concerning a hustler to the haute mode in 1920s New York who conceives a money-making scheme based on teaching joy. He plans to assemble his paying guests at an early version of a New Age spa; there he will deliver a series of lectures whose main points will be demonstrated by musicians, singers, and dancers hired from Harlem. Thus, the guru will enable his neurasthenic patrons to connect with their primitive selves by imitating the rhythms of the age (i.e., jazz): after all, "Negroes were the happiest people on earth. . . . they alone really know the secret of rhythms and of movements. . . ." He goes on to say that the music that "primitive Negroes brought with their drums from Africa to America . . . is the Joy of Life." (When this story was written, primitivism was not universally considered a negative—let alone a racist—concept; see, e.g., the writings of D. H. Lawrence.)

———. "Simple Goes on Record." *Chicago Defender,* 17 July 1948 (no pagination).

Simple is crushed when his Cousin Mabel gets religion and sells his cherished collection of jazz and blues records, including a rare Bessie Smith recording. When his buddy asks if a beer will mend his broken heart, Simple replies that the situation calls for bourbon.

Hunter, Evan. *Second Ending*. New York: Simon and Schuster, 1956; London: Constable, 1956. [Also published as *Quartet in "H."* New York: Pocket Books, 1957.]

When young jazz trumpeter Andy Silvera imposes himself on his erstwhile friend, Bud Donato, he brings havoc along with him. Bud needs to cram for exams, and Andy has become deeply involved in narcotics and consequently requires constant attention, forcing Bud into the role of nursemaid. The sections on music-making, especially in Book I, ring true; there are also frequent references to Kenton and Gillespie, among others.

————. *Streets of Gold*. New York: Harper and Row, 1974.

Yet another dramatization of the corrosive power of the American Dream. The birth-blind speaker, Dwight Jamison, is a second-generation Italian-American who abandons his study of classical piano after listening to Art Tatum recordings. After paying his dues for several years, Jamison becomes very successful, thanks largely to a fluke hit recording. At the height of his success, however, he falls victim to the corruption surrounding the music industry as well as to rock 'n' roll, which is making bebop obsolete. Jamison comes to realize that the streets paved with gold that his grandfather spoke of on his deathbed referred less to the fame and fortune connoted by the jazz musicians' street of gold, 52nd Street, than to hard-earned moral values. Although this novel concerns the melting-pot experience of an immigrant family, the second half contains much of interest for readers of jazz fiction: namely, solid discussions focusing on the mechanics of the music, several descriptions of jazz performances, and frequent references to such musicians as Dizzy Gillespie, Oscar Peterson, and George Shearing.

Hunter, Kristen. *God Bless the Child*. New York: Charles Scribner's Sons, 1964.

Apart from one extended nightclub scene (in the section titled "Them That's Not Shall Lose"), the only jazz in this truly depressing novel of growing up black and female in the ghetto is in the title and chapter headings, all of which are taken from one of Billie Holiday's signature songs, "God Bless the Child," a title also borrowed by half a dozen other books with little or no jazz content—though one could probably argue that the reader can actually *hear* Holiday sing that lugubrious song as he reads these generally hopeless works.

Hurd, Thatcher. *Mama Don't Allow*. New York: Harper and Row, 1984.

In this illustrated tale for children, young saxophone-playing opossum Miles and his critter chums—the Swamp Band—are thrilled to be playing at the Alligator Ball until they discover that Swamp Band Soup is on the menu for the post-dance repast. The band summons up all of its musical expertise and ingenuity to escape disaster.

Isadora, Rachel. *Ben's Trumpet*. New York: Greenwillow, 1979.

A nicely illustrated juvenile book about young Ben, who loves jazz and plays an imaginary trumpet until the trumpeter from a neighborhood jazz club fixes him up with a real instrument.

———. *Bring on That Beat*. New York: G. P. Putnam's Sons, 2002.

A "story" for juveniles told in rhyming couplets about the way jazz transformed Harlem in the 1930s. The graphics are such that the book doesn't really require words.

Islas, Arturo. *La Mollie and the King of Tears*. Edited by Paul Skenazy. Albuquerque: University of New Mexico Press, 1996.

Jazz saxophonist Louie Mendoza is in the emergency ward of a San Francisco hospital telling the story of his day—and, really, his life—to a stranger with a tape recorder. This unfinished novel elaborates the complexity of the Chicano condition in spicy vernacular language. Surprisingly, though Mendoza is a jazz musician, he has little to say about music.

Jackson, Jon A. *Man with an Axe*. New York: Atlantic Monthly, 1998.

A mystery featuring detective "Fang" Mulheisen of the Detroit PD. In this number in the series, Mulheisen goes in search of a collection of notebooks left behind by a late colleague; this in turn involves Mulheisen in a quest to discover what really happened to Jimmy Hoffa one long-ago weekend at an isolated African-American resort community on the Great Lakes. Mulheisen is a jazz buff, and the book contains many references to bop and free jazz and to the jazz musicians who matriculated in the "old" Detroit. One important character had played sax in Phil Woods's band, while another turns out, in a neat novelistic twist, to be the daughter of Albert Ayler. A rambling yet always interesting narrative, especially for lovers of jazz fiction.

Jacob, Charlee. "Jazz." *Stygian Articles* #4 (Winter 1995): 32–40.

Not seen.

————. "The Jazz Club." *Stygian Articles* #7 (Autumn 1996): 5–10. Not seen.

James, Stuart. *Too Late Blues*. New York: Lancer Books, 1962.
Pianist Ghost Wakefield and his quintet aren't exactly getting rich or famous playing their special brand of jazz around Southern California, but they are pretty much sustained by performing the music they love with musicians they enjoy and respect. Enter a beautiful woman, an agent or two, and a recording contract and things soon spin out of control, leaving everyone at odds with Ghost and destroying the combo. Many references to jazz musicians and several scenes set in jazz clubs and the recording studio. The fact that this book came out almost simultaneously with the movie of the same title, is a paperback original, and is copyrighted by the director/producer of the movie, John Cassavetes, and one John Smith leads one to suspect that it is what is sometimes called a novelization.

Janowitz, Hans. *Jazz: Roman*. 1927. Germany: Weidle Verlag, 1999.
Influenced by the jazz craze that swept over Germany in the mid-1920s, this novel is probably the first substantial fiction to appropriate the techniques and structures of jazz in a literary text; in short, the book attempts to translate music into words. As the speaker says, he is writing a jazz novel, not a conventional one, and so his work "is subject to different rules, just as a jazz piece is subject to different rules from those that apply to a sonata for piano and violin." The "plot" concerns a historian looking back on the turbulent 1920s from the perspective of 1999. At the center of this variegated overview are Lord Punch and his Jazz-Band-Boys, a group of five musicians who meet by chance after failing an audition. They soon land a job at a famous dance club and after a while become successful enough to rename themselves Jazz-Symphonists as they progress toward "their mission in life: translating the whole world into Jazz." The nightclub setting allows for the introduction of a wide variety of characters, moods, and events. At times, it almost seems as if the Marx Brothers were adapting John Dos Passos's *USA* to the silver screen. The narrator rejects the standard novelistic impulse to tie the sundry plot threads together at the end, saying instead:

> A jazz novel has the right to fade out quietly, and just to come to an end in the midst of a thematic repetition. To insist on this inalienable right in the first jazz novel that has been written according to the laws of jazz music is my prerogative. You may not agree, but I will now take the liberty to grant the saxophone a postlude, delicately accompanied by violin, piano, and drum; I have to leave it at that. The jazz instrument is hard to control; it likes to follow its own tonal paths. I will let it express itself one more time here, although I can't help but fear

that it might play a prank on the jazz character—against itself, if you will. But I have no means at my disposal to prevent that. In the framework of this story, I am completely at the mercy of my instruments.

The quoted passages above are taken from Cornelius Partsch and Damon O. Rarick's partial translation of the novel and can be accessed at http://cat.middlebury.edu/~nereview/Janowitz.html. The 1999 republication, in German, is accompanied by a CD and contains an annotated discography of the music referenced in the novel.

Jeffers, H. Paul. *Rubout at the Onyx*. New Haven and New York: Ticknor and Fields, 1981.

A mystery set in the 1930s in Manhattan. Jazz buff private eye Harry Mac-Neil (the "Mick Dick") undertakes to get to the bottom of a mob hit that occurred at the Onyx Club—"the best jazz joint on Fifty-second Street"—on New Year's Eve when Art Tatum was playing piano. Tatum, Paul "Pops" Whiteman, and George Gershwin have limited roles. In an "Author's Note," the writer glosses the lives of some of the real people who appear in the novel and claims that if it achieves any authenticity of mood, this is largely because of the 1930s jazz records he played while writing.

Jeffers, Honorée Fanonne. "Morning and the Last Blues Song," *Brilliant Corners* 9 (Summer 2004): 29–36.

A tone poem of a story that uses oldtime Georgia bluesman Swamp to reflect on the origin and meaning of the blues.

Jesmer, Elaine. *Number One with a Bullet*. New York: Farrar, Straus and Giroux, 1974; London: Weidenfeld and Nicolson, 1974.

A novel by a former Motown secretary about the monstrous greed and corruption that infests the music industry. Although the record firm at the book's center is black-owned, it nevertheless exploits its black artists as it strives to produce a "bullet," a hit record that promises to go on generating income. Negligible jazz content.

Jessup, Richard. *Lowdown*. London: Secker and Warburg, 1956; New York: Dell, 1958.

A Frank Sinatra soundalike, Walker Alise, cheats and connives his way to the top of the pop music world, looking 50 when he dies at 33. Although one scene takes place at the Blue Note, this novel is essentially about the sleazy mechanics of the pop music industry and of the crushing burden of fame. In short, little jazz interest.

Jeyapalan, Renuka. "The Jazz Singer." *Another Toronto Quarterly* (Fall 2000).
    http://www.anothertorontoquarterly.com/Fall2000/renuka.html (19 August
    2003).
    An interior monologue concerning a guy in a jazz club who is disturbed
that the woman (perhaps a jazz singer) he had hoped to see isn't showing up.

Joe, Yolanda. *My Fine Lady.* New York: Dutton, 2004.
    A Pygmalian story (the title puns on *My Fair Lady*) in which talented, am-
bitious "homegirl" Amani Holland falls under the tutelage of Professor Hopson, at twenty-five the youngest Ellington Fellow in the history of a black
university near Washington, D.C. Hopson had bet a colleague that he could
transform a rap singer into a traditional jazz singer in three months. Enter
hip-hopper Amani, whose parents had been jazz musicians. As Amani struggles to achieve her musical destiny, she comes to realize that her quest is actually to discover who she is—and she finds that "She wasn't rap. She wasn't
jazz. She was neo-soul." The milieu of this novel is exclusively African-
American, and the target audience is exclusively female, as witness the
opening sentence: "Where does the hope for love begin?" The jazz content
is modest.

Johns, Veronica Parker. "Mr. Hyde-de-Ho." In *Ellery Queen's Awards: 11th Se-
    ries*, edited by Ellery Queen, 106–51. New York: Simon and Schuster, 1956.
    When the speaker finds out that a jazz musician has apparently fallen in
love with her very rich, obese friend, she is first incredulous and then fright-
ened. The women soon find themselves entangled in mysteriously frightening
circumstances—a variation on the single-woman-in-distress theme. In explaining the predictably bad behavior of jazz musicians, the narrator says,
"All the talent, the fire that makes them great, burns with a bright alcoholic
flame." The speaker is a receptionist at a recording company that specializes
in jazz and "the better bop"; the story contains many references to the 1950s
jazz scene, recording sessions, and jazz clubs.

Johnson, Clifford Vincent. "Old Blues Singers Never Die." In *The Best Short
    Stories by Negro Writers*, edited by Langston Hughes, 414–27. Boston: Lit-
    tle, Brown, 1967.
    In Paris one day, a black American serviceman encounters legendary blues
singer River Bottom, who was "sporting a big fat diamond ring" and clothes
to match. This leads to reflections on race (France versus the United States,
for instance) and the majesty of the blues.

Johnson, Grady. *The Five Pennies.* New York: Dell, 1959.
    Novelization of the biopic of Loring "Red" Nichols, the Mormon cornetist
who goes to New York in the 1920s filled with musical ideas and ambitions. Af-

ter quitting his job with Wil Paradise's band, he forms the Five Pennies in order to play his beloved Dixieland jazz. At the height of his fame, Red's daughter develops polio, so he abandons his musical career and moves his family to a more salubrious climate. Considerably later, he allows himself to be persuaded to buy a small nightclub that seems destined for oblivion until some of his famous friends from the past materialize to bail him out. The novel rounds up all the usual between-the-wars suspects, including Bix Beiderbecke, Mezz Mezzrow, Miff Mole, Pee Wee Russell, Joe Venuti, and Louis Armstrong. In the film, Danny Kaye and Barbara Bel Geddes play Red and his vocalist wife.

Johnson, James Weldon. *The Autobiography of an Ex-Coloured Man.* Boston: Sherman, French and Company, 1912.
   A light-skinned boy of mixed parentage discovers a talent for music, masters classical piano, and turns classical music into ragtime, achieving success in the process. He later determines to turn ragtime into classical music—in other words, to give voice to the African-American experience through the structures and techniques of classical music. He masquerades successfully as a white, takes a white wife (blonde and blue-eyed), and leads a comfortable life, uneasily believing that he has betrayed his race, sold his "birthright for a mess of pottage." An early, important book about the trauma of confused racial identity and of the potential that music has to promote the welfare of the black artist and, by implication, the race itself. The first "pre-jazz" novel?

Jones, Gayl. *Corregidora.* New York: Random House, 1975.
   Although the first-person protagonist is a blues singer, neither she nor the novel has much to say about music (beyond the obligatory I-sing-cause-I-gotta-sing). Scattered references to blues and jazz artists. At one point, when asked what the blues does for her, the speaker reflects, "It helps me to explain what I can't explain." Much more about the legacy of slavery and black feminism than about music.

Jones, James. "The King." *Playboy* 1955. In *Eddie Condon's Treasury of Jazz,* edited by Eddie Condon and Richard Gehman, 337–49. New York: Dial, 1956.
   Probably based on the return of Bunk Johnson, this story concerns Willy "King" Jefferson, a legendary trumpeter who played an important role in the development of jazz. When King makes a comeback, he fails to generate much interest—because, frankly, he isn't playing very well and also because interest in his old-timey New Orleans brand of jazz has passed.

Jordan, Elizabeth. *Blues in the Night.* New York: Fawcett Gold Medal, 1987.
   Like the long-running soap opera it seems to be imitating, this novel has it all: geographical and historical sweep; world war and revolution (including a

walk-on by "Che" Guevara); racial conflict; booze and drugs; witch doctors and mysterious foreign gangsters; and, finally, love, love, love. In the midst of this maelstrom, we find Dessie, a blonde with a penchant for the blues, thanks in large part to her black nanny down home in South Carolina. When she goes to New York after birthing an illegitimate child, she auditions to become a jazz singer, only to be told that she would never make it in show biz unless she were willing to strip. Against all odds, she becomes a tremendous success, then falls into obscurity, at one point literally singing for her supper in Mexico. But then she begins to climb back into the spotlight and at the end seems destined to reestablish herself as the finest jazz singer of her generation. There are characters named Dizzy and Pepper, many references to jazz artists, and some music in performance—but one would have to willfully suspend disbelief in order to credit any of it.

Joseph, Oscar. "Suite for Queen." In *NOMMO: A Literary Legacy of Black Chicago (1967–1987)*, edited by Carole A. Parks, 192–98. Chicago: OBA-house, 1987.
Steve Anderson reminisces about his past while standing alone on a Harlem street playing "Suite for a Queen" on his saxophone in homage to his mother and happier days. At one point Anderson compares his solitary playing to Sonny Rollins's dropping out of public performance and practicing his horn on the Williamsburg Bridge. Much of the story attempts to approximate the bebop sounds Steve creates on his horn.

Julian, Scott. "The Jazz Pilot." *Bizarre Bazaar #2*: 52–58 (1993).
Not seen.

Kaminsky, Wallace. "The Sound-Machine." *The University Review* 31, no. 3 (March 1965): 163–74.
After being introduced to jazz by his black army buddy Buster, Nick (the narrator) resolves to become the best saxophonist on Earth; in addition, Nick feels the compelling need to be accepted by black musicians. Nick gets his chance to perform with ranking musicians and more than holds his own but loses his dear friend Buster in the process.

Kane, Henry. *Peter Gunn*. New York: Dell, 1960.
Debonair detective Peter Gunn accepts an assignment to do a background check of a jazz guitarist. As invariably happens in the hard-boiled subgenre, the simple task escalates into increasingly serious crimes, including of course murder. Cover copy proclaims "Murder to a jazz beat" and indeed the story begins at Gunn's home base, Mother's, a jazz club where Gunn's sweetheart

is the featured singer. But apart from a jam session that opens the novel and the beatnik argot of several characters, there is negligible musical interest. A novelization of the late 1950s, early 1960s television series starring Craig Stevens.

Kanin, Garson. *Blow Up a Storm*. New York: Random House, 1959.
The first-person narrator is a playwright and saxophonist; he tells the story of an old buddy from the past, Woody Woodruff, whose trumpet playing was in a class with Louis Armstrong's and Bunny Berigan's. The novel—which takes place on either side of World War II—contains many references to jazz artists and some excellent descriptions of music in the making, including a very effective scene in which seven band members blend their very different talents, personalities, and backgrounds, supporting a central theme: ". . . if we could all learn to play together . . . why is it we couldn't learn to live together?" Much emphasis on race and booze. One character, Slug (a drummer), seems to be modeled after Charlie Parker.

———. *The Rat Race*. New York: Pocket Books, 1960.
Lee Konitz had once told the hayseed protagonist, Pete Hammer, that he liked Hammer's tone, so Pete goes to New York hoping to make it big on the saxophone. When Pete is forced by circumstances to share a small apartment with a gal who had been knocked around, they fall in love and face the harsh realities of big city life together. This book is a novelization of Kanin's screenplay for the 1960 movie of the same name, and the movie was an adaptation of Kanin's and Ruth Gordon's play (1949, 1950), also of the same title.

Karp, Larry. *The Ragtime Kid.* Scottsdale, AZ: Poisoned Pen Press, 2006.
A researched, historical mystery involving white teenager Brun Campbell, a piano-playing prodigy who, upon hearing "Maple Leaf Rag," runs away from home to seek out Scott Joplin in Sedalia, Missouri, where he hopes the great ragtime musician will give him piano lessons. As he reaches his destination, he stumbles upon the corpse of a young woman and picks up a couple of items that will later play a significant role in solving the mystery of the woman's death. But, as the author explains in a postscript, "The Last Word," the deeper mystery concerns, among other things, why a conventional white businessman would agree to publish the work of a then still obscure black composer and to do so on a royalties basis—a very rare phenomenon at the time. In exploring racial issues, turn-of-the-century musical business practices, and the history of ragtime, this novel employs both fictional and real people, especially Scott Joplin and Brun Campbell (so-named "The Ragtime Kid" by Joplin).

Kawana, Phil. "Dead Jazz Guys." *Dead Jazz Guys and Other Stories*, 7–19. Wellington, New Zealand: Huia, 1996.

As he sits reading a biography of Miles Davis in the library, Mike has a chance encounter with Lee that leads to the beginning of a relationship. As Mike prepares to go to bed with Lee for the first time, he ponders the significance of listening to dead guys (John Coltrane and Don Cherry) playing jazz while he makes love. In the lovely moments that follow, Mike concludes that for now "angels [Coltrane and Cherry] arose from the grave to serenade them. From the lounge, John Coltrane's saxophone and Don Cherry's trumpet writhed and danced around each other. Supple, sinewy and alive." This story could take place with young lovers anywhere, but it is set in New Zealand, with Mike a dreadlocked Maori bone carver boy and Lee a Maori-Italian-Samoan girl.

Kay, Jackie. *Trumpet*. London: Picador, 1998; New York: Pantheon, 1998.

A first novel from the self-described "Black Scottish poet," Jackie Kay, *Trumpet* dramatizes the life and, more significantly, the death of jazz trumpeter Joss Moody, who is revealed to have been a woman—despite having been married for many years to Millie, with whom he raised their adopted son Colman. Told in flashbacks through multiple points of view, this intriguing work raises resonant questions about the indefinability of gender and identity and how these can be deeply complicated through music, as when Joss reflects on his relationship to the music he produces:

> The music is his blood. His cells. But the odd bit is that down at the bottom, the blood doesn't matter after all. None of the particulars count for much. True, they are instrumental in getting him down there in the first place, but after that they become incidental. All his self collapses—his idiosyncrasies, his personality, his ego, his sexuality, even, finally, his memory. All of it falls away like layers of skin unwrapping. He unwraps himself with his trumpet. Down at the bottom, face to face with the fact that he is nobody. The more he can be nobody the more he can play that horn. Playing the horn is not about being somebody coming from something. It is about being nobody coming from nothing. The horn ruthlessly strips him bare till he ends up with no body, no past, nothing.

Whether or not this novel was inspired by the 1992 movie, *The Crying Game*, or the even more recent revelations about real-life jazz man Billy Tipton, who turned out to have been a woman, it adds a fascinating new dimension to such works. (See Diane Wood Middlebrook, *Suits Me: The Double Life of Billy Tipton*. Boston and New York: Houghton Mifflin, 1998.)

Keithley, George. "Perdido Street Blues." *Brilliant Corners* 10 (Winter 2005): 41–56.

A period piece set in 1926 Chicago involving local politics and the death of a congressman. The story is framed by Louis Armstrong and the Hot Five setting up for a jam session at a gin joint called Bert Kelly's Stables. With Armstrong's wife, Lil, on piano, they begin the set with a song she composed, "Perdido Street Blues."

Kellerman, Jonathan. *A Cold Heart: An Alex Delaware Novel*. New York: Ballantine, 2003.

The trigger event in this psychological thriller featuring series psychologist-sleuth Alex Delaware involves the vicious death of noted blues guitarist Baby Boy Lee, whose last song gives the novel its title. Apart from this and some background concerning Baby Boy's development as a bluesman, there is very little musical interest in this story of a serial killer who chooses rising celebrities as his victims.

Kelley, William Melvin. "Cry for Me." *Dancers on the Shore*, 180–201. Garden City, NY: Doubleday, 1964.

The young narrator's Uncle Wallace comes up to New York City from the South. One night in Greenwich Village Uncle Wallace becomes outraged when he happens upon a blues/folk performer singing a song *he* had written and mangling it in the process. Uncle Wallace takes over the stage, becomes a big hit, and ends up at Carnegie Hall, where he brings together the members of the audience, black and white, in a joyous dance. This is what Simple in Langston Hughes's "Jazz, Jive, and Jam" (q.v.) advocates.

———. *A Different Drummer*. New York: Doubleday, 1959, 1962.

With a black writer who wrote a significant jazz novel and a title that implies a musical instrument, you'd expect this book to contain considerable musical reference. But there is none; rather it is a densely political novel of the civil rights movement.

———. *A Drop of Patience*. New York: Doubleday, 1965.

An affecting fable about a birth-blind horn player who leaves the South for New York and Chicago, where he is finally recognized for his seminal role in shaping the new music—undoubtedly bebop. Ludlow Washington may be a genius but his blindness, his blackness, and his total devotion to his music do not allow him to fit in anywhere. Washington cracks up after being exploited and betrayed by commercialism and racism, recovers, rejects the belated

Part 4

recognition he is receiving, and sets out to find a church—anywhere—in need of a good musician.

Kelly, Rod. *Just for the Bread*. London: Robert Hale, 1976.
     After filling in with a rock band at a society ball in London—"just for the bread"—struggling jazz trumpeter Cornelius Lefroy is seduced by the sensation-seeking hostess, Lady Gabrielle Damian. Unfortunately, their liaison is secretly filmed, and Lady Gabrielle is blackmailed. When she opens her checkbook to Lefroy to resolve the matter, he accepts for two compelling reasons: he needs the money and he is booked for a week at Ronnie Scott's famous jazz club to play opposite Freddie Hubbard, "who would blow him into the ground every night." Apart from this, however, there are only a few references to the different styles of Dizzy Gillespie and Don Cherry. In short, although this is a rare novel, it is not worth seeking out for its jazz content.

Kennett, Frances. *Lady Jazz*. London: Victor Gollancz, 1989.
     A long novel chronicling the struggles of Ida Garland to succeed as a singer in the London of the 1930s. Ida was born into a show business family and is determined to carry on the tradition of her grandfather, an African-American who came to London in the 1890s. But just as her career begins to flourish, World War II breaks out, and she leaves the stage—until love reenters her life. Given its length and subject matter, this novel contains disappointingly little jazz content.

Kerouac, Jack. *Desolation Angels*. New York: Coward-McCann, 1965.
     As usual, Kerouac's persona (or alter ego), Jack Duluoz, is in search of Truth ("God or Tathagata") and in praise of America. Passing references to such musicians as Sarah Vaughan, Breu [*sic*] Moore, and Dizzy Gillespie and a scene or two involving musical performance.

——. *Maggie Cassidy*. New York: Avon, 1959.
     Much reference to the big bands Kerouac listened to in the late 1930s.

——. *On the Road*. New York: Viking, 1957.
     Like all of Kerouac's novels, this is not, strictly speaking, a jazz fiction, though it is shot through with references to jazz musicians and contains a few scenes of music in performance. More important, the prose style of this novel attempts to emulate the spontaneity of the music.

——. *The Subterraneans*. New York: Grove, 1958.
     A confessional narrative depicting the protagonist's love affair with a black girl. Occasional references to Charlie Parker underscore the novel's hallucinatory mode.

————. *The Town and the City*. New York: Harcourt Brace, 1950.
Hipsters and bop musicians with their dark glasses and berets are mentioned.

————. *Visions of Cody*. New York: McGraw-Hill, 1972.
A companion piece to *On the Road*, with the members of the Beat Generation (before it was so named) frantically exploring the America—and the Mexico—of the late 1940s and early 1950s. Jack Duluoz, Kerouac's persona, narrates this diaristic novel that focuses on Cody Pomeray, whose endless thirst for experience, coupled with boundless energy, make him the new American hero. At one point, Duluoz follows Lee Konitz down the streets of New York, not knowing why. The book contains many other references to jazz and its artists, including Charlie Parker and Coleman Hawkins.

Kirkwood, Valerie. *Torch Song*. New York: Kensington, 1996.
A time-travel romance with only a few scattered jazz references to such artists as Benny Goodman, Louis Armstrong, and Bessie Smith.

Kitt, Sandra. *Serenade*. New York: Pinnacle/Windsor, 1994.
Alexander Morrow has devoted her existence to music but isn't making much headway until Parker Harrison reenters her life. Equally adroit at classical music and jazz, Parker had stolen—and broken—Alex's heart years ago and now sets about to repair the earlier damage. The story is set in Washington, D.C.; significant scenes take place in the famous jazz club, Blues Alley; all of the characters are African-Americans with ties to the music world; and the jacket copy claims that "Alexander Morrow has struggled long and hard to make it in the red-hot electric world of jazz." Despite all of this, the jazz content is less than negligible. In short, a "Pinnacle Romance."

Klavan, Andrew. *Hunting Down Amanda*. New York: William Morrow, 1999; London: Little, Brown, 1999.
A mid-tech, melodramatic thriller involving a heartbroken black sax player who becomes involved in a truly incredible plot, which includes, among other things, the search for a young girl with miraculous healing powers. The jazz content is limited to a solid chapter or two on the jazz man—Lonnie Blake—at work, scattered references to musicians like James Carter, and occasional chapter titles taken from such jazz standards as "'Round Midnight" and "Stardust." At one point, having been bested by Lonnie, the evil antagonist says, "I should never have sent you guys up against a jazz musician. Those guys are dangerous."

Knight, Damon. "Coming Back to Dixieland." *Orbit* 18, 1976. In *The Planet on the Table*, edited by Kim Stanley Robinson, 168–97. New York: Tom Doherty/(TOR), 1986.

A science fiction story in which several miners on Titania must overcome serious obstacles in order to compete in a musical competition fifteen million miles away. The Hot Six is a Dixieland combo that plays "old Earth-type music," but their tuba player is missing. Miraculously, they find a replacement at the last minute—a musician no one has ever heard of and who had learned his instrument on Mars. After a stunning (and well-described) performance, the boys are awarded a grant: a four-year tour of the Solar System. Music is very much at the heart of this story, with ample reference to Louis Armstrong.

Knight, Phyllis. *Shattered Rhythms*. New York: St. Martin's, 1994.
    Lesbian private investigator Lil Ritchie follows around a great Franco-American jazz guitarist, Andre Ledoux, using his music as an anodyne for her psychic wounds. When he disappears, she is hired to find him, allowing her to go to the great Montreal Jazz Festival. The book contains a few pretty good descriptions of music but as a whole it is a far-fetched, cliché-ridden, tensionless mystery with minimal jazz interest.

Kotzwinkle, William. *The Hot Jazz Trio*. Boston: Houghton Mifflin/Seymour Lawrence, 1989.
    Although the titles of the three stories in this triptych—"Django Reinhardt Played the Blues," "Blues on the Nile," and "Boxcar Blues"—imply solid musical content, there is very little. In the first story, Django Reinhardt and his Hot Jazz Trio (which becomes the Duo and a Half when Reinhardt is halved!) are performing in Paris in the 1920s; other characters in this fantasy include Cocteau, Picasso, and Sartre. In one of the chief incidents, a box falls in love with a disappearing woman. There's no musical content in the second and third stories.

Lamb, David. *The Trumpet Is Blown*. New York: I Write What I Like, 1997.
    Yet another coming-of-age narrative. Two seemingly inseparable young friends from the projects grow apart as they struggle to come to terms with their environment, the crack-and-violence–dominated world of Bedford-Stuyvesant. One of the boys, Shawn, embraces the world of drugs, while the other, Chris (later Jibril), dedicates himself to the trumpet and his adopted religion, Islam. Jibril has the good luck to be guided by Hassan, a jazz trumpet legend who teaches music with lessons drawn from basketball and religion. Many jazz references to such performers as Dizzy Gillespie, Miles Davis, John Coltrane, Art Blakey, and David Sanchez.

Lange, Art, and Nathaniel Mackey. *Moment's Notice: Jazz in Poetry and Prose*. Minneapolis: Coffee House, 1993.

The editors claim that this is the first anthology to bring together both jazz-related poetry and prose. While it inevitably duplicates some entries from earlier collections (Richard N. Albert's *From Blues to Bebop: A Collection of Jazz Fiction*, Marcela Breton's *Hot and Cool: Jazz Short Stories*, and Sascha Feinstein and Yusef Komunyakaa's *The Jazz Poetry Anthology*), it also includes works that have not been previously collected; full-page photographs are interspersed throughout the text.

Lardner, Ring. "Rhythm." *The Love Nest and Other Stories*, 163–83. New York: Scribner's, 1926.
   At the heart of this story is the question of whether it is morally reprehensible —or acceptable behavior—for jazz composers to "borrow" from classical sources for their ideas. The implication is that such borrowing is integral to the composition of jazz.

Lea, George. *Somewhere There's Music*. Philadelphia: Lippincott, 1958.
   By the time 21-year-old Mike Logan returns to his hometown in Michigan after fighting in the Korean War, he has given up swing and Dixieland for the new "cool" jazz, and he's also exchanged his clarinet for a baritone sax. As in every other soldier-back-from-battle narrative, Mike is disoriented on his return: he has no plans, prospects, or marketable skills, only an abiding love for music. This allows him to drift into the hermetic society of jazz musicians and the perfidious panacea of booze and narcotics. The novel has considerable jazz content, starting with a title taken from the very popular mid-twentieth-century jazz tune, "How High the Moon."

Lee, George Washington. "Beale Street Anyhow." *Beale Street Sundown*, 13–35. New York: House of Field, 1942.
   Matt Johnson, The Master of Revels for the annual carnival celebration in Memphis, hatches a plan to ensure that the name of Beale Street not be changed to Beale Avenue. Although street music is clearly part of the Beale Street experience, it is not given much emphasis in this story.

———. "The Beale Street Blues I'm Singing." *Beale Street Sundown*, 156–76. New York: House of Field, 1942.
   After getting his best suit and good glass eye out of hock, Mushmouth Henry returns to Beale Street where he is disappointed to discover the prevalence of the blues, which he feels has a negative impact on the street. Mushmouth does his best to uproot the blues but, ironically, becomes a blues singer himself.

———. "The First Blues Singer." *Beale Street Sundown*, 70–86. New York: House of Field, 1942.

When a daughter of Beale Street, young Alberta, takes voice lessons and demonstrates excellent potential, she is discouraged from singing the blues she loves. Alberta becomes famous as a classical artist and travels all over but cannot resist singing her beloved blues; as the narrator says after hearing her sing: ". . . I thought I heard in her voice the rhythm of the Mississippi River when it laps at the foot of Beale Street and then rolls away gently to the sea."

———. "It Happened at an Amateur Show." *Beale Street Sundown*, 36–47. New York: House of Field, 1942.
    The speaker had never enjoyed amateur nights but when he overhears a mulatto woman encouraging her dark young friend to enter a contest that night, he decides to attend. The young girl is a great hit but gets into trouble after dedicating "The Ethiopian Blues" to her white employers, who consider the song too nasty for polite (i.e., white) society.

Lees, Gene. *And Sleep Until Noon*. New York: Trident, 1966.
    Under the influence of a buddy and the zeitgeist, Jack Royal catches the jazz bug at an early age. Before long Jack is learning harmonic theory and translating repulsive pop tunes into jazz. He also does a fair pastiche of Nat King Cole as he sings along to his own piano accompaniment. Jack soon leaves Chicago for New York where he abandons the jazz he loves to pursue a career as pop singer. He becomes a great success but, in the tradition of such stories, loses any trace of humanity he once had. Enter a beautiful, intelligent Swedish journalist, whose love for Jack enables him to undergo a transformative experience. He regains the decency he had lost in his lust for fame. The early chapters focusing on Jack's jazz apprenticeship ring true, as do the late chapters involving a recording session. Author Lees has published widely on jazz and other musical matters.

Leiber, Fritz. "The Beat Cluster." In *The Seventh Galaxy Reader*, edited by Frederick Pohl, 199–214. Garden City, NY: Doubleday, 1964.
    Guitar-playing hipster, Fats Jordan, and his beatnik buddies are deported from Outer Space—"The Beat Cluster"—to Earth. On his final broadcast from space, Fat's words are accompanied by music from the Small Jazz Ensemble.

Leistra, Ben. *Het Jazz—Requiem.* [*The Jazz—Requiem.*] The Netherlands, Gopher: 2004(?).
    According to jacket copy, a novel in Dutch about saxophonist Boudewijn, who battles alcoholism as he becomes famous as a jazz musician. Not seen.

Leonard, Elmore. *Tishomingo Blues*. New York: William Morrow, 2002.

Shortly after Dennis Lenahan brings his daredevil high-diving act to the Tishomingo Lodge in Tunica, Mississippi, he witnesses a "Dixie Mafia" execution. Shortly after, he meets a Jaguar-driving African-American hustler from Detroit, Robert Taylor, and they become involved in Elmoresque shenanigans. The musical content concerns Taylor, who loves the Delta blues and talks about them at every opportunity. The wacky plot is based on the crossroads metaphor, the Faustian pact between man and the devil á la Robert Johnson. The title is taken from the Spencer Williams composition, made famous by Duke Ellington, among others.

Lewis, Ellen Jordis. "Miss Brown to You." *Brilliant Corners* 8 (Winter 2003): 15–20.

An affecting coming-of-age story about young Evelyn Brown ("Miss Brown to You") and her music-loving parents. After her mother dies, she hangs out at the jazz clubs where her father plays, drinking Shirley Temples and doing homework under her dad's loose but loving supervision. As in all such stories, she must all-too-soon move on to another stage of her life.

Lewis, William Henry. "Rossonian Days." In *Gumbo: A Celebration of African American Writing*, edited by Marita Golden and E. Lynn Harris, 631–44. New York: Harlem Moon, 2002.

Dedicated to all the jazz musicians "nobody heard," this is an impressionistic story about life on the road for unknown jazz musicians who are traveling to a gig in Denver. The protagonist sums up the situation for the nameless musicians of the time:

> Bebop has died, straight ahead Jazz is dying. The small traveling band ain't long for this road. Long Playing records play the hits, what's popular spinning on records for less than any five-piece group driving state to state. They not gonna like you out West cause you Sonny Rollins, son, they gonna like you cause they heard your record was on the tops of the Billboard and Downbeat lists. Or maybe you got an angle: Dave Brubeck and Chet Baker blowin blues like the Brothers but their blues ain't about paying the bills. Only a few will rise off the highways and land on wax.

So why do they persevere? Because through their music they can discover their own voice, express their individuality, and get in touch with their roots. The story overflows with references to jazz musicians and their music.

Lima, Orlando. *No Room for Squares*. New York: Limachips Press, 2003.

This novel comprises four parts (called "sides") and three main characters, each of whom is given a solo. The protagonist is a Wall Street broker nicknamed Gamble, whose blue suit obscures the trumpet wizard within. Gamble is a babe-magnet, who whiles away his life making money, getting drunk on twee drinks, attending strip shows, and sorting out his love life. In the time-honored fashion of such stories, Gamble soon flees this high-reward, low-content life for New Orleans. There he meets Claire, a former stripper who now reads palms by day and plays trumpet by night. Discovering Gamble's talents as a player and composer, Claire arranges for his trumpet to be flown in from New York. The instrument is run over by a streetcar, an accident that introduces character number three, known as "Rat" to his friends, who now repairs brass instruments. (Now in his 60s, he had once played drums and buddied with Dexter Gordon and Sonny Rollins. Now he is an oracular wise-man-in-rags, who proffers guidance to the favored few.) The three worthies then segue to New York, where—surprise!—Gamble turns the jazz world on its ear. At the end, he leads a band in a Harlem club, asking the audience to join him "in a round of applause for Sonny Rollins, Herbie Hancock, Horace Silver, Wayne Shorter, Lou Donaldson, Ron Carter, Milt Jackson, and Donald Byrd," all of whom are in attendance. This book is remarkable for its lack of a single fresh image, well-crafted sentence, interesting character, or believable event.

Lippman, Laura. "The Shoeshine Man's Regrets." In *Murder . . . and All That Jazz,* edited by Robert J. Randisi, 223–37. New York: Signet, 2004.

Tess Monaghan, a private investigator in a series set in Baltimore, becomes involved in a forty-year-old murder case when she intervenes in a skirmish between a country-club type and an old black shoeshine man. The *very* slight musical content surfaces on the last page when Tess solves the cold case with the help of a jazz lyric.

"Little Girl Blue: A Jazz Short Story." *Jazz Today* 2, no. 5 (June 1957): 15.

Guitarist-vocalist Tomy Gendichi calls his daughter "Little Girl Blue." When his daughter tells him she saw a rabbit, he responds that rabbits don't live in the city. Coming home from his gig the next morning, he sees a rabbit. Obviously, minimal music.

Lively, Adam. *Blue Fruit*. London: Simon and Schuster, 1988; New York: Simon and Schuster, 1989.

A time-travel novel in which John Field, a young ship's surgeon on an eighteenth-century whaling vessel, is put ashore in twentieth-century Harlem, where he is taken in by a black family. Field is befriended by Tommy, a talented, innovative saxophonist who guides Field through the jazz dives of Harlem. Several vivid descriptions of improvisational jazz in the making.

Lombreglia, Ralph. "Jazzers." *Iowa Review* 4, no.1 (Winter 1984): 51–63.
    The speaker meets his old buddy Bobby in a newly yuppified Baltimore bar, where the sounds of jazz on the stereo system distract them from the question at hand: Bobby's woman problem. Many drinks and hours later, the two guys (who had a jazz combo years earlier) get involved in a lively jam session, ultimately turning their thoughts to the possibility of forming a band and returning to music. As the title implies, the story is dominated by jazz.

London, Jonathan. *Hip Cat.* San Francisco: Chronicle, 1993.
    Miles Davis and John Coltrane are among the dedicatees of this rhythmic story for young readers about a saxophone-playing hip cat (feline variety), who goes to the big city in search of fame and fortune only to discover that all the really cool clubs are owned by powerful dogs.

———. *Who Bop?* New York: HarperCollins, 2000.
    Super-hip hare, Jazz-Bo, loves nothing better than to play his saxophone and does so exuberantly at the sock-hop, where there's nothing but dancing and fun all night long. This rhymed story for young children is dedicated to Joshua Redman, Charlie "Bird" Parker, and Lester "Pres" Young, the latter two of whom are in "sax heaven."

Loustal-Paringaux, Jacques de. *Barney and the Blue Note.* Translated by Frieda Leia Jacobowitz. Netherlands: Rijperman, 1988.
    A graphic (i.e., illustrated) novel about a sax player, Barney, who had briefly been the talk of the jazz world in the 1950s. But the more famous he became, the more he retreated from the world. After a gig with Art Blakey and the Messengers, Barney starts shooting heroin, loses his talent, retreats into a life of cigarettes, booze, hotel rooms, sex, and existential remoteness. Despite the fact that Barney is clearly a lost soul, he is irresistible to one once-beautiful woman, whose love allows him to regain his chops. Because of his instability and his unpredictable behavior, record companies refuse to record him. After sitting in at the Five Spot and being told by the black leader that he'd never heard a white man play like Barney (borrowing from an Art Pepper anecdote), Barney goes to California, disappears from the scene, kills a man over dope, spends several years in the slammer and mental institution, gets out, starts playing again, and then ODs. A *tres noir* book that exploits all of the worst jazz myths and stereotypes.

Lowry, Malcolm. "The Forest Path to the Spring." *Hear Us O Lord from Heaven Thy Dwelling Place*, 215–83. Philadelphia: Lippincott, 1961.

The narrator, a former jazz musician, decides to write a jazz symphony while trying to get his life together in the Pacific Northwest. Significant passages relating to the music and legendary performers of jazz.

———. *Lunar Caustic. Paris Review* 1963. London: Jonathan Cape, 1968.

Apart from a few glancing references to jazz and blues, the only jazz interest in this novella (which was edited into existence after the writer's death) is that the protagonist who is undergoing rehabilitation for alcoholism and psychological breakdown had been a jazz pianist and bandleader in England before coming to the United States.

Luongo, Margaret. "What Nina Wants." *Brilliant Corners* 10 (Winter 2005): 26–40.

On the advice of their third marriage counselor, Alicia and bassist Rob have adopted the personae of people they admire: Nina Simone for her, Charles Mingus for him. Their destination on this weekend is a fund-raising party at which Rob hopes to solicit significant funding for jazz; they are also using the occasion to see if they can get their relationship back together. It is clear from Rob's flirtatiousness and Alicia's reckless behavior that their secondary objective, at least, is destined to fail.

Lutz, John. "Chop Suey." In *Murder . . . and All That Jazz*, edited by Robert J. Randisi, 11–24. New York: Signet, 2004.

A period piece set in St. Louis in 1926 in which blues singer Lauralee worries whether she will ever experience enough "suffering and guilt" to achieve that "been-around sound" so essential to the music. When she finds her boyfriend in bed with her newfound "friend," she transacts some business that may one day get her all the way to the Cotton Club in the Harlem of her dreams.

———. "The Right to Sing the Blues." *Alfred Hitchcock Mystery Magazine*, 1983. In *Murder to Music*, edited by Cynthia Manson and Kathleen Halligan, 203–33. New York: Carroll and Graf Publishers, 1997.

Jazz-loving private detective Nudger is summoned to New Orleans, where legendary clarinetist Fat Jack McGee hires him to investigate the suspicious behavior of Willy Hollister, a club musician who "plays ultrafine piano." Nudger uncovers some disturbing coincidences in Hollister's past, and after relating these to his employer, Hollister mysteriously vanishes. Solid jazz content.

―――. *The Right to Sing the Blues*. New York: St. Martin's, 1986. An expansion of the story by the same title (q.v.).

Mackey, Henry B. "The Phenomenal Resurgence of the Spasm Band." *Record Changer* 9 (December 1950).
A parody of the white critics' efforts to track down legendary musicians in order to discover the so-called truth behind the origins of jazz. When the critic-narrator finally locates the legendary 193-year-old kazoo wizard, Jug-Head Brown, in Africa, he asks such questions as, "When were legitimate instruments first used in jazz, Jug-Head?" The latter replies (in part): "That was a sad day, man. The real jazz, the true jazz, man, you can't play that on no legit' horn!"

Mackey, Nathaniel. *Bedouin Hornbook*. 1986. Los Angeles: Sun and Moon, 1997.
An epistolary fiction in which "N." addresses a series of letters to "Angel Dust"; the letters are thick with jazz references and often contain lengthy meditations on various questions relating to mostly post-bop music. The following passage typifies the musical monologue at the heart of this plotless novel:

> I've been listening a lot to Pharoah Sanders's solo on the version of "My Favorite Things" on *Coltrane Live at the Village Vanguard Again!* The fellow who wrote the liner-notes quotes Trane as having said that he was "trying to work out a kind of writing that will allow for more plasticity, more viability, more room for improvisation in the statement of the melody itself." That may well be what I'm after as well. What gets me about Pharoah's solo is the way he treats the melody towards the end of it, coming on to it with a stuttering, jittery, tongue-tied articulation which appears to say that the simple amenities or naïve consolations of so innocuous a tune have long since broken down. He manages to be true to the eventual debris of every would-be composer. (Think about the movie the song is taken from.) It's as though he drank water from a rusted cup, the tenor's voice such an asthmatic ambush of itself as to trouble every claim to a "composed" approach. To me it borders on prayer, though prayer would here have to be revised so as to implicate humility in some form of détente—an uneasy truce or eleventh-hour treaty—with hubris. Part prayer, part witch's brew."

―――. *Djbot Baghostus's Run*. Los Angeles: Sun and Moon, 1993.
A continuation of *Bedouin Hornbook* (q.v.) and "volume two of *From a Broken Bottle Traces of Perfume Still Emanate*, an ongoing work." As in *Bedouin*, this unclassifiable fiction comprises a series of letters addressed to "Angel of Dust" that are punctuated with references to, and discussions of, music, especially jazz. The objectives of these experimental fictions by Mackey are obscure; any reader would welcome an explanatory note of some kind.

———. "From *Djbot Baghostus's Run.*" In *Breaking Ice: An Anthology of Contemporary African-American Fiction*, edited by Terry McMillan, 446–56. New York: Viking, 1990.

An excerpt from the novel of the same name (q.v.). This section contains substantial reference to Miles Davis's *Seven Steps to Heaven*.

MacPherson, Rett. *Killing Cousins*. New York: St. Martin's Minotaur, 2002.

The only musical interest in this genealogical mystery lies in the fact that the deceased woman whose life is being researched had been a jazz singer in the 1930s and 1940s. One of the categories the Library of Congress Cataloguing-in-Publication Data places this novel in is "Jazz singers"—one more book to place in the "Let the reader beware" file.

Maher, Jack. "Unique Record Reviews from a Mind Made Mad by Record Reviewing." In *Jazz 1958: The Metronome Year Book, 1958*, edited by Bill Coss, 60–62. New York: Metronome Corporation, 1958.

A spoof of the jazz reviews written by a writer suffering from cognitive— or aural—overload. Here, for example, are a few of the pieces comprising Al "Beef" Boeuf's *Meat-Eater Suite*: "Ribs to Spare," "Momma Don't Allow No Bouillabaisse," "Save the Bones for Henry Jones."

Major, Clarence. *Dirty Bird Blues*. San Francisco: Mercury House, 1996.

In his mid-twenties, shortly after World War II, Manfred "Man" Banks strives to put his life back together. He lives for his wife and daughter and dreams of making music the center of his life: he "used the harmonica or the sax to say what he couldn't find words to say." But racism and booze in the form of Old Crow bourbon (the titular Dirty Bird) constantly threaten to turn his life into a shambles. Man finally overcomes the obstacles that challenge his security and looks forward to a sanguine future. Man used to warm-up for Billie Holiday; the novel makes frequent reference to blues musicians and employs blues techniques in its narrative structure.

Malone, R. Pingank. "Sound Your 'A': The Story of Trumpeter Tom Stewart in Full-Length Novel Form." *Metronome* 58 (September 1942):16–17; 58 (October 1942): 14–15; 58 (November 1942): 14–15; 58 (December 1942):14–15; 59 (February 1943): 16–17.

A serialized novel focusing on a group of mostly young musicians with jazz aspirations who are reduced to playing in a pit band. One of the players, Tom Stewart, gets a chance to fill in with a name band that is unfortunately famous for its "tickety-tockety" style of music. The bandleader falls in love with Tom's corny playing, not realizing that Tom is making fun of the music.

Tom switches bands, creates envy through his virtuoso playing, and gets in fights. Many references to such popular bands of the time as Woody Herman's and Charlie Barnet's.

Manier, Stéphane. *Sous le Signe du Jazz*. Paris: Éditiones de I 'Epi, 1926.
This novel in French (which I have skimmed but only selectively translated) takes place in a French nightclub, where the dancers occasionally discover the ecstatic potential of jazz as they adjust their movements and rhythms to the syncopations of the African-American orchestra. There are references that would now be labeled racist, as when the music is said to be accompanied by apish smirking ("accompagnèrent de minauderies simiéques"), but the larger question concerns what the book has to say about cultural primitivism. Is the writer stereotyping, perhaps even caricaturing the black musicians or is he celebrating their more *feeling* response to life?

Mansbach, Adam. *Shackling Water*. New York: Doubleday, 2001.
For young saxophonist Latif James-Pearson, jazz is his life and Albert Van Horn his hero, so he leaves Boston for New York hoping to apprentice himself to Van Horn. During the day Latif immerses himself in his music, practicing his horn endlessly in his Harlem boardinghouse room. At night, he goes downtown to Dutchman's where Van Horn has an extended gig. Latif studies the musicians night after night, hoping to absorb the lessons they impart through their music and thus be worthy of joining them some day. But he also falls under the influence of a very hip drug dealer, Say Brother, and a white painter, Mona, with whom he enters into a complicated relationship. Just as Latif's life starts seriously to unravel, Van Horn takes him under wing and relates *his* remarkable life story to the troubled young man. Although this novel dramatizes questions of self-discovery, the grim reality of addiction, the nature of art, and racial and sexual politics, it is most consistently concerned with jazz: there are countless references to major musicians, several descriptions of musical performances, verbal riffs on the "meaning" of the music, and a style appropriate to the subject matter.

Manus, Willard. *Connubial Bliss*. Los Angeles: Panjandrum Press, 1990.
A raucous, raunchily sexist farce featuring the improbable, often grotesque shenanigans of a not-so-young, not-so-nice Jewish boy from the Bronx, Lenny Samuels, who spews street Yiddish and the language of high culture with equal flippancy. The modest jazz connection involves Lenny's friend Sydney, whose Uncle Sol is a jazz musician who once played with Petronius Priest (obviously based on Thelonious Monk): "A singular figure in a derby and goatee, playing his crabbed single-line notes and crazy chords with wicked humor." Sydney

also delights in showing off his record collection, which stretches from "Buddy Bolden to Ornette's *Enfante*, with a long loving stop en route for Charlie and Diz singing SALT PEANUTS, SALT PEANUTS and that Jackie McLean record with Donald Byrd on trumpet . . ."

———. "Hello Central, Give Me Doctor Jazz." *New Letters* 51, no. 2 (Winter 1984–85): 19–28.
In this section from *Connubial Bliss* (q.v.), Lenny is visiting jazzman Sol, who is taking the cure for drug addiction and doubting his ability to recover his musical talent.

Marsh, Ngaio. *Swing, Brother, Swing*. London: Collins, 1949. [Published as *A Wreath for Rivera*. Boston: Little, Brown, 1949.]
A classic British mystery with eccentric characters, a baffling crime, and the redoubtable Scotland Yard detective, Inspector Alleyn. The jazz content is limited to the first third of the novel where Breezy Bellair and his boogie-woogie band prepare to unveil a novelty number involving mock killings of various band members; the mock of course, in an elaborate twist, becomes real.

Marsh, Willard. "Mending Wall." *Southern Review* n.s. 5 (Autumn 1969): 1192–1204.
In his native Mexico during a semester break, Miguel is more or less forced to provide hospitality to some of his fellow law students while they wait for a bus. The more Miguel's Anglo friends drink, the more contemptuous they become of Hispanic culture and even of the jazz they claim to love. In Miguel's case, as in the Robert Frost poem from which this story borrows its title, "good fences *do* make good neighbors."

Marshall, Paule. *The Fisher King*. New York: Scribner, 2000.
Shortly after World War II, Sonny-Rett Payne fled New York to escape his family's disapproval of "the Sodom and Gomorrah" music he played and the racism that interfered with his art. Payne's legendary success as a jazz pianist in Europe and his subsequent death provide the background for this novel that explores the effect of his fame on the fragile dynamics of the family and community he left behind. Decades after his death, Payne's old Brooklyn neighborhood stages a memorial concert in his honor. It is in these pages (Chapters 15–17) that the jazz focus is greatest.

Marshall-Courtois, Rebecca. "The Place Where Colored Notes Play." 1 July 2004. http://www.jerryjazzmusician.com/mainHTML.cfm?page=marshall .html (5/11/05).

For 27 years Celina has tried to teach Ray how to identify the tastes available to his palate and he's spent those same "years trying to show her how to see and feel music. They complete each other or had . . ." before he became severely disabled. Now, as Celina plays a CD while she and Ray repose at the ocean, he begins actually to *see* the music for the first time, "the slithering call of the reds, the slow approach of greens, the sharp sparks of blues, and the bursts of yellow." In this place beyond words, Ray feels his soul being lifted away, "to that place where colored notes play." It's hard to tell whether synesthesia or schizophrenia is the source of Ray's experience.

Martin, Kenneth K. "The End of Jamie." *Negro Digest*, December 1964, 63–70.
 Sullen teenager Jamie leaves Harlem to visit his uncle in the South. When he returns after a year, he has changed: not only is he much taller, but he has learned to play jazz on the harmonica; in fact, he has learned to externalize his dark moods through his music. But at one point, Jamie can no longer make his harmonica speak for him and so loses hope.

Martin, Ralph G. *Skin Deep*. New York: David McKay, 1964.
 A novel (by a non-black American) that explores the intersecting lives of four African-American expatriates in Paris after World War II. Those with an interest in jazz fiction may find the first section ("Johnny") moderately interesting as it focuses on Johnny Smith, a jazz singer-composer with an equal gift for music and love-making.

Martucci, Ida. *Jive Jungle*. New York: Vantage, 1956.
 Basically a love story that incorporates jazz as background music. One character is a musician, and there are scattered references to such musicians as Barbara Carroll, Miles Davis, Howard McGhee, Kai Winding, Machito, and Stan Getz.

Marvin, Bryan. "Hath Charms to Soothe." *Esquire*, February 1944, 44, 112.
 While playing his hot variations to "St. Louis Blues," clarinetist Dmitri Stanakous "slipped in a G-sharp with the little finger of his left hand," causing a deep sense of well-being to wash over him. Dmitri had been bored and mildly depressed by the sameness of playing at summer country club functions, but now something thrilling was happening to him. The crowd took notice as Dmitri "surpassed the ordinary reaches of hot jazz" and they even evolved a new kind of dance—"a prancing bounce"—to suit the occasion. After the concert was over and the audience had gone home, Dmitri continued to play outside the club, charming the forest creatures that had come from far and wide to listen to this joyous music. Dmitri falls asleep and awakens to

find his clarinet smashed to smithereens, apparently the victim of "some very large deer."

Mason, Bobby Jo. "With Jazz." *New Yorker,* February 26, 1990. *Zigzagging Down a Wild Trail,* 3–19. New York: Random House, 2001.
Alas, the titual Jazz refers to a character who has nothing to do with the music.

Mass, Rochelle. "Rozogov and Jazz." *Paumanok* 2.3. http://www.etext.org/Fiction/Paumanok/2.3/html/mass.html (27 April 2002).
When Rozogov sees the narrator leaving a concert [in Israel?] at intermission, he asks if he can have her ticket. When she gives it to him, he says that she should listen to jazz; after all, jazz is a celebration of life. Rozogov's words stick with her, leading her to reflect on her life and on music. She decides that she left the concert early because, although Dee Dee [Bridgewater?] had remarkable presence and was exciting to look at, she took too many liberties with the music. At the end, the narrator tells her friend that she's going to keep an eye out for Rozogov: "He's an interesting type."

Matheson, Richard. "The Jazz Machine." *Magazine of Fantasy and Science Fiction,* 1963. In *The 9th Annual of the Year's Best SF*, edited by Judith Merril, 143–50. New York: Simon and Schuster, 1964.
The black musician telling this free verse narrative is approached by a white man ("Mr. Pink"), who tells the trumpeter that his music reveals that he has recently lost someone close to him. Then Mr. Pink shows the narrator a machine he invented that changes the sounds of jazz into the feelings that created them. The narrator smashes the machine with his instrument, reflecting that, although whites may continue to exploit blacks in every way imaginable, they better not "come scuffling for our souls" (i.e., the feelings they express through their music).

Maximin, Daniel. *L'Ile et Une Nuit* [*The Island and a Night*]. Paris: Seuil, 1995.
According to jacket copy, in this final installment of Maximin's trilogy, the series protagonist, Marie-Gabriel, prepares to resist a killer cyclone on Guadaloupe.

——. *Lone Sun.* Translator not given. Charlottesville: University Press of Virginia, 1989. [Originally published in French as *L'Isolé Soleil* (1981).]
A strange, post-modern mélange of dreams, narrative fragments, Creole aphorisms, diaries, folktales, and legends in the service of a novel about writ-

ing a novel whose major objective is to explore the unrecorded Caribbean past. Maximin's rhythms and themes are strongly influenced by Afro-American and Afro-Cuban jazz. The first of a trilogy, this work does indeed contain scattered references to jazz and its musicians, a couple of scenes dramatizing musical performances, and at least two extended passages on one of Coleman Hawkins' renditions of "Body and Soul." The excerpt that follows can only begin to hint at the power of these passages:

> Linked to your rhythm, Ariel, I listen to Coleman Hawkins for the first time as he plays a tune that's as tranquil as an assured despair. *Body and Soul*, Ariel says to me, and I watch his cat's eyes that fall without seeing anything beyond the golden curve of his sax. Big deep-voiced sex. "*Body and Soul*, his most recent composition." Our last dance, Ariel, I try to follow the thread of the melody in the labyrinth of improvisation, I try to follow the rhythm of your regular steps, the rhythm of your heart pounding against my chest, my head on your broad shoulder, my hands joined behind the gentle curve of your neck, almost beneath your hair that tickles my fingers. We will have said everything without a word of accusation or redemption. Perfect love ends without lawyers or judges. *Body and Soul*. "This musician is afraid of solitude, just like I'm afraid to see you again," says Ariel. "Listen to how he never goes directly to a high note without passing through a whole harmonic chain, listen to how he starts each phrase with a tremolo note, the way only a warmed-up ebony clarinet can do!" I love you Ariel, I love the way your despair doesn't block up your ears.

Author Maximin was born in Guadaloupe and has long lived in France. His novels are influenced by the negritude movement and informed, both in subject matter and style, by jazz, especially the Afro-American and Afro-Cuban forms. Kathleen Gýssels has said that in Maximin's three novels, "la musique prend une place tourjours croissante et elle s'enchévêtre de maniére toujours plus complexe dans une écriture post-moderne . . ." ("Le Jazz Dans le Roman Afro-Antillais: Consonances de la Diaspora Noire dans l'Oeuvre de Daniel Maximin." *Revue Littâeraire Mensuelle* 75 [August–September 1997], 124–33.)

———. *Soufriéres* [*Sulfur Mines*]. Paris: Seuil, 1987.
According to cover copy, a lyrical, sometimes epic suspense novel in which all of the actions and events are influenced by the imminent eruption of a volcano on Guadaloupe.

McCarthy, Albert J. "My Home Is a Southern Town." In *Jazz Parody (Anthology of Jazz Fiction)*, edited by Charles Harvey, 57–61. London: Spearman Publishers, 1948.

Grant Farber, talented blues pianist, moves north where he achieves some grudging fame from the white society that patronizes him. He returns to the South, knowing that his destiny is to be killed by the racist society he couldn't escape.

McCluskey, John. *Look What They Done to My Song*. New York: Random House, 1974.
A first-person account of a young, down-and-out black jazz musician's search for racial identity during the 1960s. He says his sound has been described in many ways: "The Eldorado drive of Stanley Turrentine, the swift glad comedy of Sonny Rollins, the steady quest of John Coltrane." Yet he finds precious few opportunities to demonstrate these laudable qualities. At the end, he is in the process of incorporating into his musical compositions every variety of "blackness" he has encountered on his odyssey.

——. "Lush Life." *Callaloo* 13, no. 2 (Spring 1990): 201–12.
Life on the road with "Earl Ferguson and America's Greatest Band." As Earl and his wonderful composer/arranger, Billy Cox, travel ahead of the band bus, they chat about what it's like to move from town to town trying to capture the interest of different audiences. After Billy tells an affecting story, Earl responds: "It's this music we play, Billy! It opens people up, makes them give up secrets. Better than whiskey or dope for that. It don't kill you, and you can't piss it away. You can whistle it the next day in new places. You can loan it to strangers, and they thank you for it. . . . It's what keeps us going all night." The story is interesting for its depiction of the creative process, as we see the two men struggle to put together a new song, wondering at the end if it will go over with their audiences. The title is taken from the Billy Strayhorn composition of the same name, and indeed the characters seem to pay homage to Strayhorn and his mentor, Duke Ellington.

McConduit, Denise Walter. *D.J. and the Jazz Fest*. Gretnor, LA: Pelican, 1997.
An illustrated book for juveniles "in commemoration of the 100th anniversary of jazz." When D.J.'s mom suggests to him that they go to the New Orleans jazz fest, D.J. thinks it's a boring idea. But when he gets there and sees Wynton Marsalis, B.B. King, and the Neville brothers and gets caught up in the excitement, he changes his mind. He is last seen, bright flag in hand, marching along with a band and, thanks to jazz, feeling special.

McKay, Claude. *Banjo: A Story without a Plot*. New York: Harper, 1929.
Lincoln Agrippa Daily is known to everyone as Banjo for the instrument he plays. The novel is set in the 1920s on the seedy waterfront of Mar-

seilles, where indigent blacks from all over the world spend their time panhandling, whoring, drinking, and playing music. Banjo's dream is to form
an orchestra, but the best he can manage is a short-lived quartet of a tiny
horn, flute, guitar, and his banjo. The novel is much interested in racial issues, including the back-to-Africa movement. At one point, his friend
Goosey chides Banjo for his instrument: "Banjo is bondage. . . . the instrument of slavery. Banjo is Dixie. The Dixie of the land of cotton and massa
and missus and black mammy. . . ." The novel is didactic, with many unlikely and lengthy philosophical discussions, but its musical content is always interesting and often provocative. One wonders whether the improvisational way the free-wheeling Banjo leads his life is intended to parallel
the jazz he so loves.

———. *Home to Harlem*. New York: Harper & Row, 1928.
   A gritty novel tracing the parallel paths of two young urban black males attempting to find their way in a racist society. Dancing, singing, drinking,
brawling, and screwing—these pretty much define the boundaries of the characters' non-working lives, which are played out largely in cabarets and
speakeasies. Music hovers over the action of the novel as jazz and the blues
provide a momentary (and often defective) crutch for the crippled lives of the
characters. The following passage demonstrates how music affects both the
mood of the characters and the style of the book:

> A "blues" came trotting out of the pianola. The proprietress bounced into Jake's
> arms. The men sprang at the two girls. The unlucky ones paired off with each other.
> Oh "blues," "blues," "blues." Black-framed white grinning. Finger-snapping. Un-
> dertone singing. The three men with women teasing the stags. Zeddy's gorilla feet
> dancing down the dark death lurking in his heart. Zeddy dancing with a pal.
> "Blues," "blues," "blues." Red moods, black moods, golden moods. Curious, syn-
> copated slipping—over into one mood, back-sliding back to the first mood. Hum-
> ming in harmony, barbaric harmony, joy-drunk, chasing out the shadow of the mo-
> ment before.

The term *jazz* and its variants are frequently used in unusual ways.

McKinney-Whetstone, Diane. *Blues Dancing*. New York: William Morrow,
   1999.
   A sexy cover of a couple doing a sultry dance, cover copy relating the author's style to jazz, and a musical title—alas, these are the only musical references in this novel. The same holds true for the author's earlier novel, *Tum-
bling* (New York: William Morrow, 1996), which would seem to have a
significant jazz component but doesn't.

McMartin, Sean. "Music for One Hand Only." *Phylon* 2 (Summer 1969): 197–202.

When Bernie McCafferty overhears an Ella Fitzgerald recording, he tracks down its owner, who, after claiming to be part black, offers to sell Bernie the record for an extortionate sum. In this futuristic story, plagues had decimated the black population of Africa, and now enormous numbers of British and American blacks have moved to Africa to repopulate the continent. It seems that what remains of black culture in the United States and the western world in general is at serious risk, threatening cultural impoverishment. Several references to black female jazz singers.

McNutt, William Slavens. "Jazz Justice." *Collier's* 5+, December 27, 1924.

Orphaned early and raised in the sticks by relatives, Shirley Horton moves to Manhattan where she becomes "a gold digger with a conscience," exploiting man after man until she meets her match in Ted Snowden:

> . . . a slim, blond, modern troubadour. The generation of jazz shimmied to his tunes in Shanghai and hummed his lyrics in London. Wherever throughout the world were orchestras and dance floors, liquor and lights, men and women, love and laughter in combination, there was the sound of a Snowden tune, savagely gay, cynically sensuous, weirdly, intoxicatingly rhythmic, a mocking, insolent, yet hauntingly wistful expression in movement and melody of the syncopated soul of Now. As a reward for the songs that bubbled effortlessly out of him he received a yearly return greater than the annual salary of the President of the United States.

Very much a tale of the Jazz Age with snappy dialogue, speedy roadsters, and high living in the big city.

McSiegel, Professor Snotty. *See* Feather, Leonard.

Mendez Carrasco, Armando. *Dos Cuentos de Jazz*. Androvari: Santiago, Chile, 1962.

This brief collection, in Spanish, contains two stories: "El Trompetista De Harlem" (9–22) and "El Conventillo Danza" (23–29). Louis Armstrong, Bix Beiderbecke, Stan Kenton, and Fats Waller are mentioned, and "hot jazz" and "jam session" figure prominently.

Merril, Judith. "Muted Hunger." *The Saint Mystery Magazine*, October 1963: 51–63.

The narrator is surprised when her detective-husband Pete (who is not a jazz fan) suggests they go to the Horn, a jazz club where a combo has been playing exciting music for a couple of months—or ever since a very hot blonde ("a bitch and a tease") started hanging out there, causing competition among the musicians on the stand. Pete is right in thinking that his wife's deep knowledge of jazz will help him solve Cindi's brutal rape and beating. An unusual story of its kind because it gives as much attention to the music as to the mystery.

Metzger, Deena. *Doors: A Fiction for Jazz Horn.* Los Angeles: Red Hen Press, 2005.
This *should* be a thoroughgoing jazz novel. After all, it involves a young American woman who becomes obsessed with the great, jazz-loving Argentine novelist Julio Cortázar and heartbreakingly determines, years after Cortázar's death, to will him into her life; the subtitle, too (*A Fiction for Jazz Horn*), strongly implies significant musical content. Alas, this metaphysical fiction on a major jazz writer contains only superficial jazz interest: a couple of substantial riffs on Cortàzar's novella about Charlie Parker, "The Pursuer," and scattered references to artists like John Coltrane, whose initials, one is led to suppose, link him on a spiritual level to the Argentine artist.

Meyers, Martin. "Snake Rag." In *Murder . . . and All That Jazz*, edited by Robert J. Randisi, 25–46. New York: Signet, 20004.
A period piece set during Prohibition in New York City. Legs Diamond asks the narrator, jazz pianist Vito Monte, to do some gangster business for him, but when Monte gets deeply involved in the assignment, he discovers that he has all along been a decoy. Quite a few musical references, and Louis Armstrong and Bix Beiderbecke have small roles.

Millen, Gilmore. *Sweet Man.* New York: Viking, 1930; London: Cassell, 1930.
Dedicated to Carl Van Vechten and very much in the vogue of *Nigger Heaven*, this novel is the story of John Henry, a black plantation worker with a weakness for booze and women. After serving in France in World War I, John Henry enters into a relationship with a blonde woman, who keeps him—hence the title. Told largely in the southern black vernacular, the novel makes only passing references to the blues and jazz-blues. The name of John Henry is, of course, a familiar one in folklore and blues.

Miller, Fred. *Gutbucket and Gossamer: A Short Story.* Yonkers, NY: Alicat Bookshop, 1950.
A 27-page chapbook story recounting a boozy weekend in 1940 for two "temporary grass widowers." Their wives elsewhere, Teddy and George get together to drink and listen to jazz; as so often happens under such circumstances, flirtations ensue. Many references to music and musicians: Mezz Mezzrow,

Sidney Bechet, Clarence Williams, King Oliver, Muggsy Spanier, and Louis Armstrong, among others.

Miller, Warren. *The Cool World*. New York: Little, Brown, 1959.
    A coming-of-age novel centering on gang life in Harlem. Perhaps because it has characters named Duke and Bebop and is told in jazzy language, this work has been cited in the scholarship regarding jazz fiction. But there are no musical scenes or jazz references. It was made into a movie (1964) with music by Mal Waldron.

Miller, William. *Rent Party Jazz*. New York: Lee and Low Books, 2001.
    A juvenile book summarized thus by the Library of Congress: "When Sonny's mother loses her job in New Orleans during the Depression, Smilin' Jack, a jazz musician, tells him how to organize a rent party to raise money they need." Not seen.

Mitchell, Adrian. *If You See Me Comin'*. New York: Macmillan, 1962; London: J. Cape, 1962.
    The events of a week are filtered through the hypersensitive consciousness of a British blues singer, Johnny Crane. Frequent references to American jazz artists and a couple of scenes depicting musical performance.

Mitchell, David. *Ghostwritten*. London: Hodder and Stoughton, 1999; New York: Random House, 2000.
    A long novel depicting episodes in the lives of nine heterogeneous people in nine far-flung places across the globe. Among these are an elderly woman who runs a tea shack in rural China; a British shyster in Hong Kong; a transmigrating soul in Mongolia; a terrorist in Okinawa; and a disk jockey in New York. What fate or destiny, the book asks, connects these disparate individuals? The "Tokyo" chapter will be of interest to readers of jazz fiction. Its protagonist is Satoru, a nineteen-year-old illegitimate child who plays tenor sax and runs a jazz CD shop, where he identifies and comments on the music he plays during the day. For instance, "It was a Mal Waldron time of day"; and, in describing a young woman he is attracted to: " . . . if you know Duke Pearson's 'After the Rain,' well, she was as beautiful and pure as that." Satoru is encouraged to interview for a better job but can't stand the thought of parting with his jazz existence.

Moody, Bill. *Bird Lives!* New York: Walker, 1999.
    Somebody's killing the Kenny G-like smooth-jazz musicians, and Evan Horne is called in—by the FBI no less—to help solve the serial murders. Horne's life is complicated by his attraction to one of the FBI agents assigned

to the case (which strains his relationship with his longtime girlfriend) and by his commitment to a recording contract he has just signed with great anticipation. As usual in this series, there is ample reference to jazz and its musicians. Dave McKenna has a brief role.

―――. "Child's Play." In *Murder . . . and All That Jazz*, edited by Robert J. Randisi, 95–108. New York: Signet, 2004.
After a gig, Wilson Childs and Quincy Simmons are driving around San Francisco when they are stopped by a cop who finds drugs and a gun in the car. Since Wilson is in line to work with Miles Davis, Quincy takes the fall and then disappears after being released on bail. A quarter-century later, after *Downbeat* had reported Quincy dead, Wilson finds his old friend in a homeless shelter and, since bebop is hot again, they go on a reunion tour and are looking toward a hopeful future in the end. A *real* jazz story.

―――. *Death of a Tenor Man*. New York: Walker, 1995.
Second in a series featuring amateur detective Evan Horne. In this novel, Horne leaves his home-base in Los Angeles to go to Las Vegas to help an English professor friend research the suspicious death of Wardell Gray, who died in Las Vegas in 1955. The jazz content is considerable and organic. The reader can make a transformative experience out of this series by playing the music that is mentioned while reading the novel. It works.

―――. "Grace Notes." In *Blue Lightning*, edited by John Harvey, 171–82. London: Slow Dancer Press, 1998; Chester Springs, PA: Dufour Editions, 1999.
Ex-junkie saxophonist Noel Coffey is hoping for a comeback after two months in rehab. Years ago Noel had played with Miles Davis and had even recorded an album with him, but then his career got lost in the shuffle. Now he has landed a gig in Germany and wonders if he will be able to pull himself back together. The last sentence is a provocative shocker.

―――. "Jazzline." *Ellery Queen's Mystery Magazine*, March 1991, 192–96.
Weston is a late-night call-in disk jockey at an FM jazz station. After awhile he starts visualizing faces for his callers, some of whom are knowledgeable jazz buffs while others just want wee-hours conversation. But the one who most intrigues him has the sultry voice of Julie London. Weston is in for a surprise when he accepts her invitation to stop by after work at 3 A.M.

―――. *Looking for Chet Baker: An Evan Horne Mystery*. New York: Walker, 2002.
Evan Horne is in London for a gig at Ronnie Scott's famous jazz club, hoping to get back into a serious music groove and leave crime detection far behind.

Unfortunately for Evan, his old chum—and series regular—Ace Buffington shows up with a problem: he has signed a contract to do a book on Chet Baker and has promised the publisher that Evan will agree to coauthor the manuscript. Although Evan refuses, he follows Ace to Amsterdam, but Ace has disappeared, leaving only his notes and briefcase behind. Since Ace had been staying in the room rented by Baker at the time of his death, Evan's search for his missing friend also involves him in unriddling the mysterious death of Chet Baker. As usual in an Evan Horne novel, jazz is ubiquitous—in the foreground, at the heart of the intersecting mysteries, in the supporting cast, and even, probably, in Horne's crime-detecting MO. The novel contains solid musical description, especially when Horne teams up with Fletcher Paige, 69-year-old veteran of the Count Basie horn section. For a genre novel, this one has some unusual features: a poem, "Chet Baker," by crime novelist-jazz lover John Harvey; a foreword by pianist-composer Russ Freeman; and an "Intro," half of which is italicized.

———. "Rehearsal." In *In the River Underground: An Anthology of Nevada Fiction*, edited by Shaun T. Griffin, 49–100. University of Nevada Press, 2001.
Having played with many of the greats, bassist Old Folks is "like a footnote in a chapter of jazz history." But he's twice as old as the next oldest musician in the combo, and Ozzie the leader wants him out so he can bring a younger player in—one who would fit better with the youth-oriented near-jazz the group specializes in. So Ozzie sets in motion a truly reprehensible plan to trap Old Folks into playing wrong notes in order to fire him. The narrator-drummer is sickened by the plan and by himself for not defending Old Folks.

———. "The Resurrection of Bobo Jones." In *B Flat, Bebop, Scat*, edited by Chris Parker, 1–19. London: Quartet, 1986.
Brew Daniels is a talented tenor sax man whose outlandish pranks get him exiled to the nether fringes of the jazz world. When his agent finally lands Brew a gig, it's at the musical equivalent of the last resort—the nicely named "The Final Bar"—where pianist Bobo Jones is trying to make a comeback after being institutionalized for mental incapacity. Anxious because of Bobo's reputation and also because he's the only white in an otherwise all-black combo, Brew nevertheless is able to help Bobo regain his musical genius. The story has a very satisfying denouement.

———. *Solo Hand*. New York: Walker, 1994.
The first in a mystery series featuring Evan Horne, a jazz pianist who became an amateur sleuth after injuring his hand in an auto accident. Here he tries to disentangle two musicians from a blackmail scam that could ruin their

careers. Characteristic of this series, the events shuttle between Los Angeles and Las Vegas and contain considerable jazz content. One of the musicians, Lonnie Cole, even named his dogs Miles and Bird. An additional point of interest is the discussion of the mechanics of the CD industry.

————. *The Sound of the Trumpet*. New York: Walker, 1997.
Jazz pianist Evan Horne turns detective while his hand, injured in an auto accident, undergoes rehabilitation. This novel—third in the series—revolves around an audiotape that may be the last recording of the legendary trumpeter Clifford Brown, who died in a car accident at 25. References to jazz and jazz musicians, especially of the bop era, are ubiquitous. Moody incorporates a series of "Interludes," in which he imaginatively recreates the final days of Brown's life. Jazz fans will find much of interest in this novel, and so will obsessive music collectors and mystery buffs. In a fascinating addendum on the life-imitating-art theme, an audio tape of one of Clifford Brown's last sessions (with Max Roach and Sonny Rollins) *was* unearthed after the publication of this novel and is expected to be produced by Blue Note.

Moore, John. "The Art of Improvisation." Identitytheory.com http://www .identitytheory.com/fiction/moore_art.html (15 July 2003).
The speaker, a copyeditor at a computer magazine, reflects (improvises?) on his life as he rides with his parents to visit his brother in prison. Although Marcus Williams is not a musician, he likes to imagine that he lives the life of a jazz musician; however, on this trip he is forced to conclude that "*this is not the life a jazz musician is supposed to lead*." Scattered but meaningful references to jazz and its artists, mostly beboppers.

Morgan, Max. *Aerobleu: Pilot's Journal*. San Francisco: Chronicle Books, 1997.
Printed in holograph font on "aged" newsprint and presented in an aluminum slipcase, this novel masquerades as the diary of a World War II pilot, Max Morgan, who is at the center of the vibrant jazz scene in Paris in the late 1940s. Max first established his jazz credentials through his impressive collection of bop records and then by operating a jazz club, Aerobleu, which was frequented by all of the "names" of the era, from Josephine Baker to Jean Paul Sartre. There's jazz chat on practically every unnumbered page, and Dizzy Gillespie and Charlie Parker play significant roles. At one point, jazz critic Hugues Panassié denounces Morgan, along with Gillespie and Parker, for promoting rebop; later Panassié claims that Morgan "was a corrupting influence on jazz, and that . . . [Morgan's] Aerobleu sessions were leading French musicians astray . . ." Although *Aerobleu* comes in book form, it is no longer than the average short story.

Morrison, Toni. *Jazz*. New York: Knopf, 1992; London: Chatto and Windus, 1992.

An exploration of the lives of several African-American characters who live in Harlem in 1926 but have their roots in the South. The triggering incident concerns Joe Trace, a married man in his 50s, and his lustful obsession with 18-year-old Dorcas, whom he kills when their affair goes awry. Joe's wife takes very unusual revenge by bursting into Dorcas's funeral and trying to slash the dead girl's face. The title of the book reflects its loose, improvisational structure more than its content, and comes from its association with sex, violence, and chaos: ". . . the music was getting worse and worse . . . songs that used to start in the head and fill the heart had dropped on down, down to places below the sash and buckled belts." And the "Music made you do unwise disorderly things. Just hearing it was like violating the law." In short, for Toni Morrison in this novel, jazz exerts a corrupting influence on the lives of blacks.

Mosley, Walter. "Blue Lightning." In *Blue Lightning*, edited by John Harvey, 183–209. London: Slow Dancer Press, 1998; Chester Springs, PA: Dufour Editions, 1999.

A couple of days in the life of ex-con Socrates Fortlow, who is offered a promotion from his low-paying, menial job in Watts. Socrates's sleep is disturbed by a trumpet in the night; later he meets with the horn man, the two of them get drunk together, and the horn man rips off Socrates.

———. *RL's Dream*. New York: W.W. Norton, 1995; London: Serpent's Tail, 1995.

Atwater "Soupspoon" Wise is an old, dying blues guitarist and singer from the Mississippi Delta living in New York. Seemingly at the bottom of his personal abyss, Soupspoon is befriended by Kiki, a young white woman who is also from the South and who also experienced a painful past. Soupspoon's most haunting memories are of playing with the legendary bluesman Robert "RL" Johnson, whose music "would rip the skin right off yo' back" and "get down to a nerve most people don't even have no more." Thanks to Kiki, Soupspoon is able to record his memories on tape and in so doing lessen the pain of both of their lives.

Moss, Grant, Jr. "I Remember Bessie Smith." *Essence*, December 1978, 66+.

Whenever the speaker thinks of Bessie Smith or hears one of her recordings, he is immediately transported in his mind back to his younger days, growing up in the South, surrounded by friends and family. He thinks especially of Miss Lily Bonner, who townsfolk claimed "could beat Bessie singing the blues." When, much later, the narrator returns home to New Hill, he is saddened to discover that Miss Bonner no longer takes pleasure from the blues: "Nothing is ever the same as it once was" is his mature realization.

Mu, Shiying. "Five in a Nightclub." Translated by Randolph Trumbull. *Renditions* 37 (Spring 1992): 5–22. [Originally published in Chinese in 1932.]

In this attack on capitalism, the lives of five disparate but affluent nightclubbers intersect at a jazz club, a scene that is deftly set: "The world of a Saturday night is a cartoon globe spinning on the axis of jazz—just as quick, just as crazed; gravity loses its pull and buildings are launched skyward." We discover that these revelers all know and fraternize with the black drummer, who is forced by economic circumstances to continue playing on this evening even as his wife lies in a coma after delivering a stillborn child earlier in the day. Although the story's emphasis is much more on politics than music, it is included here because it is one of the very few Chinese jazz stories to have been translated into English.

Muñoz Molina, Antonio. *Winter in Lisbon*. London: Granta, 1999. Translated by Sonia Soto. [Originally published as *El Invierno en Lisboa*. Barcelona: Seix Barral, 1987.]

An atmospheric novel filled with smoky saloons, bibulous musicians, and the intertwining quests for love and meaning against the backdrop of international crime in San Sebastian and Lisbon, among other places. The main character, Biralbo, is a jazz pianist who lacks the gift of genius. Another major character is American trumpeter Billy Swann, who has—or had—that gift in abundance. These and other musicians play in clubs with names like Lady Bird and Satchmo, and their performances are nicely—and unobtrusively—described. It could be argued that the unfolding of the plot mimics the complex rhythms of jazz. Obviously indebted to jazz and film noir, this novel could accurately be described as jazz noir fiction. And its frequent, always provocative meditations on music also qualify it as a philosophical undertaking. No matter how one decides to categorize or describe it, it deserves to be placed in the highest rank of jazz fictions. It won the Spanish National Prize for Literature as well as the Critics' Prize and has been translated into sixteen languages.

Murphy, Dallas. *Don't Explain*. New York: Pocket Books, 1996.

A wacky mystery featuring Artie Deemer, his cash-cow dog, Jellyroll (who is famous for his TV commercial), and his lovely sweetheart, professional pool player Crystal Spivey. Despite the title from a Billie Holiday song, the dog named after a famous jazz musician, and Artie's love of listening to jazz (which he doesn't do in this novel), there is no jazz content in this book.

————. *Lover Man*. New York: Scribner's, 1987.

The first in a series, each edition of which (so far) takes its title from a jazz standard. In this novel, New Yorker Artie Deemer discovers that his old girl-friend has been murdered; after a period of inertia, he goes in search of her killer. Artie is accompanied by his dog, Jellyroll, who (like his master) loves listening to jazz, especially bebop. Artie's favorite activity is to kick back and listen to his beloved jazz heroes, many of whom are mentioned by name in this humorous mystery.

————. *Lush Life*. New York: Pocket Books, 1992.

Artie Deemer, amateur detective, loves to listen to jazz, especially such boppers as Thelonious Monk and Charlie Parker; and when he needs to think, he plays hard-driving, brain-blasting bebop. When he goes to bed with his new sweetheart for the first time, Johnnie Hartman provides the background music, no doubt enabling the lovers' simultaneous orgasm. The title of this se-ries mystery comes from the famous Billy Strayhorn song.

Murray, Albert. *The Magic Keys*. New York: Pantheon, 2005.

This is the fourth installment in Albert Murray's ongoing saga—his Bil-dungsroman—of growing up black and gifted in America. Here, the autobio-graphical Scooter has put his musical ambitions on hold for the time being to re-turn to New York City, marry his college girlfriend, pursue a graduate degree in the humanities, and discover what he truly wants to do with his life. Through his deep and generally joyous immersion in the life of the city and his interaction with close friends (two of whom are transparently borrowed from author Mur-ray's buddies in the real world, the writer Ralph Ellison and the painter Romare Bearden), Scooter sets out in the end to become a writer. Jazz is woven into the fabric of this novel, through references to musicians and venues and Scooter's diminishing career as a bassist. It is also apparent in the style, as when, in a typ-ically high-spirited moment, Scooter says, "Hey, now, talking about some terp-sichorean riff signification. Man, we got it on the afterbeat already." Yet, al-though music is never far from the action, it is seldom at its center, either.

————. *Seven League Boots*. New York: Pantheon, 1995.

In this third volume of an ongoing work, Scooter—now "Schoolboy"— first becomes a bassist and then leaves the band to write music for the movies, after which he joins the expatriate colony in France. Book One, "The Ap-prentice," provides a vivid account of the workings of a large, successful African-American jazz band. In this and the previous two novels in the series, Murray appropriates, in syntax and structure, certain stylistic devices associ-ated with African-American music while frequently referring to jazz and the blues and their performers.

———. *The Spyglass Tree*. New York: Pantheon, 1991.
In this, the second volume of a series, Scooter matures as he matriculates in college in the 1930s.

———. *Train Whistle Guitar*. New York: McGraw-Hill, 1974.
The first novel in a series is set in Alabama in the 1920s and focuses on young Scooter, whose musical education is powerfully influenced by a pair of bluesmen.

Murray, John. *Jazz, Etc*. Hexham, UK: Flambard, 2003.
A lively novel that exuberates with jazz in its several varieties as it wobbles back and forth between Cumbria in Britain and Portugal, with a significant stop in New York City. The protagonist, Enzo Mori, is a brilliant Italian Cumbrian thoroughly in thrall to jazz and obsessed with his Oxford contemporary, Fanny Golightly, who becomes a world-famous jazz guitarist. Unfortunately for Enzo, Fanny exclusively desires a Portuguese musical legend, Toto Cebola. Enzo's father, Vince, contributes considerably to this zany novel as he harebrainedly pursues his overlapping passions of women, the clarinet, and his "trad band," The Chompin' Stompers. Sooner or later, everyone is spellbound by jazz, and the discussions and descriptions of the music are often technical. In fact, even the random digressions of the secondary characters are analyzed in musical terms, as if these characters were intentionally adapting their verbal behavior to the structures of jazz. Note, for instance, how Enzo compares the conversational styles of two supporting characters:

> Mrs. Carneiro's verbal jazz . . . was impressively arterial and branching, as ramblingly divagatory as the old Algarve rail system. Professor Alvarenga might have been capable of occasional parenthesis but on the whole his conversation was intelligently sequential and ordered and his jazz . . . was the jazz of extravagant ornamentation. Mrs. Carneiro, by contrast, picked up a theme, developed it, remembered something else, dropped the original thread and fluttered off in pursuit of a second, a third, a fourth. Nonetheless her original melody was always there and always distantly discernible through all those multiple anastomosings. The theme and the melody were the undying, painful memory of her one enduring love, the source to which she always returned. Once you understood that Daniel Carneiro was the thematic bridgehead, you were no longer flummoxed by Mrs. Carneiro's remarkable parallels with the mind-boggling freeform of a saxophonist and trumpeter called Ornette Coleman . . .

In short, this novel belongs on the short list of essential jazz fictions.

Nash, Leslie Ann. *Martini Diaries*, discovered and introduced by Alston Chase. San Francisco: Chronicle, 1997.

This title appears because it is a companion piece to Nash's *Observations from the Bar* and Max Morgan's *Aerobleu: Pilots' Journal* (qq.v.), both of which purport to document the goings-on at the Aerobleu Bar, the jazz center of Paris shortly after World War II. This brief book, on the other hand, compiles the martini recipes (with anecdotes concerning their origins) that supposedly were invented for such patrons as Miles Davis, Josephine Baker, and a friend of bandleader Meyer Davis's son. A fiction in the sense that the bar and the events are imaginary, but very little jazz content.

————. *Observations from the Bar*. San Francisco: Chronicle, 1997.

A companion-piece to Max Morgan's *Aerobleu: Pilot's Journal* (q.v.) and flaunting the same impressive gift box production values. This short novel covers much of the same ground as *Pilot's Journal* as it details, from Leslie Nash's point of view, the comings and goings at the Parisian Aerobleu jazz club of such figures as Charlie Parker and Dizzy Gillespie. The story also includes a diaristic account of Nash's falling in love with the mysterious Max Morgan, who is apparently involved in clandestine political activities. "Nash" and "Morgan" are obviously pseudonyms.

Neate, Patrick. *Twelve Bar Blues*. London: Viking, 2001; New York: Grove, 2002.

A sprawling, energetic novel spanning three continents, two centuries, and multiple points of view, all in the service of the time-honored theme of the search for identity, much complicated here by the fact that the ancestors of the main characters are unusually difficult to trace. At one center of this polyphonic romp is Fortis "Lick" Holden, descendant of slaves. In the early twentieth century, Lick becomes a pioneer in jazz, after learning to play the cornet in a home for black juvenile delinquents, where he spent much of his childhood. When he got out he played, briefly but incendiarily, with the greats of the day, including Louis Armstrong, and established himself as "the greatest horn player that was ever lost to history." All of this is played out against his obsession with his mulatto stepsister. Lick's story merges (mystifyingly much of the time) with stories of his African ancestors and descendants and his granddaughter Sylvia, a black London-reared former prostitute and currently unemployed jazz singer. The novel's second center of interest, Sylvia, journeys to the United States in an effort to unlock the mystery of her multiracial heritage and, presumably, discover who she is. This novel won Great Britain's prestigious Whitbread Award but isn't likely to garner many cisatlantic prizes: not only does the writer overload his plot and lapse too frequently into cliché, but he has New Orleans blacks in 1998 repeatedly say "sho nuff" and names an important American character "Fortnightly" because he shows up in a certain saloon every two weeks to play his blues.

Neiderhiser, Ed. "Gone in the Air." In *B Flat, Bebop, Scat*, edited by Chris Parker, 113–19. London: Quartet, 1986.

The speaker, a lover of music and a jazz performer, philosophizes over the meaning of music, especially Eric Dolphy's comment that when the music is over "It's gone in the air" and can never be heard again. Although the speaker claims not to be a mystic, he describes one zen-like experience thus: "Seated at my piano, caressing the keys and shaping the sounds, I could integrate myself in the large scope of reality, the broader perspective. I joined the music in the air and became an intimate partner in the cosmos, not a separate entity fighting its flow. And I could participate in things visible and invisible according to their design, blending my consciousness with that of the creator."

Neil, Al. *Changes*. Toronto: Coach House, 1976.

A plotless first-person narrative containing the reflections of jazz pianist, Seamus Finn, as he details his drug addiction and jazz involvement in a hallucinatory style. The speaker's comments on music are substantive and generally of the sort (when they are not predictable) to be provocative to the fan—or student—of jazz fiction. Here is one short section on the necessity for jazz to break from the prison of the past:

> It is one thing to be hip to Jelly Roll, Armstrong, Ellington, Pres and Bird but why accept what they did as valid for everyone. They most perfectly expressed their era sure enough, but that doesn't help us now does it? What we need is to free our minds of them, and move on, as Ornette is doing, unencumbered by tradition or anything else. Ornette just plays the emotion, it is pure expression, so don't try to fit him in yet, when he has only just started to free himself from Bird. Jazz can really open up now if we don't straight-jacket it too soon. Maybe there should be a moratorium on all critical articles, but then most jazz guys don't pay them any attention anyway.

Nemec, John. *Canary's Combo*. Hollywood: Tempo Publishing, 1964.

The cover of this rare "Nite-Time Original" paperback features an impressively voluptuous striptease artiste in mid-gyratic ecstasy. Behind her, a jazz combo is putting out some hot licks. We later learn that this group of Dixieland musicians is committed to the belief that they can achieve the ineffable through jazz but that "willing female flesh" interferes with their spiritual goal. "Jazz is a naked woman," we read, in a truly baffling metaphor. Clarinetist and saxophonist Joe Falcon is the leader of the band and the protagonist of the novel. He sleeps with Carmela Weims, the stripper on the cover, when he isn't sleeping with his wholesome, college-educated "canary" of the band, Ivy, or the black bombshell vocalist, Bess Diedlich, whose Cadillac becomes a bedroom at the touch of a button. The novel's first complication concerns Ivy's desire to make an honest man of Joe and settle into middle-class complacency.

The second involves the brutal murder of Joe's good friend and fellow band member, Benny Sullivan. At this point, Joe appoints himself detective, vowing to avenge the death of his buddy, who turns out, to Joe's astonishment, to have been gay. While conducting his investigation, Joe is beaten, attacked by killer dogs, poisoned, and threatened with guns, razors, and switchblades. He is also embroiled in racial matters and accused of rape. When Ivy is then raped, forcing her—with obscure motivation—to relinquish her singing career as well as her dream of marriage, Joe must find a new "canary" for his band. In no time at all, an incredibly beautiful, talented, sexy, career-oriented new singer materializes, reviving Joe's dream of achieving celestial heights through music. The final words of the novel, as Joe listens to the new vocalist, suggest that he may already be there: "Like *wow*." Jazz purists may be challenged to understand how Joe and company can hope to achieve artistic nirvana with one distractingly provocative nude dancing before them while an equally sexy gal belts out "The Muskrat Ramble" behind them. The all-male audience on the cover do not *appear* to be jazz aficionados.

Newlove, Donald. *The Drunks*. New York: Saturday Review Press, 1974.

Referred to as a "jazz fiction classic" in the jazzhouse.org/fict/newlove .html website, this novel (and its predecessor, *Leo and Theodore* [q.v.]) concerns alcoholic Siamese twins who play horns in traditional jazz bands before coming to New York in the '60s, when one of the twins resolves to kick booze and sober up. While the novel does contain scattered references to jazz, it is probably the style that has led others to regard it as jazz fiction. The following excerpts are taken from the section called "Satchmo Dead, A Jazz Era Ends":

> Blue noon over battlements of Seventh Regiment Armory on Park Avenue where Louis lies in state. Leo-Teddy in line on sidewalk—a few yards away TV reporters nab mourners coming out. Big white steamboats cruising heaven, soft wind blowin' through the pinewood trees *ba baz dab a dez ba bad a dab a doo dab a doo da dez buddya da be dad a DA ZOT! Good mawnin', everybody-y-y!* . . . .
>
> Leo-Teddy passes banks of fleshy gladiola, gazes hard on the dark face in the roses and twilight purple burgundy satin. IN SATCH WE TRUST. *I'm layin' this one on you, Rex!* Whooping Big Daddy Winesprinkler, hornblowing hillhigh dancing black goat under the goofing moon, drooling Big Baby Bacchus borne on orgasm, Dionysius unleashed in divine trance, leaping notes whipped, naked, bent, flattened, trilled, riding high, meteoric C's, D's, E's, F's wheemed in silver tones of steaming Good Time Charlie ginmill pandemonium, a pang as his spirit wings away over the grapedancers' fading frenzy in their tubs, a string snapping in Leo-Teddy's hearts, Louis so small, pale and dainty, his lip scar a white button.

———. *Leo and Theodore*. New York: Saturday Review, 1972.

A frequently hilarious coming-of-age novel about the hijinks of the eponymous Siamese twins who are born in upstate New York on the day of the stock market crash in 1929. After a happy small-town childhood, the boys experience a decidedly less sanguine young manhood. Through broken relationships and alcoholism, they cling to the dream of becoming jazz musicians—horn players. The sections describing their learning to play their instruments are vivid and realistic.

Newman, Charles. *White Jazz*. Garden City, NY: Dial, 1984.

As in Melissa Scott's *The Jazz* (q.v.), the jazz in the title refers to cybernetics rather than music. The story is a week in the life of Sandy, whose life is bounded by computer terminals by day and disco by night.

Newton, Suzanne. *I Will Call It Georgie's Blues*. New York: Viking, 1983.

In this novel for young readers, a Southern Baptist's 15-year-old son, Neal, feels compelled to hide his consuming passion for jazz because it doesn't conform to his family's rigid concept of social behavior. Neal listens to the great bebop pianists and tries to absorb their techniques without actually imitating the artists. Nevertheless, the music in this work is more plot device than topic exploration.

Novak, Mike. *B-Girl*. New York: Ace, 1956.

Fresh out of high school right before World War II, small-town gal Irene Malloy dreams of becoming a dance band singer. One night at a roadhouse dance in her hometown, she is captivated by the trumpeter Chuck Duval, who sounds to her like Harry James. Almost immediately they move in together in Seattle. She is hired to sing in the band, and it looks as if her dream might materialize. Then Chuck gets in a fight, damaging his lip and forcing Irene to quit the band and take on a variety of menial jobs in order to support Chuck until he regains his chops. Before this can happen, however, Chuck physically abuses Irene, causing her to break up with him. Finally, Irene becomes an all-purpose singer-for-hire. Just as she achieves some success and considerable satisfaction, Chuck reenters her life, but this time she recognizes him for the loser he has always been and rejects him in favor of the decent, middle-aged tavern owner who had befriended her in her B-Girl days. On the back cover Chuck is prominently (and mystifyingly, as it turns out) identified as the "Pied Piper of Hot Jazz," and indeed there is some music-making toward the beginning and end of the book but not much in-between.

O'Connor, Edward. *Astral Projection*. Toronto: Random House Canada, 2002.

A classic coming-of-age novel focusing on 15-year-old Goodwin Defoe, whose home life is in shambles: his dad's a drunk and wife-beater and his mom an adulteress. The year is 1967; John Coltrane died a month ago and within a year Miami would go up in flames as a result of race riots. Goodwin begins to take guitar lessons in order to play jazz. He forms a bond with his teacher, Chuck, and goes through the familiar teenage pattern of experimenting with sex, booze, and marijuana. Goodwin longed to find other "musicians interested in the kind of anachronistic music he loved," and in fact finds just such a friend. In Part One, *The Album*, the chapters are called "Tracks" and each is named after a famous tune: "Them That's Not," "All or Nothing at All," "Dancing on the Ceiling," "I Didn't Know What Time It Was," and so on. Review copies of the book were accompanied by a CD containing many of the classic jazz pieces mentioned in the text. The early chapters involving Goodwin's apprenticeship on the guitar are very convincing, and the male bonding through fishing at the end is affectingly impressive (though devoid of musical content).

Odier, Daniel. *Cannibal Kiss*. Translated by Lanie Goodman. New York: Random House, 1989. [First published in France as *Le baiser cannibale* by èditions Fayard-Mazarine, 1987.]

With an epigraph from Archie Shepp, sprinkled references to classic bebop musicians, a cat called Lester Young, and a protagonist nicknamed Bird, this free-form novel (which traces the picaresque adventures of its 15-year-old heroine) apparently wants the reader to believe that it is the novelistic equivalent of an inspired Charlie Parker solo. One can only hope that the writer (who is more famous in America under the pseudonym Delacorta) will resist basing his next novel on the paintings of, say, Jackson Pollock.

Oglesby, W. M. Ellis. *Blow Happy, Blow Sad*. Edmonton, Canada: Commonwealth Publications, 1995.

An espionage novel of the resistance movement to the Nazi occupation of Denmark during World War II. Black American jazz man, Chops Danielson, risks his life in war-torn Denmark, both by playing his cornet in underground jazz venues during which he sends coded military messages to England via his instrument (reminiscent of members of the French Resistance, who used the numbers of Louis Armstrong records as code) and by trying to rescue his Danish classical violinist sweetheart from the clutches of the Nazis. There are too many crosses and double-crosses to keep track of in this long, melodramatic, espionage novel.

O'Hara, John. "The Flatted Saxophone." *New Yorker* 39 (June 1, 1963): 28–29.

The meager jazz content of this abbreviated story occurs at the beginning in a discourse on flatted tenor saxophones—that is, saxophones played out-of-doors, as at weddings—causing one character to respond that if he wants to listen to good saxophone playing, he will "find out where Bud Freeman's working." The rest of the story—all dialogue—concerns marriage.

———. *Pal Joey*. New York: Duell, Sloan and Pierce, 1940.

An epistolary novel in which the title character, a seedy nightclub entertainer—a poor man's Bing Crosby—in 1930s Chicago reveals himself, through a series of letters to his successful bandleader "Pal Ted," to be a heel under his chummy exterior. Several references to musicians and, especially, the qualities of the saxophone.

———. "The Pioneer Hep-Cat." *Assembly*, 103–16. New York: Random House, 1961.

A pleasantly discursive story in which an old newspaperman addresses a high school journalism club on the topic of the music from the 1920s that might be called pre-jazz. The speaker avows that he would much rather talk about someone from Pennsylvania's coal country who rose above his circumstances and made a great success of his life, but his young audiences always want to hear about the legendary singer Red Watson, a jazz pioneer who drank himself into a shockingly early grave. The story is based on the legendary jazz singer from the Scranton area, Jack Gallagher, with whom (apparently) the author once sang a drunken duet of "Jazz Me." Considerable jazz reference to the Swing Era and the years immediately before and after.

Ohio, Denise. *Blue*. Kingston, New York: McPherson, 1993.

As the novel opens, lesbian Ricki Jones is at the site of the plane crash that killed her twin sister, Israellen. Then the novel shuttles confusingly back and forth in time, revealing the complicated relationships among the three black female characters. "Isra" had been a ballerina, Ricki a successful jazz-blues guitarist. Many jazz and blues singers are mentioned, and lines from blues songs are interspersed throughout the narrative. Racism, the civil rights movement, and music bind the novel together. It could be argued that the characters lead blues lives.

Oliphant, Robert. *A Trumpet for Jackie*. Englewood Cliffs, NJ: Prentice-Hall, 1983.

The story of Jackie Hayes, a jazz trumpeter who gives up performing to become successful in other, non-musical endeavors, all the time retaining his love for jazz.

Oliver, Chad. "Didn't He Ramble." *The Magazine of Fantasy and Science Fiction*, April 1957. In *Best Science-Fiction Stories and Novels: Ninth Series*, edited by T. E. Dikty, no. 9, 85–96. Chicago: Advent, 1958.

When wealthy old Theodor Pearsall's wife nags him to throw a party, he manages to be transported back 200 years to Storyville, where he can be surrounded by his beloved music. When he dies, he's given a rousing jazz funeral parade: "Louis was there, and Bix, and Bunk. Ory's trombone and Teagarden's. Bechet and Dodds and Fazola on clarinets. Minor Hall, his drum muffled with a handkerchief."

Olsen, Eric B. *Proximal to Murder: A Steve Raymond, D. D. S. Mystery.* 1st-Books, 2000.

Dr. Steve Raymond is an earringed, pony-tailed dentist with a passion for jazz; in fact, he'd probably prefer being a professional saxophonist, but he acknowledges certain musical limitations and so contents himself by playing soul-rock whenever he can. In the opening scene, a musician Steve is jamming with falls dead on stage, mid-gig. Later, the singer he's been having an affair with also dies mysteriously. Steve suspects a relationship between these two events as he presses himself into amateur detective service. The slight musical content of this novel comes in the occasional scenes where Steve is performing or observing music and in the references to the music he listens to whenever he has a chance: Ralph Moore, Ray Brown, Harold Land with Dupree Bolton, among others. The book ends with a satisfying reference to Steve's musical hero, Charlie Parker, as Steve listens to King Pleasure's recording of "Parker's Mood."

Ondaatje, Michael. *Coming through Slaughter*. Toronto: House of Anansi, 1976; New York: W.W. Norton, 1976.

A stunning novel in which the writer starts with the few known facts of one of jazz's "inventors," Buddy Bolden, and imaginatively recreates his disintegration. Taking us inside the head of the legendary cornetist, the author allows us to experience Bolden's schizophrenia, his obsession with women, and his relationship to the innovative music he creates. A serious novel that effectively employs modernistic techniques.

O'Neal, Cothburn. *The Gods of Our Time*. New York: Crown, 1960.

The unfinished story of Rusty Meaghan from the 1930s through the 1950s. Rusty has it all: he is a handsome, gifted athlete sure to become an all-American football player if he accepts a scholarship to one of the universities pursuing him and an equally talented jazz pianist. Unable to decide what to do with his life, he enters military service. When he gets out, he lands a nice gig in Chicago playing for a sultry blues singer. Rusty's life is complicated by family issues, not the least of which is his mother's involvement with a prominent Mafioso. The novel contains scenes set in the beatnik milieu and a fair amount of jazz content as Rusty goes in search of Truth.

Ottley, Roi. *White Marble Lady*. New York: Farrar, Straus and Giroux, 1965.
The interracial marriage between African-American Jeff Kirby (a failed composer but successful singer) and white blue blood Deborah Comstock seems doomed from the start and does indeed end tragically. Although the novel takes place in a Harlem club where music is performed, numbers several jazzmen among the dramatis personae, and features a protagonist who is deeply involved in the music scene, it contains very little jazz content.

Painter, Pamela. "The Next Time I Meet Buddy Rich." *North American Review* 264 (Spring 1979): 30–34.
Living out of a suitcase for long stretches at a time has created tension between a young drummer and his girlfriend, Gretel. The conflict is resolved after Tony has had a chance meeting with his idol, Buddy Rich: Tony chooses the hard life of the itinerant musician rather than the more conventional alternative.

Panahi, H. L. *Bebop Express*. New York: HarperCollins, 2005.
A train traveling from New York to New Orleans picks up musicians along the way until they form a rocking group. More interesting for the illustrations than the predictable onomotopoeic text. For children (5–8).

Parker, Chris, ed. *B Flat, Bebop, Scat*. London: Quartet, 1986.
A healthy collection of previously unpublished short stories and poems, many by not-so-famous writers. See entries for Biggie, Patrick; Burnap, Campbell; Cohen, Elaine; Davis, Clive; Fairweather, Digby; Finn, Julio; Grime, Kitty; Moody, William J. ("The Resurrection of Bobo Jones"); Neiderhiser, Ed; Salmon, Alice Wooledge; Tilley, Robert J. ("The Devil and All That Jazz"); and Zinik, Zinovy. Titles in parentheses are for authors with more than one entry in this bibliography.

Perlongo, Robert A. "Jollity on a Treadmill." In *Jazz 1959: The Metronome Yearbook, 1959*, edited by Bill Coss, 59–62. New York: Metronome Corporation, 1959.
Teenager Teddy nods off while reading about the glamorous people of the Lost Generation and dreams of the Dixieland scene in New Orleans on a Saturday night. He thinks he sees the ghosts of F. Scott and Zelda Fitzgerald among the crowd, so he goes out, returns with a machine gun, and mows

down all but a few of the revelers. The survivors "stand up and ordered more beer, a couple others started doing a jig, and the rest, all wounded, crawled to the bandstand and took over the instruments . . ."

Petry, Ann. "Solo on the Drums." In *The Magazine of the Year*, 105–10. New York: Associated Magazine, 1947.

Drummer extraordinaire Kid Jones has lost his wife to the piano player and deals with his grief in the best way he knows how: through his music and by identifying with that music as if "he were the drums and the drums were he."

———. *The Street*. Boston: Houghton Mifflin, 1946.

A grim naturalistic novel set in Harlem in the late 1940s, dramatizing a young black single mother's struggle to survive in a climate of violence, crushing poverty, and racial discord. The very slight musical content concerns Lutie Johnson's aspiration to succeed as a jazz singer, which would allow her and her child to escape the unspeakable world she is forced to inhabit: "Though she sang the words of the song, it was something entirely different that she was thinking and putting into the music: she was leaving the streets with its dark hallways, its mean, shabby rooms. . . ."

Phillips, Freeman. "Little Nooley's Blues." *American Mercury* 72, no. 327 (March 1951): 281–92; *Negro Digest*, June 9, 1951, 78–86.

Little Nooley Jackson is so affected by the death of his buddy Buck Manos that he loses his ability to play the trumpet, until one day he returns to Buck's grave in the company of several other New Orleans-style musicians and joyously regains his touch: "And the way Nooley's horn kicked and Ray Bone lay down the beat on the guitar case, it seemed like even the trombones would have to get up and stomp around."

Phillips, Jane. *Mojo Hand*. New York: Trident, 1969.

Eunice Predeaux, the protagonist of this grim novel, is a mulatto whose skin color is such that she is rejected by both races. The story, much of which is told in southern black vernacular ("I axed you what you wants, girl"), involves Eunice's fight to be accepted into the black community. An important character is bluesman Blacksnake Brown, who is apparently modeled after Lightnin' Hopkins. The musical frame of reference is Deep South blues, and several chapters include music in performance.

Piazza, Tom. "Charley Patton (1887–1934)." *Blues and Trouble: Twelve Stories*, 189–92. New York: St. Martin's, 1996.

An atmospheric sketch (or, perhaps, tone poem) evocative of the sights and sounds that inspire the blues: "The long-deserted street, the sun hot on the brick sidewalk, the shadows under the balconies, the dusty wine-colored hotel drapes, the red light flashing on the portable recording, the long moment of free-fall, and then the high guitar notes, again . . ." The twelve paragraphs of this "story," like the twelve stories in the collection, are doubtless intended to reflect the basic structure of the blues. Blues buffs will recognize the titular Patton as the founder of the Delta Blues. Although all of the stories in *Blues and Trouble* reflect the kinds of situations and experiences that beg to be converted into mournful music, only this one and "A Servant of Culture" (q.v.) have a direct musical connection. Author Piazza has written prominently about jazz and the blues.

———. "A Servant of Culture." *Blues and Trouble: Twelve Stories*, 47–61. New York: St. Martin's, 1996.
Arthur Golden works in publicity for a musical conglomerate but has long wanted to get into production, primarily to assemble a five-CD reissue of Lester Young recordings—an undertaking of lofty artistic pretensions but little economic feasibility. Now, however, a Japanese corporation has taken over, put a Yale-educated black man in charge of the newly created black music department, and begun downgrading the old jazz division in favor of the new, money-making black music of funk, rap, and soul. This change challenges Golden's putative color-blindness and leads him to suspect an anti-Semitic conspiracy.

Pico, Robert. *Jackson Jazz: Roman*. Paris: Le Castor Astral, 2000.
A fictionalized biography, in French, of Milt Jackson, who is here regarded as the founder of bebop. The novel is drenched in jazz references: to Jackson's many musical influences and contemporaries, to the jazz venues where he and others performed, and to the turbulent racial politics of the jazz world. The Modern Jazz Quartet (MJQ), of course, plays a central role in the narrative.

Pine, Les, and Tina Rome. *A Man Called Adam*. New York: Signet, 1966.
Novelization of the Sammy Davis, Jr., vehicle about world-class trumpeter (and world-class jerk), Adam Johnson, whose venomous character is defined by prejudice, booze, sex, violence, and music. Johnson is filled with hate—and self-hatred—and directs it at everyone, and not just whites. The focus of the story concerns Johnson's relationship with an idealistic civil rights champion, Claudia, a young woman he stole from his best "friend." Under Claudia's influence, Adam becomes almost human for a while but soon returns to his irascible ways before melodramatically dying from alcoholism at 35. Although the book is drenched in racial issues and jazz, it is far from enjoyable to read because of its thoroughly detestable protagonist. Mel Tormé and Louis Armstrong appear in the movie (but, curiously, not the book), and the film music was composed by Clark Terry.

Pines, Paul. *The Tin Angel*. New York: William Morrow, 1983.

A vividly atmospheric mystery set in New York's Lower East Side—the East Village—in the 1970s. Considerable jazz reference; indeed, a few folks associated with the jazz world, including Ted Curson and the Termini brothers, play small but significant roles. Dope is very much at the center of the book (in the ambience as well as the plot), and it is not romanticized. Author Pines actually owned a jazz club called "The Tin Angel" on the Bowery. Aficionados will find much of interest concerning the travails of operating a jazz venue.

Pinkney, Andrea Davis, with Scat Cat Monroe. Illustrated by Brian Pinkney. *Ella Fitzgerald, the Tale of a Vocal Virtuoso*. New York: Jump at the Sun: Hyperion Books for Children, 2002.

An illustrated children's book (ages 5–9) in the voice of a female narrator, Scat Cat Monroe, telling the story of Ella Fitzgerald's life and how she put scat singing on the map. The language of the narrative mimics "the infectious rhythms of scat."

Pinkwater, Daniel. *Mush's Jazz Adventure*. New York: Aladdin, 2002.

When Kelly Mangiaro asks her educated, saxophone-playing pooch Mush (from planet Growf-Woof-Woof) to tell her about how he came to Earth, he tells a long story about how his jazz band of animals stymied a robbery at their boss's jazz joint.

Plater, Alan. *The Beiderbecke Affair*. London: Methuen, 1985.

References to jazz musicians, especially their recordings, abound in this lighthearted mystery involving reluctant—and unlikely—detectives, jazz-lover Trevor Chaplin and his girlfriend Jill Swinburne. When a beautiful platinum blonde offers to sell Trevor some rare Bix Beiderbecke tapes at a very attractive price, he and his partner become entangled in an imbroglio between the local government of Leeds, England, and white marketers.

——. *The Beiderbecke Connection*. London: Methuen, 1992.

The third in a very frothy series featuring detective duo Trevor Chaplin and Jill Swinburne, who are now joined by their baby, First-Born, and babysitter, Yvonne. On this case, they are talked into helping a mysterious refugee cross the Yorkshire border: after all, Trevor reasons, ". . . he likes Bix Beiderbecke and Duke Ellington, which proves he's OK because people who like Bix and Duke obviously wouldn't do anything wrong." As usual, Trevor makes countless references to jazz artists, especially the aforementioned. But surely the novel's most intriguing jazz moment concerns one Mr. Pitt who "could sing the complete recorded works of Charlie Parker, note for note"—an accomplishment all the more precious for "being totally useless in a materialistic world."

———. *The Beiderbecke Tapes*. London: Methuen, 1986.

A sequel to Plater's *The Beiderbecke Affair* (q.v.) and once again featuring amateur sleuths Trevor Chaplin and Jill Swinburne, who, this time, become involved in crime in high places. After striking a deal with the barman of the local pub for some Bix Beiderbecke tapes, Trevor and Jill find themselves in possession of quite a different kind of tape—one that has crucial significance to British nuclear policy and thus carries serious implications for all of Europe. Many references to jazz musicians.

———. *Misterioso*. London: Methuen, 1987.

After her mother dies in a car crash, Rachel accidentally discovers that her real father isn't who she thought he was. So she goes in search of her biological father with only a few clues to guide her: he loved jazz, adopted the names of jazz musicians, and used "misterioso" as his signature word. Rachel tracks her father down at the Café Misterioso in London's Paddington section and learns, among many other things, that he's Jewish, which very much complicates her notion of who *she* is. The novel is redolent of jazz: some of its chapter titles are named after jazz standards, it has scenes of music in performance, and it contains a cornucopia of jazz anecdotes. Thelonious Monk's "Misterioso" is the leitmotif of this funny and affecting book.

Powers, J. F. "He Don't Plant Cotton." *Accent* 3 (Winter 1943): 106–13.

In Chicago (as, presumably, everywhere) a group of black jazz musicians is forced to compromise its musical integrity to cater to surly white audiences who "wanted . . . Mickey Mouse sound effects, singing strings, electric guitars, neon violins, even organs and accordions and harmonica teams instead of the music they [the musicians] were born to, blue or fast, music that had no name." In this case, the musicians cannot deal with one more request by a group of drunken southern whites to play "Ol' Man River."

Price, Kathy. *The Bourbon Street Musicians*. Illustrated by Andrew Glass. New York: Clarion, 2002.

When a creaky old mule learns that he is slated to be converted into back fat and soap, he sets out in a hurry for New Orleans and the life of a musician. Along the way he meets up with three other tawdry animals—a rooster, cat, and hound dog—and together they determine to form a ragtime quartet that will turn Bourbon Street on its ear. But a series of adventures conspires to make them remain in bayou country. For young children.

Pynchon, Thomas. "Entropy." *Kenyon Review* 22 (1960): 277–92.

This story qualifies as a jazz fiction because of its provocative (if zany) discussion concerning the relationship between jazz theory and the second law of thermodynamics. This is followed by a jam session, in which the musicians *think out* the music they would produce if they had instruments; the second composition they "play" is a variation on Gerry Mulligan's root chords.

———. *Gravity's Rainbow*. New York: Viking, 1973.

Although this is not by any means a jazz novel, it does contain a significant reference to Charlie Parker, whose music contributes greatly to the "acoustic collage" that shapes the narrative. Note how the following passage—one long, breathless sentence—projects the writer's admiration for Parker's virtuosity even as it describes his music:

> Down in New York, drive fast maybe get there for the last set—on 7th Ave., between 139th and 140th, tonight, "Yardbird" Parker is finding out how he can use the notes at the higher ends of these very chords to break up the melody into *have* mercy what is it a fucking machine gun or something man he must be out of his *mind* 32nd notes demisemiquavers say it very (demisemiquaver) fast in a Munchkin voice if you can dig *that* coming out of Dan Wall's Chili House and down the street—shit, out in all kinds of streets (his affirmative solos honks already the idle, amused dum-de-dumming of old Mister fucking Death he self) out over the airwaves, into the society gigs, someday as far as what seeps out hidden speakers in the city elevators and in all the markets, his bird's singing, to gainsay the Man's lullabies, to subvert the groggy wash of the endlessly, gutlessly overdubbed strings.

———. *V*. Philadelphia: Lippincott, 1963.

As in most of Pynchon's works, jazz is more of a felt presence and an influence on style and texture than central to the narrative. Here, the character of McClintic Sphere seems to be based on Ornette Coleman; the novel also contains scattered references to Charlie Parker.

Quattlebaum, Mary. *Jazz, Pizzazz, and the Silver Threads*. Illustrated by Robin Oz. New York: Delacorte, 1996.

Nine-year-old Calvin's wish for a pet of his own is partially fulfilled when his neighbor Jenny buys a hamster named Pizzazz for her magic act. Things perk up when Calvin is turned on to jazz; what had been a boring after-school existence has become razzmatazz.

Rainer, Dachine. "The Party." In *New World Writing 12*, 174–206. New York: New American Library, 1957.

Love finally conquers all—even the chaos of jazz—as the speaker is asked to host a party in Greenwich Village in the 1950s. The band hired for the occasion plays jazz, mostly bop, which makes dancing difficult and leads to fighting. As the narrator says, "The music has been bebop, that weird, atonal, fundamentally antimusical conglomeration of sound, and to that dancing could arise only in complete indifference to the music . . ."

Ramsey, Frederic, Jr. "Deep Sea Rider." In *Jazz Parody (Anthology of Jazz Fiction)*, edited by Charles Harvey, 39–49. London: Spearman Publishers, 1948.
Playing trumpet in New York City after World War II, Nubs Wilkens reminisces over his long life in jazz, starting with his work with Buddy Bolden around the turn of the century. When a white jazz groupie creates disharmony among the band members, Nubs resolves to go home to New Orleans in time for Mardi Gras.

Randisi, Robert J. "The Listening Room." In *Murder . . . and All That Jazz*, edited by Robert J. Randisi, 239–60. New York: Signet, 2004.
A widower now retired from the NYPD, Truxton "Tru" Lewis moved to a small town in Missouri, where an old friend calls from St. Louis to ask Tru's help. Tru is directed to a jazz club, sits through a set, goes to his friend's office. There he finds his friend with a letter opener planted firmly in his chest. Tru lends a helpful hand to the St. Louis police, and together they solve the crime. As in so many of the stories in this so-called jazz mystery collection, the music is incidental to the story.

Randisi, Robert J., ed. *Murder . . . and All That Jazz: 13 Showstopping Stories of Crime and Jazz*. New York: Signet, 2004.
Unfortunately, few of the stories in this collection are showstoppers and most have little musical content. It's as if the writers were contractually bound to produce a crime or mystery story with a jazz dimension and satisfied their contract by interpolating some casual reference to the music in their story or by setting it in the Jazz Age. See entries for Collins, Max Allan, and Matthew V. Clemens; Connelly, Michael ("Christmas"); Gorman, Ed; Harvey, John ("Drummer Unknown"); Holden, Craig ("P & G"); Lippman, Laura; Lutz, John ("Chop Suey"); Meyers, Martin; Moody, Bill ("Child's Play"); Randisi, Robert J. ("Listening Room"); Roberts, Les; Robinson, Peter ("Magic"); and, Smith, Julie ("Kid Trombone"). Titles or short titles are given in parentheses when the author is represented by more than a single entry in this bibliography.

Raschka, Chris. *Charlie Parker Played Be Bop*. New York: Orchard Books, 1992.
A picture book for preschoolers with a text designed to help young readers *hear* Parker's music in their minds.

———. *Giant Steps*. New York: Atheneum Books for Young Readers, 2002.
An unidentified narrator introduces his very young audience to the concept of John Coltrane's "sheets of sound" and then has a box, a snowflake, some raindrops, and a kitten illuminate this tricky technique.

———. *Mysterious Thelonious*. New York: Orchard Books, 1997.
Inspired by Monk's "Misterioso," this book for young children attempts to match the twelve musical tones of the chromatic scale to the corresponding values of the color wheel; in other words, it's as if Monk's music had sat for its portrait. Two "messages" evolve from this short, colorful book: that Monk played no wrong notes on the piano and that Monk's music expresses freedom.

Reed, Barbara. *High Notes Are Murder.* Long Beach, CA: Rare Sound Press, 2000.
The heroine of this soft-boiled mystery is Liz Hanlon, a serious musician reduced to performing in a dive. Just as her career seems about to take off, she discovers the body of her dead cousin and simultaneously begins to receive creepy anonymous messages that hint darkly that she may soon be the next victim. Apart from several references to "Satin Doll" and one to Count Bassie [*sic*], this novel contains disappointingly little music, which is surprising since it is set in the music world, features a multi-talented jazz pianist, and is accompanied by a CD.

Reed, Harlan. *The Swing Music Murder*. New York: Dutton, 1938.
A hard-boiled mystery set in Seattle and containing the usual ingredients: nightclubs, booze, violence, snappy dialogue, and an idiosyncratic private eye, Dan Jordan. The murder at the novel's center involves a popular purloined swing tune, "Poppy Seed Swing." Indeed, swing figures prominently toward the beginning, as Lance Grandy's Swing Swing Boys are seen in performance and in swing-music dialogue ("Man! What beautiful licks! Listen to him go out of key! Man!"). Despite the overwhelming popularity of this new music, Dan insists on requesting "Darktown Strutter's Ball" wherever he is.

Reed, Ishmael. *Mumbo Jumbo*. New York: Atheneum, 1972.
An unclassifiable, hyperkinetic text that parodies the overlapping histories of voodoo and jazz within the framework of a metaphysical mystery.

Reed, James. "The Shrimp Peel Gig." *Brilliant Corners* 2 (Winter 1997): 23–37.
The speaker and his fellow musicians play wherever they can get work: small festivals, ball games, banquets, and so forth. On the night of the story, as he prepares to play Dixieland for an after-dinner crowd, he reflects on the

life of small-town musicians like him. They have day jobs, of course, and play for the love of the music and camaraderie, poignantly aware that the clock is running out on dance bands. They are also keenly aware of the inevitable conflicts between their love for music and their familial responsibilities. A warm, nicely balanced story that gives a good sense of what it must be like to play in small-town, low-budget operations.

Reed, Jeremy. *Saint Billie*. London: Enitharmon, 2001.

A collection of poems and twenty-seven prose pieces intended to illuminate various facets of Billie Holiday's existence, primarily her inner life. The prose vignettes are mood pieces, most of which dramatize Holiday's emotions, experiences, and psychological states from her own perspective—from *inside*, in other words. Sadness, loss, drugs, and thoughts of death are ubiquitous. At the center of the book is a section titled "Billie's Novel in Ten Chapters"; like the other prose pieces, these chapters are less than a page each. All of the chapters are occasioned by quotations relating to the singer. In one of the more interesting cases, Billie ruminates over Carmen McRae's comment regarding the relationship between Holiday's life and her music. McRae had said, "Singing is the only place she can express herself the way she'd like to be all the time. Only way she's happy is through a song. I don't think she expresses herself as she would want to when you meet her in person. The only time she's at ease and at rest with herself is when she sings." In the title piece, the reader is asked to "Imagine a meeting between St. Jean Genet and Saint Billie Holiday." After speculating that these two outsiders were humiliated by their origins, the speaker reflects that

> The meeting's a self-deconstructing illusion. It's like the union of two holograms. The polarization is intense and evanescent. Saint Billie leaves a black glove in Saint Jean's hand. What he imparts is a gesture of the sadness which is inseparable from his eyes. He knows sadness as a commonplace of consciousness like light. When he looks back there is nobody there. When she looks back there are lilacs spilling over a wall, purple tusks which seem to have sprung out of the instant, like a thought showing up big in memory. She goes to a bar. He goes to a bar. All the lights blow for a moment. Then the song begins.

This typical passage nicely demonstrates both the weakness and the strength of the book's prose sections—a curious combination of quasi-pedantic language in the service of noirish poetic effect. Sometimes it works—but not often enough.

Rhys, Jean. "Let Them Call It Jazz." *Let Them Call It Jazz and Other Stories*, 100–129. London: Bloomsbury, 1995. [Published earlier in *Tigers Are Better Looking*. London: Andre Deutsch, 1968.]

The sad plight of a young mulatto immigrant (West Indian?) in London, whose only solace in her broken down life comes from the wine she drinks and the songs she makes up and sings. In jail, she hears a woman sing a song that touches her so deeply that she appropriates it as her own, only to give it away. She rationalizes that her act won't make any difference: they can call it jazz if they like and it still "won't make no difference to the song I heard." Affecting story but slight musical content.

Richards, Susan Starr. "Calling Up Billie." *Brilliant Corners* 8 (Summer 2004): 37–48.

An affecting interior monologue triggered by a 3 A.M. phone call. At first the speaker thinks her old friend Jo is calling from New York, but then she learns that it's Jo's sister with the news that Jo has committed suicide. The sister's request for the speaker to finish Jo's book on Billie Holiday sets off a series of reflections on Holiday's music, the jazz life, and the nature of loss.

Richards-Slaughter, Shannon. "The Blossoms of Jazz: A Novel of Black Female Jazz Musicians in the 1930s." Diss., University of Michigan, 1990.

The story starts with quotes from critics reviewing an album—*The Blossoms of Jazz*—that had resurfaced after half a century; this is followed by the liner notes to the album. Because of the record's success, the record company is trying to get the original trio (piano, bass, sax) back together for a nostalgic concert. Meanwhile, the daughter of one of the "Blossoms" decides to write a biography of the group, and she proceeds via recorded interviews, through which we learn, among other predictable things, that the trio had been reluctant to perform in the South. The concert is a rousing success with the cult followers of the band, though one critic found it disappointing because the combo didn't play the same selections they had played when Clark Gable was king. The slight value of this work derives from its rare subject matter—black female jazz musicians of the 1930s. Disappointingly little musical content.

Richoux, Pat. *The Stardust Kid*. New York: Putnam, 1973.

The Stardust Kid is Mike Riley, a hot high school jazz trumpeter in Connor City, Nebraska, during World War II. Mike wants to become a great professional musician, but his mother opposes him, largely because she doesn't want him to follow in his musician father's footsteps. This coming-of-age novel provides a nostalgic look at small-town America when the prospect of a one-night stand by Horace Heidt and His Musical Knights could raise goosebumps.

Rieman, Terry. *Vamp Till Ready*. New York: Harper, 1954.

In the middle (Chapter 8) of this murder mystery set among the haute monde of the classical music set, there is, apropos of nothing, a discussion of the changing nature of jazz and an appearance by the Turk Murphy band, which "is belting out the most exciting music heard in the land since Louis Armstrong joined King Oliver."

Rigter, Bob. *Jazz in Oostzee* [*Jazz in the Baltic Sea*]. Bodoni, 1995.

According to a review, this untranslated Dutch novel by a longtime jazz musician (tenor sax) concerns a protagonist who is hilariously out of place both in academia and the jazz world. The frequent jazz scenes involve, among others, Dutch jazz musicians, former Ellington trumpeter Nelson Williams, and tenor players Ben Webster, Johnny Griffin, and Dexter Gordon, and these episodes are said to be historically accurate. One enthusiastic Dutch commentator lapsed into English in his enthusiastic review: "Goed geblazen" [great chops?], yeah man, preach me the blues. This sure ain't no novel for no squares, man." *Jazz in Oostzee* has been called the first Dutch jazz novel. Not seen.

Rimanelli, Giose. *Una Posizione Sociale*. Firenze: Vallecchi Editore, 1959.

Seen but not translated. The jazzy cover of this novel in Italian features a blue trumpet, and the text refers frequently to New Orleans and the blues. There is an appendix to the music of Tony "Slim" Dominick and a section of definitions for jazz and blues terms used in the novel; e.g., "Jazz-Session," "Big Bill Broonzy," and "Parish Prison Blues."

Ritz, David. *Barbells and Saxophones*. New York: Donald I. Fine, 1989.

Twenty-seven-year-old Vince Viola lives for body-building, birds, sex, and his saxophone, and these often overlapping passions create the kind of conflicts that, along with a truly wacky family situation, lead Vince to the psychiatrist's couch. With an acknowledgment to "the many immortal saxists—Pres being the most prominent—who've brought me closer to God," author Ritz has produced a free-wheeling, frequently raunchy novel that is saturated with references to jazz, especially the age-old theme regarding the conflict between art and commerce that causes jazz musicians to compromise their integrity.

——. *Blue Notes under a Green Felt Hat*. New York: Donald I. Fine, 1989.

It's post–World War II New York, and 23-year-old Danny is obsessed with sex, hats, and jazz. In a jazz club on 52nd Street, where bebop is gaining favor over swing, Danny meets a gifted but unknown black pianist-singer, Cliff Summer, and the two of them go on a series of adventures designed primarily to make Summer rich and famous. At the end Danny is selling hats and jazz records (hence the title) from his business in Harlem. A raunchy novel with many references to jazz and the jazz scene, including a writer for *Metronome*.

Roberts, David Wyn. *The Alchemist's Song*. Winnipeg, Canada: Great Plains Fictions, 1998.

In the eighteenth century a perfectly matched pair of trumpets was forged, "the first brass instruments to be adorned with triple side-mounted Viennese valves . . . [giving] them access to the full chromatic scale over nearly three octaves." One of these remarkable instruments falls into the hands of late twentieth-century jazz musician Harry Holborn, who becomes obsessed with locating his trumpet's mate. When Harry dies in Egypt under problematic circumstances, his wife, Grace, continues his quest, which by now has clearly become a metaphysical endeavor. The scenes involving musical presentation and the discussions concerning the transcendent potential of jazz are played out against exotic locations and shot through with references to alchemy, folklore, mythology, and American Indian spiritualism.

Roberts, Les. "Jazz Canary." In *Murder . . . and All That Jazz*, edited by Robert J. Randisi, 135–60. New York: Signet, 2004.

When Kate O'Dwyer—the Jazz Canary—can't shake her menacing ex-husband, she calls her old friend, Cleveland-based series detective Milan Jacovich, for help. Milan not only solves Kate's dilemma but provides her with the hope of a secure future as well.

Robinson, Peter. "The Magic of Your Touch." In *Murder . . . and All That Jazz,* edited by Robert J. Randisi, 85–93. New York: Signet, 2004.

After playing a gig, the narrator (a jazz pianist) wanders into a junkyard, where he has been drawn by a jazz tune he has heard from a distance. When he reaches the source of the music, he finds an old black man with fire in his eyes playing a beat-up honky-tonk piano. After committing the song to memory, the speaker kills the old man and then transcribes the song, which almost immediately becomes a jazz standard, greatly improving the narrator's fortunes—until the song, in mysterious ways, begins to overwhelm his life. An epigraph from Poe signals the story's eeriness.

———. "Memory Lane." In *Blue Lightning*, edited by John Harvey, 265–79. London: Slow Dancer Press, 1998; Chester Springs, PA: Dufour Editions, 1999.

A quintet (three expatriate Brits and two Canadians) have "another shitty gig" at a nursing home in Vancouver, B.C. While they are playing, the speaker reflects back on his World War II experiences, in love and war. When an inmate dies during a rousing number, the speaker-saxophonist experiences a shiver of memento mori. The spirit of wartime big band music hovers over this story.

Roelants, Maurice. "The Jazz Player." Translated by Jo Mayo. In *Harvest of the Lowlands: An Anthology in English Translation of Creative Writing in the Dutch Language*, edited by J. Greshoff, 357–75. New York: Querido, 1945. [Originally published as "De Jazz-Speler." Amsterdam: Salm, 1938.]
The transformative experience of a boring businessman whose life is changed when he witnesses a black jazzman give an enraptured performance.

RogueStar. "Jazz." *Down-Home Charm* (November 7, 2001). http://alykat .hispeed.com/rogue/fanfic/newclaremont/jazz.shtml (25 March 2003).
An indeterminate cast of characters, in vague pairings, dance to jazz at the hottest, yet nameless, nightclub in New Orleans. One character, Gambit, tries to console Jean who is grieving over Cyclop's apparent death. This story was apparently "inspired" by a comic book, *Uncanny X-Men* #386 — yet another sign that "civilization as we know it" is near collapse.

Roos, Olle. "Naer Negerjazzen kom till Björkåsen" ["When the Negro Jazz Comes to Björkåsen"]. *Musikern* 1 (1992): 30–31.
Set in a tiny, remote village (Björkåsen) in northern Sweden, this humorous story in Swedish recounts the misadventures of young Pelle who, years apart, put together two different jazz combos that traveled the countryside and performed their music to little success. Later, he gets the great idea to bring Louis Armstrong to his village but soon discovers that the cost is prohibitive. So instead he arranges to bring an all-black orchestra to town for the annual festival. After the band gets off to a rip-roaring start, however, the audience discovers that the musicians are actually in blackface and they riot, ending the premier for black jazz in Björkåsen. Pelle moved to another community where he played in a restaurant for many years.

Ross, Sinclair. *Whir of Gold*. Toronto and Montreal: McClelland and Stewart, 1970.
Twenty-four-year-old Saskatchewan farm boy and aspiring jazz clarinetist, Sonny McAlpine, migrates to Montreal, hoping for a job in a band. Unfortunately, he speaks no French, the clarinet is out of favor, and he doesn't double

on saxophone. So he is reduced to pawning his instrument and living a down-and-nearly-out existence in a boarding house. A girlfriend and a shady neighbor further complicate his life, and his dream of improvising real music grows further from reach daily. Sonny's symbol of hope—the clarinet—is mentioned frequently, and the novel contains vivid passages of his practicing after getting it out of hock, but he doesn't get a break, so we never see him making music in the company of others.

Roy, Lucinda. *Lady Moses*. New York: HarperFlamingo, 1998.
   Nikki Giovanni's blurb reads: "I was not there when Charlie Parker started playing between the notes; I could not be there when Billie Holiday pondered the fruit of southern trees; I was unable to sit at a table when Miles Davis gave birth to the Cool but the musicians aren't the only ones who sing and I am here when Lucinda Roy makes her startling debut with Lady Moses." Given this puff and the protagonist's nickname, "Jazz," the most startling thing about this novel is that it contains not a single reference to jazz.

Rubio, Carlos. *Orpheus' Blues*. Baltimore: PublishAmerica, 2002.
   After returning from a tour of duty in Vietnam, Jack Stewart leaves his parents in Virginia to pursue a career as a jazz saxophonist in New York City. He knows the odds are against him, but he is determined to find his musical voice, become an artist, and discover who he really is. In Greenwich Village he develops a deep bond with his roommate, also a struggling jazz musician, and enters, almost simultaneously, into relationships with two gorgeous young women, one a sexual virtuoso, the other a girl-back-home type. Like every other struggling jazz performer in New York, past and present, Jack is taken under the compassionate wing of Hans, the mythically wise proprietor of the Empty Hand, a club in the Village where musicians, struggling and otherwise (Dizzy Gillespie makes an appearance), can pop in for a sandwich, a cup of tea, and a jam session at any hour. Jack, of course, is soon discovered as an artist-composer and is signed to the kind of artist-friendly contract unheard of in the real world. When he receives word that his beloved mother has died, Jack returns home, comes to terms with his past, and returns to New York. There, in an epiphany as predictable as every other element in this novel, he discovers the symbiotic relationship between life and art. With *Orpheus' Blues*, the male American novel of self-discovery has surely exceeded the saturation point.

Rundell, Wyatt. *Jazz Band*. New York: Greenberg, 1935.
   Although the protagonist is a 25-year-old banjo player and crooner in a popular dance band, the novel has much more to say about his soap opera love life than his career as a jazz musician. A misleading title.

Russell, Charlie L. "Klactoveedsedstene." *Liberator* 5, no. 11 (November 1965): 20–22.

This sad account of a rebellious young black boy who has been rejected by his mother contains no musical content whatsoever, apart from the title borrowed from a Charlie Parker composition. Rather, the story is the author's attempt "to convey the feeling he gets from listening to Parker's tune." Thus, jazz relates—very subjectively—to the mood of the story but not its style, as this typical passage should indicate: "My timing is good. I can see the bus now. It looks like a giant silver bug. It is upon me now. Will it stop? I wave my arms slowly. The bus passes me, but it is already slowing down. I run to catch it. The door is opened, and I step up into the bus."

———. "Quietus." *Liberator* 4 (November 1964): 20–25.

A story that explores the exorbitant price a black man must pay to make it in the white world. Although the jazz content is slight, a skein of telling references to Charlie Parker becomes symbolically significant. Randolph, Besso Oil's first black salesman, has an opportunity to move up the ladder. But he realizes that if he does what is expected of him, he will function to keep other blacks down—and that then there will be "no more Bird." This is made patently clear to him when he plays a Parker recording at a party of his new circle of acquaintances. The music is met with heavy silence so Randolph makes everyone happy by playing Dave Brubeck. In short, Parker in this story represents quintessential blackness—a condition no longer available to the "brother" who agrees to play by the rules of corporate (i.e., white) America.

Russell, Ross. *The Sound.* New York: Dutton, 1961.

A primer of the postwar hipster culture, this novel is a roman à clef inspired by Charlie Parker. The protagonist, white Jewish piano player Bernie Rich, is torn between going the big band college-circuit route with its financial security or the spontaneous, insecure Harlem scene where Red Travers, the Parker figure, is instrumental in transforming jazz from Benny Goodman to bop. Ross Russell's personal experience with Parker and the bebop scene gives this novel authenticity. There's much about race, a preponderance of sex and drugs, and occasional stereotyping, as when Red is described as being "fiercely possessive, with an overpowering virile odor and primitive genital force." Lots of good musical description.

Ryan, Tracy. *Jazz Tango.* Freemantle, Australia: Freemantle Arts Centre Press, 2002.

A doubly misleading title: this exploration of a woman's consciousness contains neither music nor dance (though its protagonist *is* named Jas).

Sachs, Ed. "Dogs Don't Always Eat Dogs." In *Music '59: Downbeat Fourth Annual Yearbook*, 69–71. Chicago: Maher, 1959.

Because of low attendance, the manager of a jazz club decides to incorporate a dog act into its jazz routine—with predictably humorous results.

Sadoff, Ira. "Black Man's Burden." *Brilliant Corners* 3 (Summer 1999): 15–25.

Thirty years afterward Erik remembers the summer of 1964 when he and a high school buddy, Rondel, shared an apartment in Manhattan's East Village. It was a summer of race riots, and civil rights and idealism were much in the air. When the two boys—one white, the other black—go to the Half-Note with their dates to hear John Coltrane, Erik comes to realize that bridging the gap between races is much more difficult than he had realized. Good description of Coltrane and company in action.

Salaverria, José. "The Negro of the Jazz Band." In *Ebony and Topaz: A Collectanea*, edited by Charles S. Johnson, 63–66. Translated by Dorothy R. Peterson. 1927. Freeport, NY: Books for Libraries, 1971.

The speaker, a writer, is intrigued by the black drummer in a mediocre jazz band playing at The Charm of Russia Tea Room along the far end of a European beach resort. When the protagonist later encounters the drummer, he is shocked to discover that he is actually white; the story provides an account of why (in the 1920s) an educated white American would masquerade as black.

Salinger, J. D. "Blue Melody." *Cosmopolitan* (September 1948): 50+.

A story based on the much mythicized death of Bessie Smith, and one of Salinger's lesser efforts.

Sallis, James. "Vocalities." In *Blue Lightning*, edited by John Harvey, 281–89. London: Slow Dancer Press, 1998; Chester Springs, PA: Dufour Editions, 1999.

A late-night monologue by a disc jockey that begins with the pronouncement that there won't be any music tonight and ends with his changing his mind. In between, there are reflections on life, love, and music.

Salmon, Alice Wooledge. "Correspondence." In *B Flat, Bebop, Scat*, edited by Chris Parker, 42–55. London: Quartet, 1986.

Martha and Louis had been living for a long year in Los Angeles and are now on their way home to London. While restoring themselves on a Caribbean island, Louis, a conductor, is offered a temporary position he can't resist in Tokyo, leaving Martha to resume writing the book she had abandoned. One day she is invited by a jazz musician neighbor to listen to his group play that night. Martha is so moved by the jazz she hears on this and another night that she experiences a transfiguration.

Sand, Carter. *Two for the Money*. San Diego: Trojan Classic, 1973.
    The only reason this title appears is because it shows up from time to time in references to "Fiction, jazz." It is a gay novel with no redeeming social or intellectual value whatsoever. The plot involves Phillip Denver meeting the giant stud of his dreams and falling in love with him. Things are complicated by the fact that Phillip's dreamboat is from Texas (the story begins in Manhattan) and has a wife and children; a further complication occurs when Phillip becomes involved with a handsome, older billionaire, who introduces Phillip into the world of very rough homosexual sex. Oh, Phillip is very vaguely a jazz pianist with a steady gig—to which he fails to show up in the course of the novel. This book may deserve a grand prix for smut but only a single upraised finger for jazz fiction.

Saroyan, William. "Jazz." *Hairenik Daily* [Boston]. *My Name Is Saroyan*, 90–93. New York: Coward-McCann, 1983.
    This story likens the mélange of urban street sounds to the "nervous noise" called jazz that was sweeping the country.

Sayer, Mandy. *Mood Indigo*. Sydney, Australia: Allen and Unwin, 1990.
    A vernacular novel-in-stories dramatizing ten or so years in the life of a young Australian girl, Rose, whose life and prospects are bleak. Rose loves her dad and the music he makes. Unfortunately, not many people are interested in listening to jazz piano; in fact, at one climactic moment when her dad starts to play "Mood Indigo," he's informed that it's happy hour at the bar and that his music should reflect that mood. Scattered references to jazz musicians, mostly pianists like Oscar Peterson, Count Basie, Nat King Cole, and Les McCann.

Schickele, René. *Symphonie für Jazz* [*Symphony for Jazz*]. Berlin: S. Fischer Verlag, 1929.
    This novel, in German, is set in Berlin in the 1920s and focuses on John van Maray and his wife, Johanna, who are the darlings of what would later be called, in the United States at least, the jet set. John is a renowned jazz musician and composer, and wherever he goes he is celebrated by a symphony of admiration from his many fans, whose praises are in fact even louder than the impressively loud music John makes. Johanna's announcement that she is going to leave John and marry the barely tolerable lounge lizard Herm Deutermann leads to a surrealistic, doubtless tongue-in-cheek,

denouement. This modernistic work is much more about the texture, color, and rhythm of language than it is about the mechanics of plot. Quite likely, the author was attempting to appropriate some of the properties of jazz into his prose narrative. One doesn't need to be able to read German to infer, even from the opening passage, that the author had little interest in creating yet another traditional story:

Bäbä, tu. Bäbä, tut. Tut! Bäbä.
Ein Hurra—Bäbätu
Auf das Känguruh!
Miau.
Die ganze Nacht hat es geregnet. Wie eine Mühle ging der Regen in der Finsternis,
Die Traufe machte dazu den rauhen, kurzpulsigen Lärm eines Motors: Raduwalu,
raduwalu.

Schneider, Bart. *Blue Bossa*. New York: Viking, 1998.
Framed by the Patty Hearst kidnapping in 1970s San Francisco, this novel provides a rounded portrait of Ronnie Reboulet, a jazz trumpeter and singer who, like Chet Baker, had once been famous both for his music and his good looks. But at the height of his fame, he lost everything—his teeth, his looks, his lip—to drugs. Now in the company of a strong, loving woman, he is trying to resurrect his life and career. The title is taken from a Kenny Dorham tune. Excellent descriptions of music-making and frequent references to bop era musicians; in fact, Charlie Parker has a cameo role. Among other things, this novel is about the complications of love and the never-ending search for a father. The dust jacket photo by William Claxton underscores the jazz connection.

Schneider, Christine M. *Saxophone Sam and His Snazzy Jazz Band*. New York: Walker, 2002.
Playing together in their home one day, a boy and his sister hear music and set out to track it to its source. When they reach the attic, they discover an old-time radio, which they open to find a jazz band of tiny musicians and dancers. They have been transported back to the big band era. A snazzy, ebullient book aimed at very young readers.

Schroeder, Alan. *Ragtime Tumpie*. Paintings by Bernie Fuchs. Boston: Little, Brown, 1989.
An atmospherically illustrated fictionalized biography of the entertainer Josephine Baker—"Tumpie"—up to the time when, still a young girl in ragtime-besotted St. Louis, she resolves to "never stop dancin'." For juveniles.

———. *Satchmo's Blues*. Illustrated by Floyd Cooper. New York: A Doubleday Book for Young Readers, 1996.

A sanitized fictional retelling of Louis Armstrong's young life, ending right after Louis buys his first horn at a pawn shop, aims it at the heavens, and vows to someday blow the stars right out of the sky.

Schüller, Martin. *Jazz.* Köln: Emons Verlag, 2000.
A mystery, in German, revolving around a saxophone that may have belonged to Charlie Parker. Not seen.

Scott, Melissa. *The Jazz.* New York: Tom Doherty, 2000.
Don't rush out to buy this book, thinking that you're putting your hands on the ne plus ultra of jazz novels. It is, rather, a futuristic road chase fable that takes place in the media-dominated future, and it contains no music. The title refers to the codeword for international cyberglitches.

Scott, Tony. "Destination K.C." In *The Jazz Word*, edited by Dom Ceruli, Burt Karall, and Mort Nasatir, 80–83. New York: Ballantine, 1960.
A short, ironic story told in hip jazz idiom, disclosing the author's deep admiration for Charlie Parker as railroad workers load Parker's last remains on a train destined for Kansas City. The author, a jazz clarinetist, knew and played with Parker.

Sexton, Kay. "Traveling Magic." *Jerry Jazz Musician.* http.www.jerrjazz musican.com/linernotes/kay_sexton.html (4/21/2004).
An homage to John Coltrane, this story contains the actual score of Coltrane's "Blue Train" as epigraph and provides a series of vignettes linked by train travel. The one centrally concerned with jazz dramatizes a jaded critic's rhapsodic response to a fresh new voice on the saxophone: "When Frannie Moore plays, you hear the green heart of this planet, singing out to you from the core of the woman's being."

Shacochis, Bob. "Lord Short Shoe Wants the Monkey." *Playboy*, 1982. *Easy in the Islands: Stories by Bob Shacochis*, 53–71. New York: Crown, 1985.
Set on a Caribbean island in a jazz club where "the jazz is sweet enough to keep a dying man alive," this story concerns a calypso singer named Lord Short Shoe who teams up with a vamp to pull off a scam involving an American and his beloved monkey. Jazz is relegated mostly to the background but occasionally occupies center stage.

Shahan, Sherry. *The Jazzy Alphabet.* Illustrated by Mary Thelen. New York: Philomel, 2002.
A brightly illustrated book designed to help young children master the alphabet—e.g., ". . . boogie-woogie bebop a boogaloo. Bim-bam blues!"

Shaik, Fatima. "The Mayor of New Orleans: Just Talking Jazz." *The Mayor of New Orleans*, 1–51. Berkeley: Creative Arts, 1987.

A novella in which a loquacious black horn man ("a Dixieland trumpet player, a Coltrane saxophone imitator, an appreciator of Mangione") entertains a young visitor from New York with an all-night tall tale regarding how he, Walter Watson Lameir, a street musician, became Mayor of News Orleans for four hectic months before going to jail for four hellish days. The vernacular story has the feel of improvisational jazz.

Shange, Ntozake. *Sassafrass, Cypress and Indigo*. New York: St. Martin's, 1982.

Dedicated to "all women in struggle," this is the story of three African-American sisters and their mother in Charleston. One of the girls is a poet and weaver like her mother; another is a dancer. Both are involved with jazz musicians, one of whom is on the dope fringe, the other a serious artist and composer. Although there are pointed references to jazz musicians and the jazz scene, the musical content is slight.

Shaw, Artie. "Snow White in Harlem, 1930." *The Best of Intentions and Other Stories*, 9–28. Santa Barbara: John Daniel, 1989.

When Al Snow drags his sax and clarinet uptown to Harlem late one night looking for a jam session to sit in on, he encounters a phenomenal piano player who lets Al (the only white in a black setting) show what he can do. Although the scene at the after-hours jazz club grows increasingly strange, Al thinks his dreams have come true. This story is a fictionalized account of author Shaw's first meeting with the musician who became his mentor, Willie "The Lion" Smith.

Shirley, Peter. "Drink and Be Merry . . ." In *Jazz Parody (Anthology of Jazz Fiction)*, edited by Charles Harvey, 32–38. London: Spearman Publishers, 1948.

Pianist Babe Sheridan and his fellow band members are true jazz enthusiasts; music is their life. One night during a jam session, Babe can't help noticing a beautiful, mysterious blonde in the audience. When on a subsequent evening he meets her, she tells him she knows the whereabouts of his ex-wife. Unfortunately, Babe dies on the bandstand before he can elicit the information he desires.

———. "Sweet and Hot." In *Jazz Parody (Anthology of Jazz Fiction)*, edited by Charles Harvey, 92–98. London: Spearman Publishers, 1948.

A jazz accordionist frets over what has become of jazz: how it has become the exclusive province of the blacks and the darling of the intellectuals. He blames writers for creating this situation. At the end, he promises to give a writer-friend an exclusive story and does so in a shocking way.

Shure, Jill. *Night Jazz*. San Jose, CA: Universe, 2001.

Successful ad executive Jeri Devlin rushes to New York to get to the bottom of her brother's mysterious disappearance. On her first night she is transported back to the Jazz Age—the 1920s—where she fully immerses herself in the culture of the time, especially women's fashions. This time-bending romance contains a few references to Harlem nightclubs, performances by Ma Rainey and Alberta Hunter, and the music of Gershwin and Cole Porter, but no significant jazz content: another misleading title.

Shurman, Ida. *Death Beats the Band*. New York: Phoenix, 1943.

First, despicable Andy Parker is killed just as he is getting into the groove singing his new hit, "Headlined in My Heart," and then another band member is killed before a third is assaulted with a trumpet. Since the orchestra and the patrons are marooned by a blizzard, the task of solving the several crimes falls to the band's new bassist. Considerable musical discussion and description, especially early on; in fact, the novel has several transcriptions of musical notation.

Sill, Harold D., Jr. *Misbehavin' with Fats: A Toby Bradley Adventure*. Reading, MA: Addison-Wesley, 1978.

Through the miracle of time travel, young New England white boy, Toby Bradley, is able to meet and hang out with his hero, Fats Waller, and to learn what it was like to grow up talented and black in segregated America. Frequent references to jazz musicians and several quotations from music associated with Waller.

Simmonds, Ron. "Send in the Clones." *Crescendo & Jazz Music*, no. 33 (December–January, 1996–1997): 15–16.

Bernie has a great idea for a Christmas television jazz show: he'll assemble the best studio jazz men in the land, give them rubber masks modeled after the great jazz artists of the past, and send the large audience into the throes of nostalgia. But the musicians are offended to wear masks and so hire bit actors to take their place. The heat becomes so intense that the actors behind the masks become clones of Miles Davis, Dizzy Gillespie, Benny Goodman, et al. But since the "musicians" can't play a lick, a tape recorder playing the original of Benny Goodman's recording of "Let's Dance" is brought in to save the day . . . maybe. A fantasy.

Simmons, Herbert. *Man Walking on Eggshells*. Boston: Houghton Mifflin, 1962; London: Methuen, 1962.

Black trumpeter and football player Raymond "Splib" Douglas seems to be the hope of the future but relinquishes his wonderful potential to drugs. His mother opposes his jazz from the beginning, thinking it "a lot of sentimental bunk by a bunch of shiftless people who never had sense enough to grow up." Her brother, also a trumpeter, tells her that on the contrary, "that's your history coming out of them horns!" The story takes place in and around St. Louis and also Harlem during Prohibition. Much talk of racial issues and of jazz, especially about "home boy" Miles Davis.

――――. "One Night Stand." *Gamma #1* (1963): 88–93.

Young Maury was the hottest trumpeter anyone had seen; he "made Louis, Diz and Miles sound like little boys playing with matches." But his fellow musicians worry that Maury has no interest in women—until one night he becomes infatuated with a woman in the audience and wins her over with his incredible playing.

Simon, George T. *Don Watson Starts His Band*. New York: Dodd, Mead, 1941.

Written for a juvenile audience and containing a foreword by Benny Goodman, this novel focuses on a young hayseed who determines to become a professional bandleader.

Sinclair, Harold. *Music Out of Dixie*. New York and Toronto: Rinehart, 1952.

The story of Dade Tarrent in the first two decades of the twentieth century. Raised in the slums around New Orleans, Dade is moved by music early in his life, learns first to play the piano and then the clarinet, enjoys success and suffers defeat, becomes a composer and artist, and is headed for New York at the end. Jelly Roll Morton makes a small but important appearance. Dixieland, booze, dope, violence, race.

Sklar, George. *The Two Worlds of Johnny Truro*. Boston: Little, Brown, 1947.

A long novel about Johnny Truro, a large, artistically talented youth who undergoes the usual processes and experiences on his way to discovering himself. Frequent references to Bix Beiderbecke, Kid Ory, Jelly Roll Morton, Count Basie, Wild Bill Davison, Coleman Hawkins and others; a scene in which Johnny explains to a buddy the difference between jazz and swing; and an explanation of how jazz provided catharsis and nirvana for Johnny and his chums—this is about the extent of the novel's jazz content.

Škvorecký, Josef. "The Bass Saxophone." *The Bass Saxophone: Two Novellas*, 115–209. Translated by Káca Poláčková-Henley. Toronto: Anson-Cartwright, 1977; London: Chatto and Windus, 1978; New York: Knopf, 1979.

Although jazz is outlawed, a young jazz fan dreams of playing saxophone with an orchestra. Much emphasis on the protagonist's love of jazz and on the rarity of the instrument.

———. "The Bebop of Richard Kambala." Translated by Káca Poláčková-Henley. *Rampike* 3 (1984–85): 101–4.

After an exhilarating jam session, the title character commits suicide in a particularly grisly way.

———. *The Cowards*. Translated by Jeanne Nemcová. New York: Grove, 1970; London: Gollancz, 1970; New York: Ecco, 1980.

Danny Smiricky loves jazz and plays the sax with his friends at every opportunity. The story is set in Czechoslovakia after the fall of Nazi Germany as the Russians are moving in. The content is densely political, with very little specific jazz reference—though jazz does seem to serve as Danny's anodyne against the pain and confusion of his chaotic world.

———. "Eine Kleine Jazzmusik." Translated by Alice Denesová. *The Literary Review* 13 (Fall 1969): 47–61.

The speaker and his young chums are determined, in 1940 Czechoslovakia, to put on a jazz concert—much in violation of Aryan restrictions against various kinds of music and instruments. The Masked Rhythm Bandits (as the group comes to be known) cleverly succeed in their objective but with lamentable consequences. As in other works by Škvorecký, jazz is here associated with freedom and democracy, with everything opposed to totalitarianism.

———. *The Swell Season: A Text on the Most Important Things*. Translated by Paul Wilson. Toronto: L. and O. Dennys, 1982; New York: Ecco, 1986.

In these six interrelated stories, young Danny Smiricky (surely the author's alter ego) falls in love with practically every girl he encounters. He also loves jazz and his country, Czechoslovakia of the 1940s when Nazi terrorism intruded into every corner of everyday life. Passing references to jazz and musicians and one lovely description of a Bach fugue being converted into a rollicking "Sweet Georgia Brown." This is part of a trilogy featuring Smiricky; the other two are *The Cowards* and "The Bass Saxophone" (qq.v.).

————. "That Sax Solo." 1966. Translated by Rosemary Kavan, Káca Poláck-
ová, and George Zteiner. *The Mournful Demeanour of Lieutenant Boruvka*,
25–36. New York and London: Norton, 1987.

When the sexy vocalist for a jazz band is found dead, series detective Lieutenant Boruvka investigates. Because he himself once played saxophone and
clarinet, and remembers what he learned about music, he is able to solve the
case. Readers without a technical grasp of musical notation are likely to remain puzzled over Boruvka's resolution of the mystery.

————. *The Tenor Saxophonist's Story*. Translated by Caleb Crain, Káca
Poláčková-Henley, and Peter Kussi. New York: Ecco, 1996.

Written in Prague in 1954–56, this collection of related stories depicts
the totalitarian regime in Czechoslovakia after World War II. The many
scattered references to jazz do not form a coherent pattern but nevertheless
are associated with freedom and slavery; in fact, for the protagonist, his
tenor sax hitch counterbalances "the large, shining, five-point star" of
Communism.

Smith, Andrea. *Friday Nights at Honeybee's*. New York: Dial, 2003.

Apart from their blackness, no two gals could seem more different: Forestine is 6'2" and ruggedly assembled; she comes from the Brooklyn projects
and a difficult family situation. Viola, on the other hand, is "cute" and lives
in the stultifyingly religious Deep South. But the two women are metaphorically united in their desire to be elsewhere, in order to position themselves
to pursue their passion for music. Forestine has the real goods as a blues and
jazz singer and soon starts to make a name for herself. But she is faced by a
serious dilemma after bearing a child: should she follow her dream to become a great musician or sacrifice her career to motherhood? Meanwhile Viola is ostracized from her community for sexual indiscretion and wends her
way north to Harlem, where she rents a room from homegirl Honeybee Mc-
Color. It is here that the paths of the two women converge, allowing them to
bond and set their lives in the direction of a productive future. Honeybee's
is the locus of the Harlem music scene, and every musician of note (as well
as many of little note) stops by at one time or another. In fact, Honeybee's is
like a rolling jam session where good (i.e., "soul") food and music are am-
ply available at the regular "gathers." Jazz and the blues suffuse this novel
set in the 1960s: famous, not-so-famous, and fictitious musicians are frequently referenced; Forestine's musical apprenticeship is nicely rendered;
and life on the road for marginal musicians is effectively described. Focusing on sisterhood, this folksy novel is told almost exclusively in the African-
American vernacular.

Smith, C. W. "The Plantation Club." *Southwest Review* 62 (Winter 1967): 47–63.

Trying to be cool, two young white aspiring jazz musicians ingratiate themselves with the black musicians at the Plantation Club. When the boys are busted for marijuana, they implicate one of the black musicians—a real artist—who is soon sent to jail while the boys are released, demonstrating that the so-called blindness of justice does not relate to color.

Smith, J. P. *Body and Soul*. New York: Grove, 1987.

Polish émigré jazz pianist Jerzy Wozzeck has a gig in a rundown Paris bistro known for showcasing the best jazz this side of New York. But when a Corsican gangster takes over the club, Wozzeck is forbidden to play Charlie Parker riffs, block chords, or anything that resembles bebop. To compensate for financial woes and a job gone sour, innocent Jerzy accepts a commission to deliver a seemingly harmless package. Predictably, the contents are not as untainted as advertised, and Jerzy is implicated in crime. He flees to London but discovers that his past will always be with him. Many references to jazz, especially to such luminaries as Charles Mingus, John Coltrane, Art Blakey, and Miles Davis.

Smith, Julie. *The Axeman's Jazz*. New York: St. Martin's, 1991.

Picture this: a title with a double jazz reference and a dust jacket portraying a skeleton laying down some heavy grooves on a muted trumpet. But this mystery, set in New Orleans yet, contains absolutely no jazz content. A novel set in New Orleans but containing references to neither food nor music is comparable to a book about Las Vegas that doesn't mention gambling. A clear case of false advertising and a misleading title.

———. *Jazz Funeral*. Fawcett Columbine, 1993.

Female homicide detective Skip Langdon is pressed into service when the beloved producer of the New Orleans Jazz and Heritage Festival is murdered and his young sister disappears. The novel contains a very few scattered references to jazz musicians (the Marsalises, Holiday, Vaughan), occasional blues scenes, and a nonmusical character named Flip Phillips, but Janis Joplin figures more prominently than any other real-life musical performer.

———. "Kid Trombone." In *Murder . . . and All That Jazz*, edited by Robert J. Randisi, 161–84. New York: Signet, 2004.

When New Orleans series private investigator Talba Wallis is asked by jazz singer Queenie Feran to investigate the death of her ex-husband, Talba becomes entangled in a case involving date rape, computers, contract killing, and drugs. The musical content consists mostly of references to New Orleans musicians.

Smith, Martin Cruz. *Stallion Gate*. New York: Ballantine, 1986.

A thriller set in New Mexico in the mid-1940s involving the most secret installation of World War II, the test site for the first atomic weapon. J. Robert
Oppenheimer and Klaus Fuchs are among the historical characters; the protagonist is Joe Peña, an American Indian soldier from the Southwest whose
dream is to open a jazz club after the war. Joe had played piano with Charlie
Parker on 52nd Street and is involved in a couple of jazz scenes, but music is
clearly a background element. On the other hand, the image of Klaus Fuchs
dancing a "Hapsburg ballroom number" to Joe Peña and his band's bebop
clings to the memory.

Smith, Robert Paul. *So It Doesn't Whistle*. New York: Harcourt, Brace, 1941.

Although this novel contains scattered references to such musicians as
Louis Armstrong, Bix Beiderbecke, Coleman Hawkins, Duke Ellington, and
Bud Freeman, it is mostly about the booze life.

Smith, William Gardner. *South Street*. New York: Farrar, Straus and Young,
1954.

The story of three African-American brothers whose father had been
lynched when they were very young, and of Philadelphia's South Street after
World War II. Scattered references to jazz and jazz musicians, a nice description of a jam session, and much attention to a blues singer, a central character; nevertheless, the novel is largely concerned with racial politics, particularly as they impinge on Claude Barrons, one of the brothers, who marries a
white violinist.

Sonin, Ray. *The Dance Band Mystery*. London: Quality, 1940.

Someone's been killing the members of King Grayson's London swing
band, causing Sam Underhill of the *Dance Band News* and Detective-Inspec-
tor John Adams of Scotland Yard to team up to solve the mystery. To get to
the bottom of things, and also to help prevent further murders, former jazz
man Underhill signs on as pianist with Grayson's orchestra. In this capacity
he succeeds in uncovering the killer in a case involving the distribution of potent reefers to musicians, children's dolls imported from America, and a
scorned woman. According to jacket copy, author Sonin was longtime editor
of the *Melody Maker*, "the world's leading dance band and light music
weekly newspaper."

Sorrentino, Gilbert. *Mulligan Stew*. New York: Grove, 1979.

A postmodern parody of the excesses of all things literary, containing scattered references to jazz and its musicians and a crackling riff on the (imagi-

nary) compositions of jazz drummers: "*I Caught That Chick in a Web of Love, Krupageneous . . . Will My Buddy Love Me (Now That He's Struck it Rich?), By a Cozy Coal Fire . . .*" It also contains a rhapsodic chapter, "A Bag of the Blues," singing the praises of dreamgirl Daisy.

Southern, Terry. "The Night the Bird Blew for Doctor Warner." *Harper's Bazaar*, January 1956, 101+.
A musicologist involved in writing a comprehensive book on Western music, Doctor Warner, determines to do field work in bebop by procuring heroin— with predictably disastrous consequences.

———. "You're Too Hip, Baby." *Esquire*, April 1963, 68+.
An educated white man in Paris tries to make the scene by getting close to black jazz musicians, one of whom lets him know that his overtures in the direction of friendship are inauthentic.

Spechler, Diana. "Inheritance." 1 November 2004. http://www.jerryjazzmusician.com/mainHTML.cfm?page=spechler.html (5/11/05).
Nineteen-year-old Wendy, the narrator, has a crush on a boy three years younger, Jackson, a jazz buff whose father plays sax at Harvard Square bars. Wendy and Jackson drop acid together and explore each other's sad past histories, while Jackson's dad (predictably?) comes on to his son's girlfriend.

Spicer, Bart. *Blues for the Prince*. New York: Dodd, Mead, 1950.
A hard-boiled mystery in which The Prince (Harold Morton Prince), the best jazz pianist/composer over the last twenty years, is killed and his right-hand man is charged with the crime after fraudulently claiming—or threatening to claim—that *he* had composed the music that had made The Prince famous. It turns out, of course, that nothing is as it seems. A good deal of both jazz and racial politics. In the most fully developed jazz section (Chapter 17), a group of the greatest jazz all-stars gather to memorialize The Prince in a jam session.

St. James, Blakeley. *A Festival for Christina*. New York: PBJ Books, 1983.
An extremely rare "erotic" (i.e., pornographic) romp featuring series bombshell Christina van Bell, who sets out to produce the most spectacular jazz festival of all time. To do so, she discovers, she must first locate and then sign the headliner musicians she covets. Her task is complicated by the fact that most of them seem to be in hiding in the least accessible corners of the globe. But Christina is nothing if not tenacious: she locates and engages in prodigious, polymorphous promiscuity with all of them before signing them to contracts. Interestingly, she likens her quest to the fluidity and freedom of jazz. It goes without

saying that the ensuing festival is a bacchanalian extravaganza and artistic success. Two scenes in particular linger in the mind long after the book has been returned to its plain brown wrapper. In the first of these, the transsexual soloist in a hot female group, the Jazzabelles, generates a spectacular erection while soloing center-stage; in the other, as a clarinetist plays a medley of jazz standards (including "You Go to My Head"), Christina fellates him while humming the melodies—thus, probably, sending the jazz kazoo into even deeper oblivion.

Steig, Henry. "Gertie and the Pied Piper." *Esquire*, February 1945, 44+.
   Gertie is the proprietress of the Swingland Billiard Academy in Manhattan, a snack bar and pool hall where musicians hang out. She is irritated by the musicians' nonstop chatter about jazz and other musicians. From this it is clear that her relationship with clarinetist Joe is not likely to develop into a more lasting arrangement: like his fellow jazz musicians, Joe is married to his music. The "Pied Piper" in the title likely alludes to the Greenwich Village jazz club over which James P. Johnson's group, among others, presided in the 1940s.

———. *Send Me Down*. New York: Knopf, 1941.
   A very long, discursive but nevertheless valuable novel about two working-class brothers and a buddy growing up in New York City between the wars. They study music at considerable sacrifice to their parents, become interested in jazz, and then resolve to pursue it as a career, disappointing their parents who consider such music to be trash. The brothers soon go their own musical ways, one taking to the road with a small group, the other building a big band that eventually plays Carnegie Hall. For Frank, the big band leader, success becomes a problem, but he is able to restructure his life to get back to what he most enjoys. There are references to Fletcher Henderson, Bessie Smith, and others, to the black revolution in music, and (inevitably) to the racial tensions of the time. When a black musician says to a white musician that he supposes he ought to be grateful to be in music, the white musician responds: "You certainly should . . . In almost anything else where you had a chance at all, you'd have to be five times as good as a white man. In music you only have to be, say, twice as good." A good deal about the travails of travel, the economics of the music business, and the conflict between art and entertainment. Also, significant reference to the destructiveness of marijuana in the world of swing music.

———. "Swing Business." *Saturday Evening Post*, December 19, 1936, 10+.
   The difficulties of assembling a swing band and then getting bookings for it, told in irritatingly slangy language, which, apparently, is supposed to mimic the swing argot of the 1930s, as in this typical passage: "Djever gedda nextra dime oddovim for it? No! Ain'tcha got no ambition?"

Stephens, Edward. *Roman Joy*. Garden City, NY: Doubleday, 1965.
    The title character of this long novel, Roman Joy, is a young, talented but undisciplined drummer during World War II. Romie briefly rises to fame with the Dave Eckhardt Band, but then crashes when he sets out on his own. This novel is saturated with jazz and swing references, from the tedium of building a big band and the hardships of life on the road to the actual making of music. Much is made of the differences between jazz and swing but the disparity is, curiously, never explained.

Stewart, John. "The Americanization of Rhythm." *The Black Scholar*, June 1975, 73–77.
    A sometimes surrealistic story about a white couple in Chicago who invite a black jazz drummer to their apartment for drinks. The wife has been preoccupied with the drummer's music for some time, but when he shows up it turns out that the Jewish couple—Moses and Harriet—want to use him to start a new race.

Straub, Peter. "Pork Pie Hat." *The Armchair Detective* 27 (Fall 1994): 440–467. Reprinted as *Pork Pie Hat*. London: Orion, 1999.
    The unnamed narrator of this novella was a grad student at Columbia with a passion for jazz when he discovered, to his great surprise, that legendary saxophonist "Hat" (so-called because of his signature pork pie hat) was not only alive but playing at an East Village club on St. Mark's Place. So the narrator starts to hang out at the club, listening in awe, night after night, to the extraordinary music of the great horn man. Before long the speaker ingratiates himself with Hat, who agrees, one Halloween, to allow himself to be interviewed by the young man. The jazz content, which has been impressive to this point, then gives way to a tale of terror involving, one long ago Halloween, the eleven-year-old Hat, a dead white woman in the black section of town, and several spooky events appropriate to the occasion. The narrator publishes the interview—his homage to Hat—in *Downbeat*, but does not go on to become a jazz critic as he had thought he might. Several years later he is inspired to try to substantiate some of the particulars of Hat's story and comes away from his researches dubious and confused. It is likely that Hat applied his wonderful improvisational skills to the art of storytelling. (The real "Pork Pie Hat," of course, was Lester Young.)

Street, Julian. "The Jazz Baby." *Saturday Evening Post*, July 15, 1922, 5–6+.
    A generational dispute ensues when Mrs. Merriam, an old line New Yorker, discovers that her collegiate son Lindsay has fallen in love with the saxophone, and has bought one that is "Quadruple gold plate over triple silver

plate." When Mrs. Merriam reacts to these specifications by asking if it is "a fire extinguisher, or a home-brew outfit," her son replies, "No—home blew" and then proceeds to sing a chorus of "Those Home-Brew Blues" before winding up his performance with a saxophone solo. The dispute continues when Lindsay and friend take a couple of girls uptown to the Apollo to see a show called *Jazzbo* instead of going to a more culturally respectable event in a more socially acceptable part of town. At one point Mrs. Merriam tries to analyze jazz, deciding it is "musical Bolshevism—a revolt against law and order in music. Apparently, too, the jazz Bolsheviks were looters, pillaging the treasure houses of music's aristocracy. One piece was based upon a Chopin waltz, another was a distortion of an aria from *Tosca*, another had been filched from Strauss's *Rosenkavalier*."

Suarez, Virgil. *Latin Jazz*. New York: William Morrow, 1989.

A novel of dislocation centering on a Cuban-American family trying to forge an identity. Although one of the main characters is a musician, and the novel ends with a spirited description of a salsa band in action, *Latin Jazz* contains scant reference to music of any kind. For a novel overflowing with Cuban-American music and life shortly after World War II, see Oscar Hijuelos's exuberant novel, *The Mambo Kings Play Songs of Love*. New York: Farrar, Straus, Giroux, 1989.

Summers, Barbara. "Social Work." In *Breaking Ice: An Anthology of Contemporary African-American Fiction*, edited by Terry McMillan, 601–14. New York: Viking, 1990.

Alicia has been unsuccessful in her efforts to help her lover Richard, a tenor saxophonist, overcome his drug addiction so she resolves to break with him. It was his "talent that she had fallen in love with. . . . The golden horn pumping liquid, silken sex. He wove Trane and Pharoah, Sonny Rollins, and Archie Shepp like ancestral threads into a new fabric, a new suit of clothes as sharply pressed as Lester Young, as raspy and tweedy as Ben Webster. Yet the true magic lay in removing these fine garments, that divine talent, and uncovering the naked, needy soul underneath." But apart from this resonant passage and a few more references to Coltrane, the story has little jazz content.

Sutherland, Luke. *Jelly Roll*. London: Anchor, 1998.

When their psychotic saxophone player drops out of the Sunny Sunday Sextet, the five remaining members decide to find a replacement, go on tour, and gain a new musical lease on life. They soon acquire a brilliant sax man; unfortunately, not only was he brought up in Ireland (the novel is set in Scotland) but he is black. Much of this long novel focuses on the unspeakable racism and other prejudices that are brought to the surface by the appearance of this gifted outsider. Although there are occasional descriptions of jazz in performance, the primary center of interest lies in the volatile chemistry of the band as it goes on its tour of the Highlands. Many readers will have trouble going beyond the long opening sections, which are in Scottish dialect and overflowing with obscene and assaultive language. In fact, this novel probably contains more grisly scenes, scatological language, and drug abuse than any other single work of jazz fiction. The epigraph from Marlowe's *Doctor Faustus* implies—and the novel confirms—that the writer intended his story to function as a metaphor for Hell in the modern world. He succeeded. Author Sutherland is a songwriter, musician, and vocalist.

Sylvester, Robert. "The Lost Chords." In *Eddie Condon's Treasury of Jazz*, edited by Eddie Condon and Richard Gehman, 435–47. New York: Dial, 1956.
    As Pops ("the greatest jazz trombonist of his time, which . . . meant all time") sits waiting to be interviewed for a profile in a jazz magazine, he reflects on his long involvement with the music and on its development. Bix Beiderbecke and Bunk Johnson are mentioned prominently. Although this is a well-told story, it would surely create second thoughts in anyone aspiring to a career in jazz.

———. *Rough Sketch*. New York: Dial, 1948.
    Entrepreneur Tony Fenner had become such a big name that *Current Magazine* decided to do a biography of him. The reporter finally locates four people who knew the mysterious Fenner. One of these is Walter "Pops" Jarman, "The Prophet of American Jazz" and the last of the riverboat jazz musicians. In this section of the novel there is much talk of the rise of jazz in the 1920s and 1930s; of the problems in leading a band; of the economics of the music industry; and of the effects of the record industry (which was just coming into prominence) on the music. Among other things, Fenner was a musicians' agent. Scattered references to early New Orleans jazz men like Muffle Jaw Chambers, Agile Bacquet, Yellow Nunez, Jelly Roll Morton, and Louis Armstrong; Bix Beiderbecke has a cameo part. Considerable talk of the effect of marijuana and booze on music.

Tamar, Erika. *Blues for Silk Garcia*. New York: Crown, 1983.
    Fifteen-year-old Linda Ann Garcia's only legacies from her father are a striking physical resemblance, a guitar, and a recording of a song, "Blues for Linda Ann." After learning that her father is dead, Linda Ann sets out to discover who he really was. She is at first gratified to be told that Silk reinvented jazz theory and that he was a genius of the jazz guitar. But as Linda Ann

probes further, she discovers that her dad was also a wretched human being—an irresponsible boozer and hophead, quite likely a psychopath. Linda Ann comes to understand that the only human feelings her father experienced were distilled in his music. Thus Linda Ann matures as she comes to accept her father for what he was; now she can become her own person, no longer just "the daughter of Silk Garcia."

Tate, Sylvia. *Never by Chance*. New York: Harper, 1947.

After the gal he loves dies suddenly and senselessly, Johnny Silesy learns that he didn't really know her and sets out to discover who the enigmatic woman really was. Although Johnny is apparently a ranking swing pianist, this novel has little musical content, apart from short, infrequent discussions concerning putting together charts and building a sixteen-piece swing orchestra.

Taylor, Debbie A. *Sweet Music in Harlem*. Illustrated by Frank Morrison. New York: Lee and Low, 2004.

Inspired by Art Kane's famous photograph, *Harlem 1958*, *Sweet Music in Harlem* tells the story of Uncle Click, famous Harlem horn man, and his nephew C.J., who also aspires to become a jazz musician. When Uncle Click learns that a photographer from *Highnote* magazine is on his way to take his picture, he panics to discover that his signature hat is missing and so he sends his nephew to scour the neighborhood to locate the precious item. In doing so, C.J. unwittingly sets in motion a lovely occasion of music and camaraderie. For juveniles.

Taylor, Robert Love. *Blind Singer Joe's Blues*. Dallas: Southern Methodist University Press, 2006.

Set primarily in the first quarter of the twentieth century on the Tennessee-Virginia border, *Blind Singer* embodies a diffuse narrative shot through with questions of religion, family, and eccentric behavior, all tied together by music. When Hannah Ruth Bayless gives birth to a blind son, Singer Joe, she passes on to him her supernal gift for music. It is approaching mid-century toward the end of the story when we are told that Singer Joe is now playing more jazz than blues. Fans of blues and jazz fiction will be disappointed that little attention is paid to Singer Joe's musicianship along the way (though we do learn that he once traded licks with Charlie Christian). Another character, Pink Miracle, had been beaten for plying his blues in black neighborhoods of Memphis until bluesman Sonny Boy Jimson acknowledged his talent, took him under wing, and helped him gain the approbation of Beale Street.

Thomas, Ianthe. *Willie Blows a Mean Horn*. Illustrated by Ann Toulmin-Rothe. New York: Harper & Row, 1981.

Willie's young son idolizes his dad and lives to watch him play his horn. When the boy goes to sleep at night, he dreams of the day when he will "play a lullaby to the wind," just like his dad. For young children.

Thompson, Brian. "Life's Little Mysteries." In *Blue Lightning*, edited by John Harvey, 357–75. London: Slow Dancer Press, 1998; Chester Springs, PA: Dufour Editions, 1999.

In 1961 jazzman Cliff Augur is playing in an ocean liner band, planning to defect when the ship docks in New York. On board Cliff has a brief romance with an Italian movie star, but he never loses track of his dream to seek out "Al Cohn and Zoot Sims, and blow them away." Thirty years later a young executive at Columbia records comes across an unissued 1961 recording of Cliff Augur on sax and vibes and is blown away by the music of an apparently great but altogether unknown artist.

Thompson, Charles. *Halfway Down the Stairs*. New York: Harper, 1957.

Taking place around the time of the Korean War, this is essentially a college novel with the predictable ingredients: emotionally conflicted young people in search of that ineffable "something," fast cars, booze, drugs, and jazz. The first-person narrator, Dave Pape, frequently mentions that he plays sax and often refers to jazz musicians like Stan Getz, Johnny Hodges, and Erroll Garner; in fact, his involvement with two different jazz ensembles figures prominently in his life. In the second of these, he is the leader of a combo in Manhattan but the gig flops, and Dave sells his sax. Despite all of this, the jazz content of this novel is very modest.

Thompson, Robert L. "A High Type Dissertation on Skiffle." *Record Changer* 10 (January 1951): 10, 20.

More feuilleton or casual than story proper, this piece describes in mock-serious terms the intricacies and challenges of washboard playing, the music produced by the instrument being, of course, "a very proper branch of jazz-iana."

Thorp, Roderick. *Dionysus*. New York: Coward-McCann, 1969.

Paul Thomson is a magnetic young black man who returns home after spending several years in New York and Europe as a jazz trumpeter and cornetist. Although the novel makes glancing references to jazz and contains a short but dramatically meaningful section on the frustrations of commercializing jazz, these are overwhelmed by the dramatization of racial and family dynamics, the search for selfhood, and the eternal conflict between Dionysian and Apollonian modes of behavior.

Tidler, Charles. *Going to New Orleans: A Dirty Book.* Vancouver: Anvil Press, 2004.
After landing a gig with a jazz band, Lewis "Sweet Horn" King and his nymphomaniacal girlfriend, Ms. Sugarlicq, travel from Vancouver to New Orleans. There the proliferation of sex, violence, booze, and profanity that characterizes their shenanigans in the events that follow suggest that this phantasmagorical novel is intended to symbolize yet another descent into the underworld; even before Hurricane Katrina, New Orleans is here depicted as Hell, albeit a Hell with good music and even better food. While roaming the forbidding landscape of the Big Easy, Lewis and company occupy themselves by eating, drinking, fornicating, killing, and—occasionally—involving themselves with music. Local musicians, from Buddy Bolden to the Marsalis family, are frequently referred to, and there is one nicely realized scene depicting "Sweet Horn" in musical performance, but generally there's more emphasis on the sex organ than the jazz trumpet.

Tilley, Robert J. "The Devil and All that Jazz." In *B Flat, Bebop, Scat*, edited by Chris Parker, 34–38. London: Quartet, 1986.
A fantasy reprising the Faust theme—with a twist. In this version, a trumpet player enters into the obligatory pact with the devil: his soul in exchange for surpassing talent. But this time the devil is outfoxed when the trumpeter rejects hot jazz in favor of West Coast "cool" jazz.

——. "Something Else." *The Magazine of Fantasy and Science Fiction*, 1965. In *Twenty Years of the Magazine of Fantasy and Science Fiction*, edited by Edward L. Ferman and Ralph P. Mills, 248–62. New York: Putnam's, 1970.
When Dr. Sidney Williams's spacecraft crashes on an unknown planet, he is relieved to discover that his clarinet and recording gear are in good working order. After listening to his beloved recording of Duke Ellington's "Ko-Ko," however, he is shocked to hear a facsimile of the music come back to him. He discovers that the sound emanated from an elephantine creature like nothing he had ever seen. Through the agency of jazz, they become friends, but after a while Williams is rescued and the creature dies. Several references to musicians like Art Tatum, Coleman Hawkins, and Eddie Condon.

——. "Willie's Blues." *The Magazine of Fantasy and Science Fiction*, May 1972, 54–75.

A very unusual science fiction story told in diaristic fashion by a time-traveling jazz buff, who shuttles back to the 1930s (from 2078) to locate the jazz saxophonist who had made "Willie's Blues" famous before he died.

Tormé, Mel. *Wynner*. New York: Stein and Day, 1978.

Mel Tormé gives an insider's account of the rags-to-riches story of Martin Wynner, a young singer with a golden voice. After the musical content finally kicks in about halfway through the novel, there are many references to jazz musicians and the big band scene of, primarily, the 1930s and 1940s. At one point, Wynner sings a duet with Billie Holiday.

Townley, Roderick. *Sky: A Novel in Three Sets and an Encore*. New York: Atheneum Books for Young Readers, 2004.

It's 1959 in New York City and nerdy, tongue-tied teenager Sky (né Alec Schuyler) has adolescent problems: what to do about a brainy, beautiful girlfriend and what to do with the rest of his life. Sky lives to communicate through his music, jazz piano, and is helped tremendously to achieve his potential when he is befriended by famous Honduran jazz pianist, Arturo Olmedo. But Sky's father is utterly opposed to jazz, so Sky runs away from home and stays with his newly adopted surrogate father, Olmedo. Sky matures very nicely when he does the right thing by reporting a teacher for inappropriate behavior and reconciling with his dad. The subtitle of the novel underscores its significant musical content. The three sets are "Moanin'," "'Round Midnight," and "I Should Care"; the encore is "Circle in the Rain." The book is dedicated to pianist Lennie Tristano and drummer John Weisman.

Tsutsui, Yasutaka. *Jazu Shosetsu* [*Jazz Stories*]. Tokyo: Bungei shunju, 1996.

A collection of light jazz stories, in Japanese, some of which would be better categorized as gags.

Tucker, Lisa. *Shout Down the Moon*. New York: Downtown Press, 2004.

Twenty-one-year-old Patty Taylor just wants to make a life for herself and her two-year-old son Willie, but a psychologically destructive, alcoholic mother and a scary ex-husband who wants to reenter Patty and Willie's lives provide formidable obstacles. To make matters worse, Patty lands a job as lead singer of a serious jazz quartet, forcing the band to compromise its standards in order to become commercially viable. But Patty vows to learn jazz and transform herself from pretty pop singer to respectable musician, thus gaining the respect, if not the love, of the group. Aimed at an audience of young female adults, this novel contains scattered references to jazz songs and singers (Betty Carter and Johnny Hartman, among others), and the lyrics to "I Loves You, Porgy" play an important role.

Turner, Frederick. *1929*. New York: Counterpoint, 2003.
A whirlwind of a novel stretching from sea to shining sea during one of the most tumultuous times of the twentieth century, when the Great Drunk of the 1920s segued into the Long Hangover of the 1930s. The story begins—and ends—in Davenport, Iowa, decades after the death of its most famous son, Bix Beiderbecke, the incandescent but short-lived musical genius. The occasion is the popular Bix Fest, which has attracted one of Bix's old friends, whose lengthy reminiscences provide the fictionalized biography of the legendary jazz man. We see Bix mastering his instruments in unorthodox ways without being able to read music. Later, when he begins to make his bones as a musician, Bix crosses paths with Scarface Al Capone and his inner circle of gangsters, including Jack McGurn of Valentine Day Massacre infamy. Later Bix travels to Hollywood with Paul "Pops" Whiteman's "Symphonic Jazz Orchestra" to make the first all-color musical talkie. Here he rubs shoulders with several silver-screeners of the time, including the wonderfully presented Clara Bow, with whom Bix engages in raucous sex. Now superstars, Bix and his cronies are mobbed by jazz fans as the band crisscrosses the country in a customized railroad car. As the group's fame grows, the lives of the musicians become increasingly hectic because of the exhausting schedules and endless promotional schemes. One captivating scene depicts a "battle of the bands" between Bix and company and Fletcher Henderson's band. Many notable musicians play significant roles in the novel: Louis Armstrong, Joe Venuti, Bing Crosby, Hoagy Carmichael, and the Dorsey brothers, among others. In one scene Bix takes French composer Maurice Ravel to Harlem to hear Duke Ellington. Ravel later compliments Bix on *his* piano playing by saying: "You seem always to be there—in the vicinity, so to say, of the melody." Throughout the book Bix is at the mercy of booze: he was an alcoholic even before he was a musician. He is also keenly aware of the constant pressure to improvise. When the question is raised concerning which of these brought Bix to premature death, the narrator, in the novel's final sentence, delivers a most satisfactory answer. Although *1929* is densely packed with detail and often long-winded, it is always energetic and its descriptions of music in the making range from evocative to thrilling. In short, a fitting tribute for the centennial of Bix Beiderbecke's birth and an essential jazz fiction.

"The Two Dollar Bet." *Jazz Today* 2, no. 4 (May 1957): 22.
A continuation of "Eddie and the Two Dollar Bet" (q.v.).

Ulanov, Barry, "California Dialogue: In Which Two Mythical Characters Discuss Music and Musicians on the Two Coasts." *Metronome* 62 (March 1946), 21–23+.

The subtitle pretty much says it all: this is an imaginary dialogue between an East Coaster and a West Coaster concerning the relative merits of the jazz scenes in Los Angeles and New York. Many musicians are named, with Dizzy Gillespie perhaps being mentioned most prominently. The Easterner accuses the Westerner of racism in his critique of East Coast jazz.

Updyke, James [W. R. Burnett]. *It's Always Four O'Clock*. New York: Random House, 1956.

After returning home to Gary, Indiana, following World War II, the narrator, guitarist Stan Powles, moves to Los Angeles, where he hangs out in nightclubs with the music fraternity, including the mysterious, eccentric Royal, the focus of the novel, an avant-garde pianist. These two, along with the bassist Walt and a female singer, form a group and attempt to forge a new kind of jazz. Music is central to the narrative, as is the stereotypically self-destructive artist-genius. Much booze and carousing and also much about the sporadic pleasures and frequent problems of trying to perform serious music in a nightclub.

Van Vechten, Carl. *Nigger Heaven*. New York: Knopf, 1926.

Intended to be ironic, the title refers to the far balcony in theatres where African-Americans were relegated, and by extension it also obliquely connotes Harlem. It is the time-honored story of a small-town boy who falls for a big city "Lady of Pleasure" and whose character is tested in the process. An important but controversial novel that was intended to celebrate African-Americans. James Weldon Johnson, among others, lauded the book; other members of the black artistic and intellectual communities excoriated it.

Vega Yunqué, Edgardo. *No Matter How Much You Promise to Cook or Pay the Rent You Blew It Cauze Bill Bailey Ain't Never Coming Home Again: A Symphonic Novel*. New York: Farrar, Straus and Giroux, 2003.

Young Vidamía Farrell—half Puerto Rican, half Irish—sets out to find the father she never knew and, through him, discover who she is. The journey takes her from the affluent suburbs of New York, where she lives with her status-conscious mother and wealthy stepfather, to Manhattan's Lower East Side, where her father, Billy Farrell, lives with his second family. Billy had once been a rising jazz pianist; in fact, Miles Davis had asked Billy to join his band and fumed when he joined the Marines instead. Billy's musical aspirations suffered a serious setback when he lost two fingers in Vietnam and developed post-traumatic stress disorder over the death of a buddy. Vidamía is lovingly accepted by her new family. Soon she and her newfound siblings purchase a piano for their father to get him back into the jazz scene. Billy regains his artistry, while Vidamía enters into a relationship with an up-and-coming African-American saxophonist, Wyndell Ross. Soon the Village Gate arranges a gig, with Wyn as the star attraction, backed by Billy and his precocious sixteen-year-old son, among others. Shocking and cataclysmic events interfere with this redemptive plan, but through it all Vidamía grows, accepts herself for who she is, and resolves to build a productive future. This epic novel (over 600 pages and spanning 150 years) explores at length, through myriad voices, questions of race and ethnicity, especially black, white, and Latino. It is fairly thick with references to jazz, especially bebop and Afro-Rican. There are vivid scenes of music-in-the-making, and many famous musicians play minor roles, including Billie Holiday, Miles Davis, Thelonious Monk, Charles Mingus, Charlie Parker, Dizzy Gillespie, Larry Coryell, and Buster Williams. The subtitle of what is, hands down, the longest title in the literature of jazz fiction is "A Symphonic Novel," and in the "Author's Note" at the end, Vega Yunqué states that his "intent in the novelistic structure of the work has been to pay homage to two original art forms from the hemisphere: the Mexican mural and United States jazz."

Vian, Boris. "Cancer." Translated by Julia Older. *Blues for a Black Cat and Other Stories*, 35–42. Lincoln and London: University of Nebraska Press, 1992. [First Published as *Les Fourmis*, Paris: Edition du Scorpion, 1949.]
    Dying in penury, jazz flutist Jacques (i.e., Jack) Teagarden is reduced to selling his sweat in order to survive. The sweat is poured "into bottles labeled 'Sweat from the Front' and people bought it to wash down the 99 percent burnt bread of the Service Corps." Other stories in this collection allude to jazz musicians and compositions; in fact, the title story—"Blues for a Black Cat"—carries the secondary meaning of black musicians wailing. In addition to his career as a man of letters, author Vian also played jazz trumpet professionally.

————. "A Chorus for the Last Judgement." *Jazz Hot*, 1946. In *Round About Close to Midnight: The Jazz Writings of Boris Vian*, translated and edited by Mike Zwerin, 9–16. London and New York: Quartet Books, 1988.
    A phantasmagorical narrative concerning the (apparently drunken) shenanigans inside the offices of *Jazz Hot* magazine. Much "in" talk about the recent developments in jazz, even as one of the speakers mistakes a plumber for a bassist. As Mike Zwerin exclaims at the end of his preface, "Jazzistically bizarroid."

————. "Letter to Santa Klaus." *Jazz Hot*, 1950. In *Round About Close to Midnight: The Jazz Writings of Boris Vian*, translated and edited by Mike Zwerin, 119–21. London and New York: Quartet Books, 1988.

In this spoof of a letter to Santa Claus, the writer uses phonetic language and puerile puns to promote the cause of jazz (and get in digs at certain well-known jazz figures): "Gnat Hentoff rote you a 5,000-word letter about why he deverves a Learned Father jazz index in his stocking . . . there's a wail of a whole in his discography. Plus too cases of twelve-yeer-old flatted fifths."

———. "Round About Close to Midnight." *Jazz Hot*, 1948. In *Round About Close to Midnight: The Jazz Writings of Boris Vian*, translated and edited by Mike Zwerin, 1–5. London and New York: Quartet Books, 1988.
A fantasy or, as the subtitle suggests, "A Fairly Fairy Tale," in which the speaker is awakened by Joseph Goebbels, who claims to be "special propaganda delegate to the UN Musical Commission, Jazzband Department." Goebbels's insidious purpose is to infiltrate the language via bebop jive, and his modus operandi is to unleash dreadful bebop puns, as in this typical passage: "He called the waiter and ordered wild Reece with steamin' pea-bop soup. Getting the idea, I asked for a pot of Tea-lonious. . . ."

Vining, Keith. *Keep Running*. Chicago: Chicago Paperback House, 1962.
According to his own modest self-evaluation, Jack Norman is the best jazz pianist and arranger in New Orleans—and he's damned good looking, too. But Jack has a problem—actually, several related problems: he's on weed; deeply in lust with an unbelievably beautiful, sexy singer; and, seriously out of favor with the mob. In order to save his skin, Jack must take to the road. This is a violent, crime noir novel with several musical references.

Wain, John. *Strike the Father Dead*. New York: St. Martin's, 1962; London: Macmillan, 1962.
A British novel about the barriers—philosophical, emotional, racial—that separate people. When young Jeremy commits himself to jazz at age 17, he estranges himself from his classics professor father. Through his association with Percy, a black American hornplayer, Jeremy matures in his music and in his life. This novel takes place at the moment when the new post–World War II developments in jazz were filtering across the ocean and finding congenial accompaniment in French existentialism. Good descriptions of music-making, the jazz life, and the difficulty of simultaneously pursuing an art and trying to make a living at it. The novel also embodies the familiar Western themes of the painful complexities of family relationships and the search for a father.

Wainwright, John. *Do Nothin' Till You Hear from Me*. New York: St. Martin's, 1977; London: Macmillan, 1977.
The narrator of this light mystery is wisecracking, band-leading bassist, "Lucky" Luckhurst, whose obsessive goal in life is to put together the best big

band in all of creation. Lucky's life is turned around when he receives a parcel containing a human ear and a note implying that a kidnapping is underway. Through the agency of a clarinet-playing policeman, Lucky is enlisted to help solve the crime; the denouement is improbable and unexpected. The crime/mystery dimension of this novel is pretty much submerged by Lucky's ruminations on jazz and the mechanics of building a high-quality big band.

Wallop, Douglass. *Night Light*. New York: W.W. Norton, 1953.
   Young New York widower Robert Horne loses his beloved daughter to a random killing and devotes his life to uncovering and understanding the forces behind her death. His quest takes him into the amoral world of jazz, where excessive behavior is the norm. Limited description of bop in the making, good description of the jazz scene, scattered references to musicians — Flip Phillips, Lester Young, Dizzy Gillespie, Chu Berry, Max Roach, and Stan Getz, among others. Definitely a noir novel: obsessive and feverish, like the novels of Jim Thompson.

Weatherford, Carole Boston. *Jazz Baby*. New York: Lee and Low, 2002.
   A juvenile book in which, according to the Library of Congress summary, "A group of toddlers move and play, hum and sleep to a jazz beat." Not seen.

Weik, Mary Hays. *The Jazz Man*. New York: Atheneum, 1966.
   A children's book about Zeke, a little boy who lives on the top floor of an old brownstone in Harlem. Zeke's imagination and spirits are lifted by the musician across the way — the jazz man. Zeke's mom leaves, his dad disappears, and so do the Jazz Man and his buddies. But Zeke's parents return, and Zeke begins to regain his sense of security.

Weiss, Joe. *Passion Blues*. New York: Beacon, 1953.
   Trumpeter Hank Miller leads a hot jazz combo, and indeed there are decent descriptions of jam sessions in the early chapters. There is interest, too, in the relationship between Miller and a very talented and — of course — gorgeous young singer, Sherry, who has a gift for jazz. A competent singer himself, Joe mentors her, at one point urging her to listen repeatedly to recordings by such singers as "Sarah Vaughn [*sic*], Billie Holliday [*sic*] and Doris Day" in order to develop her own style. One can but shake one's head in wonder at the creative cosmic forces that conspired to cause author Weiss to link these three names while only misspelling two of them. Inevitably, Sherry begins to consider Hank more than just tutor and surrogate father. This is complicated by the fact that Hank is also involved with two other women, one of whom, Linda, turns out — to Hank's vast surprise — to be a lesbian; when Linda then

entices Sherry into her own bed, Hank is freed to hook up with his true love, Hope, who likes Hank and his love-making so much that she sets her mother up with him, thereby gaining maternal sanction for the forthcoming marriage between Hank and Hope. The first half of this soft-porn item contains some interest for the lover of jazz fiction, but the second half focuses primarily on sexual shenanigans. The novel contains a predictably merciless portrait of a "Harvawd Yawd" jazz critic, an abundance of spanking, frequent references to the perils and pitfalls of the jazz life, and for one reader at least a large mystery: Is Hank supposed to be mulatto? Early on, as he addresses the mirror, Hank remarks on his Negroid features, and the cover art (a doctored photo?) portrays a racially ambiguous male. And if he *is* mulatto, then what? James Joyce's annotators must have had an easier job.

Weller, Anthony. *The Polish Lover*. New York: Marlowe, 1997.

Jazz clarinetist Danny meets a mysterious, enigmatic Polish woman, Maja, in New Zealand, enters into a globe-trotting relationship with her, and then reflects bitterly, ten years after the affair has ended, on the meaning of the relationship. The jazz content is substantive—many references to musicians (including a cameo appearance by Adam Makowicz), some analytical discussions (e.g., the harmonic ideas of John Coltrane), and solid description of a recording session. In fact, the improvisational nature of jazz reflects the structure and theme of the novel. Only a pretty good novel but an excellent contribution to jazz fiction.

Welty, Eudora. "Powerhouse." *Atlantic* 167 (June 1941): 707–13.

A widely anthologized and discussed story about a mythic black pianist (loosely modeled after Fats Waller) doing a one-night gig at a white dance in Alligator(!), Mississippi. As his name implies, Powerhouse is a man of exuberance and creativity, both of which traits are in ample evidence in a story Powerhouse tells during intermission. In fact, the improvisational story he tells, accompanied by verbal responses from his sidemen, is very much like a jam session translated into words. It is also a metaphor for the plight of the alienated artist.

Westin, Jeane. *Swing Sisters*. New York: Scribner's, 1991.

The frame of this very long (551-page), researched novel concerns the reunion in 1982 of the Swing Sisters, an all-woman big band that flourished toward the end of the Depression and was then "forgotten in their own time." The main narrative returns to 1937 when the band was formed against considerable odds. Serious, accomplished musicians, the gals soon learn that "pretty faces mean pretty profits"; even when the band blows off the roof in concert, the reviews focus on the musicians' clothing rather than their music. If this novel in any way reflects the reality of its subject matter (as the author claims it does), then the existence of female bands during the 1930s and 1940s must have been unbearable. The *Swing Sisters* is shot through with booze and dope, lesbian and interracial relationships, skimming managers and gangster warlords, religious fanaticism, and lengthy courtroom appearances. Even when one of the women makes it to Hollywood, her life falls apart. This novel is nevertheless valuable for its depiction of women musicians at work, a vastly underexplored region of jazz fiction. [Much lighter-hearted and set in Great Britain, the made-for-TV movie, *The Last of the Blonde Bombshells* (2000), starring Dame Judi Dench and Ian Holm among others, covers much of the same territory as *Swing Sisters*. The scriptwriter is Alan Plater, who has also written jazz novels (q.v.).]

Wheeler, Susan. *Record Palace.* Saint Paul, MN: Graywolf, 2005.

A refugee from the banality of California and an insufferable family life, scrawny blonde Cindy is studying art history in Chicago in the early 1980s, a time of political and musical upheaval. The dipsomaniacal Cindy soon gravitates to the jazz emporium of the title, a claustrophobically cramped space ruled over by Acie Stevenson, a gigantic supercool African-American with a glass eye who's going on 60. They form an unlikely alliance, leading Cindy into an entanglement with Acie's family that places her in danger. Although the novel employs three distinct voices, its unmistakable thematic thrust concerns Cindy's search for a purpose that will lead her in the direction of selfhood. Starting with its syncopated style, the book is drenched in jazz, ranging from significant references to the Art Ensemble of Chicago and Richard Muhal Abrams to the bebop that is constantly playing (and knowledgeably described) in the Record Palace. Underscoring the novel's dense musical dimension is a "Selected Playlist" at the end that lists the music referred to in the text.

Whitmore, Stanford. *Solo.* New York: Harcourt, Brace, 1955.

The two musicians at the heart of this novel represent opposing views toward their art. Ross Jaeger craves fame and success and won't be satisfied until he's acclaimed the best jazz pianist on Earth. The enigmatic, highly individualistic Virgil Jones, on the other hand, plays for the love of playing and creating—for himself, in other words. When Jones starts to achieve success, others scheme to exploit and manipulate him, but Jones resists and remains true to himself, thus achieving whatever fulfillment he's capable of. Jaeger, with his intense craving for more, can never be satisfied. Flip Phillips makes a cameo appearance, and music is frequently described and discussed—e.g., "When he [Jones] played . . . his piano was always new, always daring yet never tangled with badly conceived innovations, always a special brand of jazz that no one could imitate."

Wideman, John Edgar. "Concert." *The Stories of John Edgar Wideman,* 213–17. New York: Pantheon, 1992.

As the speaker attends a concert featuring a chamber jazz ensemble not unlike the Modern Jazz Quartet, the music has an hallucinatory effect on him, evoking a free-association of ideas, memories, and emotions. Jazz is very much at the center of this story.

———. *Sent for You Yesterday.* New York: Avon, 1983.

In its technique and thematic concerns, this is a Faulknerian novel. It employs multiple narrators who tell stories of the memorable dead from the community, Homewood, the black section of Pittsburgh, very much in decline. The key episode of the narrative, which covers half a century beginning in the 1920s, concerns the return to the community and subsequent killing by a white policeman of Albert Wilkes, a legendary blues pianist. Magically, another townsman, Brother Tate, inherits Wilkes's music: he simply sits down at the piano one day and, without prior training, begins playing, as if he were reincarnating Wilkes. Then, just as abruptly and mysteriously as he had begun, Brother Tate stops playing—and talking, too, communicating exclusively through scat singing. Although jazz is not extensively described, it is nevertheless important in the way it binds the community together and informs the style and structure of the novel. In short, the *spirit* of the music is everywhere apparent.

———. "The Silence of Thelonious Monk." *Esquire,* November 1997, 107–11.

A story in the form of a meditation (or is it the other way around?) regarding the relationship of the silences in Monk's music to the speaker's yearning and sense of loss: "When it's time, when he feels like it, he'll play the note we've been waiting for. The note we thought was lost in silence. And won't it be worth the wait." A reflective, deeply felt piece on the emotive value of Monk's music to the speaker's loss of a woman sometime in the past.

Williams, John A. *Clifford's Blues.* Minneapolis: Coffee House, 1998.

After being caught in a compromising situation with a young American diplomat in Germany in the 1930s, Clifford Pepperidge, a gay black American jazz pianist, is incarcerated in Dachau, where he remains throughout Hitler's reign. Told through a diary that surfaced nearly half a century after Clifford's ordeal, this novel dramatizes the resilience and resourcefulness of the human will *in extremis*. The germ of the story occurred when author Williams saw a photo of black prisoners of war in the museum at Dachau, leading him to research the history of black prisoners during World War II.

———. *Night Song*. New York: Farrar, Straus and Cudahy, 1961. [Published as *Sweet Love Bitter*. New York: Dell, 1966.]

The story of Richie "Eagle" Stokes, a bop saxophonist based on Charlie Parker. When Stokes disintegrates and dies, he becomes a folk hero, with graffiti—"Eagle Lives" or "The Eagle still soars"—cropping up everywhere. The novel is dense with musical reference, including how jazz musicians are exploited by the music industry; but it is primarily interested in racial issues, as the white protagonist, David Hillary, fails Stokes by not going to his aid when cops work Stokes over.

Williams, Mike. *Old Jazz*. Freemantle, Western Australia: Freemantle Arts Centre Press, 2003.

After a failed marriage and a life of indirection, loner-poet Frank Harmon has gravitated to the southern coast of Western Australia, a place well suited to the dramatic emptiness of his life. But his complacent existence is shattered when, in very short order, he receives a late night phone call from a sister he didn't know he had and then falls in love with the bisexual Canadian backpacker who tends bar at his local pub. At his sister's encouragement, Frank revisits the world he had left behind—the England of his youth. And with her help he endeavors to find out the truth about that past, especially as it relates to his parents. Frank of course learns what every reader already knows (or this novel wouldn't exist): that the past was not as it had seemed. Frank knew his dad had been a jazz musician and successful club owner, his mother a jazz singer. What he didn't know is that his father was not in fact his father, nor was he his sister's father. Thus Frank and his "sister," who all along had different mothers, are unrelated. It's a relief to discover at the end that Frank's depressive Canadian girlfriend back home in Australia has *not* committed suicide, though she has returned to Canada, which, for Frank, may be just as bad. We can only hope that he doesn't return to England next year and get close to the woman he used to call sister. The "old jazz" of the title refers to past events, which, not incidentally, revolve around music.

Williamson, Penn. *Mortal Sins*. New York: Warner, 2000.

Although this historical thriller is set in New Orleans in 1927 and its jacket copy employs such words and phrases as "living beat," "syncopations," and "hot jazz," one would have to possess the auditory acuity of the great gray owl in order to hear the music. In short, yet another example of misleading advertising.

Willis, George. *Little Boy Blues*. New York: E. P. Dutton, 1948.

The final installment in Willis's trilogy dealing with the problems of musicians. In this one, Midwestern trumpeter Low Carey aspires to have a band of his own — and meets a woman willing to bankroll him.

———. *Tangleweed*. Garden City, NY: Doubleday, Doran, 1943.

The dispiriting first volume of the author's trilogy concerning the problems faced by jazz musicians. The protagonist here, Rusty Warren, is a swing band drummer at a dive called the Union Garden in Kansas City. Rusty and his fellow musicians are serious about their music; they wish for some kind of transcendence: "Jazz was hollow. Jazz was always just about to tell you something really important. That was when somebody else jammed. When you played for yourself, you were always just going to get it off your chest, but you never did. Somehow, the orgasm never came." Rusty's life is not only complicated in this way, but also by women, booze ("tangleweed"), the desire to compose as well as perform, and the constant pressure to commercialize the music. This book is really a collection of sketches masquerading as a novel. The author himself played drums in small jazz orchestras in the Midwest.

———. "Union Garden Blues." *American Mercury*, August 1942, 176–82.

A sad story focusing on the futility of performing in a seedy nightclub surrounded by drunks and other pathetic creatures. As in Willis's longer works, there is no joy in jazz: playing "it was like loving and hating at the same time, in an agony of eternal, unsatisfied, creative tumescence." A revised version of this story becomes a chapter in *Tangleweed* (q.v.).

———. *The Wild Faun*. New York: Greenberg, 1945.

The story of a young, good-looking pianist who prostitutes his talent by hustling the middle-aged women who hang all over him at the cocktail lounge where he holds forth. This is the second volume in what the author claimed was a trilogy: *Three Musicians*. The other two are *Tangleweed* and *Little Boy Blues* (qq.v.).

Wilson, Edmund. *The Higher Jazz*. Edited by Neale Reinitz. Iowa City: University of Iowa Press, 1998.

Written in the 1940s but never finished, this novel has a misleading title; in fact, the title was chosen by the editor. The novel involves a character who would like to create a new kind of music by combining the elements of the new modernistic music (Copland, Schoenberg, et al.) with American popular music.

Winkler, Mark. *The Jazz Boxer: How We Nearly Kept the Mafia Out of Minnesota*. St. Paul, MN: Fruit of the Loon Press, 1985.

The jazz content of this hard-boiled detective fiction resides almost entirely in its title, which refers to the narrator's perception of a boxer who does his roadwork outside the narrator's window. Wired to a Walkman, the boxer seems to move according to the rhythms of jazz.

Wolfe, Bernard. *The Magic of Their Singing*. New York: Scribner's, 1961.
    In this novel of hipsters, the protagonist, a student of international affairs, goes on a disillusioning search for the meaning of hipness. After Chapter 10, jazz is always peripherally present.

Woodley, Richard. *The Jazz Singer*. New York: Bantam, 1980.
    A novel based on a screenplay that was an adaptation of a play written by Samson Raphaelson—and something, clearly, has been lost in transliteration (or whatever the process might be called); namely, the jazz that *was* present in the original Jolson movie. The story fairly suppurates with schmaltz: poor Jewish boy's father wants his son to be a cantor and sing the praises of God, but poor Jewish boy wants to be a rock star and, in fifteen minutes or so (it seems), becomes one before arriving at the painful realization that fame and fortune have no content unless they can be shared with loved ones. Although we are spared "O Mein Papa," we *are* subjected to a painfully spirited "Hava Nagilah." For jazz, we must settle for a flurry of references to Charlie Parker and two scenes depicting superstar Jess Robin (né Yussel Rabinovitch) performing his beloved blues. Heaven be praised that this "novel" isn't accompanied by a CD.

Woods, G. Arthur. *The Jazz and the Blues*. Baltimore: America House, 2000.
    A young, uptight accountant with a feel for music and modest skill on the guitar impulsively leaves his Tampa home to hit the road in search, presumably, for something that will bring meaning to his life. His travels acquaint him with a variety of unusual people and land him in (for him) exotic places, especially jazz and blues centers like New Orleans, Clarksville, Memphis, and Chicago. Along the way, he masters his instrument well enough to land regular gigs. At the end, he returns to New Orleans, where he feels close to the origins of the jazz and blues that represent to him everything that is good about America. The novel is followed by an addendum of blues lyrics based on the persons, places, and events in the story, reminding us of how unimpressive the words of even good blues songs (which these are not) can be without the music. Although *The Jazz and the Blues* contains considerable musical content, it reads as if it had never crossed an editor's or proofreader's desk.

Xu Xi. "Jazz Wife." *Tattoohighway* 6. http://www.RainTiger.com; http://www .tattoohighway.org/6/xxjazz.html (2/27/2003).

The illegitimate offspring of a black American jazz banjo player and a Chinese stripper in Hong Kong, the speaker, herself an aspiring musician, marries a jazz pianist who is the product of a black-white relationship. They move to Cincinnati where he and his band become almost famous. But life is grim for the young couple in 1978 because jazz is "dying faster than a doornail that *tings!*" The wife's life is subordinated to music—the rehearsals at their home, the criticisms of the music by the band members, the gigs before half-empty houses. In short, as the story's opening sentence proclaims, "You [the jazz wife] marry the music not the man."

———. "Manky's Tale." *History's Fiction: Stories of the City of Hong Kong,* 2nd ed., Hong Kong: Cameleon Press, 2005.
A Chinese jazz drummer cum computer programmer, Manky is at a crisis point in his life: his marriage is failing, his dad's dying, and Tiananmen Square has cast fear and anxiety over everyone. So he reminisces about happier days in Boston, when he and his wife were on the jazz scene trying to soak up what it means to be American; he remembers most poignantly the "spiritual" experience of seeing Elvin Jones play drums and how he thought at the time that his father wouldn't be able to comprehend either what seemed to him the "'crazy-foreign jazz life'" he was living or the wife he had married.

Yates, Richard. "A Really Good Jazz Piano." *Short Story* 1. New York: Scribner's, 1958: 49–70.
Two friends who had been Ivy League undergrads together, Carson and Ken, get together in France where they befriend black expatriate pianist Sid and then reject him when they discover that he is trying to land a gig in Las Vegas in order, obviously, to make a decent living. From their privileged— and decidedly unpragmatic—perspective, the boys regard Sid's desire to forge a better life as selling out.

Yerby, Frank. *Speak Now: A Modern Novel.* New York: Dial, 1969.
As the author says, "This is a novel about miscegenation—one of the two or three ugliest words in the English language . . ." Set against the background of the Paris student riots of 1968, *Speak Now* involves black jazz musician Harry (who has an ongoing gig at *Le Blue Note*) and his white, southern sweetheart Kathy, whose life is complicated by pregnancy. But in the end their love for each other gives them the courage to face the problems of a mixed marriage. Very little musical content and even less novelistic interest.

Young, Al. "Chicken Hawk's Dream." 1968. In *Hot and Cool: Jazz Short Stories.* Ed. Marcela Breton, 229–33. New York: Plume, 1990.

Ne'er-do-well Detroiter Chicken Hawk has a dream in which he retraces
Charlie Parker's footsteps through New York while playing the background
music to his own dream on alto sax. Convinced that he can blow in real life,
he arranges with some high school chums to borrow a horn in order to show
off his chops—with predictably disastrous consequences.

————. *Snakes.* New York: Holt, Rinehart and Winston, 1970.
    After being orphaned early and spending his early years in Mississippi, MC
moves to Detroit with his grandmother, Claude, where life is a bearable struggle. After hearing Coltrane, MC is turned on to music; he forms a band, they
become locally famous, the band dissolves, and MC, after getting his high
school diploma, sets out for a two-week vacation in New York—which, the
reader suspects, will turn into a lifetime of pursuing music.

Young, Steve. "Bella by Barlight." *Brilliant Corners* 1 (Winter 1996): 45–49.
    Kenneth Ayaki plays piano in an Asian jazz trio that has a running gig at
a sleazy, run-down nightclub in downtown Los Angeles. Predictably, the
patrons—a mix of Occidentals and Asians—want to hear only the most
vapid Tin Pan Alley-type music. One night an obnoxious, belligerent
American demands a song the trio doesn't know. When they mollify him
by playing a similar tune, he introduces Ken to his Filipino wife, leading
Ken to reflect on the emptiness of his own existence.

Zabor, Rafi. *The Bear Comes Home.* New York: W.W. Norton, 1997.
    Several real-life jazz musicians, including Charlie Haden and Ornette
Coleman, make cameo appearances in this sprawling, exuberant novel that
dramatizes the awesome challenges confronting the creative artist to be per-
sistently spontaneous and innovative and the joy—the grace, even, and transcendence—that derives from these challenges. The protagonist is a sax-playing, talking bear—in short, an outsider's outsider—who experiences love and
transcendent bliss through music; imagine the John Coltrane of *A Love
Supreme.* The descriptions of music-in-the-making, of the improvisational
process, of life on the road with a jazz band, and of the grim financial reality
of the professional jazz musician's life—all of these are richly and lovingly
detailed, often technical, and consistently convincing. Often reading like an
unlikely collaboration between the Saul Bellow of *Henderson the Rain King*
and the Franz Kafka of "The Metamorphosis," this novel deserves a place
alongside the small handful of jazz fictions that are worth rereading.

Zane, Maitland. *Easy Living.* New York: Dial, 1959.
    Although this novel keeps threatening to break out into a jazz fiction, i
never does so. Rather, it is the account of a porcine protagonist with a swee

tooth and his bed-hopping, hashish-smoking friends in bohemian Paris and London. One character is married to a jazz musician; there is some chatter about jazz (with specific reference to Charlie Parker); and several scenes take place in jazz clubs, but generally speaking there is very slight musical content.

Zinik, Zinovy. "A Ticket to Spare." Translated by Frank Williams. In *B Flat, Bebop, Scat*, edited by Chris Parker, 58–70. London: Quartet, 1986.

A Muscovite, Zinovy, gets a free ticket from a friend to attend a Duke Ellington concert in Kiev. At first the concert is a resounding success, with the very idea of jazz equaling freedom in the speaker's mind. But chaos soon breaks out in the concert, sending Zinovy on a surrealistic journey through the streets of Kiev on the day prayers are being offered in secret for the victims of Babi Yar, leading Zinovy to question his own identity.

Title Index

This title index can easily be used also to locate references to authors, because it includes every work of fiction annotated in part 4. One entry below after page 80 will refer to the alphabetical author entry in part 4, which will include information on date, publisher, and the author's annotation. Readers may therefore select any works of interest to them in part 4 and use this title index to find any reference to those works in parts 1, 2, and 3, and, on occasion, a comparative reference in part 4.

Titles are alphabetized by the first key word, ignoring "a," "an," and "the" and their foreign equivalents (*la, el, eine*, etc.); thereafter alphabetization is letter by letter. The novel *1929* appears as though spelled out (i.e., *Nineteen Twenty-Nine*). If the work is listed in this volume only in a foreign-language edition, an English title follows in brackets; if the work is annotated as published in both foreign and English-language editions, it is usually listed in both languages, with a *see* reference to the English-language title, unless the titles are virtually identical (e.g., *Steppenwolf, Der Steppenwolf*), in which case both titles are listed, English first.

About the Author

Associate founding editor of *Brilliant Corners: A Journal of Jazz and Literature,* David Rife grew up at a good time and place to become a jazz fan. The time was the decade following World War II when bebop offered, especially for the younger set, a welcome respite from the widespread blandness that then prevailed. The place was Elkhart, Indiana, considered at the time to be the Band Instrument Capital of the World. It was not unusual for some of the musicians who stopped by Elkhart to test their new horns to stay long enough to gig at the sock hops sponsored by the school district or the "breakfast dances" that began after midnight, lasted till dawn, and appeared to have been sponsored by guys in zoot suits. Jazz was, as they say, in the air.

Rife's undergraduate education began at Florida State University, where he went on an athletic scholarship and ended with a B.A. in English from the University of Florida. After teaching English as a second language for the U.S. Army in Puerto Rico for two years, he enrolled in the graduate program at Southern Illinois University at Carbondale, earning a Ph.D. in English. He then worked for 35 years at Lycoming College in Williamsport, Pennsylvania, teaching American literature, modern fiction, and several special courses like Crime and Mystery Fiction. He was honored to hold the first endowed chair at that institution. His writings on a variety of topics appear in such publications as *American Literary Realism, Annual Review of Jazz Studies, Dictionary of Literary Biography, Journal of Modern Literature,* and *Oxford Companion to Crime and Mystery Writing. Jazz Fiction* is his first (and likely last) book-length publication.

As a professor emeritus, Dr. Rife divides his time in retirement between Pennsylvania and Florida and plans periodically to update and extend his study of jazz fiction.